D0820249

THE CHANGING STRUCTURE
OF AMERICAN BANKING

Columbia Studies in Business, Government,
and Society, Eli M. Noam, General Editor

The Changing Structure of American Banking

Peter S. Rose

1987
Columbia University Press
New York

Library of Congress Cataloging-in-Publication Data

Rose, Peter S.
   The changing structure of American banking.

   (Columbia studies in business, government, and
society)
   Includes bibliographies and index.
   1. Banks and banking—United States. I. Title.
II. Series.
HG2491.R65 1987   332.1′0973   86-18843
ISBN 0-213-05980-9

Columbia University Press
New York   Guildford, Surrey
Copyright © 1987 Columbia University Press
All rights reserved

Printed in the United States of America

This book is Smyth-sewn.
Book design by J. S. Roberts

COLUMBIA STUDIES IN BUSINESS,
GOVERNMENT, AND SOCIETY
Eli M. Noam, General Editor

Contents

PART IV: INTERINDUSTRY COMPETITION
AND STRUCTURAL CHANGE IN BANKING

Preface

THIS IS A book about the changing *structure* of American banking in the years since World War II. It examines the tremendous changes that have occurred during this period in the numbers, relative sizes, geographic distribution, service offerings, and organizational form of American banks and attempts to assess the impact of those structural changes on bank performance in serving the public. How strong is the level of competition in the industry? Is U.S. banking becoming more or less concentrated in its control of the nation's financial resources? Does bank performance—profitability, prices, and interest rates charged; the returns paid on the public's savings; the allocation of credit, etc.—reflect predominantly the benefits of competition or the burdens of regulation and market concentration? Have the public, bank management, and bank shareholders benefited from recent structural changes, including the rapid expansion of bank holding company organizations and branch banking and a more liberal federal chartering and merger policy?

Each chapter in this book is devoted to a major topic in the field of banking industry structure and public policy. Each chapter is research oriented, summarizing and reflecting the relevant findings of several decades of research on the key competitive and structural issues facing American banking today. In the opening chapter the evolving role of the commercial bank in the economy, from the earliest narrowly focused commercial credit and payments institutions to the broadly diversified financial service firms of today, is analyzed. The most important structural trends in the industry—the size distribution of banks and concentration of banking resources, the growth of new banks and continuing spread of branch banking, the postwar dominance of holding-company organizations in both bank and nonbank financial fields, the spread of interstate banking, and the growing challenge posed by nonbank financial institutions—are all summarized in chapter 1.

Chapter 2 reviews the concepts of banking structure and organization. What do the terms *structure* and *organization* mean and why are they important to bank management and to the public? What goals do American banks pursue? What are the benefits and costs of bank competition and how can they be measured? The chapter concludes with an overview of recent surveys of the public's reaction to banks and the services they offer.

Each chapter that follows examines a different problem area within the banking structure field. Chapter 3, for example, discusses the chartering of new banks, looking at the charter process itself, the effects of new charters on the conduct of existing banks and other financial institutions, and what is known about the performance record of newly chartered banks. The latter half of this chapter focuses on bank failures—their causes, prediction, and consequences. Chapter 4 explores the effects of *internal* bank growth from the perspective of more than three decades of controversy over the possible existence and extent of economies of scale in banking. Are there benefits for bank owners and the public in terms of greater efficiency and cost savings when banks grow in size? Is the nation's banking structure likely to move toward a highly concentrated industry dominated by a handful of large banks, owing to recent technological developments? Chapter 5, on the other hand, considers the *external* growth of banking organizations through mergers and reviews what is known about the effects of banks mergers on banking institutions themselves, their stockholders, and the public. Recent changes in bank merger law and regulation, including the Department of Justice merger guidelines, are examined for their public and private implications.

Chapter 6 focuses on concentration and competition in U.S. banking markets. Traditional and newer measures of market concentration and competition are examined and the findings of recent studies of banking market concentration are summarized and evaluated. This chapter is followed by an exploration of the key organizational structures in the industry—branch banking (chapter 7), multibank holding companies (chapter 8), and conglomerate mixtures of banks and nonbanks within holding companies (chapter 9). In each case the relevant research literature is reviewed for significant evidence on the public and private benefits and costs of each form of banking organization and the unique managerial problems each seems to engender.

Banking's principal competitors are the focus of attention in chapters 10 and 11. Chapter 10 discusses the growing challenge posed by such nonbank thrift institutions as credit unions, savings and loan associations, savings banks, and money market funds. We review research evidence bearing on the impact of these nonbank thrifts on local and national markets and assess the strength of their competitive challenge for commercial banks. Chapter 11 examines the recent explosive growth of financial service conglomerates, such as Sears Roebuck, Prudential-Bache, and Shearson-American Express. The unregulated formation and expansion of these "symbiotics" present formidable competition for banks in selected markets—a competition characterized by continuing product line innovation. In this same chapter the recent counterattack launched by conglomerate banking organizations is examined from the standpoint of both the regulatory and management control problems it poses.

The book concludes with two chapters dealing with today's all-important issues of the regulation and deregulation of American banking. The history, rationale, extent, and structure of bank regulation are reviewed in chapter 12, along with recent proposals to reform the American bank regulatory structure. Chapter 13 analyzes the dominant structural trend of the 1980s—regulation and deregulation of bank services and prices. The content of recent and proposed deregulation legislation is explored, along with what is known about the effects of deregulation on the performance of banks in meeting their own objectives and in meeting the public's demand for an acceptable quantity and quality of financial service at reasonable cost.

This book is guided by two underlying presumptions. One presumption is that the traditional economic theory of markets and organizational structure applies fully to commercial banking in the United States. That is to say, the structure of banking markets—the degree of competition and concentration in American banking—and the way in which individual banks are organized *do* matter in shaping the conduct of individual banking firms and influencing their performance in meeting the public's need for convenient and high-quality financial services. This book also reflects the author's belief that the solution to today's bank management and regulatory problems lies in *research*. If we are to grapple successfully with the challenges posed by today's rapidly changing banking technology, with the impact of a more volatile economy on bank safety and soundness, and with the continuing proliferation of services and institutions within the financial sector, competent research on these problems is no longer (if it ever was) merely a luxury enjoyed by academics but is a necessity for banks, bank regulators, and the public they serve. We must know what past research has already established and what our most pressing needs are for further research in the banking structure field. Pursuit of both what is known and what is unresolved in the bank structure and competition field represents the fundamental purpose of this book.

I am indebted to numerous individuals for their helpful comments and analysis of the findings of this book and for the encouragement needed to see this project through to its completion. In particular, deep gratitude is owed to Professor Robert P. Shay; Dr. Vincent P. Apilado, Professor and Chairman of Finance, The University of Texas at Arlington; Dr. George J. Benston, Professor of Accounting, Economics, and Finance at the University of Rochester; Dr. Robert A. Eisenbeis, Wachovia Professor of Banking at the University of North Carolina; Drs. James W. Kolari and Asghar Zardkoohi of Texas A&M University; Dr. Stephen A. Rhoades, Chief of the Financial Structure Section at the Federal Reserve Board; and to the many other professionals in the banking research arena whose support, encouragement, and ideas proved indispensable. I am especially indebted to my wife Kandy and to my three sons—Robbie, Michael, and Jason—for their boundless patience and understanding through the many twists and turns of this project. Much of what is positive and worthwhile in this book is owed to them; what is not belongs only to me.

Peter S. Rose
January 1987

PART I: ANALYZING MAJOR TRENDS IN U.S. BANKING TODAY

1.

Trends in the Structure and MakeUp of American Banking

THE HISTORY of banking in the United States is a history of *change;* every aspect of the industry has been touched by the dynamism of a changing economic and financial landscape. Clearly some of the changes have been more important than others. Two, in particular, have dominated the nature and method of American banking—the geographic broadening of banking markets and an increasing level of competition, both from within and from without the industry. Obviously these two dominant trends are interrelated. As markets have broadened with improvements in communications, technology, and transportation, commercial banks have faced added competition from more distant competitors. Moreover, this intensification of competition, by threatening to trim bank profit margins, has stimulated American banks to reach even farther afield and find new markets and new services.

Broadening of Markets and Competition
in American Banking

The broadening of geographic markets is *not* unique to commercial banking. Virtually every industry has felt the impact of America's evolving, increasingly innovative, interdependent economy. In the nation's early history before the Civil War the vast majority of products and services were traded in *local* markets—cities, towns, and farming communities. Buyer and seller were usually from the same community or county, and transactions, most often, were face to face. Bartering of goods and services—payment in kind—was as common as the use of currency and coin. Checks were not popular before the Civil War; indeed, public trust in bank paper of any kind was not high and was often deservedly so. Nevertheless, commercial banks were the dominant financial institution of nineteenth-century America.

A century ago bank assets represented roughly four-fifths of the total assets of all domestic financial institutions. Most of the remaining institutional assets belonged to insurance companies that began their operations shortly before the Revolutionary War. Credit unions had not yet appeared, and thrift institutions—savings banks and savings and loan associations—grew slowly except in selected regional markets such as New York City and in New England. Thus, financial transactions were highly localized and commercial banks generally dominated local deposit and credit markets.

It was the Industrial Revolution, which blossomed during the Civil War era, that profoundly and irrevocably altered the character of American banking and that of the markets banks serve. The advent of heavy power-driven machinery and assembly line production dramatically increased the supply of goods available to American consumers at low cost. New and ever more distant markets had to be found to absorb the burgeoning supply of manufactured goods and services. Producers of goods and services and consumers became increasingly separated by both time and space. This situation mandated significant improvements in communications, transportation, and in the media of exchange between buyer and seller.

Early in the nineteenth century, roads, canals, navigable waterways, and port facilities expanded rapidly. However, these communication and transportation links were inadequate to handle the growing flood of passenger and cargo traffic, most of it headed into the Midwest. The railroads appeared, beginning in the 1830s and 1840s, and their rapid westward expansion was soon joined by a transcontinental telegraph system and an improved postal service. During and following the Civil War a nationwide rail system was put in place and further improvements in wire communication, as well as the development of the telephone, occurred.

The tangible result of these changes was, of course, to lay the foundation for a tremendous geographic broadening of markets. Goods mass-produced in the East could more easily be moved to the South and West at reasonable cost. Concomitant with these improvements in transportation to cover broader markets was the development of a national monetary system, supported by a central bank (the Federal Reserve System) created to guarantee adequate growth of liquidity and strengthen federal supervision of banks in order to promote public confidence.

These massive economic and technological changes profoundly affected commercial banks and the provision of financial services. Growing, capital-intensive industries required huge amounts of financial capital, necessitating the development of huge lending institutions that could gather and direct funds into those industrial projects offering the greatest chance for economic success. Thus, banking markets—especially those for commercial loans and deposits—expanded beyond local boundaries into regional and national markets. Branch banking and holding-company banking became more popular as a vehicle for amassing a large volume of financial resources. Concomitantly, bankers were forced to centralize and standardize their products and product delivery systems and develop specialized skills.

The Industrial Revolution also brought with it an emerging middle class of wage earners and salaried managers. These people needed an outlet for their savings and a source of credit for the purchase of homes, furniture and appliances, clothing, transportation services, and medical care. It was here that commercial banking's response to the public's developing financial needs was slow to develop and, initially, inadequate in scope. By and large, commercial banks in the nineteenth century shunned the consumer, both as a source of funds and as a credit customer. Small consumer deposits were generally viewed as too costly to process and small consumer loans as both too costly and too risky to add to bank portfolios. Indicative of this attitude, the first major bank in the country to establish a consumer credit department—National City Bank of New York, as it was called then—did not do so until 1928. Commercial banks were similarly hesitant to offer low down payment, longer term home mortgages to finance the growth of single-family housing, preferring the more liquid commercial loan to either short-term or long-term consumer financing.

Development and Expansion of Banking's Principal Competitors

Commercial banks' early preference for commercial rather than consumer accounts opened the door to credit unions (first begun in New England just before World War I) and to savings and loans and mutual savings banks (both formed early in the nineteenth century). These institutions moved in to answer the small savings account and small loan needs of a rapidly growing, increasingly urbanized middle class. And what consumer financial needs these nonbank depository institutions could not fulfill were met by life insurers and finance companies. Life insurance companies began pouring the majority of their loanable funds into both residential and commercial real estate projects, aided by the emergence of mortgage banking firms, which first identified and then serviced profitable residential and commercial property loans. Finance companies first became a prominent force in the installment loan market during the 1920s, providing funding for the purchase of automobiles, household appliances, and business inventories. The lending and fund-raising activities of life insurers, mortgage bankers, and finance companies helped to bridge local markets and weld them into an integrated, nationwide financial system. Few financial institutions, commercial banks included, could thereafter legitimately claim total isolation from the potent competitive forces of the national financial marketplace.

American banking's response to these competitive challenges was a belated one, occurring mainly in the years following World War II. Two overwhelming forces came to confront banking's traditional bias toward short-term commercial lending, funded by noninterest-bearing demand accounts and low-interest savings deposits. One was the fact that the traditional commercial loan and deposit market was rapidly eroding. The banks' largest corporate customers soon discovered that there was an effective, often cheaper, and more flexible substitute for prime bank credit—the commercial paper market. And those commercial credit accounts refused by the banks and too small or too risky for the commercial paper market were finding a warm reception from commercial finance companies, who also began to aggressively market their equipment leasing services. At the same time corporate treasurers, better trained in cash management techniques, were finding higher yielding outlets for their liquid funds than the banks were offering for corporate deposits. The result was a drastic slowing in bank deposit growth, particularly among the major money center banks. Demand deposits at major New York City banks, for example, were virtually flat during the 1950s at a time when the credit needs of businesses and consumers were growing rapidly.

COMPETITION IN THE POSTWAR FINANCIAL SECTOR

The erosion of traditional commercial banking markets was counterbalanced by burgeoning *consumer* credit and deposit markets. World War II had generated explosive growth in family incomes as women entered the labor force in large numbers and war production virtually eliminated unemployment. Much of the added income poured into family savings, however, because of war-time rationing. After the war, though, consumer spending literally exploded; purchases of automobiles, home appliances, and single-family homes led the list, fueled not only by accumulated savings but also by a baby boom and record growth in new family formations. Confronted with unprecedented opportunities for profitable installment and real estate lending and a ready source of loanable funds from family savings accounts, U.S. commercial banks for the first time in their history offered aggressive competition to nonbank thrift institutions and finance companies for consumer accounts.

Faced with a declining share of household savings accounts in the 1950s, commercial banks fought back in the 1960s and 1970s to first stem the tide and, eventually, to establish preeminence in the household market, especially in the installment lending field. In the 1980s consumers looked even *more* important to bankers because many of their traditional business customers—energy companies, farming operations, commercial real estate projects, and the developing nations—were in deep financial trouble. In contrast, the retail consumer account, especially those held by baby boomers, seemed to offer greater stability and greater profit potential if they could be priced aggressively to cover their true costs of production.

The consequences of this change in banking strategy were and continue to be enormous for both bank management and bank shareholders. It meant greater problems in managing cash flow and balancing the slower velocity of longer term, less liquid credits against more volatile, higher velocity deposits in order to protect bank profit margins. This shift in bankers' strategy toward consumers also mandated operating on a larger scale to hold down unit production costs and reduce deposit volatility. Moreover, the increased cost and volatility of bank sources of funds was exacerbated, beginning in the early 1960s, when major banks developed the large negotiable CD and later extended the CD concept into the Eurodollar market. This new "money market strategy" called for raising an increasing proportion of operating funds from short-term borrowings in the federal funds, CD, Eurodollar, and commercial paper markets. Bank profit margins, especially among money center institutions, became increasingly sensitive to interest rate fluctuations, and the largest banks in the nation no longer led the industry in profitability.

Moreover, a better educated, better informed, and more mobile consumer began to emerge in the 1960s and 1970s. This shift in consumer attitudes toward saving and managing money and credit forced banks into larger advertising programs to attract and retain consumer accounts and into extensive branch systems that followed the consumer into new, rapidly growing suburban neighborhoods. And where branching was prohibited or restricted, holding companies offered a viable alternative to branching that allowed aggressive banks to follow their customers into mushrooming residential markets.

As the 1970s and 1980s unfolded consumers demanded both neighborhood convenience and more innovative services for each and every dollar deposited. For example, just as corporations sought out more efficient cash management techniques during the 1950s and 1960s, so the consumer demanded the same kinds of financial amenities in the 1970s and 1980s. Literally, the mind set of the typical household customer changed from that of passive "saver" to active "investor," increasingly aware of financial alternatives and displaying the willingness to spread business around in pursuit of higher returns and better quality service. Predictably, bank operating costs soared, earnings margins eroded, and in the 1970s and 1980s bank failure rates climbed to postwar record levels.

SERVICE PROLIFERATION, DEREGULATION,
AND STRATEGIES FOR THE FUTURE

Thus, the complications brought to banking by the "consumerism" strategy of the 1950s and 1960s were amplified by the "financial department store" strategy of the 1970s and 1980s. Many banks elected to proliferate new services and to compete in multiple markets with their broadened service menus. One of the most serious effects of this newly evolving strategy was a surrendering of gains in operating efficiency (scale economies) that might have flowed from simply expanding the total size of banking organizations with the *same* service mix. This proliferation of new services resulted in cost increases frequently outstripping revenue growth so that operating margins dropped, particularly after 1980, when federal deregulation of depository institutions really began to take hold. Added to these pressures were an increasingly volatile economy and a new central banking strategy that opted for closer money supply control at the expense of more stable interest rates—both of which raised bank operating risks. At the same time federal regulatory authorities sharply reduced bank leveraging opportunities by demanding substantial infusions of new primary capital, an increasing proportion of which was raised by expensive security offerings in foreign markets.

Moreover, the development and adoption of new technology have introduced new uncertainties into the marketing and delivery of banking services, as microchips and plastic cards increasingly replace banker–customer contact. Most analysts today see the bank office of the future filled with computer terminals and interactive video systems, cashing checks and dispensing electronic cash, taking deposits, and providing information to customers on their credit and investment options, with additional space for hawking a wide range of nontraditional products and services ranging from groceries to recreation. Banking services will also be more readily accessible via home and office computer, through plastic ID cards with built-in microprocessors ("bank branches in the pocket"), and terminals in retail stores and shopping centers. As Professor John Kareken (1981) suggests, the bank of the future will find its traditional functions of making payments, underwriting securities, and intermediating between savers and borrowers far less in demand in a world where all transactions are intimately computer linked. Households and businesses literally become their own banks and borrowers, their own intermediaries. Transportation and communication costs will plummet, justifying increases in average bank size and fewer independent banking institutions as well as fewer electronic and brick-and-mortar branch offices. Even as banks find their payments, underwriting, and intermediation roles diminishing, their roles as financial advisor and risk appraiser for both businesses and households will expand.

Tellers will give way to financial counselors equipped with interactive computer systems capable of answering thousands of detailed questions about a mushrooming array of financial products. Some computer experts (e.g., Schank 1984) foresee artificial-intelligence advisory systems that will provide top-of-the-line banking information to *all* customers regardless of their income or social status and make loan decisions solely on the basis of fact, not personality. But will a customer used to personal human contact in a bank respond enthusiastically to these innovative mass delivery methods? The research evidence on that question is by no means compelling.

And it is likely that significant and perhaps even more startling changes lie ahead for banking and the customer. As in the past, many of these changes will be directly related to fundamental economic, demographic, regulatory, technological, and competitive forces. For example, bankers must rethink the appeal and design of their service menu for a population that today is becoming increasingly dominated by middle-aged adults (those in the 25-to-44 age bracket), and the elderly (65 years and older), even as school age and young adult populations (18 to 24 years) continue to decline. The credit and savings needs of these increasingly older, service-oriented, and information-sensitive adults will demand new user-friendly approaches and new skills centered around the computer and improved marketing techniques.

Bankers in the 1980s and beyond will continue to find their profit margins threatened by erosion from competition inside and outside the industry and by a shortage of quality loans relative to the industry's capacity for generating loans. New and improved policies and procedures for evaluating, documenting, reviewing, and working out problem loans must be developed. These new credit techniques are needed not only because a more volatile and more slowly growing economy will demand them, but also because many of banking's largest and best loan customers have either already found cheaper money elsewhere or are demanding narrow profit spreads on their loan requests. Bankers are and will continue to hunt for quality new customers and new sources of revenue in ways that expand their net returns without sharply increasing costs and capital requirements. Standby credits, wholesale trading in new and old kinds of securities, middle-market and small business clients (especially those offering innovative new products and services), government-sponsored or guaranteed loans, the personal accounts of upwardly mobile businessmen and women—all are target areas for bankers' in a continuing "flight to quality" today. These changes in banking merely reflect the volatility and uncertainty that has characterized the final quarter of the twentieth century.

At the same time bankers are entering an era of greater *constraints,* imposed not only by the vestiges of regulation from the past but also by the environment, the availability of resources, and the changing structure of roles in an American society on the threshold of the twenty-first century. Increasingly, bankers' decisions about growth and customer service will have to consider the scarcity of human and nonhuman resources and the equity with which those resources are used. Moreover, a badly bruised environment will no longer tolerate the rapid industrial expansion of the past, and this fact will reshape the attitudes of the public toward the character and makeup of American economic growth and toward the banker's role in funding that growth.

While many of the old banking regulations born in the Great Depression era are certainly dead, *new* regulations that speak more to the impact of banking on the quality of life and the quality of the environment loom on the horizon. By an ironic twist of fate federal and state regulations in the past have sheltered banking from many of the activist groups and movements that arouse and focus public opinion in the United States. Deregulation is beginning to dismantle that shield of protection and expose the industry to increased public scrutiny regarding the quantity, quality, mix, and cost of banking services. Nowhere is this more evident than in the recent upsurge of credit discrimination suits and in consumer lobbying efforts to control credit card interest charges, force the offering of life-line banking services, and speed up the availability of deposited funds.

Ahead, then, lie slower growth in the employment of people in banking, the replacement of labor-intensive personal services with automated customer information systems, new forms of regulation focused on quality and equity objectives, further credit quality and control problems and a search for higher quality credits, and increased competition posed by thrift institutions, investment houses, insurance companies, and industrial firms seeking greater diversification and new opportunities for growth. Bankers will be more visible and, therefore, more accountable in their dealings with both the competition and the customer. These trends, coupled with rapid expansion in new service lines (especially insurance, investment counseling, investment banking, and loan servicing) outside the industry's mainstream, pose many new problems for the future. An industry steeped in conservative and traditional values will have to find new solutions to these new problems. And it must do so in a financial marketplace that is both more demanding and less forgiving.

Causes of Change in Banking

This brief historical sketch of American banking points to five powerful forces that have shaped the structure and growth of the industry in the past and will continue to dominate its future. These five powerful causes of change are:

1. *economic conditions,* including the level and growth of employment, production, consumption, saving, and interest rates;
2. *demographic forces,* including shifts in population between rural and urban areas, changes in the rate of family formations, and the age and income distribution of the population served by American banks;
3. *regulation,* including legislative mandates, court decisions, and federal and state supervision of bank operations and growth;

4. *technological change,* including innovations in the production and delivery of financial services and the processing of financial information; and

5. *competition,* including the number and relative sizes of both bank and nonbank financial institutions that are rivals for credit, deposit, and service accounts in thousands of local markets across the nation.

Whereas each of these casual forces has had a potent effect on American banking, this book is devoted primarily to the last of the five—the force of *competition.* My interest in these pages is in how the competitive environment for banking has changed in recent years and is likely to change still more in the decades ahead. I shall focus in particular on a major aspect of that competitive environment: the *structure* and *organization* of the industry—how the number, relative sizes, and organizational forms of banks have changed and what those structural changes have meant and are likely to mean in future years for banks themselves and for the public they serve.

What structural trends have dominated American banking in recent years? Although this question is pursued in detail in the ensuing chapters, I pause in this opening chapter for a broad overview of the most significant structural changes in recent banking history. In a sense the following sketch of recent structural trends in American banking provides a road map of the chapters that follow.

Recent Structural Trends in U.S. Banking

The structure and organization of American banking have experienced dramatic changes in recent decades, particularly since 1960. In this period holding companies have come to dominate the industry's assets and deposits: branch banking has achieved permanent legal status in about four-fifths of the states; branch and holding-company organizations increasingly have crossed state lines to follow their customers: the average banking organization has expanded greatly in size in the wake of a record number of mergers; and conglomerate financial service organizations have proliferated in response to the changing needs of a rapidly growing, increasingly service-oriented American economy. In this section I examine these structural trends with a broad brush stroke and look at some of their causes.

SIZE DIVERSITY IN AMERICAN BANKING

        One feature of American banking that continually amazes foreign observers is the tremendous *diversity* in the size of U.S. banking institutions and the *persistence* of that diversity over time. The largest American banking organizations today are BankAmerica Corporation, whose domestic assets exceeded $82 billion at year-end 1983, and Citicorp with nearly $61 billion in domestic assets on the same date. BankAmerica operated more than 1300 domestic branch offices, and Citicorp, 331 branches at the end of 1983. The flagship banks of these huge holding companies—Bank of America, NT&SA and Citibank, N.A.—ranked first and eighth, respectively, in total assets among the world's largest commercial banks in 1983.

        At the other end of the spectrum, however, are thousands of exceedingly small, limited-service, often single-office banks serving neighborhoods, cities, and counties in both rural and urban settings across the United States. As table 1.1 shows, nearly 6,000 of the nation's 14,000 insured banks—40 percent—held assets of less than $25 million apiece in 1983, while about 9600 banks—two-thirds of the industry—

Table 1.1. Asset Size Distribution of Domestic Insured Commercial Banks in the United States. Asset Totals as of December 31, 1983[a]

Size Range of Total Assets Held	Number of Insured Commercial Banks in Size Group	Percent of All U.S.-Insured Banks	Total Assets Held by Bank-Size Groups (in $ billions)	Percent of All Industry Assets
Less than $25 million	5,820	40.2%	$82.1	4.0%
$25 to $49.9 million	3,747	25.9	134.1	6.6
$50 to $99.9 million	2,623	18.1	181.0	8.9
$100 to $499.9 million	1,836	12.7	347.6	17.1
$500 million to $999.9 million	191	1.3	132.5	6.5
$1 billion or more	256	1.8	1,150.0	56.7
All domestic insured U.S. banks	14,473	100.0%	$2,027.3	100.0%

SOURCE: Federal Deposit Insurance Corporation, *1983 Statistics on Banking.*
    [a]Columns may not add to totals, owing to rounding.

reported total assets of less than $50 million each. Billion-dollar banking institutions, dominant in the financial systems of Canada, Great Britain, and most other industrialized nations, numbered less than 300 in the United States in 1983, representing just under 2 percent of the industry's population.

While still dominated by the smallest institutions, the size distribution of American banks has been sliding *upward*. Generally all asset size categories shown in table 1.1 have increased as a percent of the industry's total population at the expense of the smallest bank size group (less than $25 million in assets). U.S. banks in the $50- to $100-million asset size range have grown most rapidly as a percentage of the industry's population since 1970, followed, respectively, by commercial banks with $100 to $500 million in total assets and those with assets of more than $500 million. The average-sized U.S. bank has grown significantly in recent years, from about $20 million in 1960 and $43 million in 1970 to $140 million in 1983. Growth in average bank size has resulted from a combination of factors: (1) increases in production and real incomes attributable to a growing and generally prosperous economy; (2) inflation, which increases the nominal value of both bank assets and deposits; and (3) acquisitions and mergers that have absorbed thousands of small banks into larger, more geographically diversified branch and holding-company systems.

The great diversity in bank size does not prevent the industry from being at least moderately concentrated. Billion-dollar banks represent just 2 percent of all American banks but hold nearly 60 percent of the industry's total resources. In contrast, the numerically dominant less than $50-million insured banks accounted for only about 10 percent of all U.S. bank assets. Indeed, all U.S. banks with less than a billion dollars in total footings—about 14,400 banks or 98 percent of the industry population—hold only about two-fifths of domestically controlled banking resources.

Throughout much of the nation's history the level of banking concentration has been gradually *decreasing.* For example, according to recent studies at the Federal Reserve Board (1970, 1978, and 1982) the ten largest U.S. banking organizations held close to one quarter of the industry's deposits in the 1930s, 20 percent at the end of the 1960s, and less than 18 percent at year-end 1980. The 100 largest banks accounted for nearly 60 percent of industry deposits during the Great Depression, 47 percent at the close of the 1960s, and 45 percent in 1980. If adjustments are made for bank acquisitions made by these largest organizations through their holding companies, the secular decline in concentration is moderated and, according to some studies, increases slightly in the most recent period. As I note in chapter 6, a trend toward declining concentration appears in bank asset and deposit data at the local level—most evidently in metropolitan areas (SMSAs)—and in many states.

GROWTH IN NEW BANKS

One reason for the apparent long-term decline in banking concentration is the continuing growth in the numbers of new banks chartered each year. Following the debacle of the 1920s and 1930s when the American bank population was more than cut in half (from more than 29,000 in 1920 to about 14,000 in 1940), the post-World War II period ushered in an era of relative stability as mergers and absorptions roughly counterbalanced federal and state charterings of new banks. For example, in 1950 there were about 13,446 insured U.S. banks operating; in 1960, 13,126; and in 1970, 13,511. However, the 1970s and 1980s were marked by rapid increases in new banks. During the 1970s alone the nation's banking population grew by more than 1000 institutions net, while new charterings accelerated to an average of more than 300 new banks a year in the early 1980s (see table 1.2).

The 1980s, however, appear to have launched a new trend in the industry's population—pressure to *consolidate* the industry's structure into fewer *independent* banking organizations. Data released by the Federal Reserve Board (1970 and 1982) indicate that, after elimination of multiple banks controlled by the same holding company from industry totals, the number of *independent* banking organizations grew slowly during the 1960s and 1970s and then fell by more than 200 in 1980. As the 1980s began there were about 12,500 independently owned banking organizations in the United States, less than at any time since World War II. With the continuing spread of interstate banking agreements, expanded financial service powers for banking's chief competitors, and more liberal federal merger guidelines, it is likely that the number of independent U.S. banking organizations will decline, albeit slowly, into the foreseeable future. This gradual decline in independent banking units will be further aided by the recent acceleration in bank failures. In 1984 alone, for example, 78 commercial

Table 1.2. Changes in the Number of Banks in the United States, 1969–1983[a]

Years	Number of Banks at Beginning of Year	Newly Organized Banks	Banks Reopened[b]	Effects of Mergers, Consolidations, and Absorptions of Banks Converted to Branch Offices	Other Losses	Supervision of Operations	Voluntary Liquidations	Other Changes	Number of Banks at End of Year
1969	13,679	134	—	−128	−18	−4	−1	—	13,662
1970	13,662	185	—	−127	−23	−1	−8	—	13,688
1971	13,688	201	1	−83	−13	−4	−3	−1	13,706
1972	13,786	265	—	−106	−10	−2	−2	−1	13,930
1973	13,930	344	—	−87	−10	−3	—	—	14,174
1974	14,174	405	1	−105	−13	—	—	−3	14,459
1975	14,459	275	3	−82	−13	−3	—	−8	14,631
1976	14,631	190	—	−128	−13	—	−2	−6	14,672
1977	14,672	200	—	−159	−2	—	—	−7	14,704
1978	14,704	180	—	−154	−16	—	—	−2	14,712
1979	14,712	237	—	−217	−16	—	−2	−6	14,708
1980	14,708	266	—	−117	−18	−3	—	—	14,836
1981	14,870[a]	253	—	−216	−5	—	—	+11	14,913
1982	14,913	373	—	−290	−7	—	−3	+8	14,994
1983	14,994	405	—	−359	−22	—	—	+29	15,047

SOURCE: Board of Governors of the Federal Reserve System, *Annual Report*, various issues, and *Annual Statistical Digest*, 1970–1979 and 1980; Donald T. Savage, "Developments in Banking Structure, 1970–81," *Federal Reserve Bulletin* (February 1982), pp. 77–85; and Federal Deposit Insurance Corporation, *1983 Statistics on Banking*.

[a]Figures include savings banks and small numbers of nondeposit trust companies reporting to the FDIC.
[b]Discontinuity in series reflects a difference in classifications used by each banking agency.

banks failed, only to be exceeded in 1985 and 1986, when more than 100 banks collapsed—the largest annual number of insured bank closings since the founding of the Federal Deposit Insurance Corporation in 1934. Indeed, the newest trend is characterized by the gradual emergence of regional banking conglomerates covering four to five states, offering intense competition in both middle-market business services and in consumer banking.

CONTINUING SPREAD OF BRANCH BANKING

Over the past century the most pervasive long-term trend in American banking has been the spread of branch banking organizations. At the turn of the century less than 1 percent of American banks operated even a single branch office. However, the broadening of agricultural and industrial markets, coupled with the failure, merger, or absorption of thousands of small single-office banking institutions in the 1920s and 1930s, gave great impetus to the spread of branch banking systems. Further impetus to branching activity was provided during the decades after World War II when the suburbs grew and when businesses and households began to migrate south and west in larger numbers. Commercial banks followed with mergers and branch offices where the law allowed.

Whereas Congress granted the states full authority to decide if banks could branch within their territories with passage of the McFadden Act in 1927, few states authorized unlimited full-service branching until recent decades. During that time numerous states along the eastern seaboard and in the upper Midwest moderated or eliminated their restrictive branching statutes. For example, New York gradually moved from allowing limited branching within counties and special districts to statewide branching in 1977. New Jersey preceded the Empire State with a similar rule change in 1973, following a move from branching in head-office counties to district-wide branching in 1969. New Hampshire and Virginia followed New York in 1979 and 1978, respectively, with full-service branching across the state. Virginia had moved as early as 1962 to permit statewide branching by merger and further liberalized its law in 1978 to permit more *de novo* branching. Ohio authorized statewide branching in 1979 to take effect in 1989. Arkansas moved from the prohibition of full-service branching to countywide branching in 1973. Florida allowed countywide branching activity in the same year and then followed with statewide branching via merger in 1979—a position also adopted by Nebraska. By 1986, 21 states and the District of Columbia had acted to permit branching statewide and another 20 allowed at least limited branching by banks operating within their borders.

Even some states that still prohibit or restrict branching activity have moved to ease the restrictions on limited-service facilities (such as drive-in windows and automated tellers) or to permit the upgrading of some limited-service units to full-service capability. For example, Texas authorized off-premises automated tellers at customer-convenient locations in 1978 and then in 1983 permitted one full-service branch within a prescribed narrow radius of the home office with regulatory sanction. Minnesota authorized banks to upgrade as many as two limited-service outlets to full-service branches in 1980. In 1986 there remained only nine states in which full-service branching was prohibited.

These and other changes in state branching laws, coupled with powerful economic forces, led to a dramatic rise in the number of

Table 1.3. Growth of Branch Banking Offices in the United States[a]

Year	Number of Branch Offices	Number of U.S. Banks Operating Branches	Number of U.S. Banks Without Branches (Unit Banks)
1900	119	87	12,340
1910	548	292	24,222
1920	1,281	530	29,761
1930	3,522	751	22,928
1940	3,531	959	13,575
1950	4,721	1,241	12,905
1960	10,483	2,329	11,143
1970	21,424	3,994	9,694
1972	24,872	4,459	9,491
1974	28,705	5,186	9,295
1976	31,405	5,741	8,958
1978	34,857	6,393	8,348
1980	38,779	6,858	8,012
1981	40,838	7,053	7.860
1982	39,835	7,037	7,957
1983	40,913	7,054	7,993
1984	41,907	7,068	7,428

SOURCE: Federal Deposit Insurance Corporation, *Annual Report*, various issues, and Gerald C. Fischer, *American Banking Structure* (New York: Columbia University Press, 1968), p. 35.

[a]Includes a small number of branch offices operated by nondeposit trust companies.

branch offices nationwide and in the number of banks operating branches. In fact, as table 1.3 shows, the number of branches nearly quadrupled between 1960 and 1981, fell back slightly in 1982, and then reached a record total of almost 41,000 in 1983. The annual growth rate in total branch offices slowed dramatically in the 1980s, however, as office closings increased relative to the opening of new branches.

This deceleration in the construction of conventional full-service branches stands at the confluence of significant economic, demographic, and technological currents. New communications technology allowing customers to access their accounts and communicate with their bank via telephone, computer terminal, and microprocessor-equipped plastic cards offers significantly less expensive alternatives to conventional brick-and-mortar service delivery systems. At the same time, average bank deposit interest costs have surged upward due to deregulation and increased financial institutions' competition. Moreover, wage and salary costs have increased more rapidly than inflation as the industry strives to add managers better trained in computers, marketing, financial planning and counseling, and funds management. These cost pressures have promoted the adoption of capital-intensive service delivery methods and spurred on the pursuit of high-volume operations to utilize new equipment more efficiently.

Recent trends in commerical bank branching and service delivery systems also represent a competitive counterreaction to the challenges posed by nonbank thrift institutions—savings and loan associations, mutual savings banks, and credit unions. As the thrifts acquired bank-like powers through legislation, their often extensive branching systems became more effective substitutes for bank branch facilities. For example, the number of U.S. savings and loan branch offices quadrupled between 1970 and 1984, climbing to almost 18,000 in the latter year. Savings associations were also authorized to operate mobile branches during the 1960s and automated or manned mini-branches in shopping centers and other customer-convenient locations during the 1970s. Thus, the unique competitive advantage commercial banks once enjoyed through their extensive, neighborhood-convenient, full-service branching systems has been seriously eroded by the combined forces of improved technology, liberalized regulations, and intensified competition.

Table 1.4. Bank Holding-Company Expansion in Recent Years

Selected Years	Number of Holding Companies Registered with the Federal Reserve System	Commercial Banks Affiliated With Registered Companies	Percentage of All Domestic U.S. Banks Acquired	Percentage of All Domestic Bank Offices Controlled by Registered Companies	Percentage of All U.S. Domestic Bank Deposits Held by Holding-Company Banks
1960	47	426	3.2%	6.1%	7.9%
1970	121	895	6.5	11.8	16.2
1971	1,567	2,420	17.7	36.1	55.1
1974	1,752	3,462	23.9	47.6	67.9
1976	1,913	3,793	25.9	49.4	65.5
1980	2,905	4,954	33.9	56.8	76.7
1983	5,371	—	—	—	87.0[a]
1984	6,146	—	—	—	89.0[a]

SOURCE: Federal Deposit Insurance Corporation, Annual Report, selected issues; Board of Governors of the Federal Reserve System, Annual Report, selected issues.

[a]Percentage of total assets held by domestic U.S. banks.

POSTWAR DOMINANCE OF THE BANK HOLDING COMPANY

The 1960s and 1970s witnessed the rapid rise and eventual dominance of the *holding company* as the premier organizational form in American banking. By 1980 banks affiliated with these companies held three quarters of industry deposits and controlled nearly three fifths of all domestic bank offices. (See table 1.4.) A bank holding company, under federal law, is a corporation owning stock in or otherwise controlling at least one commercial bank. All corporations that hold at least 25 percent of the equity shares of at least one bank or are found to exercise a "controlling influence" over at least one bank (regardless of the percentage of that bank's stock actually held) must register with and be open to examination by the Federal Reserve Board.

Whereas only those companies holding the stock of or controlling at least two banks—multibank companies—were required to register with the Board before 1971, the 1970 Amendments to the Bank Holding Company Act brought even one-bank holding companies under Federal Reserve supervision and regulation. At the time the 1970 Amendments were passed, there were about 1350 holding companies known to be controlling only one bank and 121 registered multibank companies. By year-end 1980 there were 361 multibank companies and 2544 one-bank companies, but each segment held almost equal shares of the industry's assets.

The number of *both* multibank and one-bank companies continued to grow rapidly during the 1980s. In 1983, for example, there were 526 multibank companies and 4499 one-bank firms. By 1986 multibank holding companies were permitted in 43 states and allowed to operate under certain legal restrictions in 7 others; only one state (Mississippi) prohibited multibank holding companies at that time. A dozen of the states allowing multibank companies, however, placed a "cap" on the percentage of statewide deposits any one company could control. These "caps" ranged from 8 percent of the state's total bank deposits in Iowa to 20 percent of statewide deposits in New Jersey and West Virginia.

One of the principal changes brought about by the 1970 Amendments to the Bank Holding Company Act was validation of the authority of holding companies to acquire or start *nonbank* business ventures. However, fearing that many of the nonbank firms owned and operated by bank holding companies might be excessively risky and threaten the solvency of banks held by the same company, Congress imposed two major limitations: (1) the *closely related test,* stating that any nonbank businesses added to the company must be closely related to banking as determined by the Federal Reserve Board; and (2) the *public-benefits test,* requiring that any such acquisitions must reasonably be expected to result in greater public convenience, improved efficiency, or other gains outweighing any possible adverse effects (including unsound banking practices or diminished competition). Companies that acquired or started nonbank businesses not meeting these tests before June 30, 1968, were given until year-end 1980 to divest themselves of such activities or to sell the commercial banks they controlled.

As I note in subsequent chapters, highly diverse sets of nonbank business ventures are legally permitted and presently controlled by both large and small bank holding companies. The ability to expand into such activities further diversifies the permissible services banks can offer and, potentially at least, reduces the risk of fluctuating bank earnings. Even more significant, these nonbank businesses can venture across state boundaries, operate in any region of the nation, and thus allow the holding company through its nonbank ventures greater geographic diversification than domestic commercial banks are currently able to achieve. Moreover, several states have recently moved to expand the permissible nonbank activities of banking organizations operating within their borders, in part to create more local employment opportunities. For example, Alaska and North Carolina have moved to allow commercial banks to enter the insurance, management consulting, real estate, securities, and travel agency fields, while California has expanded banking powers in the management consulting, real estate, securities, and travel agency fields. These state-sanctioned ventures have significantly heightened public and regulatory concern over the safety and soundness of commercial banks linked to new business ventures.

INTERSTATE BANKING

The eroding geographic barriers to holding-company nonbank business expansion spawned a veritable explosion of interstate banking activities in the 1970s and 1980s. As previously noted, prohibitions against *interstate* branching—unless specifically authorized by the state to be entered—have been in place since the 1920s. In 1957 the Douglas Amendment to the Bank Holding Company Act restricted acquisitions of bank stock by out-of-state holding companies to less than 5 percent of an individual bank's outstanding common equity. Nevertheless, numerous practical loopholes were found around these legal barriers. Some banking organizations had already established an interstate presence (e.g., First Interstate Bancorporation of California, which controlled subsidiary banks in 10 other states) and were thus exempted under the grandfather provisions of the relevant federal statutes. A study by Whitehead (1982) identified 45 U.S. grandfathered banking organizations controlling 141 out-of-state banks with 1,396 branch offices as of June 30, 1982.

Interstate banking has been facilitated also by recent provisions in federal law and antitrust policy that allow rescue of failing banks or thrifts through mergers with larger and sounder out-of-state banking organizations. The well-known mergers of Citicorp with Fidelity Savings and BankAmerica with SeaFirst, as well as Chase Manhattan's acquisition of troubled Ohio thrift institutions, are cases in point. Individual *states* also have granted permission for outside entry by either banks or bank holding companies, sometimes to provide a limited range of services and usually on condition that their own banks are granted reciprocal treatment by other states. Examples include Delaware and South Dakota, which recently provided an avenue for out-of-state entry to extend credit card services; Alaska, Arizona, and Maine, which sanctioned entry by out-of-state bank holding companies; and Indiana, Kentucky, Maryland, and Ohio, where entry by out-of-state banks is permitted subject to reciprocal treatment provisions. A gradual phase-in of nationwide interstate banking triggered by regional branching agreements between states has received some support in Congress, especially when combined with restrictions on interstate acquisitions by the largest banking corporations and by financially weak institutions. A June 1985 ruling of the U.S. Supreme Court further strengthened the legal basis for emerging regional interstate banking compacts.

Adding to the bewildering maze of interstate banking operations, foreign-owned banks had become a potent competitive factor in U.S. urban markets during the 1970s and 1980s, especially in the competition for large commercial and real-property loans. Whitehead (1982), for example, identified some 53 foreign banking organizations with 103 interstate branches as of June 30, 1982. When 22 foreign-owned international banking (Edge Act) offices and 116 agency offices are included, Whitehead found a total of about 250 interstate bank-related offices controlled by foreign institutions. So rapid was the expansion of foreign bank activities across state lines in the 1970s that Congress responded with passage of the International Banking Act of 1978, placing their future territorial growth under essentially the same rules that confront domestic banks. Foreign-owned agency and branch office operations henceforth were governed by the terms of the Bank Holding Company Act, and the deposits held by the largest foreign banking organizations were subject to the same Federal Reserve requirements and interest rate ceilings as banks.

U.S. banks countered this interstate "invasion" by foreign banking organizations with the rapid expansion of their own Edge Act subsidiaries—international banking corporations that federal law permits national banks to establish across state lines. Some 143 U.S.-owned Edge Act corporations had established offices in 16 states by the end of 1982. Even more extensive were U.S. bank loan production offices (LPOs) established across state boundaries that can generate both international and domestic accounts for their bank's home office but are prohibited from accepting deposits. Whitehead (1982) counted 202 LPOs in 1982, operating in 34 states.

As extensive as these various interstate organizational vehicles had become by the 1980s they were dwarfed in importance by the interstate expansion of nonbank businesses operated by bank holding companies. Often called 4(c) (8) subsidiaries after the section of the Bank Holding Company Act that defines their legal status, the depth and breadth of holding-company controlled nonbank activities reached truly epic proportions by the early 1980s, as observed by Whitehead (1982). He counts nearly 11,000 different business activities provided through the interstate offices of holding-company 4(c) (8) subsidiaries at year-end 1982, including such services as commercial and consumer finance, mortgage banking, credit card operations, factoring, loan servicing, trust operations, financial advising, leasing, data processing, management consulting, insurance underwriting, and insurance agencies. Offices of 4(c) (8) businesses outside the home state of their holding company numbered about 5,500 and were present in all 50 states. In total, Whitehead (1982) identified 7,742 out-of-state bank-related offices scattered across the nation at the end of 1982.

In addition to the foregoing vehicles for interstate expansion, a number of contractual arrangements were made between bank holding companies and banks in other states in the event interstate branch banking is legalized by Congress or by the various state legislatures. Purchases of up to 4.9 percent of the outstanding common stock of out-of-state banks, which may be made today without regulatory approval, have become common, particularly in the Midwest. Other expectational arrangements involve the purchase of up to 24.9 percent of an out-of-state bank's equity capital—often nonvoting stock convertible into common equity once interstate branching rules are changed. Still another conditional interstate agreement is the "merger of equals" whereby banking organizations headquartered in different states formally contract to forge an interlocking relationship once federal or state branching rules are altered (as happened in Ohio in 1985, for example) and take an immediate but limited equity interest as a foundation for the future. Further expansion of interstate banking operations in the years ahead will depend heavily on two key factors: (1) enabling legislation and (2) the sensitivity of bank service production costs (and, therefore, profits) to changes in the size of interstate banking operations.

RISE OF NONBANK COMPETITORS AND DEREGULATION

The rapid expansion of banking organizations nationwide and the lure of continuing rapid growth in the public's demand for financial services has spurred *nonbank* institutions into entering the banker's marketplace. Nonbank thrift institutions—savings and loan associations, mutual savings banks, credit unions, and money market mutual funds—have launched a frontal competitive assault against banking's most traditional services—credit, payments, and safekeeping of funds. Nondeposit financial conglomerates—ranging from insurance, credit card, and brokerage companies to manufacturers and retail chain stores—elected to aggressively challenge banks for both their conventional credit and deposit accounts and for new service lines, especially in insurance agency, real estate and security brokerage, and loan-servicing activities.

Some of the nondeposit financial conglomerates ("symbiotics") exceed the nation's largest banking corporations in overall size, range, and intensity of activity. For example, the 1983 net income of Sears, Roebuck & Company was half again as large as Citicorp's, while the net incomes of both American Express and Cigna exceeded that reported by BankAmerica Corporation in the same year. As reported by the American Bankers Association (1985), the combined assets of leading nonbank competitors Aetna Life and Casualty, American Express, Cigna, John Hancock Mutual Life, Merrill Lynch, Metropolitan Life, Prudential Insurance Company of America, and the Travelers Corporation exceeded the combined assets of America's top three bank holding companies—BankAmerica, Citicorp, and Chase Manhattan Corporation—by nearly $20 billion at the close of 1983. Many nonbank firms were sheltered and even encouraged by federal legislation that, on the one hand, continued to restrict commercial banking essentially to its traditional lines of commerce while granting increased bank-like powers to some of the industry's most formidable competitors in the deposit-taking field.

In March 1980 Congress passed and President Carter signed into law the Depository Institutions Deregulation and Monetary Control Act that permitted nonbank depository institutions (as well as commercial banks) to offer third-party payments services in all 50 states, including interest-bearing NOW accounts, share drafts, and automatic funds transfer services (ATS). Thus, the long era in which commercial banks exercised virtually exclusive control over payments services in the American economy was brought to an end. At the same time major new credit powers, including the offering of credit cards and commercial and consumer loans, were granted savings and loans and savings banks, and these new powers were further expanded when the Garn-St Germain Depository Institutions Act was passed in October 1982. Among the few concessions granted commercial banks under the 1982 deregulation law was the authority (along with nonbank thrifts) to offer money market deposit accounts (MMDAs) to compete with share accounts offered by money market mutual funds. The incredible success of MMDAs, expanding to more than $300 billion less than six months after their inauguration, halted and partially reversed a decade of dramatic growth by money market funds at the expense of both commercial banks and nonbank thrifts.

This experience with the MMDAs pointed to what commercial banks could do in competing against nonbank financial service firms if regulations were eased to permit all suppliers of these services to compete on a "level playing field." Banks sought to level the playing field further in the mid-1980s, particularly with reference to insurance companies and brokerage and investment firms, seeking authority to offer an expanded menu of brokerage, insurance, and underwriting services. As we shall see in a later chapter, however, these expanded service powers are likely to come about slowly, owing to Congressional and regulatory fears over bank solvency and heightened concern over eroded public confidence in a system buffeted by a dramatic increase in bank failures. The problem bank list maintained by the Federal Deposit Insurance Corporation reached unprecedented length in the early and mid-1980s, further dampening deregulation moves that might allow commercial banks into more risky service lines. Indeed, the outlook for further broadening and liberalizing of the playing field for banks seems clouded and highly uncertain at this time. It may even be that the pendulum that swung so forcefully in the direction of deregulation will swing back toward *reregulation,* propelled by extensive publicity surrounding the industry's most conspicuous failures and by political opposition from those groups who have the most to lose from unfettered competition with the nation's commercial banks.

What Is a Bank?

The massive structural and organizational changes I have discussed have led today to an *identity crisis* in banking. The simple question "What is a bank?" has become exceedingly difficult, if not impossible, to answer. Bankers have found it far more difficult in today's financial marketplace to find their real service niche vis-à-vis those institutions that represent their principal competition.

To a large extent bankers themselves have changed the nature of banking. However, law and regulation have also recently redefined the industry's role and responsibility. It is safe to say that what we understand as the business of banking today will be substantially altered in the next decade and perhaps be unrecognizable in a generation. The changes now occurring—some would call it a *revolution*—are rapid because the industry today is at the confluence of unprecedented economic, demographic, technological, competitive, and regulatory changes.

A bank is, after all, what a bank does. But what a bank does—or more precisely, what it is *allowed* to do—is a matter of law and regulation. And this codified character of the banking firm is in a state of flux today to a degree unparalleled in the nation's history. Traditionally, commercial banks were defined in law as corporations empowered to accept funds and other valuables (such as securities) for safekeeping, to make payments to a third party on behalf of a customer, to exchange one form of currency and coin for another, to grant direct loans to businesses and individuals for legitimate purposes, and to discount commercial notes. These simple functions were performed by banks for centuries stretching back to medieval Europe and, in the view of many scholars, even to Athens, Rome, and other cities of the ancient world where the professional ancestors of modern bankers sat in open-air markets to profit from trading coins and discounting commercial notes.

This traditional view of a bank and its functions was codified into both federal and state banking statutes during the nineteenth century. Commercial banks were distinguishable from other domestically chartered corporations under law by their authority to (1) accept demand deposit accounts that could be transferred to a third party in settlement of debts and (2) grant credit to individuals and institutions, either through direct loans or through the discounting and redemption of notes. The payments (or demand-deposit) power was particularly significant because, so long as banks were its sole possessors, the banking system had virtually exclusive control over the nation's money supply and payments mechanism. These exclusive demand-deposit powers were, in fact, both a blessing and a curse for bankers because they brought with them extensive government regulation to safeguard money creation and the flow of funds needed to support commerce and industry.

This two-piece definition of a bank—demand-deposit acceptor and loan maker—was given a slightly different twist when the Bank Holding Company Act was passed in 1956 and subsequently amended in 1966 and in 1970. That law, as we have seen, was designed primarily to regulate the veritable explosion of corporations holding bank stock and of nonbank business ventures allied with banks. In the 1956 version of the holding-company law, banks were defined essentially by *who chartered them*. Thus, national associations were banks if they received their authority to organize and commence operations from the Comptroller of the Currency in Washington, D.C. State-chartered corporations were banks if their charters were issued by the state banking commissions.

Later, in 1966, the Bank Holding Company Act was amended to include as banks only those institutions with demand-deposit powers, and most savings-oriented intermediaries such as credit unions, savings and loans, and mutual savings banks were thereby excluded. Thus, the 1966 amendments changed the legal identity of a "bank" from where it received its charter to the content of its services.

This refocusing of the banking concept was sharply narrowed in 1970 when new amendments to the Bank Holding Company defined the bank as an institution that accepted demand deposits and made *commercial* loans. In the legal sense, at least, banking was taken back to its earliest origins when it dealt almost entirely with business firms.

In a paradoxical way the 1970 Amendments both narrowly defined the business of banking and provided a channel for future expansion of that definition. The Federal Reserve Board was granted authority to add future services and functions that it saw as "so closely related to banking or managing or controlling banks as to be a proper incident thereto." Nevertheless, the narrow legal definition of banking expressed in the 1970 version of the Bank Holding Company Act created an obvious loophole for expansion-minded financial service companies. By either disposing of a commercial bank's demand (checking) accounts or by selling off its commercial loan portfolio, the institution involved ceased to be a *bank* for purposes of federal regulation. Therefore, it would not be bound by federal restrictions against interstate branching, the offering of security brokerage and underwriting services, and the sale of insurance. Several financial conglomerates soon marched adroitly through that legal loophole—for example, Merrill Lynch, which controlled a New Jersey bank, began disposing of that bank's demand-deposit accounts and refused to accept new demand deposits.

As the number of such "nonbank banks" grew, the Federal Reserve Board moved to halt the trend by broadening the definition of "bank" for purposes of holding-company regulation. The Board's Regulation Y was revised, effective February 3, 1984, to state that "demand deposits" would be defined to include any deposit with transactions capability that, as a matter of practice, is subject to payment on demand through presentation of a check, draft, negotiable order of withdrawal, or other similar instrument. The net effect was to bring *all* forms of interest-bearing checkable deposits (such as NOWs) under the general label of "demand deposit" and the organization controlling them under the umbrella of Federal Reserve supervision. And, to close other loopholes in the federal regulatory net, "commercial loans" were redefined to include broker call loans, or the purchase of retail installment loans or commercial paper, certificates of deposit, bankers' acceptances, federal funds loans, and similar money market instruments, or the deposit of any interest-bearing funds.

These broader definitions of "bank" were immediately challenged in federal court by Dimension Financial Corporation on grounds that the Federal Reserve Board had exceeded its authority and gone beyond the intent of Congress. In 1984 the Federal Reserve Board reluctantly approved the application of New York's Bankers Trust Company to open a nonbank in the State of Florida. In the same year U.S. Trust Corporation of New York was allowed to convert its nondeposit Florida trust company to a nonbank depository institution—taking demand deposits and granting *consumer* loans. And, in 1986 the Supreme Court affirmed the unregulated status of *nonbank banks* and ruled that the Federal Reserve Board had exceeded its authority in trying to hamper the expansion of these institutions. This opened the door to a possible flood of applications to charter limited-service banks.

Within a month following the Board's first approval of these unique institutions, 28 companies had applied to set up 165 nonbank-bank facilities across the nation. Approved nonbank banks were opened and operated by such well-known companies as Sears Roebuck, J.C. Penney, E.F. Hutton, Citicorp, and Control Data Corporation. Because they did not qualify as banks under the terms of the Bank Holding Company Act, nonbank banks ostensibly could launch nonbank business ventures forbidden to bank holding companies and legally operate banks in more than one state.

An interesting dilemma confronted Congress when the Garn-St Germain Depository Institutions Act was being debated in the summer and fall of 1982. That bill brought about a significant expansion in the powers of nonbank thrift institutions, granting them commercial loans, checking accounts, and trust operations that historically were reserved for commerical banks alone. Would not any nonbank thrift choosing to offer these services become a commercial bank, subject to both federal and state banking laws and especially to the terms of the Bank Holding Company Act? Because the answer was likely to be "yes," Congress moved in the Garn bill to exclude from the term "bank" any institution whose deposits were insured by the Federal Savings and Loan Insurance Corporation (FSLIC) or that received its charter from the Federal Home Loan Bank Board (FHLBB). This action only added to the confusion over what a bank is for it shifted the focus of that definition. Instead of defining a bank in terms of its *function*—i.e., the services it provides as stipulated in the Bank Holding Company Act—this historic institution now was to be identified by the *government agency* selected to regulate it. Such an approach was obviously flawed, conducive to both regulatory inequity and public confusion, and likely to be quickly outmoded by the force of events.

It has become abundantly clear from these recent developments that a complete reexamination of the role and function of banks and other financial institutions within the nation's financial system is imperative. Equally imperative, the structure and role of the federal and state regulatory system surrounding the operation of financial institutions need revamping and overhaul. Perhaps more than at any time in the nation's history we face the danger that a regulatory structure designed to benefit the public, promote competition and efficiency, and preserve the soundness and stability of the financial system is ill suited and potentially destructive of that end. The continuing debate and discussion over "What is a bank?" is not, therefore, merely a philological exercise but also the opening chapter of a saga laced with powerful economic, demographic, technological, and political undercurrents. The question of the proper nature and role of banks and their competitors in our financial system will not go away and it can no longer be ignored as we turn to confront the future. It is an issue to which we shall return time and again in the chapters that follow.

References

American Bankers Association. 1985. "The Financial Services Scene: An American Banker Scorecard." *American Banker* (January 4).

Board of Governors of the Federal Reserve System. 1970. "Recent Changes in the Structure of Commercial Banking." *Federal Reserve Bulletin* (March), pp. 195–210.

—— 1978. *The Bank Holding Company Movement in 1978.* Staff Study (September).

—— 1982. "Developments in the Banking Structure, 1970–1981." *Federal Reserve Bulletin* (February), pp. 77–85. Prepared by Donald T. Savage.

Di Clemente, John J. 1983. "What Is a Bank?" *Economic Perspectives* (January-February), pp. 20–31. Federal Reserve Bank of Chicago.

Federal Reserve Bank of Dallas. 1984. "Ruling Spurs 'Nonbank' Applications." *Roundup* (June), p. 1.

Fischer, Gerald C. 1979. "The Structure of the Commercial Banking System, 1960–1985." *The Journal of Commercial Bank Lending* (May—October).

Gurwitz, Aaron S. and Julie N. Rappaport. 1984–85. "Structural Changes and Slower Employment Growth in the Financial Services Sector." *Quarterly Review* (Winter), pp. 39–45. Federal Reserve Bank of New York.

Kareken, John H. 1981. "Technical Change and the Future of Banking: One Man's View," in Golembe Associate Reports, Washington, D.C., June 12, pp. 1–8.

King, B. Frank. 1984. "Interstate Banking: Issues and Evidence." *Economic Review* (April), pp. 36–45. Federal Reserve Bank of Atlanta.

Schank, Roger C. 1984. *The Cognitive Computer.* Reading, Mass: Addison-Wesley

Talley, Samuel H. 1974. *The Impact of Bank Holding Company Acquisitions on Aggregate Concentration in Banking.* Board of Governors of the Federal Reserve System.

Whitehead, David D. 1982. "Interstate Banking: Taking Inventory." Federal Reserve Bank of Atlanta. Staff Study.

2.

Organization and Structure: Two Key Factors Shaping Bank Performance

THE BANKING INDUSTRY, like any other, is made up of a collection of both organizations and structures. The term *organization* in this sense refers to the individual firm—how its lines of authority and decisionmaking are arranged and how its resources are arrayed to produce and sell goods and services. Over the centuries banking has developed a wide array of organizational forms in response to external pressures—principally competition, technological change, regulation, economic and demographic conditions—and internal pressures—principally the availability, price, and quality of resources under management's control. These organizational forms range from small single-office, locally oriented banks to huge multiple-office, multimarket holding companies—each a chosen response to the confluence of competitive, technological, regulatory, and resource constraints presented by the external and internal environment.

The term *structure,* on the other hand, looks beyond the individual firm to the marketplace—the channel through which firms (suppliers) communicate with their customers (demanders) on the availability and pricing of goods and services. Structure refers to the numbers of banks and competing nonbank financial service firms serving a given market, the particular services they offer in that market, the size distributions of banks and bank customers, the degree of horizontal and vertical integration of banks, barriers to market entry, and geographic dispersion of both banks and their customers. Just as the organizations of individual banks vary widely, so do banking market structures—from markets served by many banks relatively equal in size with strong competitive rivalry (i.e., a market structure approaching pure or perfect competition) to markets served by one bank that is the sole supplier of financial services (i.e., a monopoly). Market structure, like bank organization, responds to competition, technological change, regulation, and economic and demographic conditions.

The Structure-Conduct-Performance and Organization-Conduct-Performance Models

This book is devoted to the structure *and* organization of American banking. Why are they important? In what ways do market structure and bank organization really matter? Part of the answer lies in one of the most fundamental concepts in economics—the *structure-conduct-performance model*. Economists generally believe that the structure of a market influences the conduct (behavior) of individual firms. And the conduct of those firms, coupled with market demand for goods and services, shapes the performance of firms in serving the public (table 2.1).

COMPETITION AND COLLUSION IN THE SCP MODEL

The structure-conduct-performance (SCP) model presumes that market structures characterized by *many* firms supplying the same or similar products and services, with all firms relatively *equal* in size, are pro-competitive markets generating superior performance. Buyers in such markets are more likely to find the best selection of goods and services, produced at the lowest cost in terms of scarce resources (i.e., greatest efficiency) for given level of quality. Moreover, in highly competitive markets excess profits beyond a "normal return" (necessary to preserve the viability of the firm) are quickly eliminated by old and new competitors.

This happy result follows because no one firm or small group of firms is likely to dominate such a competitive market. Collu-

Table 2.1. The structure-conduct-performance model

External Factors ⟶	Structure ⟶	Conduct ⟶	Performance
Available technological methods for the production and delivery of financial services Regulation by federal and state authorities Economic conditions (level and growth of production, availability and cost of productive resources, elasticity and growth of demand, and the price and availability of substitute products and services) Demographic factors (distribution, growth, and social profile of the population to be served)	Structure of banking markets (number and relative sizes of competitors supplying and demanding banking services, entry barriers, and geographic dispersion of suppliers and demanders)	Bank management strategy and objectives (including pricing behavior, marketing programs and goals, new service innovations, and the development of new production and delivery systems)	Price, quantity, and quality of financial services offered to the public

sion to fix prices and market shares or to protect excess long-run profits cannot long succeed. Conversely, as Scherer (1982) points out in a comprehensive review, the SCP model presumes that markets served by one or a few firms with significant disparities in firm size are more likely to be characterized by coordination of policies and collusive agreements. The result is inferior performance in terms of the quality and quantity of goods and services produced, higher prices, and profits that exceed a normal return.

THE ORGANIZATION-CONDUCT-PERFORMANCE MODEL

For several decades bankers, economists, and financial analysts have argued that the structure-conduct-performance framework must be supplemented by a second model—the organization-conduct-performance (OCP) model—if we are to more fully explain bank behavior. This view contends that the internal organization of a bank—especially whether or not it operates branch offices or joins a holding company—significantly affects its conduct in serving the public. The key linkages in this model are:

External Factors →	*Organizational* *Form*	→ *Conduct*	→ *Performance*
(Technology,	(Unit bank,	(Bank man-	(Price, quan-
competition,	branch bank,	agement	tity, and quality
regulation, eco-	holding com-	strategy and	of financial ser-
nomic condi-	pany, etc.)	objectives)	vices offered
tions,			to the public)
demographic			
factors)			

Unfortunately, these linkages between bank *organization*, conduct, and performance are not as convincingly grounded in theory as is the *structure*-conduct-performance model. In fact, as we shall see in this and subsequent chapters, the question of whether particular kinds of banking organizations really influence bank conduct and ultimately performance in the financial marketplace has been a subject of great research interest and intense public debate for decades. Because banks that branch or organize holding companies tend to be larger and operate in markets where only a few leading banking organizations control a majority of assets and deposits, it is frequently assumed that such complex multiple-office organizations generate inferior public performance (especially higher prices and excess profits). Other analysts argue, however, that such organizations by virtue of their greater resources and stability produce superior public performance—a wider array of services, more conveniently and efficiently provided. In later chapters of this book I evaluate these arguments and examine the available research evidence in detail. For the moment, however, let us examine the major organizational forms used in American banking.

Principal Organizational Forms in Banking Today

Unlike many other countries, banks in the United States are private
business organizations, pledged under their federal or state-issued charters to serve *both* the public interest and their stockholders. What is a
business organization?

That seemingly simple question has aroused growing interest among economists and financial analysts in recent years because
the earlier literature in economics has tended to focus on *markets* rather
than on the character of individual-firm organizational arrangements.
Today, however, an elaborate theory of organizational behavior is
emerging, much of it viewing business organizations, to quote Jensen
(1983), "as a nexus for a complex set of contracts (written and unwrit-
ten) among disparate individuals." Thus, each business organization
serves as a centralized location for unilateral contracts between cooperating agents—owners of land, labor, and capital—who desire to
produce and sell products or services for economic benefit. As Jensen
and Mechling (1976) observe, within each organization, contracts
specifying the rules of the economic game have three dimensions—
the assigment of decisionmaking authority, a reward system, and a
performance evaluation system. The nature of the contracts between
cooperating agents within the organization and between the organization and its customers distinguishes one type of business organization
from another and places it at a competitive advantage or disadvantage
relative to those organizations sharing the same marketplace.

Commercial banking in the United States is characterized
by six major organizational forms: (1) unit banks, (2) branch banking
organizations, (3) banking chains (discussed in a later section), (4)
multibank holding companies, (5) one-bank holding companies, and
(6) financial conglomerates. The history of American banking has
been characterized by a gradual shift of emphasis away from unit and
small branch banks toward larger and more complex conglomerate
organizations that span markets, diversifying both geographically and
by product line.

UNIT AND BRANCH BANKING

Unit banks are corporations offering their full range of
credit and deposit services from a single office. There are no offices

apart from the head office where customers may obtain access to a full range of services offered by the bank. Unit banks may, however, operate satellite limited-service facilities, such as drive-in windows and auto-mated teller machines, linked electronically or by pneumatic tube to the head office.

Branch banks offer a full complement of services from more than one office. Usually there is a designated home or head office with branch offices scattered among neighborhoods in the same community, within the same county and perhaps into neighboring counties or statewide.

A branch banking organization is similar to a unit banking organization in that both, in their purest form, are single banking corporations rather than multiple corporations linked together. Re-gardless of the number of branch offices a branch banking organization operates, it has but one corporate charter, one set of capital accounts, one board of directors that sets policy for the whole organization, and one senior management staff. In contrast, the remaining types of banking organizations—holding companies and conglomerates—are multiple corporate entities, bringing together firms each of which possesses its own corporate charter, capital account, board of directors, and management staff. As we shall see, this distinction is important from a management control point of view.

HOLDING COMPANIES AND FINANCIAL CONGLOMERATES

Multibank holding companies are corporations that hold all or part of the equity shares of more than one bank. Often these organizations are formed to skirt around laws prohibiting or restricting branch banking because most states do not limit or regulate bank holding-company activity. In contrast, one-bank holding companies hold all or a portion of the equity shares of a single bank. Both multibank and one-bank companies may also acquire stock in nonbank businesses provided these are "closely related to banking" and produce "public benefits."

The legal capacity of bank holding companies to acquire businesses offering different financial products allows these organiza-tions to become financial conglomerates. Among the most important banking conglomerates today are those that bring under the same corporate umbrella both wholesale-oriented (commercial) and retail-oriented (consumer) banks, finance companies, mortgage companies, leasing companies, data processing firms, and venture capital affiliates. A wide variety of other nonbank business activities is also permissible, as we shall see in chapter 9. The principal objectives of such conglomerations of disparate firms and services are (1) reduction of risk through geographic and product-line diversification, (2) avoidance of restrictive regulations against organizational expansion, and (3) synergistic benefits from more efficient usage of available resources. With these alleged benefits, however, may come additional costs related to the span of management control and other factors.

Many of today's banking conglomerates were put together as a response, at least in part, to the rapid development of nonbank conglomerates—*symbiotics*—offering both financial and nonfinancial products and services. Familiar examples today include Sears Roebuck and Company, General Motors Corporation with its GMAC finance company subsidiary, Shearson-American Express, and the Prudential-Bache insurance securities conglomerate. I discuss more fully the challenge to banking posed by the symbiotics in chapter 11.

Forms of Ownership and Management

With the exception of a few private banks established in the nineteenth and early twentieth centuries that were proprietorships or partnerships, virtually all U.S. banks today are *corporations,* owned by their stockholders with policies dictated by a stockholder-elected board of directors. And the overwhelming majority of those stockholders hold common equity shares that carry voting privileges and the right to claim any net earnings left over after all legal obligations are met. Very few banks have issued forms of equity other than voting common stock. Nonvoting preferred stock, for example, represents less than 1 percent of industry net worth, though the volume of preferred issues has accelerated in recent years with the development of variable-rate preferred shares.

BREADTH OF BANK OWNERSHIP AND CONTROL
The ownership of bank common stock is not widely dispersed but is narrowly held in most instances—often by members of

the same family or by close friends and business associates. While that is changing with the continuing spread of branch banks and holding companies, it nevertheless remains true that the majority of American banks rank among the most closely held of all U.S. corporations. The identity of bank stockholders, particularly in the case of smaller independent banks, is not generally known, except in confidential bank examination reports where the principal shareholders are listed. Occasionally surveys are carried out by the federal banking agencies or Congress, most of these looking into the extent of *chain banking* arrangements.

Banking *chains* exist where two or more banks have the same individual or group of individuals as common stockholders. Thus, chain banking is a loose, informal association that may exercise actual control over a group of banks or may simply hold bank stock as an earning asset. Chains are *not* regulated unless they have effective control over banks and that control is officially recognized by the Federal Reserve Board, which would then require the chains to register as bank holding companies. However, most are unregulated, which makes it very difficult to gauge the size and importance of bank chain arrangements. Two dated surveys—one by the House Banking and Currency Committee in 1964 and the other by the federal banking agencies for the Senate Committee on Banking, Housing, and Urban Affairs in 1978—provide a rough measure of the extent of chain arrangements. The 1964 House study, for example, indicated that about 2300 banks—18 percent of the industry—with $53 billion in assets were involved in chain relationships (i.e., at least one stockholder held 5 percent or more of the outstanding stock of two or more banks or the same director or officer was common to at least two banks in the group).

Because many chain arrangements represent indirect attempts by larger banks to control smaller institutions, Congress directed the federal banking agencies during the 1970s to examine and report those instances in which the officers, principal stockholders, or directors of a bank were granted loans to acquire the stock of other banks. Stock loans became very popular during the 1920s in the Midwest and South, where branch banking was restricted or prohibited, forcing larger banks interested in controlling smaller ones to settle for informal control through friendly stockholders (Cartinhour 1931). The federal banking agencies reported in 1978 that about 6700 commercial banks (roughly 48 percent of the industry) had bank stock loans outstanding. Many of these chain arrangements were converted subsequently into holding companies when it appeared that federal regulation would be imposed in those instances where the Federal Reserve Board detected effective control. Clearly, if we ignore chain relationships in a given banking market—and the vast majority of research studies do so because of lack of information—we may substantially underestimate the extent of market concentration and considerably overestimate the extent of banking competition. Many bank merger and holding-company acquisitions may be approved by federal authorities even though the public interest would dictate otherwise.

BANK GOALS AND MANAGEMENT OBJECTIVES
        Whereas most American banks are closely held instead of having their stock widely dispersed in the market, management styles and strategies seem to differ markedly. Unfortunately, we still have only limited research evidence about how closely managed American banks really are and the effects of differing management styles. For example, what goals does bank management typically pursue? Are most American banks profit or stock value maximizers as is often assumed in banking market studies? Economists generally argue that a market-oriented economy functions most efficiently with maximum consumer welfare when the management of each firm seeks the highest possible return for its owners.
        But are Americans banks and their managements really driven by the goal of profit or maximization of shareholder return? We do not really know. Researchers in the bank structure field typically assume that, if markets are reasonably competitive, each bank will be pushed toward the profit goal and toward improved customer service. However, bank researchers in recent years have begun to raise serious questions about bank management styles and goals with much of the work centered upon the behavior of regulated firms.
        More than two decades ago Becker (1957) and Williamson (1963) posed the argument that, under suitable conditions, managers are free to pursue objectives that maximize their utility but are *not* necessarily consistent with maximum profits. For example, management may engage in *expense preference* behavior, incurring extravagant expenses that go beyond the profit-maximizing level. A utility-maxi-

mizing manager may prefer a larger staff and other executive "perks" (e.g., elaborately decorated offices and country club memberships) to increasing stockholder returns. What conditions might give rise to this situation? Regulated industries where owners' property rights are partially attenuated in the public interest, imperfect markets, and widely disbursed ownership of a firm's stock that grants management virtually complete control—all have been cited as causal factors for expense preference behavior.

Is there evidence of such behavior in banking? Edwards (1977) found such evidence among urban banks in a labor market test of 44 metropolitan areas (SMSAs). He detected higher wage and salary expenditures in those local markets dominated by large banks during the years 1962, 1964, and 1966. Edwards' view—that diminished competition, coupled with close regulation of the industry, leads to greater managerial emoluments—was later confirmed by Hannan (1979a) and Hannan and Mavinga (1980).

More recently, research has shifted toward the related issues of whether owner-dominated or management-dominated banks perform better and whether *agency costs* must be incurred by stockholders to prevent bank management from adopting expense preference behavior. For example, Glassman and Rhoades (1980) analyzed the profitability, deposit growth, expense per employee, and facilities' expense ratios of 1406 banks, each one the lead bank in a holding company. Including measures of the degree of owner control in their regression analysis, Glassman and Rhoades found that owner-controlled banks averaged higher profits (measured by return on assets) than management-controlled institutions. However, they uncovered less clear evidence that management-dominated banks incurred greater expenses or substituted growth for profits.

Because smaller banks tend to have a higher level of owner control, expense preference behavior by management should be more common among larger U.S. banks. However, Glassman and Rhoades' (1980) analysis of profitability ratios among the nation's 200 largest banks found no consistent linkage of bank expenses to the degree of owner control. These conclusions are roughly consistent with those of Hannan and Mavinga (1980), who find that management-controlled banks (in which no single shareholder has 10 percent or more of outstanding common stock) tend to have higher occupancy and furniture equipment expenses but not necessarily higher labor costs than banks with greater control by the owners. More recently, Arnould (1985) finds evidence of positive agency costs in the form of higher salaries for chief operating officers among management-dominated banks.

Not all the research evidence supports the expense preference theory of bank management, however. For example, Smirlock and Marshall (1983) found *no* relationship between monopoly power and discretionary behavior among bank managers in 38 metropolitan markets located in unit banking states. They argue that competition among managers inside and outside a management-dominated firm would tend to eliminate wasteful expense behavior and that carefully designed incentive plans can encourage bank managers to prefer maximum profitability over other goals. Moreover, bank size appears to be a key factor in what goals a bank, its management, and its owners pursue. Whitehead and Lujytes (1982) find that small banks often pursue increased market share at the expense of profits; yet, such banks are more likely to be owner dominated. In contrast, they observe that larger banks, at least those examined in the Southeastern region of the nation, attempt to maximize profitability and market share simultaneously.

It is evident from the foregoing discussion that U.S. banks pursue multiple goals. Some try to maximize profits; others focus on the related objective of maximum stock price; still others pursue growth and market share goals, while another significant group apparently places management satisfaction at the top of the list. Many banks mix these various goals into some form of combined strategy that balances the interests of owners, managers, regulators, and customers. Clearly, no simple label applies to the goals and management strategies employed by American banks today.

INTERNAL BANK MANAGEMENT POLICIES:
CONSOLIDATION OR LOOSE CONFEDERATION?

Just as there is much ignorance about bank goals, we also know very little about trends in internal bank organization and the degree of management control exercised within the banking firm. This is a particularly important issue in the case of multiple-office and conglomerate banking organizations because effective internal controls would seem to be vital to their efficiency and competitiveness in an increasingly deregulated financial marketplace. Economists often argue that the degree of centralized control and consolidation is a key benchmark differentiating branch and unit banks from holding company, chain, and conglomerate organizations. The former organizations, allegedly, tend to be close-knit, highly centralized institutions where all key decisions are made by a central management team, whereas holding companies, conglomerates, and chains are closer to loose confederations with limited centralization of decisionmaking.

Indeed, there *is* some research evidence on the control features of holding-company banking. One of the most important studies in this field was carried out by Lawrence (1971) for the Federal Reserve Board. He surveyed all domestic registered multibank holding companies, focusing principally on their operating policies toward non-lead banks inside the organization and on interlocking directorates. Lawrence also looked for possible centralization of budgeting, dividend policies, capital management, loan participations, money market borrowings, loan and security portfolio management, price setting, personnel policies, and accounting, marketing, and planning programs. He found that multibank companies exercised their greatest control over affiliated bank investment policies and correspondent relationships and the least control over individual loan decisions, the mix of bank loan portfolios, and service prices, apparently because of concern over possible antitrust violations. The degree of centralized control over subsidiary banks varied markedly from bank to bank and appeared to be unrelated to holding-company size or maturity or to bank size and geographic location. Lawrence concluded that each banking organization's management policy and practice and its performance in serving the public have to be examined on a case-by-case basis rather than rely on sweeping generalizations about the industry as a whole.

In a follow-up study Lawrence (1974) explored the operating policies and management styles of 27 bank holding companies controlling *nonbank* businesses. These holding companies controlled some of the largest banks in the nation (including six of the top ten U.S. banking companies). He found "close control" over nonbank subsidiaries carried out by supervisors from the lead bank and through control of a majority of the boards of directors of the nonbank firms. Moreover, he found that holding-company lead banks generally provided important support services (e.g., accounting, auditing, and personnel management) for their nonbank subsidiaries, which were generally operated as profit centers. In fact, control of nonbank businesses was as tight or even tighter than the control exercised over affiliated banks, probably owing to the added risk of nonbank ventures and management's relative lack of experience in most nonbanking fields.

Lawrence's pioneering studies of holding-company operating policies, management styles, and their linkages to the performance of affiliated banks spun off several research studies during the 1970s. For example, Mayne (1976) compared the management of liquidity, investments, loans, deposits, expenses, capital, and risk, as well as pricing and profitability, of centrally managed holding-company banks versus independently owned banks. Using Lawrence's rating system for degree of centralized management control, she found few performance differences among independent banks, bank subsidiaries of decentralized holding companies, and banks associated with holding companies practicing centralized decisionmaking. Mayne saw little gain from a regulatory point of view from including "the internal management structure of a banking group as an important factor" in approving or disapproving holding-company applications to acquire more banks (p. 48).

Whether banks affiliated with different holding companies do, in fact, perform differently, implying differences in management policy and control, was further pursued by Fraas (1974) and by Rose and Scott (1984). Fraas correlated the performance of affiliated banks in Colorado and Ohio with a set of dummy variables indicating the particular holding-company organization to which each bank belonged. He found significant performance differences between affiliates associated with different holding companies, rejecting the notion that all affiliated banks have common features that outweigh their individual differences. Rose and Scott followed Fraas' lead, examining the performance of 715 affiliated and independent banks in five key holding-company states—Florida, Michigan, Missouri, Ohio, and Texas. They concluded that

few holding companies appear to control their affiliates tightly; for most holding companies, affiliates do not appear to perform as a homogenous group. . . . The absorption of an independent bank or a *de novo* bank by a holding company (BHC) will change its performance, if it does change it, more in response to the characteristics of the acquiring BHC than in response to its simply becoming a member of the BHC sector. Therefore, Congress should not view the bank holding company movement as monolithic when it deliberates the issue of interstate banking (p. 12).

The implications of these few existing bank ownership and management studies seem abundantly clear. American banking is not monolithic but diverse in organizational form, in the distribution of ownership and management styles, and in its goals and objectives. Moreover, decentralized control and decisionmaking is a frequent characteristic of multiple-office banking organizations, particularly in the holding-company sector. Whether the decentralized character of many banking organizations will persist in the future in view of recent pressures toward industry consolidation is problematical, however, and clearly must await further detailed research.

Bank Market Structure in Theory and Practice

While organizational form, management style, and internal control policies *may* shape the conduct and performance of banks, most economists and financial analysts would argue that the *structure* of banking markets and the competitive rivalry within those markets are at least as powerful a determinant of how well banks serve the public. Indeed, the linkages among market structure, bank conduct, and performance have been empirically tested in dozens of studies, covering thousands of different markets across the nation. In the balance of this chapter my focus is on the underlying *theory* behind those empirical investigations—the theory of competition in the financial marketplace.

WHAT IS COMPETITION?
Most commercial banks offer their services in markets still mainly *local,* confined largely to the boundaries of a city, county, or metropolitan area. However, technological change in the form of automated teller machines, wave transmissions, on-line computer linkages, etc., is rapidly broadening banking markets and tearing down the old constraints imposed by geography and time. Yet, however narrow or expansive banking markets happen to be at any given time, the *marketplace* represents the milieu within which management decisions

and policies must be carried out. And it is competition in the marketplace, along with economic conditions, that determines the success or
failure of bank management decisions and policies.

Competition from one vantage point refers to individual
firm *conduct*, specifically the presence of *interfirm rivalry*. This view of
competition looks at the willingness of individual firms to search out
the needs of their customers and to respond with products and services
whose qualities and prices are designed to attract a substantial share of
the available market.

An alternative view of more recent origin stresses the
structural character of a market. Competition exists where there are a
sufficient *number* of firms present selling a homogeneous product (or,
at least, one for which there are relatively close substitutes) so that
buyers have a wide range of choices. And, each firm must be so small
relative to the total market that it cannot perceptibly influence market
price simply by varying its own output.

These two views of competition—conduct versus structure—are *not* mutually exclusive. Rivalrous conduct can exist among
market-leading firms in a concentrated market that does not meet the
structural definition of competition. Rivalrous conduct may also be
present in a market that looks structurally competitive.

In banking, competition is increasingly being evaluated by
the behavior of *prices* for credit, deposits, and other financial services—
a prime target of the deregulation movement. Before recent deregulatory actions, however, *nonprice* competition in the form of increased
customer convenience, bonuses, and "free" services was more common
than outright price competition, especially in the taking of deposits.
The tremendous increase in bank branch offices during the 1960s and
1970s is prime evidence of the historical importance of nonprice competition in U.S. banking. Banks prevented by regulation from using
favorable prices to attract customer accounts offered greater convenience (i.e., lower transactions costs) instead.

PUBLIC BENEFITS OF COMPETITION

For nearly a century now federal government policy as
expressed in the Sherman Antitrust Act of 1890 and the Clayton Act
of 1914, as well as more recently in the 1960 Bank Merger and 1956
Bank Holding Company Acts, has attempted to ensure the presence

of competition in the production and sale of goods and services. Supporting these laws is the expectation of significant public benefits in the form of greater efficiency in the allocation and use of scarce resources, increased innovation in developing new and better quality products, and product prices that approach true long-run unit costs of production. As Benston (1973) notes:

competitive markets provide suppliers with the motivation to serve the public and use resources efficiently. If one bank does not provide services to meet the needs of customers, another bank can prosper by doing so. If a bank operates inefficiently, its owners and managers forfeit the resources wasted (p. 221).

Competition conserves, rather than wastes, resources because production decisions by individual firms are, as Scherer (1980) observes, "responsive qualitatively and quantitatively to consumer demands" (p. 3).

COMPETITION IN BANKING MARKETS

Competition in banking or in any other field takes place within the confines of a market. What is a *market?*

Markets are *not* places with geographic or territorial boundaries but rather *mechanisms* through which buyers and sellers of goods and services communicate the availability of products and their desired terms of sale. For example, economists Browning and Browning (1983) observe: "markets. . . refer to the interplay of all potential buyers and sellers involved in the production, sale, or purchase of a particular commodity or service" (p. 6). A more specific definition is offered by Houck (1984):

A market is a collection of actual or potential buyers of a specific good or service. This collection has two characteristics: (1) none of the buyers has the option to purchase the item from sellers outside this collection and (2) none of the sellers has the option to sell the item to buyers outside this collection. The interaction of these buyers and sellers generates a set of interrelated prices and conditions of sale or use. The principles or facts determining which buyers and sellers are in this collection identify the market spatially, temporally, and politically (p. 356).

Communication between potential buyers and sellers may be personal and face-to-face, as when customer and banker negotiate the terms of a loan. Buyer-seller communication may also be remote and impersonal, as in an auction market (e.g., the market for U.S. Treasury bills), where prices and availabilities are posted continuously and shift frequently in response to changing demand and supply pressures. In either case the fundamental *purpose* of the market mechanism is clear: *To allocate scarce resources and products in the most direct and efficient manner to those willing to bid the highest prices for them.*

Demand Elasticities. How far do markets extend? How can bankers decide who their competitors are in any given market? In economics the concept of *cross-elasticity of demand* was developed to deal with these questions. Banks and other financial firms serve the same market when they respond to each other's initiatives in changing the availability of financial services and the terms of sale. For example, suppose the management of Bank A decides to sell its money market deposit accounts more aggressively by offering higher interest rates, resulting in a significant impact on Bank B's market share. B responds by publishing a new schedule of deposit rates to protect and possibly expand its own market share. Clearly, these two banks serve the *same* market, for the actions of one in setting prices and other terms of sale affect the quantity of financial service sold by the other. The degree or intensity with which one bank's actions produce reactions by other banks is a measure of the boundaries of the marketplace and of the degree or intensity of competition in that market.

The Justice Department's Demand Elasticity Approach. The cross-elasticity of demand concept relates closely to the approach used recently by the U.S. Department of Justice to define product and geographic markets. As explained by Guerin-Calvert (1983), these markets are defined using an assumed 5 percent increase in prices posted by firms seeking to merge. Justice Department analysts try to determine if merging companies could profitability increase their prices by 5 percent or if customers would respond to those higher prices by shifting their purchases to other products, negating the price increase. If consumer shifting does occur, the other products purchased are considered to be within the *same* product market. Similarly, the geographic boundaries of a market depend on whether a 5 percent price increase would result in customers shifting their purchases to companies outside the immediate area. If this shifting occurs, the geographic boundaries of the market area need to be expanded to include other producers. Thus, a market would be accurately delineated from a geographic point of view when all firms that could prevent any one firm from profitably increasing its prices by 5 percent are included in the market's boundaries.

Transactions Costs. The cross-elasticity of demand concept defines markets essentially from the suppliers' point of view. We may also view banking markets in terms of the *transactions costs* that buyer and seller are willing to pay to make trading possible. Transactions costs include the time and expense incurred in searching for information concerning product availability and prices, the costs of communications and delivery, and any commissions or fees needed to enlist the services of a broker or dealer. The magnitude of marginal transactions costs relative to the benefits received by both customer and bank from searching the market shapes market boundaries.

For example, household checking accounts are predominantly a *local* financial service because the benefit (expected profit) to a bank from selling each additional deposit unit and the marginal benefit (expected savings) to a customer in searching for alternative sources of *deposit* supply are low relative to the marginal transactions costs that must be incurred. In contrast, the market for home mortgage loans tends to be broader in scope than for household checking accounts because the additional benefits from identifying the optimal mortgage loan terms are substantial, especially for the borrowers, relative to the additional transactions costs involved.

Size as a Market Determinant. Both customer and bank size also influence the dimensions of a market. Generally the larger the customer (measured, for example, by sales or income) and the larger the bank, the larger the market in which each will trade. Thus, loans to large corporations are generally traded in national or international markets. In contrast, loans to households for the purchase of home appliances are serviced predominantly by small local banks.

The Problem of Multiple Markets. The *multiproduct* nature of banking adds significantly to the problem of defining the scope of banking markets. The same bank often competes in both the local market for household checking accounts and installment loans and in

the national or international market for commercial loans and government bonds. Moreover, many banking services are cross-sold and are
therefore interdependent. For example, the bank may insist that a loan
customer also keep his checking and savings deposits with that bank.
Research studies on bank structure and competition usually choose
between studying the market for *one* banking service or viewing banks
as offering a unique *bundle* of services within the boundaries of a single
market area. No guidelines exist on the relative costs and benefits of
these two widely used approaches for studying commercial banks and
the markets they serve.

       Most Damaged Market. While the cross-elasticity of de-
mand, the transactions cost/benefit ratio, and the other concepts discussed above are conceptually appealing as measures of a market's
boundaries, their appeal as practical management and policy instruments leaves much to be desired. Indeed, these concepts pose serious
operational problems given the limitations of real-world data. For
example, the derivation of even a crude approximation for the cross-
elasticity for a single banking service would require detailed studies of
individual bank behavior in thousands of different bank locations over
lengthy time intervals. The time and resource constraints surrounding
most management and public policy decisions require "quick approximations" of real-world markets. These practical constraints have led to
conventional measures of bank market boundaries, most of them narrowly focused on the "most damaged market" concept.

       It is the *small* bank customer—household or small business
firm—that is, presumably, most in need of protection against monopoly
and collusion, for that customer possesses few realistic alternatives.
Thus, banking markets are typically defined by the geographic areas
within which households and small businesses shop for checking accounts, loans, and savings deposits. By convention this is presumed to
be the *local market* fenced in by the boundaries of a city, county, or
metropolitan area. In short, *proximity* has come to dominate the operational definition of banking markets.

       Admittedly, such a pseudo-market definition introduces
untold distortions into the banking research process. We may wonder
with good reason how our research findings and public policy decisions
might be altered at some future point when we are able to cast aside
our present crude surrogates for the scope of real-world banking markets. City, county, and metropolitan boundaries are used basically for

convenience and because much supporting economic and demographic data are available for those geographic units. Unfortunately, as Wolken (1984) observes, market definition techniques have been slow to change and new methods of market delineation are seldom tried.

Yet, financial service markets are changing rapidly today with continuing improvements in communications and transportation methods. Some recognition of these technologically driven changes was taken by the Federal Reserve Board in 1980 when it defined certain major banking markets by the extent of their Ranally Metro Area (RMA)—a growth area containing a central city or cities and surrounding communities or built-up area having a population density of at least 70 per square mile and where at least 20 percent of the labor force commutes to the central city or cities. However, there is little evidence that the courts or other regulatory authorities responded in any substantial way to recent market-shaping economic and technological trends. Whether any portion of the barrage of county and metropolitan data we often use to assault bank structure issues is truly relevant and revealing of the answers we seek is a question few choose to raise and even fewer attempt to resolve.

ALTERNATIVE FORMS OF COMPETITION IN BANKING MARKETS

Pure or Perfect Competition. Ideally, public policy today is designed to promote *pure* or *perfect* competition in as many markets as possible. A purely competitive market is one in which:

1. Each firm supplying the market produces an identical set of products or services so that the output of each supplier is a perfect substitute for the outputs of all other suppliers.
2. The entry of new firms and the exit of existing firms either by merger or failure is free and unrestricted.
3. Each firm and each buyer is a price taker, rather than a price setter, in that there are so many firms supplying the market and so many potential buyers that no one individual or institution has sufficient market power or is able to successfully collude with others to impose its wishes on competitors.

4. Each firm seeks to maximize its long-run profitability or the wealth of its shareholders.
5. Production economies are not characterized by continuously positive returns to scale such that the largest size firm possible is not the most efficient (i.e., a natural monopoly); rather, there must be constant or diminishing returns to scale or, at least, scale economies that are small relative to the size of the market.

The concept of *perfect* competition adds to these conditions the absence of any barriers to the flow of resources between firms and industries, infinite divisibility in productive resources, and perfect knowledge by all market participants.

Economic theory contends that a marketplace in which these conditions are met leads to maximally efficient production, at lowest resource cost, for a given level of quality in the long run. The marginal cost associated with producing and supplying the last unit of output in a purely competitive market will, in the long run, equal the market price actually charged consumers for purchasing that last unit. Excess economic profits will be eliminated so that producers of goods and services receive only those profits necessary to efficiently generate the equilibrium quantity of output demanded by the marketplace. Each firm's level of output will be pushed to that level at which the average cost of production is lowest. Those suppliers unable to produce at minimum average production cost will begin taking losses and, in the long run, will cease their production.

If the conditions necessary for a purely competitive market are *not* met, poorly managed firms will probably survive. Frequent innovation in production techniques and in products is unlikely, and successful collusion is more likely. There will be some wastage of resources, higher prices for given level of quality, and excess profits. Expense preference behavior of the kind discussed earlier may also be more common. If a *natural monopoly* exists, eventually the marketplace will be served by only one firm, and the public will have no alternative sources of supply.

Tradeoffs Among Pure Competition, Safety, and Efficiency. But pure competition is an ideal seldom achieved and, historically, has often been pushed aside by other valued objectives. For example, concern over the *safety* of the public's deposits and the stability of the financial system has given rise to regulation of both entry into and exit from banking. Moreover, it is not clear that resource efficiency is always promoted by a marketplace that freely admits the entry of new firms and thereby prevents any one firm from achieving optimum (minimum cost) size. If substantial returns to scale arise from allowing banks to expand significantly in size, then a more enlightened public policy would promote the growth of mergers and acquisitions to yield a few efficient-size producers and thereby avoid waste. In these circumstances a monopolist or oligopolist will be able to produce at a lower cost per unit than can many small, inefficient producers operating under pure competition. Perhaps, too, less than perfectly competitive markets promote innovation in production techniques and in the development of new products because they more adequately shelter firms from risk.

Profits and Competition. Profits may be higher in imperfectly competitive markets owing to collusion and entry barriers. However, recent research suggests there may be other explanations for above-normal profits than imperfect competition alone. For example, high rates of return may be explained by risk differentials between firms, as argued by Stigler (1963) and by Cootner and Holland (1970). Then, too, recent research by Demsetz (1973) and Peltzman (1977) suggests that high rates of return may be as closely associated with superior efficiency and innovativeness as they are with collusion and joint maximization of profits. Still other research studies of imperfectly competitive markets (e.g., Brozen 1971) imply that variations in firm growth rates account for a substantial proportion of observed differences in profitability because demand may outrun production capacity in the short run. Moreover, a direct correlation may exist between advertising volume and profitability owing to product differentiation effects, as argued by Bloch (1974).

Barriers to Perfect Competition in Banking. Even with a vigorous public policy designed to promote aggressive competition in local banking markets across the nation, there are significant practical barriers to the attainment of perfect competition. Each bank, for example, sells, not an identical, but a slightly differentiated package of services as defined by the confluence of its location and convenience to the customer, the personalities of its staff, the nature of its advertising program, etc. Moreover, in few local banking markets is the number of competing financial service firms so large that each has no perceptible influence on market price.

Perhaps even more significant are the entry barriers in banking. These include the formal, legal restrictions imposed by state and federal statutes, which, nominally at least, require a demonstration of public need and of the absence of substantive damage to competitors. These restrictions have, however, been vitiated to a considerable extent in recent years by more liberal chartering and merger policies at the federal level. More formidable today are the entry barriers associated with *product differentiation* in the form of an existing network of bank-customer relationships, as previously discussed by Alhadeff (1954), Hodgman (1963), VanHoose (1983), and Wood (1975). As I observe in more detail later in this chapter, bank customers are often reluctant to shift their traditional banking relationships, in part because of the risks of financial disclosure to new parties and because of transactions costs. The result is a substantial entry barrier that tends to perpetuate market concentration and protects existing market shares. Not surprisingly, then, banking as a whole displays relatively high market share stability.

Thus, a substantial gap exists between theory and real-world banking markets with only limited applicability of general market concepts to any given local market situation. This fact of life became of special concern to bank regulatory authorities in the 1930s owing to the emergence of the federal government as an active regulator of the structure of local banking markets. Federal banking authorities moved to exert closer control over mergers, acquisitions, and new bank charters. Without an underlying theory to guide decisions on the supervision and regulation of imperfectly competitive markets, public policy was in danger of becoming unrealistic and irrelevant, if not positively harmful.

Theories of Imperfect Competition. Fortunately, the 1930s ushered in new concepts of market structure and behavior that recognized both the existence of elements of monopoly power and of competition in most real-world markets. These newer models were designed to account for market dominance by a handful of leading firms or to deal with the fact that individual firms through advertising, product innovation, etc., rarely sell products or services viewed as "identical" by their customers. Moreover, many firms produce multiple products and are able to practice some degree of price discrimination among separable groups of customers with varying elasticities of demand.

Two economists—Edward Chamberlin (1933) and Joan Robinson (1933)—began the development of a theory of imperfectly competitive markets. Later Clark (1940) developed an influential standard for policy decisions known as "workable competition." The development of these models of imperfect competition led other researchers—most notably Chandler (1938), Alhadeff (1954), Hodgman (1961), and Shull (1963)—to apply the models to the commercial bank as a multiproduct, price-discriminating firm and to banking markets where there were elements of monopolistic behavior.

Today we recognize the existence of several different kinds of market structure, depending on the number of suppliers of products and the degree to which those products are alike (homogeneous) or differentiated. Scherer (1980), for example, presents a five-way classification scheme (table 2.2). The degree of product or service differentiation is generally measured by the degree of *substitutability* among the offerings of different suppliers as viewed by their customers. If products are viewed by customers as perfect substitutes, they are *homogeneous*. When one supplier's product or service is preferred over those turned out by competing firms, even at the same price (owing perhaps to locational convenience or image), then product *differentiation* exists. In this case the product's price can be raised relative to rivals' prices and positive demand will still be present for the higher priced product.

The distinction between markets characterized by few or by many supplying firms depends on whether firms view themselves as affected by each other's actions. Where there is perceived interfirm influence, markets are considered to be *oligopolistic*. In pure competition each firm is a price taker and has no perceptible influence on price; in contrast, imperfectly competitive market structures—monopoly, oligopoly, and monopolistic competition—are characterized by the fact that each firm serving the market believes it can influence market price by changing the quantity of goods or services it produces. Thus, each firm in an imperfectly competitive market encounters a downward-sloping demand curve, requiring it to lower its price in order to expand its sales volume, and the price paid by its customers is greater than the firm's marginal cost of production. In the long run positive economic profits can emerge, especially if entry is restricted.

Development of the Structure-Conduct-Performance Model.
During the 1940s and 1950s an important extension of market structure concepts appeared in the form of the *structure-conduct-performance* (SCP) model discussed earlier. This theory of individual firm behavior under varying market structures was refined theoretically and empirically in the path-breaking work of Bain (1951, 1956, and 1968). He searched for a statistically significant relationship between profitability and concentration across a broad cross-section of U.S. manufacturing

Table 2.2. A Scheme for Classifying Market Structures

Degree of Product or Service Differentiation	Number of Sellers Supplying the Market		
	One	*A Few*	*Many*
Homogeneous product	—	Homogenous oligopoly	Pure competition
	Pure monopoly		
Differentiated product	—	Differentiated oligopoly	Monopolistic competition

industries. Subsequently, important empirical studies and conceptual refinements of the SCP model were carried out by Stigler (1963), Weiss (1971, 1974), Scherer (1970, 1980), Shepherd (1972), Williamson (1975), Kahn (1971), Blair (1972), and many others.

These studies of manufacturing and industrial market structure have tended to focus on three major areas: (1) the effects of conventional market structure indicators (such as the number and relative sizes of firms present in each market) on prices and profits; (2) the impact on costs, pricing, and profitability of entry restrictions against new competitors; and (3) the effects of changing market shares or market growth on conduct, pricing, and profit margins. Recent empirical studies with few exceptions suggest that, where the structure of a market contains few competing firms and significant entry barriers against new firms, the conduct of firms serving that market is more likely to include attempts to levy excessive prices and generate suboptimal output with possible joint maximization of earnings.

Is Structure Endogenous or Exogenous? More recent research has tended to question one of the underlying assumptions of the SCP model, namely, that the structure of a market is an *exogenous* factor in shaping the conduct and performance of individual firms. A newer "noncausal" alternative view has emerged contending that structure is, in part, an *endogenous* result of firm conduct. For example, firms achieving greater efficiency may drive less efficient firms from the market, resulting in an increase in market concentration. Proponents of this latter view tend to focus on the Lerner index of monopoly power—the price charged the customer less the marginal cost of production—as a key measure of individual firm and industry performance. Nevertheless, as noted in recent studies by Clarke and Davies (1982), Geroski (1982), and Donsimoni, Geroski, and Jacquemin (1984), proponents of the newer view generally argue that measures of market structure, such as the concentration ratio, are still a useful tool for evaluating firm and industry performance in responding to the public's demand for efficient and high-quality service.

Application of Structure and Competition Models to Banking. Whereas the applicability of the SCP model to nonfinancial markets was established convincingly as early as the 1940s and 1950s, it was not until the 1960s and 1970s that the basic validity of the SCP model was demonstrated in banking. The fact that banking was a regulated industry and, many analysts believed, not subject to strict application of the antitrust laws discouraged research on banking structure. However, that situation changed dramatically with passage of the Bank Merger Act in 1960 and a series of Supreme Court decisions, beginning with the landmark Philadelphia National Bank case in 1963, that emphasized the necessity of preserving and promoting competition in banking, even within the boundaries defined by federal and state regulation. The result, as we shall see in the ensuing chapters of this book, was a veritable explosion of bank market structure and competition studies mirroring earlier industrial studies. Overwhelmingly, these studies have concentrated on the relationships among bank market structure, the key *prices* in banking—the rate of interest on loans and the promised rate of return on deposits, and bank profitability as barometers of how well or how poorly the public is being served by American banks.

Other Structure Theories:
Potential and Future Competition
and Contestable Markets

The theories of bank structure detailed to this point focus on the status and effects of *existing* competition in a given marketplace. As noted by Shepherd (1984), such theories examine the character of *internal* market conditions where "internal conditions embody the degrees of actual competition and monopoly among firms already existing inside the market" (p. 574). In recent years the attention of economists has been directed more intently at conditions *external* to any given market. The basic notion here is that business firms not currently operating in a particular market may attempt to enter that market in some future period. This *threat* of outside entry presumably causes firms inside the market to behave differently than if they were not operating under such a threat. Theories of external conditions generally fall into three groups—potential competition, probable future competition, and a relatively new theory called "contestable markets."

POTENTIAL COMPETITION AND LIMIT PRICING

In the 1950s and 1960s the theory of potential competition became a significant factor in bank regulators' decisions. *Potential* competition requires the courts and regulatory authorities to assess the competition that is *likely* to develop between banks in the future. Is it likely, for example, that two banks in two different markets proposing to merge would, through growth and expansion of either of the institutions, become significant competitors in the future? If so, approval of the proposed merger would eliminate a potential increase in competition through future market entry. Because it does rest on the notion of *structural probabilities*—what is likely to happen to both concentration and bank performance in the future—the doctrine of potential competition has not received a warm reception from courts and regulators (except for the Federal Reserve Board) who must apply theory to real-world situations.

In the past the courts and regulatory agencies have tried to develop a set of objective criteria that can be used to assess the probability of potential competition developing into actual competition. Among the issues typically raised in these cases are the following:

1. Have the banks involved been active in the past in acquiring or branching into new markets?
2. Are the market areas involved economically attractive so that significant penetration into those markets is likely in the future?
3. Does existing federal or state law prohibit or restrict entry into the markets involved?
4. How is the structure of the markets changing and how concentrated are those markets today?
5. How significant in their own markets are the banks that are applying to merge or form a holding company?
6. Is the elimination of potential competition likely to be outweighed by the benefits to public convenience and public need if the proposed transaction is permitted to occur?

Concrete evidence of potential competition developing into actual competition is limited. One of the most frequently cited studies was prepared for the New York State Banking Department by Kohn and Carlo (1970). These researchers conducted a detailed examination of 14 bank merger and holding-company applications in New York State that were *denied* during the 1961–63 period. In 10 of those cases Kohn and Carlo concluded that potential competition became actual competition (on average, within four years), the institutions involved becoming "more effective competitors than they had been previously" (p. 3). In most cases competition increased because the large bank involved in the denied application eventually branched *de novo* into the other bank's area or acquired a smaller bank there, or the targeted institution was acquired by a third bank not previously represented in the target market. Kohn and Carlo concluded that "large, expansion-minded banking organizations are not easily discouraged. If blocked from entry by one method into a market they find attractive from an economic standpoint, they are likely to seek alternative means of entry" (p. 5).

The late 1960s and 1970s ushered in a rash of potential competition cases, the federal banking agencies and Department of Justice frequently moving to block market extension mergers and acquisitions using the doctrine. This upsurge in court cases stimulated further research work on the nature and likelihood of potential bank entry into new markets. For example, Gilbert (1973) inquired whether the regulatory agencies used the same criteria for evaluating the likelihood of future market entry as private banking organizations did and found they did not. Therefore, it was not clear to Gilbert that the regulators were realistically assessing potential competition in bank mergers across multiple markets.

Hannan (1979) tested the theory of *limit pricing*, which argues that firms operating in imperfectly competitive markets will keep their prices below levels that would invite entry by potential competitors. Tobit analysis of the threat of entry by banks branching in Pennsylvania indicated that the presence of greater numbers of large banks (more than $300 million in deposits) with branching potential raised the interest rate on passbook savings deposits paid by existing banks in the local market. Moreover, the threat of entry by outside banks appeared to have more impact in less competitive, more concentrated markets. However, with only this limited evidence to support the potential competition doctrine, its importance declined drastically as a basis for rejecting proposed mergers on competitive grounds, especially after the Federal Reserve Board lost a 1978 Michigan case on appeal, as discussed by Connor (1985).

PROBABLE FUTURE COMPETITION

In the 1970s and early 1980s the Reserve Board developed a concept related to potential competition for mergers across markets (i.e., market extension mergers). It is called *probable future competition.* As explained by Winer (1982), the Board has applied the future-competition concept to oligopolistic markets where a small group of financial firms has sufficient power to set price. A banking organization attempting to acquire one of these oligopolistic firms would not be likely to improve competition in the relevant market but would merely *replace* an existing firm. However, if such a merger were prohibited, the applicant company presumably would enter the relevant market by acquiring a much smaller firm (a "toehold acquisition") or by building a new office (*de novo* entry). Thus, Winer observes, approval of such a market extension merger would eliminate an "opportunity for improvement and could also solidify the anticompetitive structure of the market" (p. 528).

The future-competition doctrine has not been well received by the courts. In two famous 1980 holding-company cases—the

Mercantile Texas Corporation (Dallas) acquisition of Pan National Group, Inc. of El Paso and the Republic of Texas Corporation (Dallas) acquisition of Citizens National Bank of Waco—the Federal Reserve Board *denied* these bank acquisitions on grounds of probable future competition. Both denials were subsequently vacated by the U.S. Fifth Circuit Court of Appeals, the court ordering the Board to demonstrate (1) that the target market was already concentrated, (2) whether a large or small pool of potential market entrants existed, (3) whether there were persuasive reasons to suggest the acquiring institution would prefer to enter the market *de novo* or via a toehold acquisition or would make investments elsewhere if the merger application were denied, and (4) whether independent entry would carry substantial likelihood of promoting competition or of deconcentrating the target market. In light of these high evidentiary barriers the Federal Reserve *approved* both holding-company acquisitions by majority vote.

It is difficult to assess the outlook for the probable-future-competition doctrine. Recent research has found some supporting evidence that a substantial proportion of merger applications in relatively concentrated markets is subsequently followed by more procompetitive entry methods after the merger requests were denied. For example, Rhoades and Yeats (1972) and Rhoades (1981) find that of 22 bank merger and acquisition applications denied by the Federal Reserve Board and the Federal Deposit Insurance Corporation during the 1960s, predictions of future market entry by these agencies turned out to be correct 68 percent of the time. Yet, as Stutzer (1984) argues, it is by no means clear that the application of the doctrine would increase the public's welfare over and above the regulatory costs involved.

The Federal Reserve Board's approach to the future-competition concept has been attacked by the Department of Justice. Justice's 1982 merger guidelines (discussed in chapter 5) appear to be much more liberal than the Board's approach to deciding if future competition applies in any particular case. In view of the recent trend toward more liberal interpretation of the antitrust laws it seems unlikely that the probable-future-competition doctrine will be vigorously applied in the future. There is more support in the judiciary today for prohibiting mergers and acquisitions on grounds of avoiding an *increase* in market concentration rather than for proactive steps to *decrease* concentration.

THE THEORY OF CONTESTABLE MARKETS

Early in the 1980s a new theory of the linkages among competition, size of firm, and market performance appeared—*contestable markets,* the contribution of Baumol, Panzar, and Willig (1982) following several years of study of the cost structures of multiproduct industrial firms. While still awaiting extensive application in banking, contestable markets holds some promise for future bank competition research because it deals with scale economies in a multiproduct framework—one of the key problem areas for bank management and for regulatory control over bank expansion.

Contestable markets posits that conditions *external* to a market dominate conditions *internal.* The theory assumes free entry and exit of competitors who can rapidly enter or leave any market without losing their capital (i.e., sunk cost is zero) and possess the same cost functions as firms that already serve the market. New entrants can duplicate any existing firm and completely replace it without significant costs or time lags. Technology, customer loyalty, and size are not significant entry barriers. Thus, potential competitors cannot enter a market with price cutting and be profitable, but the fact that there are always potential entrants with identical cost functions as existing firms prevents existing companies from earning excess profits. Entry can be forestalled if existing firms in the market become efficient in production and restrained in their pricing policies. Thus, *threat of entry nullifies monopoly power.*

In contestable-markets equilibrium, no firm currently serving the market will suffer losses, and neither can any firm—existing or potential competitor—find an output mix that generates excess profits. An industry that is not minimizing production costs invites costless entry, eliminating inefficiencies, as well as excess profits. Thus, as Shepherd (1984) notes, contestable markets is a theory essentially of "ultra-free entry" resulting in "efficient outcomes," including zero excess profits, optimal prices, and efficient production and innovation even in purely monopolistic markets (p. 572). This presumes, of course, that market demand reacts instantly to changes in posted prices and to any differences in posted prices between firms currently supplying the market.

While contestable-markets theory contains a number of problems yet to be resolved and its empirical validity remains an open question, it would appear to hold considerable promise for an analysis of the efficiency, cost structures, and market performance of multi-product firms, particularly those in the financial services field. In many aspects of financial services, for example, entry and exit have been made relatively easy, sunk costs are relatively minor, and capital appears to be readily shiftable among multiple uses. Unfortunately, very little work has yet been done addressing the possible linkages between banking and contestable markets.

Studies of Selected Banking Markets and Customer Preferences

The structure of banking markets and the organizational forms individual banks adopt are subject to close regulation. Changes in the number of banks, branch offices, and holding-company affiliations, and changes in the package of financial services offered are all regulated to promote competitive efficiency and public convenience. Yet, how often have banking regulators checked into the *actual benefits* of bank regulation? Is the public really better served today after decades of extensive bank regulation? Are we getting really effective banking competition and the fruits of competition predicted by theory? It is surprising how few published studies have inquired into the public's view of its own banking service needs and how well those needs actually are being met by American banks today.

   One of the earliest such studies was prepared by Luttrell and Pettigrew (1966) who surveyed a random sample of nonbank businesses in the St. Louis metropolitan area (SMSA). These researchers found that the largest local businesses ($200,000 or more in net worth) tended to use one of the three largest metropolitan banks as their lead bank, while factors other than bank size—convenience, banking hours, drive-in windows, availability of parking, and fast service—guided smaller firms in selecting their principal bank. Nearly three-fourths of the small firms surveyed banked within three miles of their place of business. Even among the largest firms the nearness of their principal bank to their business location was a key factor, though the size of the bank chosen and its credit policies were even more important than nearness.

One third of the businesses with $200,000 or more in net worth had banking connections outside the local market. More than 70 percent of these large firms had checking accounts at more than one bank compared with only about one quarter of the smaller firms. In fact, from the Luttrell-Pettigrew survey it was quite evident that the larger the firm, the more likely it was to shop around for both credit and deposit services and to maintain multiple banking connections. However, among all sizes of businesses there was strong *loyalty* to existing banking relationships. For example, the largest size companies had done business with their principal bank an average of 26 years; among smaller firms the average principal-bank relationship extended over about 15 years. However, despite evidence of strong loyalty, most firms showed little hesitancy to open new accounts and subdivide their banking relationships.

Luttrell and Pettigrew concluded that the business services market is *bifurcated* into a market for large banks and large businesses that extends beyond a single metropolitan area and a second fragmented market (with numerous submarkets) for small banks and small businesses. The market devoted to the largest firms appeared to be intensely competitive because of the willingness of even long-term bank customers to open new accounts elsewhere, while maintaining their traditional banking connections. On the other hand, the importance of *convenience* in the small-firm market serves to limit competition because of the availability of few banks within close proximity to the customer, giving local banks a substantial competitive advantage. As Luttrell and Pettigrew observe:

the question of bank competition for business accounts may thus turn not so much on concentration of resources in a few banks as on whether more than one or two banks are effectively competing for the business of small firms and households in the neighborhood shopping centers and sub-areas of the SMSA. Furthermore, the number of large banks may not be an important competitive factor. Actual and potential competition from large banks in other metropolitan areas may not be an important competitive factor (p. 12).

The St. Louis survey was followed in 1967 by the publication of three metropolitan-area surveys of bank customers in Elkhart, Indiana; Cedar Rapids, Iowa; and Appleton, Wisconsin, performed by Kaufman (1967 a, b) and Stiles (1967) on behalf of the Federal Reserve Bank of Chicago. The Stiles study focused on 151 business firms selected in a stratified sample (by size and industry type) from the business community in Cedar Rapids, Iowa. The large majority of business customers reported satisfaction with the array of bank services available to them and, as in the St. Louis study, there was little evidence of "shopping around"— often described by business customers as "unnecessary." Among the possible reasons for this attitude, as cited by Stiles, may be the small number of prospective suppliers of financial services for smaller businesses and the required disclosure of sensitive financial information to a new bank when the customer seeks a new source of credit. Another factor is the ability of the customer's initial bank to "outbid" its rivals for the customer's account because it has already incurred the expense of credit investigation. A new bank must incur a higher marginal cost to make a "tender offer" to a new customer. The Cedar Rapids study suggested that a "traumatic experience" (such as the denial of an important loan request) is the kind of jolt that "may be necessary to provoke an active canvass of alteratives. . . on the part of business customers of banks" (p. 26). *Convenience* was again stressed as a key factor in the initial choice of a banking relationship and as a key reason for persistent customer loyalty.

The Elkhart, Indiana, and Appleton, Wisconsin, studies by Kaufman (1967 a, b) were broader in scope, focusing on both business and household customers—each group the target of a random mail survey. Both studies found a strong bias among households and smaller businesses toward choosing a *local* bank for their principal banking relationship. (In Appleton, for example, 92 percent of the businesses and 97 percent of the households used an institution within the local community as their primary bank.) Firms using banks outside the local community were primarily larger businesses (in Elkhart, more than $2.5 million in annual sales) or branches of corporations headquartered elsewhere, while households generally used banks out of town only when a member of the household was employed outside the local community. When asked to name possible alternative banks, both sets of customers mainly chose other *local* institutions.

Roughly half the respondent businesses and households in the Appleton and Elkhart communities had accounts at more than one bank. Convenience and service quality once again dominated the bank selection process for both businesses and households with strong loyalty to the initially chosen bank on the part of both customer groups. The large majority—60 percent or more of households—rated bank service quality as *excellent*. Interestingly enough, about one fifth of the firms and two fifths of the responding households used one or more services (especially credit) from *nonbank* financial institutions, such as savings and loan associations.

More recently, customer surveys by Eisenbeis (1970), Gelder and Budzeika (1970), Lundsten and Mandell (1977), Whitehead (1980), Watro (1981), Glassman (1982), and Scott and Dunkelberg (1984) have tended to confirm the earlier Midwest bank customer studies. Once again, customers strongly emphasize *convenience* to home and office in their banking choices. But local banks are *less* dominant the *larger* the city they serve.

Credit availability and customer satisfaction apparently are not significantly different between city and rural banking markets. In fact, in the one study by Scott and Dunkelberg (1984) looking into the matter, small businesses in rural communities ranked their principal bank's performance above that of urban banks in knowing the customer's business, in reliability, and in personal service (due, in part, to lower employee turnover rates at rural institutions). This study found no evidence that rural banking markets are any less competitive than urban markets in serving small businesses. Differential service and service pricing between rural and urban markets is *not* a well-researched area, however. In view of the trend today toward significant interstate expansion by large banking organizations this is an area very much in need of further inquiry.

The more important and more financially significant the service, the wider the geographic area over which the customer is willing to search for the best terms available. Thus, auto and home loan markets are wider than the markets for checkbook accounts, small savings deposits, and safety deposit rentals. However, nonlocal financial competitors appear to have increased in importance, especially in suburban areas, and particularly for small business customers and for loans more than deposits. Moreover, if service terms are perceived to be the "same" or "highly similar" from bank to bank, the customer is less likely to venture far afield in choosing where to bank. This suggests that continued deregulation of financial services will contribute to a broadening of banking markets if customers perceive greater disparities from bank to bank in service terms and service menus.

In summary, the few published studies of the opinions of bank customers on the quality, cost, and availability of financial services come to remarkably consistent conclusions. By and large, the quality of bank credit and deposit services is *favorably* rated by the public and *convenience* is the dominant factor in choosing a bank for both businesses and households. This convenience factor plus the risks (such as alienating the first bank) and the costs of "shopping around" (including the financial disclosure requirements) discourage changing banks frequently among the large majority of bank customers. The net result is to limit most banking markets to primarily *local* areas, often as narrowly defined as the neighborhood (particularly for households and locally owned businesses). Thus, competing alternatives are narrow and neighboring banks have a clear competitive advantage. The resulting disadvantage for distant banks can generally be overcome only by offering significantly better price or nonprice terms or, more commonly, when the initial bank denies an important customer request (especially a loan application).

The customer opinion studies are at once both encouraging and disturbing— encouraging, because there is little evidence in the surveys of customer needs unmet, of poor service quality, of arbitrary and capricious customer treatment, or of general public dissatisfaction with banking services. There is, on the other hand, a disturbing note because the strong emphasis on convenience and the hesitancy of most customers to change banks (though not to open multiple accounts) bespeaks *imperfect markets* with the potential for substantial discrimination and excess prices and profits. One obvious caveat that must be kept in mind, however, is the age of most of the customer surveys. Much has changed recently in the technology of communication, increasing the ease with which customers can reach distant financial institutions. Moreover, those studies reviewed here provide information only as of a single point in time and do not capture how well banks are dynamically responding to the rapidly changing, increasingly sophisticated financial needs of their business and household customers.

Many analysts would find in the customer opinion studies the need either for a strong regulatory watchdog role over local market structures on the part of bank supervisory authorities or for an aggressive legislative and regulatory effort to increase the number of institutions offering competing financial services in local markets. As I discuss more thoroughly in the chapters that follow, it is predominantly this *latter* route that Congress and the federal regulatory agencies have chosen in recent years.

Summary and a Look Forward

In this chapter I have taken a broad overview of banking *organizations*—their arrangement and management styles—and of the *structures* of banking markets and their implications for public policy. Each organizational form in banking—unit or branch, holding-company affiliated or independent, conglomerate or narrowly focused—is a response to significant external pressures that continue to shape the industry, including technological changes, regulation, the pricing and availability of scarce productive resources, and demographic trends. The same is true of the varying market structures through which banking services are sold, from highly competitive with intense rivalry to highly concentrated with one or a handful of suppliers of financial services sometimes acting in concert to protect their earnings and market shares. Here, too, changing technology, regulation, demographic shifts, and resource availability and cost shape the character of banking markets and, through the market mechanism, dictate how well the public is supplied with the financial services it needs.

My principal focus in this chapter has been on the *expected* (theoretical) links between form of bank organization, structure of banking market, and the performance of banks in responding to the public's demands. At the core of any such discussion is the *structure-conduct-performance model* derived from the economic theory of markets. It suggests that in markets where banks agree to act in concert to protect their individual positions and refuse to aggressively compete, individual bank conduct is unlikely to yield financial services in optimal quantity and quality at prices that reflect the efficient use of scarce resources. In the past the principal goal of bank regulation has been to avoid such suboptimal market structures and to prohibit or restrict those organizational forms that, allegedly, lead to poor performance in meeting the public's demand for financial services. Increasingly today, however, the regulatory factor is being supplanted by competition and the free interplay of market forces in shaping market structures, bank organizations, and performance.

This shift of emphasis in public policy from a dominant role for regulation to a dominant role for competition raises a number of intriguing issues. For example, does the structure-conduct-performance model still apply to banking? Are banks today truly responsive in terms of service availability and pricing to changes in market structure and organization that promote greater competition? If so, *which* changes in structure and organization are best in a performance sense in today's financial markets? Should those changes be achieved by promoting the growth of large conglomerate financial service firms or smaller, narrowly focused suppliers of conventional banking services? Should existing financial service firms be encouraged to expand their activities significantly—perhaps through more lenient public policies toward mergers and acquisitions—or should the entry of new, relatively small firms be encouraged along with more vigorous enforcement of antitrust standards? *None* of these questions is new. It is rather their *importance* that has increased with the inauguration of government policies that rely more on the market and less on regulatory dictum. In the chapters that follow I explore each of these questions and attempt to assess the content and quality of research directed at answering them.

References

Alhadeff, David A. 1954. *Monopoly and Competition in Banking.* Berkeley and Los Angeles: University of California Press.

—— 1974. "Barriers to Bank Entry." *Southern Economic Journal,* 40:589-603.

Arnould, Richard J. 1985. "Agency Costs in Banking Firms: An Analysis of Expense Preference Behavior." *Journal of Economics and Business,* 37:103–112.

Bain, Joe S. 1951. "Relation of Profit Rate to Industrial Concentration in American Manufacturing, 1936–1940." *Quarterly Journal of Economics* (August), 65:293-324.

—— 1956. *Barriers to New Competition.* Cambridge, Mass.: Harvard University Press.

—— 1968. *Industrial Organization.* Rev. Ed. New York: Wiley.

Baumol, William J., John C. Panzar, and Robert D. Willig. 1982. *Contestable Markets and the Theory of Industry Structure.* New York: Harcourt, Brace Jovanovich.

Becker, G. 1957. *The Economics of Discrimination.* Chicago: University of Chicago Press.

Bedingfield, James P., Philip M. J. Reckers, and A. J. Stagliano. 1985. "Distributions of Financial Ratios in the Commercial Banking Industry," *The Journal of Financial Research,* 8(1):77-81.

Benston, George J. 1973. "The Optimal Banking Structure: Theory and Evidence." *Journal of Bank Research* (Winter), pp. 220–37.

Blair, John M. 1972. *Economic Concentration.* New York: Harcourt Brace Jovanovich.

Bloch, Harry. 1974. "Advertising and Profitability: A Reappraisal." *Journal of Political Economy* (March-April), 82:267-86.

Browning, Edgar K. and Jacquelene M. Browning. 1983. *Microeconomic Theory and Applications*. Boston: Little, Brown.

Brozen, Yale. 1971. "Bain's Concentration and Rates of Return Revisited." *Journal of Law and Economics* (October), 14:351–69.

Cartinhour, Gaines T. 1931. *Branch, Group and Chain Banking* (September). New York: The MacMillan Company.

Chamberlin, Edward H. 1933. *The Theory of Monopolistic Competition*. Cambridge, Mass.: Howard University Press.

Chandler, Lester V. 1938. "Monopolistic Elements in Commercial Banking." *Journal of Political Economy* (February), 46(1):1–22.

Clark, John M. 1940. "Toward A Concept of Workable Competition." *American Economic Review* (June), 30:241-256.

Clarke, R. and S. Davies. 1982. "Market Structure and Price-Cost Margins." *Economica* (August), 49(3):277–88.

Clemens, Eli W. 1950–51. "Price Discrimination and the Multiple-Product Firm." *The Review of Economic Studies*, 19:1–11.

Connor, Michael C. 1985. "The Redirection of Power in American Banking." *Mergers & Acquisitions* (Winter), pp. 48–53.

Cootner, Paul and D. Holland. 1970. "Rate of Return and Business Risk." *Bell Journal of Law and Economics and Management Science* (Fall), 1:211–26.

Darnell, Jerome C. 1966. "Chain Banking." *National Banking Review*, no. 3, pp. 307–31.

Demsetz, Harold. 1973. "Industry Structure, Market Rivalry, and Public Policy." *Journal of Law and Economics*, 16(1):1–9.

Donsimoni, Marie-Paule, Paul Geroski, and Alexis Jacquemin. 1984. "Concentration Indices and Market Power: Two Views." *Journal of Industrial Economics* (June), 32(4):419–34.

Ederington, Louis H. and Samuel L. Skogstag. 1977. "Measurement of Banking Competition and Geographic Markets." *Journal of Money, Credit and Banking*, 12:469–82.

Edwards, Franklin R. 1977. "Managerial Objectives in Regulated Industries: Expense-Preference Behavior in Banking." *Journal of Political Economy* (February), 85(1):147–62.

Eisenbeis, Robert A. 1970. "A Study of Geographic Markets for Business Loans: The Results for Local Markets." *Conference on Bank Structure and Competition-Proceedings*. Federal Reserve Bank of Chicago.

Fraas, Arthur G. 1974. *The Performance of Individual Bank Holding Companies*. Staff Economic Study no. 84. Washington, D.C.: Board of Governors of the Federal Reserve System.

Gelder, Ralph H. and George Budzeika. 1970. "Banking Market Determination: The Case of Central Nassau County." *Monthly Review* (November). Federal Reserve Bank of New York, pp. 258–266.

Geroski, P. 1982. "Interpreting A Correlation Between Profits and Concentration." *Journal of Industrial Economics* (March), 30(3):319–326.

Gilbert, Gary G. 1975. "An Analysis of Federal Regulatory Decisions on Market Extension Bank Mergers." *Journal of Money, Credit and Banking*, 5:81–92.

Glassman, Cynthia A. 1982. "Evidence from the Banking Side." *Economic Review* (April), 67:54–58. Federal Reserve Bank of Atlanta.

Glassman, Cynthia A. and Stephen A. Rhoades. 1980. "Owner vs. Manager Control Effects on Bank Performance." *The Review of Economics and Statistics* (May), 62:263–70.

Guerin-Calvert, Margaret E. 1983. "The 1982 Department of Justice Merger Guidelines: Applications to Banking Mergers, "*Issues in Bank Regulation*, Winter, pp. 18–25.

Hannan, Timothy. 1979a. "Expense Preference Behavior in Banking: A Reexamination." *Journal of Political Economy* (August), 87:891–95.

——— 1979b. "Limit Pricing and the Banking Industry." *Journal of Money, Credit and Banking* (November), 11(4):438-46.

Hannan, Timothy and Ferdinand Mavinga. 1980. "Expense Preference and Management Control: The Case of the Banking Firm." *Bell Journal of Economics* (Autumn), 11:671–82.

Hodgman, Donald R. 1961. "The Deposit Relationship of Commercial Bank Investment Behavior." *Review of Economics and Statistics* (August), 43:257–68.

——— 1963. *Commercial Bank Loan and Investment Policy*. Champaign, Illinois: Bureau of Economic and Business Research.

Houck, James P. 1984. " 'Market': A Definition for Teaching." *Western Journal of Agricultural Economics*. 9(2):353–56.

Jensen, Michael C. 1983. "Organization Theory and Methodology." *The Accounting Review* (April), 58(2):319–39.

Jensen, Michael C. and William H. Meckling. 1976. "Theory of the Firm: Managerial Behavior, Agency Costs and Ownership Structure." *Journal of Financial Economics* (October), 3:305–60.

——— 1979. "Rights and Production Functions: An Application to Labor-Managed Firms and Codetermination." *Journal of Business* (October), 52(4):469–506.

Kahn, Alfred E. 1971. *The Economics of Regulation*, vol. 1 and 2. New York: Wiley.

Kalish III, Lionel. 1972. *The Influence of Current and Potential Competition on a Commercial Bank's Operating Efficiency* (January). Working Paper no. 15. Project for Basic Monetary Studies. Federal Reserve Bank of St. Louis.

Kaufman, George G. 1967a. *Customers View Bank Markets and Services: A Survey of Elkhart, Indiana*. Staff Economic Study no. 37, Washington, D.C.: Board of Governors of the Federal Reserve System.

——— 1967b. *Business Firms and Households View Commercial Banks: A Survey of Appleton, Wisconsin* (September). Federal Reserve Bank of Chicago.

Kildoyle, Patrick Page. 1971. *A Study of Bank Customers in Central Nassau County* (June). Banking Studies Department. Federal Reserve Bank of New York.

Kohn, Ernest and Carmen J. Carlo. 1970. *Potential Competition: Unfounded Faith or Pragmatic Foresight?* (March). New York State Banking Department.

Lawrence, Robert J. 1971. *Operating Policies of Bank Holding Companies—Part 2* (March). Staff Economic Study no. 59. Washington, D.C.: Board of Governors of the Federal Reserve System.

—— 1974. *Operating Policies of Bank Holding Companies—Part 2: Nonbanking Subsidiaries* (March). Staff Economic Study no. 81. Washington, D.C.: Board of Governors of the Federal Reserve System.

Lundsten, Lorman L. and Lewis Mandell. 1977. "Consumer Selection of Banking Offices—Effects of Distance, Services, and Interest Rate Differentials." *Conference on Bank Structure and Competition-Proceedings*. Federal Reserve Bank of Chicago. pp. 260–86.

Luttrell, Clifton B. and William E. Pettigrew. 1966. "Banking Markets for Business Firms in the St. Louis Area." *Review* (September), pp. 9–12. Federal Reserve Bank of St. Louis.

Mayne, Lucille S. 1976. "Management Policies of Bank Holding Companies and Bank Performance." *Journal of Bank Research* (Spring), pp. 37–48.

Mote, Larry R. 1967a. "Competition in Banking: The Issues." *Business Conditions* (January), pp. 8–16. Federal Reserve Bank of Chicago.

—— 1967b. "Competition in Banking: What Is Known? What Is the Evidence?" *Business Conditions* (February), pp. 7–16. Federal Reserve Bank of Chicago.

Peltzman, Sam. 1977. "The Gains and Losses from Industrial Concentration." *The Journal of Law and Economics* (October), 20(2): 229–63.

Perlick, Walter W. and Charles L. Barngrover. 1975. "Interlocking Directorates and Commercial Banks: Implications for Competitiveness in Alternative Banking Structures" (April). Paper Presented at the Eastern Finance Association, Columbia, South Carolina.

Rhoades, Stephen A. 1977. *Structure-Performance Studies in Banking: A Summary and Evaluation*. Staff Economic Study no. 92. Washington, D.C.: Board of Governors of the Federal Reserve System.

——1981. "Probable Future Competition and Predicting Future Entry in Bank Merger Cases." *Issue in Bank Regulation* (Spring), pp. 30-36

——1982. *Structure-Performance Studies in Banking: An Updated Summary and Evaluation* (August). Staff Economic Study no. 119. Washington, D.C.: Board of Governors of the Federal Reserve System.

Rhoades, Stephen A. and A. J. Yeats. 1972. "An Analysis of Entry and Expansion Predictions in Bank Acquisition and Merger Cases." *Western Economic Journal* (September), 10(3):337-345.

Robinson, Joan. 1933. *The Economics of Imperfect Competition*. London: MacMillan.

Rose, Peter S. and William L. Scott. 1984. "Heterogeneity in Performance Within the Bank Holding Company Sector: Evidence and Implications." *Journal of Economic and Business*, 36:1-14.

Scherer, F.M. 1970. *Industrial Market Structure and Economic Performance*. Chicago: Rand McNally College Publishing.

——1980. *Industrial Market Structure and Economic Performance*, ed. 2. Chicago: Rand McNally College Publishing Company.

Scott, Jonathon A. and William C. Dunkelberg. 1984. "Rural versus Urban Bank Performance: An Analysis of Market Competition for Small Business Loans," *Journal of Bank Research*, Autumn, pp. 167-178.

Shepherd, William G. 1972. "The Elements of Market Structure." *Review of Economic and Statistics* (February), 54:25-37.

——1984. "Contestability vs. Competition." *American Economic Review* (September), 74(4):572-87.

——1982. "Monopoly Profits and Economies of Scale." In John Craven, ed. *Industrial Organization, Antitrust, and Public Policy.* Boston: Klumer Nijhof.

Shull, Bernard. 1963. "Commercial Banks as Multiple-Product Price-Discriminating Firms." In Deane Carson, ed. *Banking and Monetary Studies*, pp. 351-68. Homewood, Ill.: Richard D. Irwin.

Smirlock, Michael and William Marshall. 1983. "Monopoly Power and Expense-Preference Behavior: Theory and Evidence to the Contrary." *Bell Journal of Economics* (Spring), pp. 166-78.

Stern, Louis W. and John R. Grabner, Jr. 1972. *Competition in the Marketplace.* Glenview, Ill. Scott, Foresman.

Stigler, George J. 1963. *Capital and Rates of Return in Manufacturing Industries.* Princeton, N.J.: Princeton University Press.

Stiles, Lynn A. 1967. *Businesses View Banking Services: A Survey of Cedar Rapids, Iowa.* (March). Federal Reserve Bank of Chicago.

Stutzer, Michael J. 1984. "Probable Future Competition in Banking Antitrust Determination: Research Findings." *Quarterly Review* (Summer), pp. 9-20. Federal Reserve Bank of Minneapolis.

U.S. Congress, House Committee on Banking and Currency, Subcommittee on Domestic Finance. 1964. *Twenty Largest Stockholders of Record in Member Banks of the Federal Reserve System.* 88th Congress, 2nd Sess., Washington, D.C.: U.S. Government Printing Office.

U.S. Congress, Senate Committee on Banking, Housing and Urban Affairs. 1978. *Special Survey of Bank Stock Loans to Officials, and Major Stockholders of Other Banks, Inside Loans and Overdrafts.* U.S. Senate, March 16, 1978. Washington, D.C.: U.S. Government Printing Office.

VanHoose, David D. 1983. "Monetary Policy Under Alterntive Bank Market Structures." *Journal of Banking and Finance*, 7:383-404.

Watro, Paul R. 1981. "How Should Banking Markets Be Delineated?" *Economic Commentary* (December 1). Federal Reserve Bank of Cleveland.

Weiss, Leonard. 1971. "Quantitative Studies of Industrial Organization." In Michael D. Intriligator, ed. *Frontiers of Quantitative Economics.* Amsterdam: North-Holland Publishing.

——1974. "The Concentration-Profits Relationship and Anti-Trust." In H. J. Goldschmid, H. Michael Mann, and J. F. Weston, eds. *Industrial Concentration: The New Learning.* Boston: Little, Brown.

Whitehead, David D. 1980. "Relevant Geographic Banking Markets: How Should They Be Defined?" *Economic Review* (January-February), 65:20-28. Federal Reserve Bank of Atlanta.

Whitehead, David D. and Jan Lujytes. 1982. "An Alternative View of Bank Competition: Profit or Share Maximization." *Economic Review* (November), pp. 48-57. Federal Reserve Bank of Atlanta.

Williamson, O. 1963. "Managerial Discretion and Business Behavior." *American Economic Review* (December), 53:1032-57.

——1975. *Markets and Hierarchies: Analysis and Antitrust Implications.* New York: The Free Press.

Winer, Anthony S. 1982. "Applying the Theory of Probable Future Competition."
    Federal Reserve Bulletin (September), pp. 527-33.
Wolken, John D. 1984. *Geographic Market Delineation: A Review of the Literature.*
    Staff Economic Study no. 140. Washington, D.C.: Board of Governors of the
    Federal Reserve System.
Wood, John. 1975. *Commercial Bank Loan and Investment Behavior.* London: Wiley.

PART II: IMPACT OF NEW ENTRY AND GROWTH ON BANK PERFORMANCE

3.

Entry and Exit
in American Banking

COMMERCIAL BANKING has always been a regulated industry in the United States. Some observers have referred to the extensive regulations confronting banks in recent years as "cradle to grave" supervision. No bank today can be organized and open its doors for business without federal or state regulatory approval, and in most instances, *both* are required. Nor can banks liquidate their assets and go out of business without government sanction. In between the opening and closing of a bank, both the management and the operations of each banking corporation are closely scrutinized by federal or state regulatory agencies and sometimes both. The regulation of existing banks is considered in subsequent chapters. In this chapter, however, the focus is on the beginning and the end of the bank regulatory process—the chartering of new banks and the relatively few banks that fail each year. (See table 3.1.) Both processes are heavily influenced by regulation and, perhaps most importantly, by the underlying current of economic conditions.

Table 3.1. Entry and Exit in U.S. Banking

Charters Issued for New Commercial Banks

Years	Total for All Commercial Banks	National Bank Centers	State Bank Charters			
			Total	State Member	Nonmember Insured	Noninsured
1946–49	407	67	340	34	247	59
1950–59	880	181	699	49	543	107
1960–69	1,854	822	1,032	51	843	138
1970–79	2,482	575	1,907	180	1,453	274
1980–84	1,758	744	1,014	181	523	310

Number of Commercial Bank Failures

Year	Insured	Noninsured	Total	Year	Insured	Noninsured	Total
1946	1	1	2	1965	5	4	9
1947	5	1	6	1966	7	1	8
1948	3	0	3	1967	4	0	4
1949	5	4	9	1968	3	0	3
1950	4	1	5	1969	9	0	9
1951	2	3	5	1970	7	1	8
1952	3	1	4	1971	6	0	6
1953	4	1	5	1972	1	2	3
1954	2	2	4	1973	6	0	6
1955	5	0	5	1974	4	0	4
1956	2	1	3	1975	13	1	14
1957	2	1	3	1976	16	1	17
1958	4	5	9	1977	6	0	6
1959	3	0	3	1978	7	0	7
1960	1	1	2	1979	10	0	10
1961	5	4	9	1980	10	0	10
1962	1	2	3	1981	10	—	10
1963	2	0	2	1982	42	—	42
1964	7	1	8	1983	48	—	48
				1984	79	—	79

SOURCE: Federal Reserve Board and Federal Deposit Insurance Corporation, *Annual Report*, various issues.

The Bank Charter Process
in The United States

EARLY HISTORY OF BANK CHARTERS

During the colonial period of American history there were few domestic banks as we know them today and, according to Krooss and Blyn (1971), none appeared before 1750. British banks discounted most of the commercial notes arising from trade with the colonies and held the deposits of large trading companies and wealthy colonial landholders. In the domestic economy trade was generally carried on by barter and, therefore, bypassed local banks. Moreover, the colonial population was small and widely dispersed, nine out of every ten persons working on farms. Lending was largely confined to sales on account with merchants extending credit to their customers on a short-term basis.

One of the most pressing financial needs that did give rise to a number of limited-service banks during the colonial period was the profusion of different forms of currency in circulation. Many immigrants to the American colonies brought their own coin and currency with them. The result was a wide variety of different exchange media in circulation—Spanish pieces of eight, British pounds, French francs, etc. Some colonial merchants began to offer currency exchange services, usually in conjunction with their main business line. A few merchants found currency trading profitable enough to specialize in that service—a practice that led quite naturally (as it had earlier in Europe) to the making of loans and, ultimately, to accepting deposits.

The colonial banks—most of which were land banks making loans against real estate rather than true financial intermediaries—remained small and few. Commerce and trading were limited in the colonial era because many farming operations were self-sufficient. Capital was scarce in the absence of a well-developed financial system or a large class of savers who might supply loanable funds to fuel business growth and expansion. As noted earlier, British merchant banking institutions supplied most of the capital required for international trade, and the early American banks were in no position to offer competition to these large and well-established merchant lenders—a fact of American financial life that persisted well into the nineteenth century. Added to these problems was the public's suspicious and frequently hostile attitude toward the business of banking—a phenomenon evident in many quarters even today. Some of this feeling was grounded in religious philosophies that, at least as far back as the Middle Ages, viewed the lending of money at interest as sinful. A number of times in history banks have been burned to the ground by irate mobs opposed to professional banking practices.

When governments were established in the original thirteen colonies and especially after the states were brought under the Constitution, procedures were established for the chartering of new banks. In fact, as Krooss and Blyn (1971) note, by 1800 every state except Georgia, New Jersey, North Carolina, and Vermont had chartered at least one commercial bank. Beginning in the 1830s eighteen states, led by Michigan (1837), Georgia (1838), and New York (1838), passed "free banking" legislation that made entry into the industry quite easy, subject only to minimum capital requirements and, in some instances, the pledge of securities behind any bank notes issued. A few states established commissions to review applications and issue new charters. Frequently, however, the charter decision was left to the state legislatures and, thus, became heavily infused with politics. Some charters were issued to groups of organizers simply to pay off political debts or to win popular support. Predictably, such banks often failed and shook the confidence of the public in the viability of other local financial institutions.

Equally frustrating to the public was the profusion of paper currency (notes) issued by early American banks. Before the widespread acceptance of deposit banking, commercial banks made loans simply by printing and issuing notes bearing the name or stamp of the issuing bank. These notes circulated as currency, but their value depended heavily on the quantity issued and the reputation of the issuing bank. Several states tried to control the issue of bank notes by requiring the pledge of state and federal bonds behind them and the redemption of notes in specie upon customer demand. However, owing to their low production cost, notes frequently were overissued so that it became virtually impossible to redeem many of them in gold, silver, or other forms of money in which the public had more confidence. Many so-called "wildcat banks" situated themselves in remote locations and opened for only a few hours a day—devices designed to make conversion of bank notes into gold, silver, or hard currencies as difficult as possible.

The result was that many bank notes circulated at substantial discounts from par. When a state bank failed and it did not have any remaining assets of value to be liquidated, its notes became worthless to the holder, adding to the public's confusion about which forms of money were sound and freely redeemable and which should be avoided.

ESTABLISHMENT OF FEDERAL CHARTERING RULES

It was in this environment of public confusion and dissatisfaction with many of the state chartering and regulatory systems that the federal government began its own system to charter and supervise commercial banks. Faced with both the problem of an unstable banking system and a pressing need to find dollars to finance the Civil War, Congress enacted a landmark banking law in 1863—the National Bank Act—and made further amendments to that Act in 1864. The result was the creation of a nationwide system for chartering federal banking associations, each receiving its authorization to issue bank notes, grant loans, and accept deposits from a newly created federal bureau—the Office of the Comptroller of the Currency.

Housed within the U.S. Treasury Department, the Comptroller (known also as the Administrator of National Banks) set up a series of regional offices across the country and drafted regulations governing the chartering, examination, and continuing supervision of national banks. Specifically, the Comptroller's regulations required that a new bank charter could be issued if (1) there was a demonstrated public need for a new bank; (2) the proposed new bank would be profitable within a reasonable period of time (as a practical matter, within three years); (3) the proposed new bank would not endanger the continued viability of other banks in the area; (4) the management and organizers of the proposed new bank appeared to be competent and of good moral character; and (5) the organizers and management of the proposed bank agreed to abide by all the regulations of the Comptroller's office and all federal statutes. Federal law also required the Comptroller to make sure the new bank's organizers had pledged adequate capital and that chartering another bank promoted competition and a sound banking system.

Stiff capitalization requirements were imposed relative to

those levied by the states. Because these requirements would have discouraged most bank organizers from seeking federal charters, a 10-percent tax was placed on the issue of bank notes by state-chartered banks. (National bank notes were *not* taxed but had to be collateralized with government bonds.) Predictably, hundreds of state banks applied for federal charters in the years following the Civil War, and it appeared that the state banking system would eventually disappear. However, deposit banking gained widespread popularity after the war, and the state banks began making loans by creating deposits rather than through the issue of bank notes. The remaining state banks survived, and their numbers grew to such an extent that by 1900 they surpassed the population of federally chartered banks.

The process of chartering and opening a new national bank is a long, involved, and expensive procedure, though recently the Comptroller has streamlined the process, contributing to an upsurge in new federal charters. The set of instructions mailed on request by the Comptroller's regional offices to bank organizers includes a detailed application form requiring information on the backgrounds of the organizers, their personal financial statements, who has pledged to buy stock, and an economic analysis of the local market area, along with an assessment of public need. When a bank holding company applies to charter a bank, the Comptroller reviews whether the banks it already controls have been successfully and prudently managed, though federal regulations are more liberal toward holding companies applying for bank charters on the presumption that their banking expertise is beneficial to a new bank. Notice of a charter application must be published in a newspaper of general circulation in the community involved, and interested persons have 30 days to comment or request a hearing.

Approval of a charter application (which normally occurs within 60 days of filing) is only the initial phase of a lengthy process that culminates on opening day. Management must first be hired and approved by the Comptroller's office, office facilities must be erected at the proposed site, and the necessary capital, as promised in the bank's charter application, must be raised within the year following preliminary approval. Finally, a minimum of two weeks before opening day, the Office of the Comptroller of the Currency must examine the bank to ensure that it meets all federal requirements. If that examination is satisfactory, the Comptroller grants a charter and the bank is cleared to open its doors.

THE STATE CHARTER DECISION PROCESS

The chartering process for state banks varies from state to state owing to differences in governing statutes and operating rules. Most states, however, share the requirement that each organizing group seeking a charter of incorporation must demonstrate (1) that significant public need exists for a new bank, either because of locational convenience or the offering of new services not provided by existing banks in the area; (2) that there is a strong likelihood that the proposed new bank will be profitable within a reasonable time period, as demonstrated by the organizers' projections of revenues, expenses, loans, and deposits; (3) that the proposed new bank will not cause "undue harm" to existing banks in the area; and (4) that adequate equity capital is being pledged. Applicants are normally required to pay a substantial filing fee (e.g., $2500) and often must reimburse the state for the costs of investigating the charter application. An economic report showing the number and characteristics of market area businesses and households, the local employment situation, and the number and location of financial institutions serving the local community must usually be filed, along with financial statements, resumes, and capital contributions of the organizers. Existing banks in the same area that may be affected by the new charter must be notified to give them an opportunity to protest the application if they so desire. And many states require a public hearing on the application with testimony from area banks and the general public invited. Any officers of the proposed bank must frequently be approved by the state banking commission to ensure they are qualified.

AUTHORIZING NEW BRANCH OFFICES

State-chartered banks must seek approval of their state banking department to open a new branch office. Similarly, national banks must obtain the written consent of the Comptroller of the Currency. Under the terms of the McFadden Act (1927), however, national banks cannot branch outside the limits imposed by state law. As I discuss more thoroughly in chapter 7, this has meant that in states that prohibit multiple branch offices, national banks also are prohibited from branching. In states restricting branch offices to cities, counties, or special districts, national banks must conform to those same legal boundaries in their own branching activities. Many banks have, of course, gotten around this limitation through bank holding company organizations, as I explore in greater depth in chapter 8.

Establishing branch offices is generally much easier then chartering a new banking corporation. Economic barriers are lower because less capital is needed and a branch office typically has a lower break-even point. Historically, fewer branching organizations have experienced failure than unit banks, owing, in part, to the ability of branch banks to diversify over a wider variety of markets with different economic characteristics than would be true of single-office banks. Related to this risk advantage, the regulatory authorities require substantially less detailed information in passing upon branch applications than for new charters.

This last conclusion was supported by Selby and Flournoy (1982), who found that official and unofficial discouragement of new charters was generally more common than discouragement of branch office applications. Deteriorating economic conditions, declining bank earnings and/or rising bank costs, and capital adequacy problems were most frequently cited by state banking commissions as reasons for restricting the awarding of charters for new banks. Interestingly enough, as J. T. Rose (1983) observes, state and federal authorities appear to be about equally liberal in approving new branches, provided branching is limited to a bank's own local market. In contrast, national bank regulators appear to be more liberal than state authorities in approving new branches outside a bank's home territory.

RATIONALE FOR THE CHARTER REGULATION PROCESS

The economic debacle of the 1930s ended a long era of "free banking" in the United States during which there were few *legal* barriers to bank entry. Provided the organizers of a new bank pledged an adequate amount of equity capital and agreed to abide by federal and state banking laws, a charter would usually be issued. However, the failure of thousands of banks and the ultimate collapse of the banking system during the Great Depression led to two important conclusions: (1) America was "overbanked" relative to the scarce capital funds available, for if commercial banks had been able to attract adequate capital, many more would have survived; and (2) "excessive competition," particularly in the form of price competition for deposits, had led the industry to excessive risk taking in the search for earning assets. These arguments provided a rationale for restricting the awarding of new bank charters and thus limited competition for scarce bank capital and for high-cost deposits.

As Peltzman (1965) observes:

Bank entry restriction was designed to . . . [insure] against a high rate of failure. Entry restriction is supposed to accomplish this in two ways. First, it weeds out those applicants who value their own chances more highly than do the regulators. . . . Second, it reduces interbank competition generally. In this way, . . . the whole distribution of profit rates in banking will be greater than it would be under free entry, and fewer banks will incur losses that will cause them to fail (p. 172).

An added barrier to price competition for deposits, federal deposit interest rate ceilings, were imposed on commercial banks during the 1930s. Although the public might well receive a less than optimal supply of banking services at competitive prices, presumably the benefits of controlling the number of new banks and strictly supervising those that were chartered would outweigh the costs of regulation.

Certainly the conventional view today would argue that regulation of bank entry and strict controls over bank behavior have improved the *safety* of American banking. Interestingly enough, however, a fresh perspective on the costs and consequences of banking regulation has emerged in recent years that questions certain elements of the conventional wisdom. Advanced by Fama (1980), Karaken and Wallace (1978), McCulloch (1981), Rolnick and Weber (1983), and others, this newer perspective suggests that regulation of entry may have contributed to *instability* in the banking system owing to nonoptimal pricing of deposit insurance, capital adequacy regulations, and the stimulation of maturity intermediation. Moreover, Rolnick and Weber (1983) find evidence that depositor losses during the free banking era have been overstated and that law enforcement and regulatory practices may have generated some of the instability that characterized early American banking. These findings suggest the need for a fresh look at existing controls over entry and other bank regulations in order to assess their *true* impact on the stability of the nation's banking system.

ECONOMIC BARRIERS TO NEW BANK ENTRY

The legal barriers to new bank entry erected during the 1930s were an addition to already substantial economic barriers. The most significant of these centered on the cost of physical facilities—plant and equipment—and the cost of attracting scarce managerial talent. Bank buildings are usually among the most costly and imposing structures in the local community if, for no other reason, to convey an image of safety and security. Because money attracts crime, bankers feel compelled to set up elaborate security systems and to carry a heavy burden of insurance. And in an era of increasing reliance on the computer and electronic storage and transfer of financial information, bankers have a strong competitive motivation to acquire the latest in automated facilities that may significantly increase the break-even point for most banking transactions.

The shortage of scarce managerial talent is an even more potent barrier to new bank formation. To be successful in banking requires a unique combination of social and technical skills. Management must be adept not only at analyzing complex customer financial statements but also at assessing the intangible element of human character that plays a key role in the timely repayment of loans. Larger banks enjoy the advantage of being able to attract and train personnel skilled in either or both attributes. Smaller banks, with more limited market contacts and resources, often have a difficult time finding and retaining competent management. Thousands of smaller banking institutions have been merged or absorbed in recent years owing to the classic problem of *management succession*—the inability to find new skilled management to replace those who leave or retire.

Research Studies of New Entry Markets

While regulation undoubtedly has been the chief impediment to new bank formations in the decades since World War II, economic barriers also rank high. A number of recent studies have attempted to determine the characteristics of those markets where *de novo* entry has occurred, mainly as an aid to merger and acquisition decisions by the regulatory authorities who must decide if future market entry is likely by some other, more competitive means than merger or acquisition.

For example, Hanweck (1971) examined new bank formations in 220 U.S. metropolitan areas (SMSAs) over the 1968–1969 period. He found that more concentrated banking markets generally discouraged entry, while overall market size was *positively* related to the entry of new banks. Later, Gilbert (1974) studied 67 counties in 12 states that prohibited branch banking but in which new national banks were chartered during 1964. He found that new entry markets grew faster in population than the state as a whole and, partly as a result, the population-to-bank-office ratio for new entry counties was greater than statewide averages.

These conclusions were supported by Rose and Fry (1976), who reviewed all new commercial bank charters occurring over the 1973–75 period. They found that half or more of new charters were in unit banking states that prohibited full-service branching; only about one quarter occurred in limited branching states, and less than a fifth of all U.S. bank charters took place in statewide branching states. Five states—California, Colorado, Florida, Illinois, and Texas—accounted for about half the chartering activity, and three of these ranked among the leading states in population growth. The charterings were concentrated in the largest cities, which had a median population of more than 200,000. The counties where new bank entry occurred had a mean decennial population growth rate approximately twice the national average and tended to be retail and service, rather than manufacturing, oriented with high median family incomes.

Boczar (1975) attempted to find a set of factors that contributed to the entry of new banks and to acquisitions by multibank holding companies. Examining 15 Florida urban markets over the 1967–1972 period, Boczar found that market structure had a significant influence on the bank entry process, more concentrated markets discouraging new entry. However, high levels of deposits per banking office, elevated bank profit levels, and high per-capita personal income encouraged new entry. In contrast, Savage (1982) found that state branch banking and holding-company laws did *not* significantly affect new bank income or growth. Finally, J. T. Rose (1977) formulated and tested a model of new bank entry into 20 smaller SMSA markets in Texas, 1962–73, using average market profitability (ROE and ROA), total market deposit size, market growth, per-capita personal income, the three-bank concentration ratio, and the number of bank holding-company acquisitions by established banks in the local market as possible explanatory factors. He found that increases in marketwide deposits, a higher long-run market growth rate, and greater average bank profitability (measured by ROA) stimulated new entry, with market concentration a significant *negative* factor. Thus, bank entry in the

United States appears to be market selective, and both economic and market structure conditions can pose significant barriers to new bank formation.

Technology as an Entry Barrier

Before concluding on this point, however, I must take note of the widely held view that recent technological developments in banking—especially the spread of automated information processing and service delivery systems—pose substantial barriers to the entry of new banks. As Kaufman, Mote, and Rosenblum (1982) point out, it may be that not only new banks but also many other financial institutions incapable of casting aside old methods of financial service production and delivery will be "shaken out" of the industry by organizations large enough to invest in the latest capital equipment and technical expertise. Perhaps today's technology (and especially the current speed of technological innovation) poses the ultimate, insurmountable barrier to newly chartered banks, especially for charterings of new independent banks, which in the past, have been the principal source of new bank charters.

Although the technological barriers argument sounds logical and convincing, it cannot go uncontested. For example, Metzker (1982) argues that American banking is likely to conform to the *divisibility theory.* As has happened in other industries (such as retail groceries), the latest electronic products appear to be spreading out to smaller and smaller banks, often through pooling and time-sharing arrangements. Moreover, inexpensive microcomputers have appeared with computing capacity comparable to main-frame systems of only a few years ago. At the same time the cost of automated tellers and office equipment has declined sharply in the wake of improved production methods. While many large banks have rushed ahead to make substantial capital commitments to electronic hardware and software, smaller banks, as Metzker (1982) notes, "are buying what they need, in the quantity they need, when they need it" (p. 63). This is a lower risk approach in an environment where technological change appears to be unfolding at an exponential rate. In brief, the continuing divisibility and increasing availability of data-processing and information transfer technology need not pose insurmountable barriers to new bank entry nor, necessarily, threaten the economic viability of smaller financial service firms.

Potential Effects of New Bank Charters

If there are significant barriers—legal, economic, or technological— to the entry of new banks, there may also be significant benefits from *de novo* entry. The benefits, if they exist, center on the fresh breath of *competition*—i.e., a new bank in the local market offers the public another alternative source of supply for financial services. Existing banks in the local community may have become lethargic in improving their services and facilities. Indeed, if the contestable-markets theory discussed in chapter 2 is correct, just the *threat* of possible outside entry can bring many of the benefits of competition to local banking markets.

I recall a bank charter case in which I was called to testify as an expert witness. One bank had served a local community of about 10,000 people for 30 years without facing significant competition. Those who found that institution's services inadequate or less than accommodating were forced to travel 30 miles to a neighboring metropolitan area. A common complaint from local citizens centered on the bank's inadequate drive-in facilities, which generated long traffic lines and were open for only short periods of time. Led by the mayor, a local group of citizens applied first to federal and then to state authorities for a second bank charter. Immediately the established bank in town announced plans for a doubling of its drive-in facilities, increased lobby space, and longer hours of operation. Both charter applications were subsequently turned down.

If the established banks in town have operated for a long period of time, "mutual understandings" may have emerged with respect to market shares, service offerings, or pricing schedules and tactics. Commercial banking has a long history of cooperative relationships among individual banks—centered mainly in correspondent arrangements and often arising from practical necessity. Occasionally, however, those communications may drift beyond the boundaries defined by the antitrust laws.

Still, there is no open and shut case regarding the benefits of new bank charters. As discussed in chapter 2, competition is *not* a matter of numbers; it is a matter of behavior. How aggressively do existing banks pursue new customers, create and promote new services, seek to lower prices to attract new business, and react to the marketing initiatives of their competitors? Aggressive rivalry may characterize a banking market where there are 100 banks or only two. Each market situation is different and must be analyzed on a case-by-case basis. If the existing banks are already highly competitive, the entry of a new bank in the local area may do little to improve the competitive climate.

Moreover, as suggested earlier, the addition of new competitors can work against both the banks and the public they serve. The entry of a new bank may prevent institutions serving the local market from reaching efficient size and thus raise unit production costs for all. In addition, small and moderate size banks face a limited market for new equity capital; there are few buyers for their stock on a continuing basis. This forces smaller local institutions to rely heavily on earnings retention to raise equity capital to the level desired. The addition of a new bank to the local market may significantly increase the bankruptcy risk of all or most local banks and thus add more instability than is in the public interest.

The Performance of New Banks

Whether new bank charters represent a net gain or net loss to any given market is a matter for empirical research. As noted earlier, there are convincing arguments on *both* sides of the issue—centered principally on the benefits of competition versus the costs of increased risk and reduced operating efficiency. In this and the following section I examine the available evidence along several dimensions: What is the track record of newly chartered banks? Do they survive and prosper in the majority of cases or is their failure rate high (as it is for most new nonfinancial business ventures)? Does the public benefit? What is the impact of new charters on existing banks serving the same market? Is their growth or profitability significantly reduced? Does service availability improve? I turn first to look at the new banks themselves.

STUDIES OF THE PERFORMANCE OF NEW BANKS

One of the earliest new bank studies was conducted by David Motter (1965) for the Office of the Comptroller of the Currency. Motter did a detailed performance analysis of 64 national banks chartered in 1962. He found that the principal problem faced by banks just opening is *attracting deposits,* though across his sample they were quite successful in doing so. Indeed, for most new banks represented in Motter's study, deposit growth exceeded the organizers' initial projections. Loan growth, initially at least, was even more rapid than deposit growth. Customers unhappy with existing banks in the local community or preferring to trade with a smaller institution apparently generated ample loan demand for Motter's new banks. There was also a cadre of clientele who seemed to enjoy the "novelty" of dealing with a new institution in a new building. However, credit risk appeared to be higher among new banks than among existing banks in the same community, probably because a large proportion of new loan customers previously had been turned down by other banks in the local area. Nevertheless, the added credit risk did not prevent the new institutions from becoming profitable—in most instances during their second year of operation.

A similar study by Shea (1967) reviewed the performance of 32 new banks chartered in Massachusetts. These new institutions, like those in Motter's study, typically faced immediate competition from established banks, but none was judged to be in financial difficulty. Nevertheless, start-up costs were high, principally because the new banks felt compelled to offer innovative and expensive new services (such as loan rebates, high deposit yields, free or low-cost checking accounts, and longer hours of operation). Shea found that the early failure or success of a new bank is often determined even before it opens for business. The ability of a bank's organizers to generate deposit pledges and attract local support before the doors open apparently is critical to its performance over the first few years of operation. This finding was supported by Selby (1981), whose detailed study of six Georgia banks opening during the 1975–77 period showed that director deposits accounted for more than a quarter of total deposits received shortly after opening day and significantly affected first-year bank growth.

Several studies focusing on the *growth* of new banks appeared during the 1970s. For example, Yeats, Irons, and Rhoades (1975) selected a random sample of new banks chartered during the 1960s and estimated a deposit growth curve for each bank. The annual percentage growth of total deposits was regressed against the age of the bank, disposable family income, and the number of banks entering the local market after the sample bank had received its charter. The regression equations were statistically significant, suggesting that individual bank deposit growth could be predicted within broad limits, thus making it possible to anticipate bank personnel and capital needs. Among the most important factors appearing in their regression equations were family disposable income, whose growth was positively related to bank deposit growth, and numbers of banks subsequently entering the same local market, which slowed individual bank deposit growth.

Using a larger sample Austin and Binkert (1975) studied the deposit growth rates of 351 commercial banks, starting with their charter dates. The authors found that a majority of the new institutions grew less rapidly than their organizers and the chartering authorities had projected. For example, a clear majority of the new banks (241 of 361, or 68 percent) reported deposit totals below $10 million from two to four years following their charter dates. Austin and Binkert noted, however, that none of the new banks examined had been declared insolvent or were in serious financial trouble. Still, they concluded, bank entrepreneurs appear to have an upward bias when it comes to estimating the growth of newly chartered banks and early expectations are often *not* realized.

Probably the broadest of all new bank studies was conducted by Alhadeff and Alhadeff (1976), who looked at the growth records of more than 1000 new banks in branch banking and unit banking states over the 1948–1970 period. The principal factors influencing new bank growth were the size of communities entered and the number of banking offices opened by the new institutions. As expected, the Alhadeffs found that the mortality rate—mergers and liquidations—was substantially greater and the new charter rate substantially lower for banks in branching states than in states where branches were forbidden or restricted.

SUMMARY OF NEW BANK PERFORMANCE
It seems clear from the few studies available that recently chartered banks in the United States have performed reasonably well with a substantially lower failure rate than characterizes most new

business ventures. Deposit and loan growth has generally been moderate to rapid, loans tending to outstrip deposits in the early years. Income levels in the local area and the extent of competition from other banks and from nonbank institutions do apparently play significant roles in shaping the growth record of new banks. However, there is no convincing evidence that new banks are dangerously intimidated by established financial institutions. Generally speaking, if management is capable and willing to compete, new banks can survive and grow even in highly competitive markets.

IMPACT OF NEW BANKS AND BRANCHES
ON EXISTING INSTITUTIONS

One question that emerges in every bank charter decision by federal and state authorities is: what effect is the awarding of a charter likely to have on banks and other financial institutions already serving the local market? The key phrase in most law and regulation in this field is "undue harm." Will local institutions be damaged *unduly*—especially in terms of their long-run survival—if another charter is granted? Other, equally important issues usually raised include: will the *public* benefit in any concrete way from a new charter (such as through lower prices for financial services, greater convenience, or enhanced availability of financial services)? Do the expected benefits outweigh the possible damaging effects, especially the risks to established institutions?

RESEARCH STUDIES ON PROFITS, PRICES, AND SERVICES

Several studies have examined these issues over the past two decades and the results are generally *positive*. For example, Chandross (1971) conducted a study of 98 one-bank communities that subsequently became two-bank towns through the awarding of a new charter. He found an increase in loans relative to total assets and time and savings accounts relative to checkbook deposits at the established banks as these institutions generally became more aggressive with the appearance of new competition.

Similarly, McCall and Peterson (1976) reviewed the impact of entry by a new bank in one-, two-, and three-bank rural communities in which both branch banks and unit banks were operating. They found that earnings levels of the existing banks declined relative to their expenses. As a result, returns on assets and equity decreased with most of the decline experienced by unit banks. In contrast, branch banks' return on assets and on equity appeared to be unaffected by new entry. However, a study by Hannan (1983) of the *threat* of entry by branch banks in Pennsylvania finds the expected negative relationship to bank profitability measured by after-tax return on assets. Moreover, regression tests on 351 banks suggest that the threat of entry has a greater impact on those banking markets that are more concentrated.

In *no* case did these research studies find evidence that existing banks were threatened with failure specifically as a result of the awarding of a new charter. A similar study by Motter (1965), which looked at the effects of new national bank charters for a group of ten banks serving what were formerly one- and two-bank communities, reached similar conclusions. Moreover, Motter observed that the average interest rate offered on time and savings deposits by existing institutions *rose* above the mean deposit interest rate offered by all U.S. insured banks in the same size group following the entry of a new competitor.

The effects of new bank entry do not appear to vary significantly from one region of the nation to another. Evidence in support of that conclusion was provided by Fraser and Rose (1972) in a study of banks in the Southwest (centered mainly in Texas). These researchers focused on 34 unit banks serving what were formerly one-, two-, and three-bank communities until a new bank appeared. As suggested by earlier studies, these unit banks increased their loans relative to other assets and offered more interest-bearing deposits, while earnings remained largely unaffected by the appearance of new competition.

Most new bank studies find little effect on bank loan rates stemming from the awarding of new charters. An exception is an inquiry by Marlo (1983) into the determinants of home mortgage rate differentials between urban (SMSA) markets served by both commercial banks and savings and loan associations. Relying on a regression model that holds loan value ratios and loan maturities constant, Marlo finds that entry by both new banks and new branches (which may capture economies of scale) *lowers* single-family mortgage rates. He foresees significant public benefits from a relaxation of branching restrictions and other legal entry barriers. This result was essentially corroborated in a much earlier study by Motter and Carson (1964) of outside entry by branch banks. These two researchers looked at Nassau and Westchester Counties in the state of New York after entry by branching from New York City banks was permitted in 1960. Average rates charged on consumer installment loans by Nassau County banks declined in the wake of market penetration by New York City banks. Interestingly enough, however, no evidence of a change in average service charges on checking accounts was observed.

GROWTH EFFECTS OF NEW ENTRY

Economic theory suggests that the *growth* of established banks might be significantly reduced in the short run as these banks are forced to share the existing market for loans and deposits with a new competitor. In the longer run, however, the expected outlook for growth is uncertain. If the appearance of a new bank leads to more rapid growth in local loans, supporting new construction and expansion of the local economy, then *all* banks may grow faster. On the other hand, if market growth stays the same or slows down, existing banks may well have to settle for smaller portions of the local credit and deposit pie.

Thus, the growth impact of new bank entry can be *mixed,* which is exactly what existing research studies suggest. A good example is a study by Kohn and Carlo (1969) that looked at the establishment of new branches by commercial and savings banks in New York. These researchers found that deposits grew more slowly, on average, at commercial banks, mutual savings banks, and savings and loans in those counties where a new branch office appeared. Both long- and short-run bank profits were, however, apparently unaffected.

A more recent study by Spong and Hoenig (1977) looks at the determinants of growth for both small and large banks in the Tenth Federal Reserve District. Finding straight-line projections of time trends in deposit growth to be inaccurate, these researchers estimated annual demand and time and savings deposit percentage growth for the 1967–74 period, using the percentage change in the number of banks in the local market over the preceding three years, the change in local market shares of savings and loans, lagged total deposit growth of each bank compared to overall market growth, the spread between Treasury bill rates and average bank time deposit rates, and the annual percentage growth in market permanent income as key variables. They found that *all* of these factors influenced bank deposit growth and the appearance of new banks in the local area had a measurable *negative* impact on the growth of deposits of existing banks. However, the explanatory power of their regression model was low in several instances, especially for the smallest banks in the sample, suggesting the need for further research on the determinants of individual bank growth.

COMPETITIVE RIVALRY AND MARKET SHARES

A unique study by Rhoades (1980) explored the degree of rivalry among leading banks in local metropolitan markets and its possible links to new entry. Specifically, Rhoades studied 184 SMSAs over the 1968–1974 period to determine if changes in the rankings of the five largest banks in each market were related to *net* bank entry—that is, new charters less bank closings due to mergers, failure, and other factors. Rhoades was *not* able to find a linkage between either mobility or turnover among the top five banks in each metropolitan area and market entry (after holding constant market growth, size, branching laws, and the presence or absence of bank holding companies). This suggested to the author that regulatory attempts to encourage new entry would be unlikely to have procompetitive influences on major banking markets, at least in the short run. Rhoades also observed, however, that such findings might be influenced by the relatively small scale of new bank entry (due, in large part, to regulatory controls) or by potential competition.

More recently, a collection of studies by King (1979, 1982) and J. T. Rose and Savage (1982) found a general trend toward declining local market shares among large banks reaching back into the 1960s. After exploring various possible explanations for this trend, the authors concluded that entry by new banks accounted for a significant proportion of declining local market concentration. This finding was corroborated by Duncan (1985) for entry by new branches and new banks into metropolitan areas in 13 statewide branching states. The King and Rose and Savage studies suggest, however, that *de novo* entry appears to exert its greatest impact on large rather than on small banks. Smaller existing banks faced with new competition generally maintained their profitability and continued to gain market share at the expense of larger institutions serving the same local market.

Nonetheless, some potentially good news for larger banks following a relaxation of market entry barriers is implicit in a study by Beatty, Reim, and Schapperle (1985). These researchers find that purchase premiums (i.e., the ratio of purchase price to book value) on banks targeted for acquisition tend to fall once banking organizations—usually the largest—are permitted to enter a new area through branching or holding companies. Extrapolating their findings for Pennsylvania and New Jersey to the nation as a whole, they argue that legalization of interstate banking will *reduce* the purchase prices, premiums, and the shareholder wealth of banks targeted for acquisition, and this reduction would tend to promote increased interstate expansion by the largest banks.

A General Assessment of New Entry in Banking

As noted in the foregoing paragraphs, research studies of new entry in banking cover a wide variety of time periods and market situations. The findings, too, are varied. Yet a few reasonably "safe" conclusions seem to emerge. In general, neither the worst fears of established banks nor the fondest hopes of economists and regulators concerning the appearance of new competition are realized. Little or no evidence exists that established banks are endangered by the entry of new banks or new branches. In some cases growth slows and market shares of existing institutions—particularly the largest banks—decline, but rarely are profits affected. Contrary to the dictates of the pure competition model, prices of bank services typically do not change, but service availability often *does* change (particularly the availability of local loans and interest-bearing deposits). In general, then, several positive and few negative effects seem to follow the entry of new banks and branches in local urban and rural markets.

One unfortunate gap in the literature centers on the *dynamics* of markets experiencing new entry. Existing studies generally focus on the short run—what happens one, two, or perhaps three years after a new competitor appears—while the possible long-run effects can only be guessed. Certainly new entry upsets an existing equilibrium in the market, frequently setting in motion the offering of new services, new hours of operation, and new price schedules by both old and new institutions. However, it might well be that over time the established banks reach an "understanding" with the new institution, stabilizing market shares and rigidifying pricing schedules once more. This important issue—whether new entry produces only temporary, short-range benefits or lasting, long-range advantages—must await the verdict of further research.

Bank Failures in the United States

Just as commercial banks cannot enter the industry without regulatory approval, they also cannot leave the banking business without government sanction. State-chartered banks can be closed once they are declared insolvent by the state banking commission that chartered them. Federally chartered banks, on the other hand, must be declared insolvent by the Comptroller of the Currency. Because more than 98 percent of all U.S. banks are insured by the Federal Deposit Insurance Corporation, the FDIC is also involved in most bank closings. Once an insured bank is declared insolvent the FDIC takes control of its records, assets, and liabilities.

In most cases the troubled institution will be merged with a larger and, presumably, healthier bank in order to avoid disruption of banking services. This approach also avoids a potentially severe drain on federal insurance funds, which amount to a minor fraction of all eligible bank deposits. In fact, an estimated three fifths of all U.S. bank deposits fall within the $100,000 insurance limit and, therefore, represent *potential* claims against the insurance fund. In a few cases, however, a deposit payoff becomes necessary if no suitable merger partner can be found or the FDIC wishes to promote market discipline of bank risk taking by uninsured depositors (as in the case of Penn Square Bank of Oklahoma City in 1982).

As I discuss more thoroughly in chapter 12, federal banking policy since the mid-1930s has stressed *safety* and *avoidance of failure risk* in the management and supervision of the nation's banking system. Typically, this risk avoidance strategy has resulted in some lessening of competition because a free and competitive marketplace implies that some firms (particularly the inefficient ones) will fail as prices and quantities of output respond to shifting public demands. Nevertheless, it has been argued for five decades and more that such a policy is justified by the *adverse consequences* of widespread bank failures—loss of public confidence in the banking system, loss of savings (especially the accumulated funds of individuals and families), and loss of efficiency in the intermediation process as the public fearfully withdraws its funds from both troubled *and* sound banks. As Mayer (1975) and Horvitz (1975) observed, banking is held to be unique because of "spillover" effects ("psychological externalities"), in which the financial and op-erating problems of one bank are visited upon those banks that share the same market and sometimes invade other markets as well.

THE DOMINO OR SPILLOVER EFFECT
OF BANK FAILURES
      This argument for a so-called "domino" or "spillover" effect from bank failures on otherwise sound banks has persisted for decades despite widespread agreement that, as noted by Kaufman (1985), "the introduction of federal deposit insurance broke the close link between the failure of an individual bank and that of the banking system" (p. 1). For example, when troubled Continental Illinois National Bank had to be propped up by the FDIC with a $4-billion-plus rescue plan, fear was expressed by all three federal bank supervisory agencies that a national, even international, banking crisis would result. Yet, there is evidence that this domino or spillover effect has been greatly dimin-ished (though not completely eliminated as evidenced by several recent failures among savings and loan associations in the nation's mid-section).

      One aspect of the spillover debate that has received recent attention is the *financial market effects* of bank failures and problem bank announcements. In particular, what happens to debt and equity funding costs for all banks when a major bank failure occurs? Do the money and capital markets detect evidence of bank financial problems, perhaps even before bank examiners do? The research results, unfor-tunately, are conflicting and provide only limited guidance for public policymakers and investors. For example, Pettway's study (1976) of the impact of the failures of New York's Franklin National Bank and United

States National Bank of San Diego on bank equity financing costs detected only a *temporary* rise in these costs, though the volume of bank equity offerings available for study makes any conclusions questionable. A more recent study by Simpson (1984) of six large bank failures during the 1970s found *no* evidence of accurate stock market prediction of impending failure before on-site examinations. Simpson suggests that insider information associated with recent large bank failures exists but does not reach the market in timely fashion.

Interestingly enough, however, this last conclusion of Simpson's—that the bank equities' market contains a substantial element of inefficiency—was rejected in an earlier study by Pettway (1980) of seven banks collapsing during the 1972-1976 period. Analysis of required returns for these institutions with returns for 24 nonfailed banks suggested that the equities' market had detected unfavorable information as much as two years before the actual bank closings. Pettway concludes:

> The examination and classification information of the regulatory authorities was not found to be uniquely important. The markets for equities of these large failed banks exhibited characteristics of efficiency as they quickly translated increasing potential for bankruptcy into share prices and returns. Since the required returns for these failed banks were increased above the level required of other large nonfailed banks, the market provided an incentive to bank managers to avoid increases in the potential for bankruptcy. Thus, the markets did play a role in bank regulation (p. 235).

A more recent study by Aharony and Swary (1983) finds that the spillover impact on bank stock values depends critically on whether investors perceive the causes of a bank's failure to be specific to the individual bank involved (as in the case of San Diego's United States National Bank and Hamilton National Bank of Chattanooga, where illegal transactions allegedly occurred) or whether the problems afflicted several similar banks or the industry as a whole (as in the case of New York's Franklin National Bank, where foreign exchange dealings resulted in substantial losses to several other banking institutions as well). Comparing the stock prices of solvent and failing banks, they found no spillover effects from the failure of a dishonestly run bank but did find an unfavorable spillover effect on even solvent bank stock prices from a problem perceived to affect several large banks at the same time. Abnormal stockholder losses, however, were observed for only a few weeks following the bank failures.

Only a handful of studies have considered the possible spillover effects of bank failures on bank borrowing costs. For example, Fraser and McCormack (1978) detected a rise in the cost of long-term bank debt following the collapse of Franklin National Bank of New York in 1974 but were not able to establish the duration of this debt market effect. More recently, Stover and Miller (1983) opened up a promising field of inquiry by looking at the *money market* effects of bank failures, focusing specifically on the impact of the Franklin failure on borrowing costs in the bankers' acceptance, commercial paper, and Federal funds markets relative to T-bill rates. Analysis of yield spreads spanning the period 12 months before to 12 months after Franklin's closing showed evidence that money market investors had distinctly anticipated Franklin's collapse, but the duration of the market impact was short (at most one to two months) and was more closely associated with a negative examination report a year earlier than with the closing itself.

Thus, no evidence was seen that one of the largest bank closings in U.S. history had permanently affected default risk premiums on short-term bank borrowings. On balance, I conclude that there *are* spillover effects of bank failures on the financial markets but, taken one at a time at least, their effects on investor attitudes toward the riskiness of bank securities appear to be short-lived.

CONSEQUENCES OF FAILURES
FOR THE DEPOSIT INSURANCE SYSTEM

In recent years Congress has expressed fears that the recent upsurge in the number of bank failures might jeopardize the federal insurance system. Indeed, there is some basis for this concern. Between 1943 and 1974 commercial bank failures averaged three per year, before climbing to an average of nearly 13 per year between 1975 and 1981. In 1982 a postwar record 34 commercial banks were closed, only to be topped in 1983 when 48 banks failed—a record beaten again in 1984 and 1985. Thus, as deregulation has progressed, Congress has simultaneously expanded the powers of the principal federal deposit insurance agencies—the FDIC and the FSLIC—in order to deal with bank failures, especially those involving the largest money center institutions.

An interesting proposal appeared in 1982 and 1983 to realign the federal insurance system so that riskier depository institutions would pay correspondingly higher insurance fees. Under the original insurance plan, all banks qualifying for federal insurance coverage pay the *same* assessment fee—a low, fixed percentage of their eligible deposits. As discussed by Bierwag and Kaufman (1983), this procedure grants a subsidy to banks electing to take on riskier portfolios at the expense of more conservative institutions. While the matter is embroiled in political discussion and debate at present, it seems likely that some form of risk-adjusted deposit insurance will be put in place in the near future.

GEOGRAPHIC AND STRUCTURAL FACTORS
IN BANK FAILURES
          The cause or causes of bank failures have been a matter for public debate and research investigation for well over half a century. Much of the ongoing debate has centered on the issue of whether or not bank failures can be predicted sufficiently far in advance of actual closing to permit remedial action, either by management or by the regulatory authorities. I consider this issue in the next section. Another important issue has, however, focused on the possible role of geographic and structural factors in the bank failure event. Do more small banks fail than large banks? What are the comparative bank size group failure rates? And is bank failure significantly correlated with location or with organizational structure?
          As Rose and Scott (1978) observe, small *rural* banks appear to be more prone to failure than either large or small banks headquartered in major metropolitan areas. Looking at the 1946–1975 period, these authors observed that

85 percent of the banks failing since 1945 were situated in markets with a median income below $5,000. Forty percent of the failed banks were in markets with declining population the decade prior to their closing (pp. 6–7).

Regarding the bank size effect, these authors found, for the same 1946–1975 time period, that

three-quarters of the banks failing since World War II have had, at the time of closing, total deposits of less than $4 million. More than one-half have held deposits of less than $2 million at the time of their failure. In contrast, less than 10 percent of all failures have occurred at banks with more than $10 million in deposits (p. 7).

Of course, large absolute numbers of failures among small banks does not prove that their failure *rate* (i.e., the number of bank failures relative to the total number of banks in a given size group) exceeds that of large or medium-size banks. There are many more small banks to begin with. However, when comparing all bank failures in various size groups, 1946–1975, with the total bank population per size group in 1973, Rose and Scott found that the failure rate was about seven times greater for banks with deposits of $10 million or less compared to banks with deposits exceeding $10 million. Further, the authors concluded that the majority of bankrupt institutions (by a ratio of roughly 3 to 1) were state chartered rather than national banks and nonmembers rather than members of the Federal Reserve System. Consistent with all of the foregoing failure patterns, Rose and Scott found bank failures to be concentrated in states limiting or prohibiting branch banking, these located principally in the Midwest and South (especially Texas, Georgia, Illinois, and Michigan). Measured by historical failure rates (relative to each state's total bank population), however, several coastal and Rocky Mountain States rank fairly high (e.g., California, Colorado, Idaho, Maine, Oregon, Utah, and Wyoming).

While small-bank failures have historically been more numerous in terms of both the failure rate and in absolute numbers, not everyone agrees that small banks are more risky than large banks today. For example, an interesting review of the evidence on comparative risk and bank size by Whitehead and Schweitzer (1982) finds "no systematic evidence . . . that small banks are at a competitive disadvantage in terms of risk" (p. 34). When they divided banking risk into five categories—credit risk, interest-rate risk, operating risk, management risk, and overall (bankruptcy) risk, the authors found largely *offsetting* degrees of risk among large and small institutions. For example, small banks are more exposed to credit risk associated with specific industries (e.g., farming), while large banks have a greater information problem, owing to their more diversified portfolio and greater incidence of international loans. Moreover, there is evidence that larger banking organizations willingly accept greater credit risk (Mingo 1975), while interest rate risk appears to be distributed about equally between large and small institutions (as noted by Flannery 1981). Operating and management risk are viewed as relatively balanced between the two types of institutions, smaller banks facing simpler operating problems but also having greater difficulty in attracting the best managerial talent. Finally, whereas bankruptcy risk may be greater among smaller banks, they also tend to hold more capital as a protective cushion. Quite correctly, Whitehead and Schweitzer (1982) conclude that banking risk deserves much more study than it has received to date.

PREDICTING BANK FAILURES AND DETECTING PROBLEM BANKS
FROM FINANCIAL STATEMENT DATA

A long-standing argument in bank research is whether bank financial statements—balance sheets and income/expense reports—convey telltale information of solvency problems and ultimate collapse. Two major arguments have been offered against the successful application of financial statement analysis to bank solvency problems. One argument contends that most bank failures are due to internal management error or crime (such as embezzlement or fraud) and are highly unlikely to be detected in conventional financial statements. For example, the former chairman of the FDIC, Robert A. Barnett (1972), contended:

There are common factors that usually are found in all of the closed banks: weak, disinterested, uninformed or fraudulent management; insufficient internal routines, controls and operating systems; and "poor housekeeping."

And Sinkey (1977a) concludes:

For over 167 years, the major cause of bank failures, dishonest bank managers, basically has remained the same. The form has varied but the driving force has not changed.

Presumably, conventional bank financial reports are inappropriate vehicles to fully convey such problems, especially where criminal mischief is involved, which, by its very nature, thrives on secrecy. Indeed, a confirming study by Rose and Scott (1981) of the prefailure risk return characteristics of eleven of the largest bank failures in U.S. history finds that a conventional financial ratio analysis model is *not* able to statistically identify these banks as population outliers.

Another argument against the use of financial statements as barometers of bank failure centers on the presumed immediacy of the failure process. The contention here is that, while financial statements may detect a probable failure situation, such signals are usually not clear-cut until a few weeks or months before the failure event. Thus, there is little or no "early warning" of impending failure to give management or the supervisory agencies time to turn a deteriorating situation around. The troubled bank dies of an external or internal shock before any remedy can be applied effectively.

Indeed, once either jaundiced financial reports or rumors of impending trouble begin to circulate, the troubled bank may lose substantial funds in a matter of hours or days. For example, a study by Sinkey (1975b) examined the effects of adverse publicity before the closings of Franklin National Bank of New York and United States National Bank of San Diego. Sinkey found that Franklin's time and savings accounts dropped about 52 percent in the six months following the bank's announcement of a suspension of stock dividend payments. USNB lost substantial amounts of IPC demand deposits in short order, but interestingly enough both collapsing banks recovered a significant portion of their initial deposit losses before closing occurred—a phenomenon observed by Kurtz and Sinkey (1973) in other cases of adverse bank publicity. Moreover, disclosure of problem status need not adversely affect bank stock prices, as noted by Johnson and Weber (1977). Thus, on balance, the great secrecy surrounding many bank financial reports submitted to the regulatory agencies, grounded in the fear of severe damage to neighboring institutions if the public only knew the "whole truth," is probably overblown. The *benefits* of public disclosure of a bank's true financial condition—including better informed investment decisions by depositors and equity holders, increased competition, more uniform industry accounting practices with better data for both legislative and research purposes, and a more optimal allocation of scarce resources in the banking sector—appear to outweigh the *costs* from public overreaction, misinterpretation, and misuse of disclosed financial data.

BANK FAILURE AND PROBLEM BANK STUDIES
With all the foregoing problems in attempting to secure and use bank financial reports to predict troubled bank situations, how much success at identifying problem or failing banks have researchers had? The evidence is mixed, but on the whole encouraging.

Incidentally, research using financial statements to generate "early warning" indices of troubled banking institutions is *not* new. Its roots go back to the 1930s when Secrist (1938) tried unsuccessfully to use financial-statement information to predict individual bank failures. There was little bank failure research after the Great Depression, however, until the 1970s, when a large number of studies appeared. These studies may be divided into two broad categories: (1) attempts to predict or discriminate between healthy banks and those on the regulatory agencies' problem bank list and (2) attempts to discriminate between banks that ultimately failed and healthy institutions.

Problem Bank Studies. From the point of view of depositors, stockholders, and bank management the so-called problem bank studies, which try to accurately flag nonfailed institutions while they are still solvent but on some regulatory agency's trouble list, are most relevant, for it stands to reason that the earlier survival-threatening problems can be discovered, the greater the chance that management will be able to turn the institution around. Thus, problem bank studies have generated a great deal of interest in the banking community. Moreover, the results of a number of these studies are reasonably consistent and encouraging of further inquiry.

For example, a study by Sinkey and Walker (1975) identified substantial differences between problem and nonproblem banks in capital adequacy, earnings, efficiency, liquidity, and loan risk at least a year before the problem banks were red flagged by examiners. As expected, banks on the FDIC's problem list were found to have deficient earnings (net income to capital), lower efficiency ratings (operating expenses to operating income), lower liquidity (U.S. Government securities to assets), and greater risk (total loans to assets, loan revenues to operating income, and equity capital to assets) than comparable nonproblem institutions. Similar findings were reported by Sinkey (1975a) in an FDIC-sponsored study that, incidentally, did not find bank size a significant determinant of problem status.

Another encouraging study from the standpoint of providing early warning of bank financial problems was prepared by Shick and Sherman (1980). These two authors explored the feasibility of developing an early warning system based on bank stock prices. Using equity price movements for 25 large U.S. banks experiencing changes in financial condition as reflected in examiner ratings, a modified single-factor capital asset pricing model was tested for at least 60 months around the date of the observed shift in examiner ratings. The sample banks all exceeded $200 million in assets as of year-end 1976. Shick and Sherman found a significant downward trend in a bank's stock price for a period of 15 months *before* adverse examiner ratings appeared, suggesting that "stock prices would have signaled problems long before the examiners confirmed their existence. . . ." (p. 145). While encouraging, these findings are certainly in need of testing over a longer time period with a larger sample of banks. Moreover, as the authors note, it is not clear whether bank stock prices yield effective *ex ante* prediction, rather than *ex post* prediction as was tested in their study. Another key problem centers on the fact that only a small minority of U.S. banks have an active resale market for their stock.

More recent problem bank studies have concentrated primarily on improving the methodology of early warning models. For example, West (1985) developed a factor-analytic model and tested it on approximately 1900 Midwest banks from seven states over the 1980-1982 period. Drawing 19 different variables from financial statements and examination reports, West's factor analysis reveals six key dimensions of bank performance that may flag banks about to assume "problem" status—capital adequacy, asset quality, earnings, liquidity, loan mix, and deposit mix. Factor scores were employed as variables in a maximum likelihood logit model to predict problem status. His model achieved about 90-percent prediction accuracy. Capital adequacy, asset quality, earnings, and liquidity emerged as dominant predictive factors, though not all the relationships found were consistent with theory, and the prediction lead time (zero to one year) may be too short to be of much practical use. The West study is, however, consistent with earlier research (such as Sinkey 1978) in finding that data from examination reports are a useful barometer of problem bank status, though it is not clear that examiners' information can be used successfully to spot actual failures (as suggested by Bovenzi, Marino, and McFadden 1983 and Korobow and Stuhr 1983, 1985).

Failing Bank Studies. In those studies examining banks headed toward ultimate collapse, the earliest comprehensive and successful study appears to be Meyer and Pifer's (1970) analysis of 30 bank failures occurring between 1948 and 1965. Arguing that the causes of bank failure are likely to include employee integrity and the quality of management, which should be captured in the figures on bank balance sheets, Meyer and Pifer constructed 30 matched pairs of failing and surviving banks on the basis of age, deposit size, location, and regulation. Stepwise linear regression analysis was applied to 32 financial variables, specified alternately as levels one and two years before bankruptcy, growth rates, standard errors, and coefficients of variation. The Meyer-Pifer model achieved 80 percent classification accuracy. Two financial variables which stood out in their regressions were the ratio of consumer loans to total assets and the net-operating-income-to-total-assets ratio. However, Meyer and Pifer were able to achieve significant classification accuracy no earlier than *two years* before the failure event, suggesting that the financial collapse of a bank as reflected in its published financial statements occurs with little prior warning.

In two notable studies in the mid-1970s Sinkey (1974, 1977b) searched for telltale financial indicators of what were at that time the two largest bank closings in U.S. history—U.S. National Bank (USNB) of San Diego (1973) and Franklin National Bank of New York City (1974). Employing a combination of univariate and multivariate statistical methods Sinkey found that, relative to the largest branch banking organizations in California, USNB proved to be a statistical outlier. The follow-on Sinkey study of Franklin National Bank also achieved success at tagging that bank as an early outlier, using such variables as operating earnings and net operating income to total assets, capital and bad debt reserves to total assets, U.S. Government and municipal bonds to total assets, and operating expenses relative to total assets.

Later Sinkey (1979) analyzed a broad cross-section of failing banks, using a matched sample of 37 failing and solvent institutions covering the 1970–1975 period. A key finding of this study was the prominence of *expense control* problems in pointing toward ultimate failure. While failing institutions actually reported larger ratios of gross operating income to assets than nonfailed banks did, the troubled banks displayed significantly lower ratios of *net* operating income and *net* after-tax earnings to total assets. In addition, the ratio of total equity capital plus reserves to total loans was deficient for up to four years before collapse. Applying linear and quadratic multiple discriminant analysis, Sinkey was able to correctly classify at least 80 percent of the banks in his study up to six years before failure. Unfortunately, however, the set of variables used as predictors was *not* consistent from year to year—a not uncommon feature of bank failure studies but one that sends financial analysts and regulators confusing signals about how far any given bank might have progressed along the failure path.

Rose and Scott (1978) tested a matched-pairs sample of 69 failing and 69 solvent banks covering the 1965-1975 period. Beginning with 110 different financial ratios representing profitability, liquidity, asset mix, capital structure, prices, and costs, the authors narrowed the list of relevant bank performance measures to 34 ratios, which were tested individually. Several mean financial ratios proved to be statistically different between the two groups of banks for at least six years before failure. These ratios included net after-tax income to total assets, total (gross) loans to total assets, interest and fees from loans to operating revenue, state and local government securities to total assets, and net available assets to total assets. However, the authors produced much less satisfactory results from a statistical point of view when these variables and other ratios were incorporated in a series of stepwise multiple-discriminant (MDA) models. No MDA model achieved classification accuracy greater than 75 percent, and by the sixth year, the predictive power of the models had reached the chance level.

Nevertheless, both the Sinkey (1979) and Rose and Scott (1978) studies suggest that the forced exit of commercial banks from the industry is not necessarily a *sudden* event but may be preceded by a series of telltale financial setbacks stretching over one or more years. Although different financial ratio indicators are used by different researchers, the consensus of findings points to expense control problems, deteriorating liquidity, and declining capital cushions as telltale signs of deepening financial trouble for a commercial bank.

BANK FAILURE THEORIES

One of the continuing, unresolved problems in the bank failure area is the lack of a credible *theory* of the bank failure process. A promising start on this problem was provided by Hanweck (1977), whose study for the Federal Reserve Board was aimed at the development of a bank "screening" program to identify troubled banks between examinations. Hanweck defined a failed bank as one in which the present value of its earnings stream is negative and developed a probability density function that depends on variables representing the ratio of bank market value relative to book value (i.e., asset quality), the present value of net income to asset book value, and the ratio of equity capital to total assets. Probit analysis was then applied to a random sample of 177 insured commercial banks that did not fail during the 1973–1976 period compared with 23 that did. Predictor variables included net operating income to assets, capital to assets (book value), the rate of change in total assets (book value), the loan-to-capital ratio (book value), and the logarithm of total assets. Of 177 solvent institutions Hanweck's model correctly labeled 176 of these and 8 of 12 failing banks in a holdout sample. Hanweck did *not* find bank liquidity measures to be a significant factor in predicting bank failure, but the ratio of loans to equity capital was significant, along with net earnings performance.

A handful of other studies have appeared recently in an effort to supply a much needed bank failure theory. In addition to Hanweck (1977), other recent theoretical contributions have been made by Ho and Saunders (1980), Dothan and Williams (1980), and Santomero and Vinso (1977). The Ho and Saunders *catastrophe model* looks particularly promising because it does not assume the path toward bankruptcy is a smooth and continuous one, but considers the possibility of an explosive collapse stemming from interactions between depositors, regulators, and bank managers. Dothan and Williams, on the other hand, develop a two-period state-preference model that generates a number of unique conclusions worthy of further exploration, such as the finding that the probability of bankruptcy can be controlled by regulating the individual bank's security portfolio rather than its loans. Finally, Santomero and Vinso develop a cross-sectional risk index based on the probability distribution of future bank capital values. They find that a two-dimensional screen consisting of a bank's capital-to-asset ratio and its coefficient of variation in capital is statistically effective in discriminating between "safe" banks and those more vulnerable to failure.

These and other recent studies offer some hope that a bank failure theory soon will emerge that yields effective empirical models for bank supervisory purposes and for research. However, a whole legion of problems are strewn across our path in reaching this desirable point. These problems include continuing uncertainty about the degree of efficiency or inefficiency in bank securities' markets; the proper conceptual framework for dealing with a partially regulated, partially unregulated financial firm; and the role and justification for bank intermediation within the broad framework of existing portfolio theory, which itself is now undergoing significant revision.

EVALUATION OF RECENT RESEARCH ON BANK FAILURES

Quite obviously, much more work needs to be done if management, regulators, depositors, and stockholders are to have a better grasp of the bank failure process and to have the capability to predict when and where failure may occur. The ideal situation would be to have an early warning system of manageable size with a consistent set of predictor variables that performs at a high enough level of classificatory efficiency to minimize both the risk of losses due to bank closings and the use of supervisory resources. Such an efficient and effective warning system would allow federal and state examining agencies to concentrate their supervisory time and resources on the minority of truly endangered institutions. However, judging by the number of recent costly failures, the regulatory agencies have a long way to go in devising an effective early warning system of bank closings—a conclusion strengthened by Rose and Kolari's (1985) evaluation of the FDIC's Integrated Monitoring System (IMS).

Nevertheless, substantial progress has been made, as noted, for example, by several authorities at a recent conference sponsored by the Federal Reserve Bank of Atlanta on monitoring individual bank condition (Koch and Cox 1983). The future role of early warning systems in assessing banking risk is promising but in need of further refinement through research. Among the areas for future research cited at the Atlanta conference were the influence of lead failure prediction times on the particular variables used as early warning devices, the impact of bank size and organizational structure on early warning model design, and the bank failure process itself (including the role of the financial marketplace and investor behavior in that process).

Interestingly enough, even as concern grows inside the regulatory community over our comparative inability to predict and head off bank collapse, the whole thrust of recent changes in banking appears to be moving away from close "cradle to grave" monitoring of bank financial condition toward a deregulated financial system in which bank risk taking is controlled by the free market. A recent study by Gendreau and Prince (1986) of national bank failures prior to 1934, when the FDIC began insuring deposits, showed that the costs of bankruptcy to stockholders and creditors are high enough to influence risk-taking (especially debt assumption) by small and medium-size banks (though the largest banks' use of debt may not be significantly impacted by the legal and administrative costs of bankruptcy). With deregulation, perhaps some banks need to be allowed to fail as part of the *price,* as Benston (1984) notes, of a dynamic and innovative financial marketplace. American banks increasingly may find themselves in a "sink or swim" regulatory climate where the principal consequences of greater risk taking will be higher borrowing costs, stiffer insurance premiums, and increased public disclosure of their vulnerable financial condition.

References

Aharony, Joseph and Iszhak Swary. 1983. "Contagion Effects of Bank Failures: Evidence from Capital Markets." *Journal of Business* 56 (July): 305–22.

Alhadeff, David A. 1962. "A Reconsideration of Restrictions on Bank Entry." *Quarterly Journal of Economics,* 76: 249–50.

Alhadeff, David A. and Charlotte P. Alhadeff. 1976. "Growth and Survival Patterns of New Banks, 1948–70." *Journal of Money, Credit and Banking* (May), 8(1):199–208.

Austin, Douglas V. and Christopher C. Binkert. 1975. "A Performance Analysis of Newly Chartered Commercial Banks." *The Magazine of Bank Administration* (January), 51(1):34–35.

Barnett, Robert A. 1972. "Anatomy of a Bank Failure." *The Magazine of Bank Administration* (April), 48(4):20–23 and 43.

Beatty, Randolph P., John F. Reim, and R. Schapperle. 1985. "The Effect of Barriers to Entry on Bank Shareholder Wealth: Implications for Interstate Banking." *Journal of Bank Research* (Spring), pp. 8–15.

Benston, George J. 1984. "Financial Disclosure and Bank Failure." *Economic Review* (March), pp. 5–12. Federal Reserve Bank of Atlanta.

Bierwag, G. O. and George G. Kaufman. 1983. "A Proposal for Federal Deposit Insurance with Risk-Sensitive Premiums." Staff Memorandum 83–3. Federal Reserve Bank of Chicago.

Boczar, Gregory E. 1975. "An Empirical Study of Multibank Holding Company Activity in Local Markets." *Atlanta Economic Journal* (November).

Bovenzi, John F., James A. Marino, and Frank E. McFadden. 1983. "Commercial Bank Failure Prediction Models." *Economic Review* (November), pp. 14–26. Federal Reserve Bank of Atlanta.

Chandross, Robert H. 1971. "The Impact of New Bank Entry on Unit Banks in One-Bank Towns." *Journal of Bank Research* (Autumn), 2:22–30.

Dothan, Uri and Joseph Williams. 1980. "Banks, Bankruptcy, and Public Regulation." *Journal of Banking and Finance,* 4:65–87.

Duncan, F. H. 1985. "Intermarket Bank Expansions: Implications for Interstate Banking." *Journal of Bank Research* (Spring), pp. 16–21.

Fama, Eugene F. 1980. "Banking in the Theory of Finance." *Journal of Monetary Economics* (January), 6:39–57.

Flannery, Mark J. 1981. "Market Interest Rates and Commercial Bank Profitability: An Empirical Investigation." *Journal of Finance* (December), pp. 1085–1101.

Fraser, Donald R. and Peter S. Rose. 1972. "Bank Entry and Bank Performance." *The Journal of Finance* (March), 27:65–78.

Fraser, Donald R. and Patrick McCormack. 1978. "Large Bank Failures and Investor Risk Perceptions: Evidence from Debt Market." *Journal of Financial and Quantitative Analysis* (September), pp. 527–32.

Gendreau, Brian C. and Scott S. Prince. 1986. "The Private Costs of Bank Failures: Some Historical Evidence," *Business Review,* Federal Reserve Bank of Philadelphia, March-April, pp. 3–14.

Gilbert, R. Alton. 1974. "Measures of Potential for *De Novo* Entry in Bank Acquisition Cases: An Evaluation." *Bank Structure and Competition,* pp. 159–70. Federal Reserve Bank of Chicago.

—— 1985. "Recent Changes in Handling Bank Failures and Their Effects on the Banking Industry." *Review* (June/July), pp. 21–28. Federal Reserve Bank of St. Louis.

Hannan, Timothy. 1983. "Bank Profitability and the Threat of Entry." *Journal of Bank Research* (Summer), pp. 157–63.

Hanweck, Gerald. 1971. "Bank Entry into Local Markets: An Empirical Assessment of the Degree of Potential Competition Via New Bank Formation." *Bank Structure and Competition,* pp. 161–172, Federal Reserve Bank of Chicago.

Hanweck, Gerald. 1977. "Predicting Bank Failure," *Research Papers in Banking and Financial Economics,* Division of Research and Statistics, Board of Governors of the Federal Reserve System, November.

Ho, Thomas and Anthony Saunders. 1980. "A Catastrophe Model of Bank Failure." *Journal of Finance* (December), 35(5):1189–1207.

Horvitz, Paul M. 1975. "Failures of Large Banks: Implications for Bank Supervision and Deposit Insurance." *Journal of Financial and Quantitative Analysis* (November), 589–601.

Johnson, James M. and Paul G. Weber. 1977. "The Impact of the Problem Bank Disclosure on Bank Share Prices." *Journal of Bank Research* (Autumn), pp. 179–82.

Karaken, John H. and Neil Wallace. 1978. "Deposit Insurance and Bank Regulation: A Partial-Equilibrium Exposition." *Journal of Business* (July), 51:413–38.

Kaufman, George G. 1985. *Implications of Large Bank Problems and Insolvencies for the Banking System and Economic Policy.* Staff Memorandum 85–3. Federal Reserve Bank of Chicago.

Kaufman, George, Larry Mote, and Harvey Rosenblum. 1982. "Product Lines in Geographic Markets." *Bankers Monthly Magazine* (May 15), vol. 94, pp. 19–23.

King, B. Frank. 1979. "Entry, Exit, and Market Structure Change in Banking." Working Paper Series (March). Federal Reserve Bank of Atlanta.

—— 1982. "Changes in Large Banks' Market Shares." *Economic Review* (November). Federal Reserve Bank of Atlanta, pp. 35–39.

Koch, L. Donald and William N. Cox, eds. 1983. "Warning Lights for Bank Soundness: Special Issue on Commercial Bank Surveillance." *Economic Review* (November). Federal Reserve Bank of Atlanta.

Kohn, Ernest and Carmen J. Carlo, 1969. *The Competitive Impact of New Branches.* New York State Banking Department (December).

Korobow, Leon and David P. Stuhr. 1983. "The Relevance of Peer Groups in Early Warning Analysis." *Economic Review* (November). Federal Reserve Bank of Atlanta, pp. 27–34.

—— 1985. "Performance Measurement of Early Warning Models." *Journal of Banking and Finance,* 9:267–73.

Krooss, Herman E. and Martin R. Blyn. 1971. *A History of Financial Intermediaries.* New York: Random House.

Kurtz, Robert D. and Joseph F. Sinkey, Jr. 1973. "Bank Disclosure Policy and Procedures, Adverse Publicity and Bank Deposit Flows." *Journal of Bank Research* (Autumn), pp. 177–84.

Ladenson, Mark L. and Kenneth J. Bombara. 1984. "Entry in Commercial Banking, 1962–78." *Journal of Money, Credit and Banking* (May), 16(2):165–74.

Marlow, Michael L. 1983. "Entry and Performance in Financial Markets." *Journal Bank Research* (Autumn), pp. 227–30.

Mayer, Thomas. 1975. "Should Large Banks Be Allowed to Fail?" *Journal of Financial and Quantitative Analysis* (November), pp. 603–10.

McCall, Allan S. and Manfred O. Peterson. 1976. *The Impact of De Novo Commercial Bank Entry.* Working Paper No. 76–7. Federal Deposit Insurance Corporation.

McCulloch, J. Huston. 1981. "Misintermediation and Macroeconomic Fluctuations." *Journal of Monetary Economics* (July), 8:103:–15.

Metzker, Paul F. 1982. "Future Payments System Technology: Can Small Financial Institutions Compete?" *Economic Review* (November), pp. 58–67. Federal Reserve Bank of Atlanta.

Meyer, P. A. and H. W. Pifer. 1970. "Predictions of Bank Failures." *The Journal of Finance* (September), pp. 853–68.

Mingo, John J. 1975. "Regulatory Influence on Bank Capital Investment." *Journal of Finance* (September), 30:1111–21.

Motter, David C. 1965. "Bank Formation and the Public Interest." *The National Banking Review* (March), 2:299–350.

Motter, David C. and Deane Carson. 1964. "Bank Entry and the Public Interest: A Case Study." *The National Banking Review* (June), 1:469–512.

Peltzman, Sam. 1965. "Bank Entry Regulation: Its Impact and Purpose." *National Banking Review* (December), 3:163–77.

Pettway, Richard. 1976. "The Effects of Large Bank Failures Upon Investors' Risk Cognizance in the Commercial Banking Industry." *Journal of Financial and Quantitative Analysis* (September), pp. 465–77.

——— 1980. "Potential Insolvency, Market Efficiency, and Bank Regulation of Large Commercial Banks." *Journal of Financial and Quantitative Analysis* (March), 15(1):219–36.

Pettway, Richard and Donald T. Savage. 1982. "Bank Holding Company *De Novo* Entry and Banking Market Deconcentration." *Journal of Bank Research* (Summer), 13:96–100.

Rhoades, Stephen A. 1980. "Entry and Competition in Banking." *Journal of Banking and Finance*, 4:143–50.

Rolnick, Arthur J. and Warren E. Weber. 1983. "New Evidence on the Free Banking Era." *The American Economic Review*, 73(5):1080–91.

Rose, John T. 1977. "The Attractiveness of Banking Markets for *De Novo* Entry: The Evidence from Texas." *Journal of Bank Research* (Winter), pp. 284–93.

——— 1983. "Branch Banking and the State/National Charter Decision." *Journal of Bank Research* (Summer), pp. 170–72.

Rose, John T. and Donald T. Savage. 1982. "Bank Holding Company *De Novo* Entry and Banking Market Deconcentration." *Journal of Bank Research* (Summer) 13:96–100.

Rose, Peter S. and Clifford L. Fry. 1976. "Entry Into U.S. Banking Markets: Dimensions and Implications of the Charter Process." Paper Presented at the Western Finance Association, Honolulu (June).

Rose, Peter S. and James W. Kolari. 1985. "Early Financial Warning Systems as a Monitoring Device for Bank Condition." *Quarterly Journal of Business and Economics* (Winter) 24(1):43–60.

Rose, Peter S. and William L. Scott. 1978. "Risk in Commercial Banking: Evidence from Postwar Failures." *Southern Economic Journal* (July), pp. 90–106.

——— 1981. "Eleven Largest U.S. Bank Failures." *Review of Business*, 16(2):1–11.

Santomero, Anthony M. and Joseph D. Vinso. 1977. "Estimating the Probability of Failure for the Banking System." Research Paper No. 29. Federal Reserve Bank of Philadelphia.

Savage, Donald T. 1982. "Branch Banking Laws, Deposits, Market Share and Profitability of New Banks." *Journal of Bank Research* (Winter), pp. 200–6.

Scott, William L. and Peter S. Rose. 1977. "The Bank Failure Problem Reexamined." *MSU Business Topics* (Winter), pp. 5–10.

Secrist, H. 1938. *National Bank Failures and Nonfailures: An Autopsy and Diagnosis.* Bloomington, Indiana: Principia Press.

Selby, Edward B. Jr. 1981. "The Role of Director Deposits in New Bank Growth." *Journal of Bank Research* (Spring), pp. 60–61.

——— and Barbara Flournoy. 1982. "Restrictions on Bank Charter and Branch Approvals in Economically Troubled Times." *Issues in Bank Regulation* (Spring), 5(4):21–24.

Shea, Maurice P., III. 1967. "New Commercial Banks in Massachusetts." *New England Business Review* (September), pp. 2–9. Federal Reserve Bank of Boston.

Shick, Richard A. and Lawrence F. Sherman. 1980. "Bank Stock Prices as an Early Warning System for Changes in Condition." *Journal of Bank Research* (Autumn), pp. 136–46.

Simpson, W. Gary. 1983. "Capital Market Prediction of Large Commercial Bank Failures: An Alternative Analysis." *The Financial Review*, (February), pp. 33–55.

Sinkey, Joseph F. 1974. "The Failure of United States National Bank of San Diego: A Portfolio and Performance Analysis." *Journal of Bank Research* (Spring), pp. 8–24.

—— 1975a. "A Multivariate Statistical Analysis of the Characteristics of Problem Banks." *Journal of Finance*, (March), 30:21–36.

—— 1975b. "Adverse Publicity and Bank Deposit Flows: The Cases of Franklin National Bank of New York and United States National Bank of San Diego." *Journal of Bank Research* (Summer), pp. 109–12.

—— 1977a. "Problem and Failed Banks, Bank Examinations, and Early Warning Systems: A Summary." In Edward I. Altman and Arnold W. Sametz, eds. *Financial Crises: Institutions and Markets in a Fragile Environment.* New York: John Wiley and Sons.

—— 1977b. "Identifying Large Problem/Failed Banks: The Case of Franklin National Bank of New York." *Journal of Financial and Quantitative Analysis* (December), pp. 779–800.

—— 1978. "Identifying "Problem" Banks." *Journal of Money, Credit, and Banking* (May), 10(2):184–93.

—— 1979. *Problem and Failed Institutions in the Commercial Banking Industry.* Greenwich, Conn.: JAI Press.

Sinkey, Joseph F. and David A. Walker. 1975. "Problem Banks: Identification and Characteristics." *Journal of Bank Research* (Winter), pp. 208–17.

Spong, Kenneth and Thomas Hoenig. 1977. "An Examination of Individual Bank Growth: An Empirical Analysis." *Journal of Bank Research* (Winter), pp. 303–10.

Stover, Roger D. and James M. Miller. 1983. "Additional Evidence on the Capital Market Effect of Bank Failures." *Financial Management* (Spring), pp. 36–41.

West, Robert Craig. 1985. "A Factor-Analytic Approach to Bank Condition." *Journal of Banking and Finance*, 9:253–66.

Whitehead, David and Robert L. Schweitzer. 1982. "Bank Size and Risk: A Note on the Evidence," *Economic Review*, Federal Reserve Bank of Atlanta, November, pp. 32–34.

Yeats, Alexander J., Edward D. Irons, and Stephen A. Rhoades. 1975. "An Analysis of New Bank Growth." *The Journal of Business* (April), 48:199–212.

4.

Impact of Internal Bank Growth: Economies of Scale

THE MANAGEMENT of a commercial bank today involves asking and answering a number of complex but important questions. One of those key questions is: How large should the bank be? Do larger banks have significant advantages over smaller banks, especially in being able to operate at a lower unit cost of production (i.e., economies of scale)? From the standpoint of minimizing costs, and given current technology, what size bank achieves the minimum operating cost per unit of financial service provided?

In more practical terms, does it pay the bank's shareholders if the institution grows in size? If a bank can reduce operating costs per unit of service as it grows, this gives the institution a distinct advantage over competing financial institutions that have not yet reached their most efficient size or perhaps have grown so large that they have passed the efficient size point, subjecting them to "diseconomies" of scale. Efficient production of banking services benefits bank *customers* in the form of lower prices for financial services, increased quantity and quality of services, and greater safety if superior efficiency leads to improved earnings.

In the United States the most profitable banks (measured by return on assets) are neither the largest nor the smallest but typically lie in the $50 million to $300 million asset size range. Could this

U-shaped pattern of profitability reflect an approximately U-shaped cost curve in which unit operating costs reach a low point somewhere in the $50 to $300-million asset size range? Whereas this profit information may provide a clue about the behavior of bank costs, I hasten to add that maximum bank profits do not necessarily occur at that output level where unit operating costs are minimized unless perfect competition prevails.

Cost of Producing Bank Services and Operational Efficiency

The cost of producing bank services for sale to the public is dependent on the production process used by individual banks. We can represent each bank's service output (SO) as a function of the productive factors—labor time (L), managerial skills (M), natural resources (R), and real capital (K)—the bank must employ to generate any given level of output. Thus:

(4.1) $SO = F[L, M, R, K]$

Suppose each productive factor is doubled in amount, and service output (SO) *more* than doubles. In this case the increase in output is greater than the change in aggregate production costs needed to produce that output. As Stigler (1966) observes, economies of scale occur "when a doubling of output does not require a doubling of every input" (p. 153).

Economies of scale are present whenever a smaller quantity of productive factors is required to produce each additional service unit. The cost of indivisible factor inputs is spread over additional units of output, and inputs of greater efficiency (but with greater indivisibilities) are substituted for less efficient inputs. In contrast, diseconomies of scale are present when service output changes proportionately *less* than the change in aggregate production costs. With scale diseconomies, average cost rises faster than output, owing principally to control and management inefficiencies.

Where the production of banking services does result in significant scale economies, a limited number of large banks will be able to operate at reduced resource cost compared with the cost of producing the same quantity of financial services with a large number of small banks. With positive scale economies larger banks can offer lower prices on their services or expand the quantity of financial services they make available to the public. In this case an unregulated market would, in the long run, contain only a few relatively large and efficient banks. Unfortunately competition might be lessened as a result unless there was a significant threat of entry by new competitors.

Problems in Measuring Bank Service Output and Efficiency

Economies of scale are defined in terms of the individual bank's production process. Obviously, accurate measurement of the volume of bank production requires a precise measure of what it is that banks produce—the problem of *output definition*. Unfortunately, commercial bank output can neither be easily defined nor easily measured. First of all, banks produce an intangible product—financial services—that is difficult to unitize. Consider the problem of trying to compare along the same measurement scale large corporate loans, single-family home mortgage loans, and installment loans to consumers. Some services are more conveniently (and perhaps more accurately) measured by dollar volume (e.g., deposits, loans, or security investments), while others appear more amenable to a frequency measure, reflecting the number of transactions or number of accounts serviced (e.g., check clearings, balance inquiries, and withdrawals). As we shall see, research studies that use the number of transactions or number of accounts often reach different conclusions about scale economies in banking compared with studies employing a dollar measure of bank output.

A second key problem is that banks are multiproduct firms. Each type of bank service output may have a different dimension and measure. Therefore, measurement of economies of scale for the whole banking firm requires a single index that serves as a common denominator for each dimension of bank output. One such index might be:

$$(4.2) \qquad \sum_{i=1}^{n} P_i S_i = P_1 S_1 + P_2 S_2 + \ldots + P_n S_n$$

where S_i represents each financial service produced and sold and P_i represents the market price for each service. With this index of total bank output, market price (value) serves as the common denominator for each service offered.

As Greenbaum (1966) observes, one potentially useful value-weighted index of bank output is *current operating earnings*—a measure of gross receipts or sales. It does have limitations, however, as does any weighting scheme relying on market values to measure physical output. For example, some of the observed variation in bank output is due to differences in service output and some to variations in market price. All banks do not charge the same price for the same service. This price difference reflects, in part, the fact that each bank is not only a multiproduct firm but also a *multimarket* firm. A bank sells household checking accounts in a different market, one primarily local, than the market in which it offers corporate cash management services—a market that is regional, national, or even international. And the bank may face a different set of competitors in each service market, as well as different demand schedules, leading to price differences form market to market.

One of the most important advantages of using sales, earnings, or or other market value measures of bank output is that they reflect flow of production within the bank. Bank output is a *flow*—a continuous-process in which inputs are transformed into outputs through the application of existing technology. Therefore, studies of economies of scale that attempt to measure bank output with *stock* variables (e.g., total assets, loans, deposits, number of accounts opened on a given date, etc.) do not fully reflect the character of a bank's production process.

The Form of Bank Production Functions

Beyond the problem of measuring multi-dimensional output, there is the fundamental issue of how *specifically* to link inputs and outputs. In other words, what is the character of a bank's *production function* that defines how many units of output will result from the application of specified quantities of various inputs? Over the past three decades numerous studies have expressed this input-output relationship in the form of a mathematical equation. The simplest mathematical production function would be *linear in form:*

(4.3) $SO = a_1L + a_2M + a_3R + a_4K$

where the coefficients a_i indicate the absoulte numerical effect on total service output (SO) of changing a given input by one unit. Each a_i is, then, a measure of each input's marginal productivity in generating units of output, on the assumption that all other inputs are fixed. For example, if labor time (L) is increased by one unit, but management skill, capital, and natural resources are fixed, coefficient a_1 defines how much service output (SO) will increase owing to the unitary rise in L.

The linear production function assumes that bank output always changes in the same proportion no matter how many input units are applied. Clearly, such a simplified representation of bank service production may fail to capture *any* existing scale economies. One solution to this problem is to introduce a constant term, a_0, into the linear production function. Thus, total bank service output becomes

(4.4) $SO = a_0 + a_1L + a_2M + a_3R + a_4K.$

For economies of scale to exist a_0 cannot be zero. If a_0 *is* zero, that bank experiences *constant* returns to scale so that output and inputs always change at the same rate. There are no cost savings from expanding output but also no diseconomies from bank growth.

A more realistic approach to defining a bank's production function is to use the log-linear equation:

(4.5) $lnSO = A_0 + A_1lnL + A_2lnM + A_3lnR + A_4lnK$

where output and all inputs are measured in percentage terms rather than in absolute units. In this Cobb-Douglass functional form the input coefficients A_i are all positive and fixed, regardles of input levels. The numeric value of the sum of the input coefficients (Σ_i) indicates by what percentage output will change when each input is changed by a given percentage, holding everything else constant. Thus, the presence or absence of economies of scale is indicated by ΣA_i. If this sum is *greater than one, economies of scale* (i.e, increasing returns to scale) are present; service output increases more in percentage terms than any given percentage increase in the collective inputs. Similarly, if the input coefficients add to *less than one,* the output increases less in percentage terms than any given percentage change in inputs (i.e., decreasing returns to scale) and diseconomies of scale are present. Finally, a sum of input coefficients *equal to one* indicates *constant returns to scale;* a given percentage change in all inputs results in an equal percentage change in bank service output. The log-linear equation is, thus, relatively easy to interpret because each coefficient represents the elasticity of bank output with respect to changes in the inputs. Unfortunately, the Cobb-Douglas form is still too restrictive because it limits the elasticities of substitution between productive factors and restricts permissible cost-curve shapes, allowing only for uniform scale characteristics. In particular, the elasticity of bank output with respect to factor inputs remains constant regardless of bank size.

The choice of form for banking's production function is crucial to the accurate estimation of scale effects in the industry. Yet, this question of correct functional form remains an unresolved empirical issue in banking, though the bulk of existing research studies have used some version of a log-linear model. As Kim (1985) and Diewert (1971) point out, a properly specified production function must contain the properties of linear homogeneity in the prices of productive factors, second-order concavity in factor prices for output levels, and a demand relationship for productive factors that is monotonically nonnegative with own-price elasticities of demand for factors that are not positive. Existing cost-function models typically violate one or more of these conditions, and it is not yet clear what the consequences of such violations are, especially for the managerial and public policy conclusions drawn by most studies in the field.

Moreover, with the greater intrusion of electronic equipment in financial service delivery in recent years, the fundamental character of banking's production process may be changing. Thus, it is not clear just how relevant earlier research studies will be for future management decisionmaking. Moreover, real-world data frequently do not fit the production concepts delineated by economic theory. There is no readily available data series, for example, on man-hours applied to the production of various bank services, the quantity and quality of managerial skill, or the amount of land and other natural resources applied in any given production situation.

A commonly used surrogate for actual inputs of resources, as well as the quantity of service output, is *balance sheet entries.* For example, if we view banks as financial intermediaries attracting debt and equity funds and making loans and security investments—data readily available from periodic reports of condition—bank output can be related to dollar quantities such as total time deposits, savings deposits, demand deposits, and equity capital. The production function would then indicate how much output (e.g., operating earnings) rises per dollar of deposits or of equity capital. However, these input measures are, at best, crude approximations of the underlying productive factors of labor time, managerial skill, capital equipment, and natural resources. Balance sheet numbers are indicators of the size of an organization, but size is not necessarily synonymous with output. Moreover, as noted above, balance sheet proxies for resource inputs are stock rather than flow measures and their values are set in different markets, reflecting price and quantity differences from bank to bank.

With all the limitations imposed by real-world complexities and imperfect information, it is surprising that studies of bank scale economies emerge with any useful and consistent conclusions. Yet, as we shall see in the sections that follow, while far from homogeneous in method and approach, the body of literature in this field leads to reasonably consistent managerial and public policy implications for banks and banking.

Research on Economies of the Total Banking Organization

Economies of scale studies in banking have fallen into three broad groups: (1) studies concentrating on cost-size relationships across *all* banking services—that is, looking primarily at the banking organization as a whole: (2) studies exploring the cost-size relationship for individual bank services (such as demand deposits); and (3) comprehensive studies that have focused on *both* individual services and on aggregate economies for the banking organization as a whole. We look first in this section at the methods and conclusions of the broader organization-wide studies and then at specific-service scale studies in the section that follows.

Statistically sophisticated studies of economies of scale began in the early 1960s with the work of Gramley (1962) and of

Schweiger and McGee (1961). Using the multiple regression technique to relate total bank costs (as reflected in aggregate operating expenses relative to bank asset size) to various bank size groups these researchers found substantial scale economies in commercial banking. However, branch banking organizations were found to have higher operating costs relative to assets than unit institutions. These pioneering studies both suffered from an important methodological deficiency, however: they assumed that loans of all sizes carried equal production costs per unit of loans made. This assumption clearly favored large, commercially oriented banks over smaller, retail-oriented institutions in terms of production costs.

One of the best early studies of scale economies for the banking organization as a whole was prepared by George Benston (1965b). Using the Federal Reserve's Functional Cost Analysis data for the first time Benston analyzed the output of 80 banks during the 1959–1961 period. The largest bank in his sample held total assets of $55 million, and the smallest, $3.4 million. Service output was defined as the average number of deposit accounts and loans processed during the year with size (average balances), type of account, activity level, local wage level, and number of branch offices held constant. Scale elasticities generally proved to be less than one, indicating that average operating costs increased more slowly in percentage terms than output did (measured by the percentage change in the number of accounts serviced). However, the calculated scale economies were slight and consistently significant for only one or two bank services, though all services except business loans and overhead costs displayed some evidence of scale effect.

A larger study by Bell and Murphy (1969), also relying on Functional Cost Analysis (FLA) data, examined more than 200 banks, ranging up to $800 million in total assets for 1963–1965. These researchers found *modest* average scale economies for their sample banks: a 10 percent increase in aggregate output (weighted by average account activity levels for each service) was associated with only a 9.3 percent increase in total operating costs. (This elasticity estimate was later refined by Murphy [1972] to 9.5 percent.) However, larger banks experienced diminishing cost advantages as service output increased. Interestingly, both Benston in an earlier study (1965a) and Bell and Murphy (1969) found that unit banks tended to have lower operating costs than branch banks. Yet, branch bank expansion did not appear to result in higher production costs. Thus, branch banks could offer greater convenience to their customers at little or no additional resource cost.

Taking this last conclusion a step farther Greenbaum (1967) found U-shaped declining cost curves for both branch and unit banks. However, this study of more than 1100 banks operating in the Kansas City and Richmond Federal Reserve Districts emerged with the conclusion that large unit banks have higher operating costs than larger branch banks, suggesting that growth eventually pressures banks into branching activity to minimize service production expenses—a finding that seems consistent with later work by Kalish and Gilbert (1973). Yet, Powers (1969) study of banks in the Chicago Federal Reserve District and Schweitzer's (1972) examination of more than 1300 banks in the Minneapolis District found scale *diseconomies* once a banking organization expanded beyond $25 million in assets.

A 1975 study by Adar, Agmon, and Orgler addresses the problem of banks as multiproduct firms by developing a joint production model and suggesting ways to test it. Their model is based on a nonlinear, nonadditive profit function where the marginal cost of each service output depends on the levels of output for all banking services. Thus, these researchers focus on bank production cost interdependencies arising in those cases where there is joint use of at least some inputs (such as financial information) to produce more than one financial service. They argue that "most bank cost studies explicitly or implicitly assume the special case of separable cost functions" (p. 241), which can lead to erroneous managerial and public policy decisions. The authors suggest a variety of tests for joint costs, including a pseudo-production function developed by Samuelson (1966), nonlinear regression estimation with interaction terms, and engineering cost studies. Their idea, while difficult to carry out empirically, is certainly relevant to the scale economies issue. As developed somewhat further by Osborne (1982), it deserves further investigation in subsequent research.

In the same year as the Adar et al. paper Mullineaux (1975a) presented the results of a study of relative production efficiency across different organizational structures—holding companies and independent banks—and different state branching-law environments. The Mullineaux study approaches the scale economies problem through the duality relationship between bank profit functions and production functions, using the profit function to test for differences in economic efficiency. Sample banks numbering 812 in 1971 and 859 in 1972 are drawn from Functional Cost Analysis (FCA) data supplied by all 12 Federal Reserve districts. The dependent variable—bank profits (operating revenue minus operating expense net of occupancy costs)—is regressed against output prices (including real estate, installment, and commercial/agricultural loan rates and safe deposit rental fees); input prices (including wage and deposit rates); fixed-factor quantities (including the number of full-service and limited-service branches, paying and receiving stations, and the presence of computers on bank premises); organizational structure (multibank and one-bank holding companies); and the relative numbers equivalent as a measure of market structure.

Mullineaux (1975a) concludes that the production function for banks in limited-branching and statewide-branching states displays constant returns to scale, while banks in unit banking states face increasing returns to scale. (This result was expanded by Mullineaux [1975b] using 1970 FCA data for banks in three Federal Reserve districts along the East Coast with a finding of branch-bank diseconomies and unit-bank economies.) For example, a 100-percent increase in all inputs in unit banking areas would result in an increase in output of 122 percent, on average, though legal restrictions against creating full-service branch offices prevent full capture of all these scale advantages. Holding-company affiliates, both one-bank and multibank, proved to be more profitable than independent banks in the sample, leading Mullineaux to argue that they are more economically efficient. However, at least a portion of this profitability advantage may be traceable to the presence of imperfect competition because Mullineaux found that market structure affected bank profits. The author properly acknowledges several limitations to his study, including the fact that FCA-participating banks may not be representative of the industry as a whole, fixed productive factors are assumed to be homogeneous without quality adjustments, average prices rather than market prices are used, and risk was not included explicitly in the profit function. Mullineaux notes that *risk* has not been adequately considered in the majority of scale studies to date.

A more recent study by Benston, Hanweck, and Humphrey (1982b) uses innovative methods to improve on previous studies of overall bank costs. Two measures of total bank output are employed: (1) the sum of the number of demand deposit, thrift deposit, consumer installment loan, and business loan accounts and (2) the number of each of the foregoing accounts weighted by their relative costs. A translog cost equation is constructed of the form

$$lnTC = a_{TC} + a_Q lnQ + b_{QQ} 1/2(lnQ)^2 + a_b lnB + b_{bb} 1/2(lnB)^2 +$$
$$b_{BQ} lnBxlnQ + a_A lnA + b_{AA} 1/2(lnA)^2 + b_{AQ} lnAxlnQ + a_H H +$$
$$b_{HB} HxlnB + \Sigma_j a_j lnP_j + \Sigma_j b_{jQ} lnP_j lnQ + \Sigma_j \Sigma_k w_{jk} 1/2[lnP_j \times lnP_k]$$

where TC represents total bank operating costs for five deposit and loan functions; Q measures total output as previously defined; B is the number of banking offices; A, mean-size deposit and loan accounts; H, a holding company dummy variable; and P represents the prices of capital (K) and labor (L) inputs. While a Cobb-Douglas production function can be derived from this general functional relationship by specifying the relevant parameters, Benston, et. al. recommend the more general and more flexible translog form, which, as Kim (1985) notes, overcomes the restrictiveness of the widely used Cobb-douglas form.

The authors find the traditional U-shaped cost curves predicted by economic theory. What is surprising, however, are the low levels of total bank output at which significant economies and diseconomies appear. For example, examining unit and branch banks separately, they find that significant *diseconomies* begin above $50 million in total deposits in unit banking states, while the minimum cost branch office probably holds total deposits of between $10 and $25 million. Banks in all size ranges in branch-banking states experienced scale economies in the number of deposit and loan accounts serviced, but when the vehicle for growth (either increasing the number of accounts or the number of branch offices) was held fixed, banks operating in both unit and branching states displayed scale *diseconomies* above the $50-$75 million deposit size range. While larger banks in branching states appeared to have lower average costs than similar size banks in unit-banking states, smaller banks (with deposits below $75 million) reported similar average costs in both branch and unit areas. Thus, branch and unit banks were observed to incur about the same costs per individual account once an adjustment was made for the greater cost of servicing customers with larger accounts. Small branch and small unit banks appeared to be more efficient than larger banks regardless of organizational structure. Finally, the foregoing relationships appeared to be unaffected by time period or holding-company affiliation. Thus, Benston et al. conclude that "smaller banks are, at the least, *not* at an operational disadvantage with respect to large banks. As a result, mergers appear unlikely to result in operating cost savings" (p. 21). The authors are careful to note, however, that their statistical results and conclusions do not reflect any customer-borne costs, especially inconvenience related to the availability of banking facilities and collateral services offered by the same bank.

The Benston et al. (1982) study represents a significant step forward in methodology applied to estimates of economies of scale for the banking firm as a whole. However, as Kim (1985) observes, serious methodological hurdles remain in satisfying the conditions laid down by production theory and by the real-world setting in which bank service production is carried out. Kim suggests a promising lead in the form of a multiproduct cost function that includes endogenous outputs and is one component of a system of equations encompassing cost share and revenue share relationships. While promising, however, Kim's three-stage least squares model does not appear to be fully specified. Moreover, the Benston et al. and a number of earlier studies have encountered multicollinearity and endogeneity problems with input variables, and this outcome tends to confound the relationship between bank costs and output. These problems need further study if we are to obtain results more consistent with both theory and banking practice.

At least some of the issues raised by Kim and Benston et al. have been approached recently by Gilligan and Smirlock (1984) who apply a translog cost function to test the hypothesis that bank production of service is characterized by *jointness.* The concept of "jointness" or *economics of scope* is defined by Samuelson (1966) as the capability of a single firm to produce multiple outputs at lower cost than would be true if the same outputs were divided among single-product firms. This concept, developed more thoroughly by Panzar and Willig (1978), seems particularly applicable to banking, where the same technological methods, management skills, natural resources, and capital are used to offer the same set of customers a wide range of services.

Gilligan and Smirlock (1984) estimate a translog cost function for a multiproduct firm but impose nonjointness through the addition of a nonlinear restriction. Employing a nonlinear multiple regression technique, they test for economies of scope in total operating expenses across a sample of more than 2,700 unit banks located in the Mid-West during the 1973-1978 period. Bank service output is measured alternately be demand and time deposit volume and by loan and security volume. The result is a U-shaped cost curve regardless of which measure of bank output is used. Significant scale economies are discovered for banks with deposits of less than $25 million, but larger banks display increasing *diseconomies* of scale as either output or earning assets increase. Gilligan and Smirlock recommend that future public policy decisions on permitting new bank services consider the impact of those new services on total bank costs viewed jointly.

The fact that Gilligan and Smirlock do find *some* economies of scope in banking, but only a *limited* impact from these economies on the configuration of total operating costs seems to coincide with what we now know about scale economies for nonbank thrift institutions, such as savings and loans. Because the thrifts tend to offer a much more limited range of financial services than commercial banks, these institutions should be less efficient than commercial banks, owing to smaller economies of scope. However, the scale economies literature for savings and loans (S&Ls), as reflected in studies by Atkinson (1979), Carron (1981), and Morris (1978), for example, does *not* find that S&Ls are less efficient than commercial banks. It suggests, in fact, that thrifts experience declining costs over a much broader range of output, perhaps up to about $500 million in total assets, than seems to be the case for commercial banks. Though the projected cost savings are modest, the presence of significant scale economies among the more narrowly focused thrift institutions casts doubt on the proposition that economies of scope are a potent force in determining commercial bank efficiency. It suggests, too, that the current expansion of bank service offerings cannot be expected to contribute significantly to either bank profitability or efficiency by driving down operating costs.

Finally, as we try to piece together the rapidly expanding literature on production economies for the banking organization as a whole, we must not lose sight of one of the enduring questions in the field—what impact does *organizational form* have on bank production costs? Does branch banking, holding-company banking, or unit banking yield the optimum cost savings outcome? The Gilligan-Smirlock (1984) study I have just reviewed provides no guidance on this question because it looks only at unit banks. And, unfortunately, we can find only limited satisfaction in the research to date dealing with this perennial issue.

For example, Alhadeff (1954), Gramley (1962), and Gilligan and Smirlock (1984) all find that branchless unit banks experience significant scale economies. In contrast, Benston, Hanweck, and Humphrey (1982) and Longbrake and Haslem (1975) find evidence of diseconomies of scale beyond fairly low levels of output for unit institutions. Thus, there is a clear conflict concerning the cost behavior of unit banks. In contrast, branch banks in the opinion of most researchers emerge as cost *inefficient* institutions. Benston et al. (1982), Benston (1965a), Bell and Murphy (1969), and Greenbaum (1967) uniformly find branching an expensive way to grow. However, Longbrake and Haslem (1975) find only indirect effects on average operating cost from variations in the number of branches each bank operates. Moreover, each branch office seems to experience significant scale economies as its volume of transactions expands.

More recently, Nelson (1985) has attempted to resolve at least a portion of these conflicting findings on branch banking by incorporating branching variables (as surrogates for customer convenience) into the production function. Substantial scale economies are found at the level of the individual branch office, but no significant cost savings are found from proliferating branches. As Nelson concludes: "convenience and economies of scale interact in a way that makes efficiency consistent with an enduring range of bank size and considerable variety in the extent of branching" (p. 91). Even if interstate banking becomes a reality nationwide, small banks will *not* automatically be driven from the financial services marketplace because of production cost disadvantages.

An even more recent study by Berger, Hanweck, and Humphrey (1986) analyzes scale and scope economies at two levels—at the plant or banking office level and at the firm-wide level for both state-chartered unit and branch banks. Relying on cross-section Functional Cost Analysis data for 1983, the authors find that banks of *all* sizes in branching states are competitively viable; however, large unit banks are not found to be competitively viable, particularly under the assumption of legalized interstate banking, because of scale diseconomies at their "overcongested" offices. They argue that large state-chartered unit banks may need to change their output configurations to remain viable under an interstate banking regime. Somewhat surprisingly, modest service mix and scope diseconomies are found for *both* branch and unit banks. This apparent conflict with earlier research studies is attributed to shortcomings in the methods used in previous studies and to joint service demands of bank customers which provide an economic rationale for banks to diversify their asset and liability portfolios.

Research on Economies of Scale in the Provision of Individual Banking Services

A number of recent studies have examined the cost structure of individual banking services. Among the most important services considered in the literature are demand deposits, time deposits, consumer installment loans, mortgage loans, business loans, security holdings, trust services, and safe deposit facilities. In fact, all of the foregoing services were examined by Bell and Murphy (1968) in their study of 210 to 283 banks during the years 1963–1965. The majority of services displayed elasticities of less than one, suggesting modest scale economies. However, only demand deposit accounts and real estate loans displayed statistically significant scale economies on a consistent basis.

The study cited earlier by Benston (1965b) analyzed data for 80 banks in each of three years, 1959–1961. Scale effects were estimated for nine different cost-generating functions—demand deposits, time deposits, real estate loans, installment loans, business loans, investment securities, administrative expenses, business development costs, and occupancy costs. Multiple regression techniques applied to the sample banks' cost functions indicated that investing in securities displayed the greatest returns to scale with an average operating cost elasticity across all sample years of 0.742. Demand deposits ranked second with an average cost-to-output elasticity of 0.877, followed by installment loans at 0.879. All nine bank functions showed positive returns to scale, except business development, whose average elasticity was 1.01. In general, the cost elasticities of indirect operating cost items averaged higher than the elasticities for direct operating costs.

Concerned that early scale studies failed to capture the effects of changing technology, especially the growing use of computers and other automated equipment, a number of later studies concentrated on those banking services most likely to be automated, particularly demand deposits. A good example is the work by Daniel, Longbrake, and Murphy (1971), which examined 956 commercial banks, including some of the largest institutions yet studied (of which the biggest bank serviced more than 100,000 demand deposit accounts) using Functional Cost Analysis data. Although economies of scale appeared to decline modestly after computers were put in place, positive economies were found among computer-oriented institutions—a 10-percent increase in output led to a 9.29-percent rise in unit costs, on average. And computerized banks held distinct advantages over banks without computers. In fact, noncomputerized institutions, represented by 268 banks in the sample, displayed significant *diseconomies* of scale; a 10-percent rise in their output resulted in a 10.43-percent increase in their unit costs. Daniel et al. concluded that the adoption of computerized techniques narrowed the operating advantage of larger over smaller banks where both possessed computers. However, banks that had not computerized their checking account function appeared to be at a significant operating disadvantage.

Other studies of the effects of computers on bank cost efficiency include those by Longbrake (1974) and Yawitz (1969). Both studies examined the argument that computers lower bank operating expenses because the same volume of operations can be carried out with less labor time. The presumption is that savings in wages and salaries will outweigh the increased costs associated with automation. Yawitz detected significant reductions in the number of bank personnel processing demand deposit transactions (in the 10-percent to 70-percent range) when computer processing was introduced. Moreover, his survey of 40 banks suggested that the net savings in labor over automation costs grew as additional experience was gained with computer processing.

However, Longbrake's statistical analysis tended to contradict Yawitz' survey findings. One of his models attempted to assess the effects of different features of computer usage (such as employing on-premises or off-premises machines and the length of time a computer had been in use) on such bank functions as demand deposits, time deposits, installment loans, and real-property loans. Estimates of a Cobb-Douglas production function did not support a finding of lower operating costs from automation. However, a second model did identify lower operating expenses for demand and time accounts in those instances where a bank was large enough to operate several branches with a sufficiently large volume of accounts handled through each branch. In this case on-premises computers are more economical than off-premises machines, though the reverse appeared to be true for smaller scale operations.

Longbrake concluded that use of computers reduced bank production costs when demand accounts exceeded $15 million and when time deposits exceeded about $50 million. Less favorable effects from computers were found for installment loans or real estate loans, however. In fact, Longbrake concludes "while a computer tends to reduce demand deposit operating costs when a bank has more than $15 million in demand deposits, a computer may be a luxury item for other types of operations in all except the very largest banks" (p. 381). This conclusion must be viewed with caution, however, because the data in Longbrake's study were gathered from the Federal Reserve's Functional Cost Analysis program in 1968, and more recent advances in electronic circuitry and software may have altered both the relative benefits from and the costs of automated processing.

A subsequent study by Longbrake and Johnson (1975) estimated cost functions for seven different services—demand and time deposits; business, real estate, and installment loans; investments in securities; and safe deposit boxes—and two operations areas—administrative expenses and occupancy costs, which are labeled nontraceable operating expenses. Longbrake and Johnson estimate a total of 36 cost functions segregated by four different organizational forms: (1) independent unit banks, (2) holding-company-affiliated unit banks, (3) independent branch banks, and (4) holding-company-affiliated branch banks. The volume of bank operations is represented by the number of accounts processed. Total costs for each service are related to (1) the average number of deposit or loan accounts per bank office, (2) the number of offices in each banking organization, (3) average account size and activity level, (4) the mix of accounts involved in each service, (5) the average revenue generated per dollar of service item or per safety deposit box, (6) mean annual employee wages per service, (7) and a cost interaction variable for the expenses associated with producing more than one service. A total of 967 banks were chosen from the Federal Reserve's 1968 Functional Cost Analysis data file.

Longbrake and Johnson find that the most significant economies of scale are associated with occupancy costs, administrative expenses, business loans, and security investments. For example, a 10-percent increase in office size results in an increase in business lending costs of 8.9 percent at independent unit banks, an 8.6-percent rise at holding-company-affiliated unit institutions, and only an 8.2-percent increase in business loan expenses at nonaffiliated branch institutions. However, the offices of affiliated branch banks actually show *diseconomies* in business lending, both as office size increases and as the number of branch offices grows. Longbrake and Johnson find that economies of scale for changes in office size are largest for branch banks and smallest for unaffiliated unit institutions, affiliated banks lying in between. However, a particular bank organizational form was not found to be most efficient under all circumstances. For example, Longbrake and Johnson find that independent unit banks appear to be more efficient than offices of other types of banking organizations for deposit sizes below $10 million. But, as office size grows, independents show declining efficiency and branch offices with more than $50 million in deposits display significantly greater efficiency than unit banks. Similarly, independent unit banks appear to be more efficient than affiliated unit banks when office deposits are less than $30 million.

Longbrake and Johnson conclude that small unit banks can continue to survive and operate efficiently and do not require protective laws (e.g., antibranching statutes). However, mergers among well-operated unit banks will probably reduce efficiency and may also impair competition. Similar conclusions apply to mergers among branching systems. They argue that proliferation of branch offices is inefficient unless the average branch holds more than $15 million in deposits. Holding-company acquisitions of unit banks below $30 million in deposits are also not recommended by these researchers. In contrast, affiliation of branch banks with holding companies appears to enhance cost efficiency, though a holding company embracing small branch banks seems to be more cost efficient than one large branch banking organization. Longbrake and Johnson conclude that

a mixed banking structure containing unit banks, branch banks, and to a lesser extent holding companies is consistent with achieving cost efficiency in the production of banking services. Furthermore, vast differences in markets make it entirely possible that different organizational forms will be most efficient in markets of various types (p. 38).

Concern over the specific form of the production function assumed for specific banking services has been expressed by Dugger (1975). He argues that "virtually all" empirical cost and production studies assume bank production functions are homothetic—that is, a declining average cost curve is presumed to imply increasing returns to scale. Thus, it is assumed that if two or more banks are brought together by merger or holding-company acquisition, average cost will fall when all banking inputs are increased to scale. Dugger observes that "the reduction in average cost (increasing returns) may well come about, but it is unlikely that it is a consequence of a proportional (to scale) increase in all inputs as is required by the definition of 'increasing returns to scale' " (p. 1). Input composition, particularly input differences between small and large banks, may affect the operating results from changes in bank style.

Dugger tested the assumption of production homotheticity over the 1966–1970 period, estimating production functions for five banking services: (1) demand deposits, (2) time deposits, (3) installment loans, (4) business loans, and (5) mortgage loans. The number of banks involved—all participants in the Federal Reserve's Functional Cost Analysis (FCA) program—ranged from 845 to 1,025 more than 90 percent of which had less than $50 million in total deposits. The scale measure is the average number of deposit accounts of record each month and the total number of loans made during the year. The production functions for the five services do not appear to be homothetic (based on ordinary least squares estimates of each function), suggesting significant technological differences among banks. Thus, it is difficult to draw generalizations about the production cost effects of bank growth without taking into consideration the composition of individual bank inputs and other institutional characteristics.

Evaluation of Bank Scale Studies

Although they are serious and often well-designed efforts to deal with a complex issue, bank economies-of-scale studies leave much to be desired. Two obvious problems that plague all of these studies is the lack of suitable proxies for bank output and resource inputs. I cannot yet assess the extent to which the empirical proxies employed for output and input variables have biased the statistical results and, therefore, led to erroneous managerial and policy implications. There is also the danger that the rapidly changing technology of service delivery will make earlier studies increasingly irrelevant to current bank cost and efficiency problems.

The economies-of-scale studies to date, with few exceptions, have been narrowly focused. Their concern is directed at the manner in which production costs vary with bank size—certainly a critically important issue from a public policy standpoint because it relates directly to how and why banking markets should be structured to promote both efficiency and competition. Unfortunately, however, the narrow focus of these studies has not sufficiently encouraged researchers to look for other ways in which variations in bank size influence individual bank and market behavior. For example, larger banks may reap the advantages of greater size in the form of reduced risk and lower earnings variance. Moreover, internal growth has encouraged American banks to proliferate service offerings. To the extent that these additional services result in greater public convenience, they represent returns to scale independent of what happens to production costs.

Moreover, largely because of data limitations, the scale studies have tended to concentrate on financial service output representing only a *portion* of total bank operations. Key areas of bank operations not considered in the majority of studies include trust services, cash management operations (for the bank's own cash position and those of its customers), correspondent services, leasing, and financial counseling. Economies may exist in these largely unexplored service areas, offsetting potential diseconomies in other important sectors of bank operations. Limited evidence in this direction, for example, was provided by Flannery's (1983) study of economies in correspondent services, which suggests that failure to account for these interbank services has led to an understatement of bank operating costs by as much as 15 percent and an overestimate of branch bank scale economies. A related problem is that few really large banks (for example, those with more than $1 billion in assets or deposits) are included in existing studies, and these are the very institutions that offer a number of financial services that have not yet been tested statistically for scale effects. As Flannery suggests, if cost functions are not homogeneous across the range of bank sizes, simultaneous estimation of operating costs for both small and large banks may yield inaccurate estimates and, of course, inappropriate prescriptions for public policy.

Further evidence that economies-of-scale researchers may be searching in the wrong places was provided by Reingaum and Smith (1983). Using stock market data on market value portfolios extracted from the University of Chicago's CRISP tapes for 1500 to 2500 firms, 1964–1978, they examined the relationship between capital market returns, risk, and firm size. Reingaum and Smith found that larger firms have significant capital-raising advantages over smaller firms. Even after the effect of nondiversifiable risk was removed, they found that investors still demonstrate a "statistically significant and economically important" preference for securities issued by larger companies (p. 1). Capital market investors appear to assign greater value to the earnings of larger firms such that smaller companies face a greater required rate of return and, therefore, capital-raising diseconomies of scale. The authors conclude that concentrated market power in selling the firms' products does *not* explain this size-related difference in cost of capital. Moreover, the study implies that even purely financial conglomerate mergers among smaller firms may be economical because they would tend to lower the cost of equity capital. Of course, these findings do not address the possibility that larger firms, especially in banking, tend to proliferate new services, which may result in a squandering of any size-related capital market efficiencies. Indeed, as noted earlier, if the more narrowly focused savings and loans possess greater scale economies than commercial banks do, I can conclude that growth in banking is not an unmixed blessing when it stimulates careless proliferation of services.

Whereas Reingaum and Smith were able to exclude market concentration as a factor in generating capital raising economies, Stevens (1983) has argued that in banking markets where concentration is increasing, the remaining institutions will slide along their average cost curves and capture any gains in efficiency that may be present. Thus, building on the earlier concept of X-inefficiency suggested by Liebenstein (1966), if greater concentration does reduce competition, banks in more concentrated markets may trade off efficiency and cost minimization for the benefits of reduced risk, management emoluments, etc., leading to an upward shift in the individual bank's average cost curve. Using sample data from 129 SMSAs located in unit and limited branching states in 1976, Stevens found that increased banking market concentration was associated with higher average bank costs, when population density, bank size, asset and deposit composition, and state branching laws were held constant. By implication, a public policy that reduces the degree of concentration in banking markets will also lower production costs. Prohibition of concentration-increasing mergers and acquisitions presumably would improve both production efficiency and allocative efficiency.

Finally, there remains the issue of the continuing relevance of past scale studies for an industry undergoing a technological revolution. At the heart of banking services is the storage and transfer of information—a function increasingly being automated. Nowhere perhaps is this more evident than in the payments mechanism. As more and more banking functions and services are automated, this transformation will alter the industry's production process, probably somewhat in favor of the largest institutions, because more capital-intensive production processes generally require high volume for maximum efficiency. Unfortunately, we still have extremely limited research evidence on the operating effects of this technological transition.

Perhaps, however, an indication of at least the *direction* in which automation will shift bank cost curves is provided by recent studies of scale economies for Federal Reserve payments services. For example, a study by Humphrey (1982) of average cost curves for Federal paper check processing, electronic-check processing at automated clearinghouses (ACH), and wire funds transfers, used a translog cost function for annual cross-section data, 1968–1976, with a time trend variable to capture the effects of technological change. Humphrey found that check processing over the study period was characterized by *diseconomies* of scale, while ACH processing of payments items was characterized by scale *economies* and wire transfers by *constant* average production costs. Humphrey concludes that "ACH processing can and should replace paper-check processing over time" (p. 15). If so, the long-run result is likely to mean significant economies from higher volume operations.

An earlier study by Walker (1978) looked for significant economies associated with retail banking machines—cash dispensers and automated tellers. Walker estimated average and marginal cross-sectional cost curves for a sample in excess of 300 banks to determine if and how rapidly costs fall as customer transactions volume increases. Application of a log-linear model with additive binary arguments that attempt to hold constant bank location, branching activity, and organizational form yields positive economies for cash dispenser operations. However, non-electronic fund transfer system (EFTS) costs are found to be significant in shaping cash-dispensing machine expenses, and larger banks report higher non-EFTS costs. Moreover, Walker finds that the marginal cost of cash dispensing is so low that his sample banks could offer electronic cash withdrawals at prices close to zero, suggesting greater future customer usage as nonelectronic banking costs continue to rise. Turning to automated tellers, Walker again finds that larger banks incur higher costs, probably related, as before, to higher EFT card expenses. But, there *are* significant scale economies from the use of automated teller machines (ATMs), at some banks.

On balance, the cost outlook for EFTS at the retail level is optimistic but not conclusive. It is not yet clear that larger banks possess a significant advantage in the electronic payments field once all costs—EFTS and non-EFTS—are considered. Indeed, a recent study by Metzker (1982) concludes that, because of advances in less expensive microcomputers and the divisibility features of new information-processing and transfer technology, "future payments system technology should not hinder the competitiveness of small institutions" provided they are well managed. Whereas it seems clear that complete elimination of paper transactions will favor larger banking operations, the probable impact across all banking services and, therefore, on the total cost structure of the individual bank is an unknown very much in need of further investigation.

Implications of Bank Scale Studies

What is particularly fascinating about the evolving economies of scale literature in banking is, on the one hand, the considerable improvement in research methodology that has occurred in recent years. Yet, on the other hand, the findings and implications of both new and old studies remain much the same. This field has marched on toward the use of more flexible and conceptually superior translog cost functions to answer its crucial questions; yet, the answers to those questions have changed little in either quantitative or qualitative terms. The most efficient production process appears to be reached at a relatively low level of bank output. A public policy that limits or prohibits mergers among the nation's largest banks should not damage the efficiency of individual banking institutions in using society's scarce resources unless it can be shown that economies of scope resulting from mergers or other, as yet unspecified, factors shift bank cost curves downward.

Moreover, the operating costs of newly chartered single-office banks are not necessarily greater than the costs of new branches, suggesting little gain in efficiency from adopting a branch banking system as opposed to a unit banking one. In fact, diseconomies from growth achieved via more branch offices tend to offset and, in the case of small branch banks, overwhelm economies from internal growth through processing more accounts. However, once a branch bank is established, it does appear to have more opportunities for scale economies from growth in service volume at individual branches than unit banks do.

On the other hand, the impact of holding-company affiliation on bank cost structures is so heavily in dispute that almost any generalization or conclusion today about holding-company scale effects appears hazardous.

A good example of the conflict in research findings concerning holding-company-related efficiencies is provided by Schweitzer (1972) and Kalish and Gilbert (1973). Schweitzer detected *lower* operating costs flowing from large holding-company affiliation. Kalish and Gilbert reported that holding company affiliates possessed *higher* costs than branch banking organizations (except for the smallest institutions). Longbrake and Haslem (1975) found that affiliated unit banks operated with higher production costs then did independent branch banks, but the reverse was true for affiliated versus independent branch banks. Benston and Hanweck (1977) detected more modest scale economies for affiliated institutions, though the affiliates displayed lower average costs per account than the independent banks (particularly for checkable deposits).

Of course, the foregoing observations do not *necessarily* imply there will be no significant consolidation of smaller banking organizations into larger ones as time passes. Forces other than cost effectiveness have led and will lead to fewer independent banking organizations over time, including the barriers confronting smaller institutions in raising capital, continuing shortages of skilled management, and the need to diversify geographically and by product line in order to reduce risk. (It is worth noting, however, as Whitehead and Schweitzer 1982 suggest, that evidence that larger banks have a significant risk advantage over smaller banks is unconvincing.)

Another key factor supporting further consolidation is *customer convenience*, which shapes the magnitude and direction of customer demand for banking services. Other factors held equal, the average bank customer will choose the principal bank that minimizes his or her transactions cost. Thus, a branch banking or holding-company system may generate higher unit production costs than a unit banking system but result in lower transactions cost for the average customer. And if branch banks or holding-company-affiliated banks produce a greater array of services and/or more offices, customers may experience lower transactions costs through their ability to use a wider menu of collateral bank services. Over time, then, customer demand will favor more consolidated banking organizations in many banking markets even in the absence of significant production economies.

In summary, bank cost studies to date suggest there *are* statistically significant scale economies in banking. However, as McCall (1980) observes,

most studies indicate that economies of scale in banking are relatively small, diminish rapidly with size increases and vary with organizational structure and product lines. Overall, the slight economies of scale from increased office size (output) are smallest for unit banks and larger for branch banks. The scale economies of branch banks, however, are more than offset by cost increases if the larger size results from the addition of branch offices rather than from growth of existing offices. . . . Scale economies of independent unit banks appear to be somewhat less than those of unit banks affiliated with holding companies, while those of branch banks do not seem to vary with affiliation status.

In general, unit banks can produce the same service mix at about the same resource cost for the average customer as multiple-office banking organizations. Smaller banks of any organizational type are more efficient than larger banks. Among individual bank service offerings the most substantial economies appear to stem from an expansion of loan output (particularly for business and real-property loans rather than consumer loans) and demand deposits but not from growth of time deposits or from the few peripheral services (except possibly trust operations) studied to date.

Economically relevant scale economies seem to be limited to a bank size range of no larger than $100 million in deposits, and some studies suggest deposits of $25 or $50 million are closer to the point where scale economies cease to be a significant factor in explaining the behavior of bank costs. Our knowledge of cost configurations at the upper end of the bank size distribution is far less well researched, but diseconomies of scale do *not* appear to be great enough to discourage the growth of the largest banks. As McCall and Savage (1980) note, "scale economies would not appear to be a major factor leading to the consolidation of banking organizations if branching laws were repealed" [p. 70]. And more recent research provides at least a hint—one that very much needs further corroboration—that large commercial banks may benefit from economies of capital raising and risk reduction that offset increased operating costs. Even with these potential size-related benefits, however, there is no evidence to suggest that commercial banking is a natural monopoly or is ever likely to be a natural monopoly. Thus, numerous banking institutions diverse in size, output mix, and organizational form have survived and are likely to continue to survive as viable firms in meeting the public's ever-changing and multifaceted demands for financial services.

References

Adar, Zvi, Tamir Agmon, and Yair E. Orgler. 1975. "Output Mix and Jointness in Production in the Banking Firm." *Journal of Money, Credit and Banking* (May), 8(2):235–43.

Alhadeff, David A. 1954. *Monopoly and Competition in Banking.* Berkeley, Calif.: University of California Press.

Atkinson, Jay F. 1979. "Firm Size in the Savings and Loan Industry." Research Working Paper No. 29 (December). Federal Home Loan Bank Board.

Bell, Frederick W. 1968. *Cost in Commercial Banking: A Quantitative Analysis of Bank Behavior and Its Relation to Bank Regulation.* Research Report No. 41. Boston: Federal Reserve Bank of Boston.

Bell, Frederick W. and Neil B. Murphy. 1968. "The Impact of Market Structure on the Price of a Commercial Service." *Review of Economics and Statistics* (May), 51:210–13.

Benston, George J. 1965a. "Branch Banking and Economies of Scale." *Journal of Finance* (May), 20:312–31.

—— 1965b. "Economies of Scale and Marginal Costs in Banking Operations." *The National Banking Review* (June), 2:507–49.

Benston, George J. and Gerald A. Hanweck. 1977. "A Summary Report on Bank Holding Company Affilation and Economies of Scale." *Proceedings of a Conference on Bank Structure and Competition.* Federal Reserve Bank of Chicago.

Benston, George J., Gerald A. Hanweck, and David B. Humphrey. 1982a. "Operating Costs in Commercial Banking." *Economic Review,* pp. 6–21 (November), Federal Reserve Bank of Atlanta.

Benston, George J., Gerald A. Hanweck, and David B. Humphrey. 1982b. "Scale Economies in Banking: A Restructuring and Reassessment." *Journal of Money, Credit and Banking* (November), 13 (part 1).

Berger, Allen N., Gerald A. Hanweck, and David B. Humphrey. 1986. "Competitive Viability in Banking: Scale, Scope, and Product Mix Economies." Research Papers in Banking and Financial Economics, Board of Governors of Federal Reserve System (January).

Carron, Andrew S. 1982. *The Plight of the Thrift Institutions.* Washington, D.C.: Brookings Institution.

Daniel, Donnie L., William A. Longbrake, and Neil B. Murphy. "The Effect of Technology on Bank Economies of Scale for Demand Deposits." *Journal of Finance* (March), 28:131–46.

Diewert, W. Erwin. 1971. "An Application of the Shephard Duality Theorem: A Generalized Leontief Production Function." *Journal of Political Economy,* 79:481–507.

Dugger, Robert H. 1975. *The Nonhomotheticity of Commercial Bank Production Functions.* Research Paper in Banking and Financial Economics, Board of Governors of the Federal Reserve System. (March)

Flannery, Mark J. 1983. "Correspondent Services and Cost Economies in Commercial Banking." *Journal of Banking and Finance* (March), 7:83–99.

Gilligan, Thomas W. and Michael A. Smirlock. 1984. "An Empirical Study of Joint Production and Scale Economies in Commercial Banking." *Journal of Banking and Finance* 8:67–77.

Gramley, Lyle E. 1962. *A Study of Scale Economies in Banking.* Kansas City, Mo.: Federal Reserve Bank Kansas City.

Greenbaum, Stuart I. 1966. "Costs and Production in Commercial Banking." *Monthly Review* (March–April), pp. 11–20. Federal Reserve Bank of Kansas City.

—— 1967. "A Study of Bank Cost." *National Banking Review* (June), 4:415–34.

Horvitz, Paul M. 1963. "Economies of Scale in Banking." In *Private Financial Institutions.* Englewood Cliffs, N.J.: Prentice-Hall.

Humphrey, David B. 1982. *Cost, Scale Economies, Competition, and Product Mix in the U.S. Payments Mechanism,* Staff Study No. 115 (April), Board of Governors of the Federal Reserve System.

Kalish, Lionel and R. Alton Gilbert. 1973. "An Analysis of Efficiency of Scale and Organization Form in Commercial Banking." *Journal of Industrial Economics* (July), 21:293–307.

Kim, Moshe. 1985. "Scale Economies in Banking: A Methodological Note." *Journal of Money, Credit and Banking* (February) 17(1):96–102.

Leibenstein, Harvey. 1966. "Allocative Efficiency vs. X-Efficiency." *American Economic Review* (June), pp. 392–416.

Longbrake, William A. 1974. "Computers and the Cost of Producing Various Types of Banking Services." *Journal of Business* (July), pp. 363–81.

Longbrake, William A. and John A. Haslem. 1975. "Productive Efficiency in Commercial Banking: The Effects of Size and Legal Form of Organization on the Cost of Producing Demand Deposit Services." *Journal of Money, Credit and Banking* (August), 7:317–30.

Longbrake, William A. and Marcia K. Johnson. 1975. "Economies of Scale in Banking." *The Magazine of Bank Administration* (July), pp. 32–38.

McCall, Alan S. and Donald T. Savage. 1980. "Branch Policy: The Options." *Journal of Bank Research* (Summer), 7:122–26.

McCall, Allan S. 1980. "Economies of Scale, Operating Efficiencies and the Organizational Structure of Commercial Banks." *Journal of Bank Research* (Summer), pp. 95–100.

McNulty, James E. 1982. "Economies of Scale in Banking: A Case Study of the Florida Savings and Loan Industry." *Economic Review,* Federal Reserve Bank of Atlanta (November), pp. 22–31.

Metzker, Paul F. 1982. "Future Payments System Technology: Can Small Financial Institutions Compete?" *Economic Review* (November), pp. 58–67. Federal Reserve Bank of Atlanta.

Mullineaux, Donald J. 1975a. "Economies of Scale of Financial Institutions: A Comment." *Journal of Monetary Economics* (April), 1:233–40.

Mullineaux, Donald J. 1975b. *Economies of Scale and Organizational Efficiency in Banking: A Profit Function Approach* (October). Department of Research, Federal Reserve Bank of Philadelphia.

Murphy, Neil B. 1972. "A Re-estimation of the Benston-Bell-Murphy Cost Functions for a Larger Sample with Greater Size and Geographical Dispersion." *Journal of Financial and Quantitative Analysis* (December) 7:2097–2105.

Nelson, Richard W. 1985. "Branching, Scale Economies, and Banking Costs." *Journal of Banking and Finance,* 9:177–91.

Osborne, D. 1982. "The Costs of Servicing Demand Deposits." *Journal of Money, Credit and Banking* (November) 14:479–93.

Panzar, J. C. and R. Willig. 1978. "Economies of Scope, Product Specific Returns to Scale, and Multiproduct Competitive Industries." Unpublished paper, Murray Hill, N.J.: Bell Laboratories.

Powers, John A. 1969. "Branch Versus Unit Banking: Bank Output and Cost Economies." *Southern Economic Journal* (October), 36:153–64.

Reingaum, Marc R. and Janet Kilholm Smith. 1983. "Investor Preference for Large Firms: New Evidence on Economies of Size." Research Paper No. 10. Department of Finance and Business Economics. University of Southern California.

Samuelson, Paul A. 1966. "The Fundamental Singularity Theorem for Non-Joint Production." *International Economic Review* (January), 34–41.

Schweiger, Irving and John S. McGee. 1961. "Chicago Banking: The Structure and Performance of Banks and Related Financial Institutions in Chicago and Other Areas." *Journal of Business* (July), 34:203–366.

Stevens, Jerry L. 1983. "Bank Market Concentration and Costs: Is There X-Inefficiency in Banking?" *Business Economics* (May), pp. 36–44.

Stigler, George. 1966. *The Theory of Price.* New York: Macmillan.

Walker, David A. 1978. "Economies of Scale in Electronic Funds Transfer System." *Journal of Banking and Finance.* 2:65–78.

Whitehead, David D. and Robert L. Schweitzer. 1982. "Bank Size and Risk: A Note on the Evidence." *Economic Review* (November), Federal Reserve Bank of Atlanta, pp. 32–34.

Yawitz, Boris. 1969. *Automation in Commercial Banking: Its Process and Impact.* Graduate School of Business Dissertation Series, Columbia University. New York: Free Press.

5.

Impact of External Growth: Acquiring Other Banks

AMERICAN BANKING has passed through waves of *merger* activity since World War II. The first significant wave struck during the 1950s as larger U.S. banks struggled to keep up with burgeoning loan demand and sluggish growth in deposits. Many bank mergers also were touched off by businesses and consumers moving out of the central cities into the suburbs. Threatened with a loss of both commercial loans and consumer deposits, larger banks targeted hundreds of smaller banks in suburban locations as a convenient and quick way to branch through merger. Tighter federal controls over banking combinations in the 1960s and 1970s cooled off the merger trend, but the 1980s and a more liberal federal regulatory policy ushered in a new merger wave. During 1982 through 1985, for example, banking ranked first among major U.S. industries in the total number of merger transactions and ranked in the top ten industries in the aggregate value of all merger combinations.

Each merger wave has profoundly affected the American banking structure. Mergers have contributed to a consolidation trend in hundreds of local banking markets. Moreover, these business com-

---

Portions of this chapter are based upon the author's earlier article (1984) in the *Canadian Banker*. The material is used with permission from the publisher.

binations have enabled the nation's one hundred largest banking organizations to slow the erosion of their share of the industry's resources despite the rapid growth of smaller banks in the southern and western sections of the nation. Many recent mergers have been aimed at the goals of territorial expansion, market dominance, a desire to offer new services, and an effort to reduce operating costs through scale economies. Some banks have viewed the merger vehicle as a way to reduce noninterest costs and offset rising interest expenses associated with deregulation.

Federal and State Law and the Regulation of Bank Mergers

Mergers involve the absorption of the assets and liabilities of one bank by another. The bank whose assets and liabilities are absorbed loses its corporate identity and ceases to operate as an independent firm. An infrequently used alternative to merger is *consolidation,* in which all participating banks surrender their separate corporate identities to form one organization. As Rose (1984) observes, recent bank mergers in the United States have generally fallen into one of four categories: (1) wholesale intraindustry combinations among larger metropolitan banks, aimed primarily at expanding corporate banking services; (2) wholesale-retail intraindustry combinations where large metropolitan banks acquire smaller, outlying banks in an effort to expand more deeply into consumer markets; (3) retail-oriented intraindustry combinations among two or more smaller, consumer-oriented institutions to provide new capital and management, increase efficiency, and expand services; and (4) intraindustry combinations that combine bank and nonbank institutions (such as savings and loans), often to aid a troubled firm or formalize a long-standing relationship.

STATE LAWS AND REGULATIONS

Bank mergers in the United States are controlled by both federal and state law. The states generally have limited bank merger activity through their control over the power of banks to branch or to form holding companies. For example, if state law prohibits branching, the merger of two banks in that state means one of the banks must close its office. Similarly, where branching is limited by state statute to cities, counties, or districts, bank mergers outside those geographic boundaries are discouraged because, again, one of the banks must close its facilities after the merger is consummated.

Not surprisingly, most U.S. bank mergers have occurred in states with relatively liberal branching rules—a fact supported in a study by Rhoades (1982) that categorizes states by the intensity of merger activity (1960–1975) within their borders. In states that prohibit or severely restrict branching, acquisitions of banks by holding companies have served as an alternative to full-fledged mergers. Thus, state law exerts an *indirect* influence (through branching and holding-company rules) on bank mergers, though the impact of the states on national merger trends has been substantial.

FEDERAL LAW AND REGULATION

Federal law has a profound impact on bank mergers in a very *direct* way. Section 2 of the Sherman Act (1980) forbids the creation of a "monopoly" in any line of commerce through mergers or other joint actions, and Section 7 of the Clayton Act (1914) prohibits any business combination "tending to create a monopoly" or that "may substantially reduce competition." In order to prevent possible damaging effects on competition, all mergers today involving federally insured banks must be approved by one or more federal regulatory agencies.

For example, any merger in which the resulting bank is a national bank must be approved by the Comptroller of the Currency. The Federal Reserve Board must be consulted on mergers in which the resulting institution is a state-chartered member bank, while the Federal Deposit Insurance Corporation must approve combinations involving state-chartered insured banks, mutual savings banks, and uninsured banks. Finally, the Department of Justice must approve any bank merger from the standpoint of its actual or potential effects on competition in the relevant market area to be served. Each federal banking agency must request advisory reports on competitive factors from the attorney general and the two remaining federal banking agencies.

A study by Eisenbeis (1975) suggests that the three federal banking agencies have *not* been uniform in their merger decisions, with the Comptroller of the Currency most likely to approve merger applications and the Federal Reserve and Department of Justice least likely to grant approval. However, even the strictest regulatory agency was found to approve about 90 percent of all cases appearing before it (owing, in part, to informal discouragement of questionable merger applications before a formal application is filed).

Analysis of prior merger decisions by the regulatory agencies suggests that the *probable impact on competition* is the dominant factor in the approval or denial of a bank merger application. Velk (1976) also finds, in a review of Federal Reserve merger decisions, that approval is more likely where there is strong unmet public demand for more or better quality bank services (supported by objective data), where the acquiring bank offers a menu of services substantially wider than the acquired bank, and where common ownership ties already exist between the merging institutions. Denial of a merger application, on the other hand, is more likely where applicants share any geographic market and the resulting competitive effect is judged to be "substantially adverse," where the combined size of the applicant banks is large relative to the total market, and where the acquiring bank's "financial health" is in question (such as when the ratio of net current operating expenses to total assets is relatively high). In addition, entry through merger into new markets that are already highly concentrated seems to carry a high probability of approval in an effort to bring new competition into such markets.

These findings are generally supported by Carey (1975) in an extensive study of competitive factors discussed in the merger decisions and advisories of the Comptroller of the Currency, Federal Deposit Insurance Corporation, Federal Reserve Board, and the Attorney General. Carey observes a long-term trend among the agencies of finding fewer anticompetitive effects, with the Comptroller of the Currency and the FDIC more liberal in this regard than the Attorney General and the Federal Reserve Board. In addition, Weiss (1980) observes that the federal banking agencies and the Justice Department do *not* discriminate in their merger and holding-company acquisition decisions between foreign and domestic bank acquirers. Apparently nationality is a "neutral factor" for federal authorities in deciding to approve or deny a merger or acquisition in a U.S. banking market.

The elaborate regulatory approval process in place today is a relatively recent phenomenon. Indeed, for most of the nation's history there was considerable controversy about the proper role of government in bank mergers. When the Sherman and Clayton Antitrust acts were passed near the turn of the century there was considerable doubt that these laws had any bearing on mergers in a regulated industry. Moreover, because most banks at that time served primarily local markets and many of the acquired institutions were relatively small, the possible damage from anticompetitive banking combinations was thought to be of little consequence. Then, too, many bank mergers involved failing institutions and were, therefore, frequently aided and abetted by the regulatory agencies to prevent bank runs and the draining of federal insurance reserves.

COURT DECISIONS

The uncertainty surrounding the applicability of federal antitrust laws to banking was dispelled by the Supreme Court in the landmark *Philadelphia National Bank* case, decided in 1963 (374 U.S. 321, 363). Philadelphia National Bank attempted to acquire Girard Trust Corn Exchange in a combination that, the Department of Justice argued, would have resulted in a significant diminution of local market competition. The percentage of all bank assets in Philadelphia County held by the largest bank would have jumped from 25 to 39 percent. Justice sued to block the merger, and on appeal, their position was upheld by the Supreme Court, which applied Section 7 of the Clayton Act. The Court defined "commercial banking"—the unique bundle of services offered by banks—as the relevant line of commerce with which to delineate the structure of banking markets, excluding any nonbank financial institutions from consideration. The relevant market was defined to be the *local* area within which businesses and individuals normally would go to secure banking services because they found it inconvenient to travel to more distant banks. In effect, the Court adopted a familiar proposition in banking (citing an earlier study by Alhadeff 1954) that *the size of a bank's customers determines the scope of its market area.* One of the most important consequences of the Supreme Court's decision in *Philadelphia National Bank* was to cause a rise in intermarket (i.e., market extension) bank mergers rather than mergers within the same market.

The landmark Philadelphia decision still left open the question, however, of whether mergers involving small banks in smaller communities were as vulnerable to antitrust prosecution as billion-dollar institutions such as Philadelphia National Bank. That question was answered in the affirmative when the *Phillipsburg* case reached the Supreme Court in 1967 (399 U.S. 350). The court held that *any* combination in *any* relevant market, especially that for local deposits and local loans, that would significantly damage competition was a violation of the Clayton Act. The proposed Phillipsburg merger, in which the resulting bank would have captured at least 15 percent of the relevant market, was denied. Moreover, the Court reaffirmed the principles behind this decision seven years later in a case involving *Connecticut National Bank* (418 U.S. 662), adding as well that nonbank thrift institutions could *not* be considered full-fledged competitors with commercial banks until they were legally granted the power to offer all major bank services and actively offered those services. Recent research by Murphy and Rogers (1984) in New England suggests that excluding thrift institutions from the relevant market may be a serious error because many customers do not view banks and thrifts as separate institutions, though it must be said that New England thrifts historically have played a much greater role in local bank credit and deposit markets than appears to be true in most other parts of the nation. Moreover, as noted by Welker (1986), the Federal Reserve Board and the Department of Justice have begun to include at least a fraction of thrift deposits into calculations of relevant banking markets when antitrust issues are under consideration.

THE BANK MERGER ACTS

Congress has tended to lag behind industry and the courts in drafting new legislation affecting bank mergers. In 1960 the Bank Merger Act was passed as a belated response to the accelerated growth of bank mergers during the 1950s. The 1960 statute required any merger involving federally supervised banks to be approved by the banks' principal regulatory agency. The new law placed prime emphasis on the *competitive effects* of any pending merger transaction, stipulating that mergers having a "significant adverse" effect on local market competition must be challenged in court, if necessary. Federal regulators were also compelled to review the financial history and condition of the merger applicants (especially their capital adequacy, strength of management, and future earnings prospects), as well as the probable impact of the merger on public convenience (particularly the availability of banking services in the community to be served). Thus, the Bank Merger Act of 1960 represented a relatively restrictive federal regulatory attitude toward banking combinations, mindful of the restrictive measures taken against bank holding companies four years previously with passage of the Bank Holding Company Act (1956).

Congress moderated its restrictive stance toward bank mergers in 1966 when a series of amendments were made in the 1960 law. The Bank Merger Act of 1966 was really a belated response to the Philadelphia National Bank decision. In that case the Supreme Court had come down heavily on the side of *competition* as the controlling factor in a bank merger decision. In the 1966 amendments Congress broadened and ranked the criteria under which federal regulatory authorities could approve bank merger applications in an effort to promote regulatory uniformity. The competitive effects of a proposed merger remained the principal criterion; however, mergers with anticompetitive effects might still be approved if those adverse effects were "clearly outweighed" by expected public benefits, including greater convenience in the availability of key financial services.

JUSTICE DEPARTMENT GUIDELINES
Passage of the Bank Merger Acts in 1960 and 1966 was followed in 1968 by the publication of Department of Justice guidelines for banks and other corporations proposing to merge. These initial guidelines, which remained nominally in effect until revised in June 1982, were designed to block any merger that would eliminate a significant independent bank competitor, result in a significant increase in market concentration, or allow one bank or group of banks to dominate a local market. Justice was also concerned about the effects of market concentration or dominance on barriers to the entry of new banks and on the growth of smaller banks toward larger market shares.

In general, as Di Clemente and Alemprese (1983) point out, the regulatory agencies employed the Justice Department's guidelines in their own analyses of the competitive effects of proposed mergers and holding-company acquisitions. These analyses typically began by defining the relevant market area, determining the number of competitors offering banking services in that particular market, and calculating the share of *deposits* held by the largest banks. On the basis of market shares and other data the agencies would decide if the proposed merger would affect competition to a "substantially adverse," "adverse," "slightly adverse," or "insignificant" degree. An adverse competitive impact under the terms of the Bank Merger and Bank Holding Company Acts must be "clearly outweighed" by public benefits (such as a gain in operating efficiency or avoidance of a bank failure) before the proposed merger can be approved. In most instances mergers in relatively concentrated markets would be permitted only if the acquiring bank was a *new* market extrant. If the acquiring bank was already represented in the market, acceptable mergers would normally be limited to *foothold acquisitions* (i.e., banks with a small market share) or to *de novo* banks.

Reflecting recent court decisions, relevant research, and gradually changing policies within the Justice Department, U.S. Attorney General William French Smith announced new merger guidelines on June 14, 1982. (See table 5.1, which compares the old and new Justice merger guidelines.) A number of major changes in federal antitrust policy are evident in these more recently published guidelines. The 1968 guidelines used the proportion of market area assets, deposits, or sales held by the four largest firms (i.e., the four-firm concentration ratio) as the principal measure of market structure and concentration. In contrast, the 1982 guidelines rely on the Herfindahl-Hirschmann index—the sum of the squared market shares of all firms in the relevant market—as the relevant concentration standard. Moreover, the Herfindahl index is computed as it would appear *after* the merger, rather than before, by adding the change in the index following the merger to its premerger value. Arithmetically this means that the change in the Herfindahl index would be equal to two times the product of the market shares of the firms involved in the merger. The new guidelines clearly focus on the *change* in the Herfindahl index if the merger is approved.

It is now clear that the Justice Department's 1982 guidelines will result in many mergers going unchallenged that would have been challenged under the old standards, as Gagnon (1982), Guerin-Calvert (1983), and Di Clemente and Alemprese (1983) observe. Guerin-Calvert estimates that about 4,000 *fewer* bank mergers would likely be challenged, due principally to a modest increase in market share levels

Table 5.1. Old and New Merger Guidelines of the U.S. Department of Justice

Guidelines Announced in 1968 Specifying Which Market Conditions and Shares Would Invite a Legal Challenge			Guidelines Announced in 1982 For Postmerger Levels of Concentration That May Invite a Legal Challenge		
Status of Relevant Market	Market Shares of Acquiring Firms	Market Shares of Acquired Firms	Postmerger Status of Relevant Market	Value of Herfindahl-Hirschmann Index of Market Concentration	Change in Market Concentration and Likelihood of Justice Department Challenge
Highly concentrated market: four-firm concentration ratio ≥ 75%	4% 10% ≥15%	4% or larger 2% or larger 1% or larger	Highly concentrated	Above 1,800	Likely to invite challenge if Herfindahl-Hirschmann index change resulting from the merger > 100
Less highly concentrated market: four-firm concentration ratio < 75%	4% 10% 15% 20% ≥25%	5% or more 4% or more 3% or more 2% or more 1% or more			If Herfindahl-Hirschmann index change is from 50–100, ease of entry, product line, firm conduct, and other factors will be considered before a challenge is made

Market where concentration is increasing (market share of largest two to eight firms has increased 7% or more over the past five to ten years)	Acquisition of a firm having a market share of 2% or more may be challenged		
Moderately concentrated		1,000 to 1,800	If Herfindahl-Hirschmann index change is less than 50, a legal challenge is unlikely
			Challenge likely if Herfindahl-Hirschmann index change > 100, but other factors will be considered
			Challenge unlikely if Herfindahl-Hirschmann index change is ≤ 100
Unconcentrated		Below 1,000	Any change in Herfindahl-Hirschmann is unlikely to be legally challenged
Leading company rule			If leading firm has market share ≥ 35% and is about twice the size of second largest firm in the relevant market and the firm to be acquired has a market share ≥ 1%, a legal challenge is likely

SOURCES: Department of Justice and Federal Reserve Bank of Chicago, *Economic Perspectives* (September-October 1983), pp. 14–23.

permitted for both acquired and acquiring firms. She predicts that across all banking markets, only about 10 percent of mergers will be challenged by the Department of Justice, though a higher proportion of mergers will probably be challenged in banking than in other industries due to the higher levels of existing concentration in many banking markets.

For markets designated as "unconcentrated," mergers will, in all probability, go completely unchallenged—a *safety zone* not present in the old guidelines. Even for "highly concentrated" markets, however, mergers involving the acquisition of a small firm (even if the market leader is involved) *could* go unchallenged. And a number of mitigating factors—such as favorable firm conduct, lack of significant entry barriers, imminent failure, and the ready availability of market information—may be used to override otherwise questionable concentration levels, especially where, in the judgement of Justice Department lawyers, the likelihood of collusion is low.

Motivations for Bank Mergers

Why do firms, especially banks, merge? What motivates certain firms (usually the largest corporations in a given market) to seek out other firms to acquire? Equally important, what motivates a firm (usually a smaller company) to sell out to the acquiring institution?

One important economic reason is *expected profitability.* An offer to merge may permit stockholders of the acquired bank to realize a significant capital gain on sale of their stock plus, where stock is exchanged, the opportunity to earn more favorable rates of return from the stock of the acquiring bank. This may be particularly important where the market for the acquired bank's stock is so small that its shares may be undervalued.

From the vantage point of shareholders of the acquiring bank the merger may increase the stream of expected future profits and/ or *reduce the risk* (variability) *of future returns,* especially where the acquired institution serves a different market than the acquiring one. Thus, mergers may augment projected cash flows of acquiring banks, reduce cash flow risk, or both. Indeed, management and the owners may prefer reduced risk to added profitability, especially in those markets where competition is weak. Either way, the price of the acquiring institution's ownership shares should rise, *ceteris paribus*, increasing the market value of the stockholders' investment.

Related to profitability are the potential *tax benefits* of a merger. The acquisition of a bank with strong growth potential offers shareholders of the acquiring bank the option of substituting capital gains income, taxed at more favorable rates, for ordinary income. Similarly, owners of the acquired firm can capitalize their future earnings by trading their shares for those of the acquiring company. There are other potential tax benefits flowing from increased depreciation charges and from buying businesses with substantial tax losses and thus sheltering some portion of the acquiring firm's taxable earnings (as discussed by Weston and Chung 1983).

A merger may improve the *marketability* of stock for the shareholders of both the acquired and acquiring banks. If additional shares must be issued to consummate the merger, the stock may become more actively traded. Usually the most significant benefits here are reaped by shareholders of a small acquired bank who often find that there is little or no market for their stock and that the current market price does not adequately reflect the bank's profit potential.

For many large banks, growth has slowed significantly; thus, a merger offers the potential for *accelerated growth*, particularly through the acquisition of deposits. Then, too, many large banks have been outdistanced by the rapid growth of their borrowing customers. They bump up against regulatory lending limits in attempting to respond to the credit needs of major corporations. Merger provides a vehicle to expand legal loan limits and, thus, retain valued customers. Because most acquired banks are very small relative to the size of acquiring institutions, however, the deposit growth and lending limit arguments appear to be secondary considerations and, indeed, an expensive vehicle for such growth.

Related to the foregoing merger motivation is the problem of keeping up with the *geographic expansion of the bank's customer base.* As population moves to suburban and rural areas or to distant cities, banks unable to branch through merger are faced with the costly alternatives of losing former customers to more conveniently located institutions or of opening new banks in new markets. Branching by merger is particularly attractive where the bank to be acquired has good community relationships and a good physical location. As Smith (1970) notes, branching via merger brings the acquiring bank the "goodwill" that an established bank already commands and a greater share of the local market than opening a new branch would bring in the near term. The Alhadeffs (1955) point out that acquiring an existing bank is likely to solve staffing problems and does not require the same demonstration of public need as chartering a new bank or opening a new branch would require.

An added element here is the desire of management and owners to improve their market position in the event new federal or state legislation permitting more branch banking or holding-company activity is passed. For example, a number of bank holding companies in Texas acquired minority interests in Colorado and Wyoming banks during the late 1970s and early 1980s in anticipation of some relaxation in either the McFadden Act or the Bank Holding Company Act regarding interstate acquisitions.

Many mergers seem to represent a *defensive and imitative reaction* to the actions of competitors, as noted by the Alhadeffs (1955). Banks not planning to merge may find their market shares eroding to competitors who have already launched an acquisitions program. By opening up new sources of profitability and reduced risk via diversification, merging banks may attract stockholders away from competitors as equity investors are drawn toward those institutions "where the action is." Retaliatory mergers often occur, therefore, simply to defend threatened market positions.

Operating inefficiencies also may play a role in bank mergers. Both the acquired and acquiring institution may feel they are below optimum size for their market, resulting in higher costs and lower profitability. Merger may offer a quicker route than *de novo* entry to an efficient operating volume.

Related to the efficiency argument, the risks and costs associated with *offering new services* may prohibit a bank from offering a full range of services in response to market demand. If the bank does not respond via a merger or in some other way to customer demands for new services, such inaction invites competitors to enter. To the extent customers prefer securing a bundle of both new and old services from the same bank, those institutions not providing full services will experience an erosion of their customer base.

For many small banks, especially in rural areas and smaller cities, *management succession* has been a strong motivator for selling out to a larger organization. This is particularly true where the small bank is closely held and management has been unable or unwilling to bring in qualified managers from outside. There may be no capable replacements for an aging senior management team within the bank's own market area. This proved to be a particularly serious problem in the first two decades after World War II because many young and talented executives, looking at the catastrophic bank failures of the 1930s, did not consider banking a viable career path. A related problem may be fear on the part of the bank's owners that the government will place an unexpectedly high value on the business for purposes of estate taxation. Moreover, a merger can bring about substantial salary increases and improved fringe benefits for existing employees and thus help to retain the best of experienced management while opening up a broader market for new management.

Impact of Mergers on Bank Performance

A few studies have appeared over the years in an effort to discern the controlling motives for mergers and to assess their effects on banks, bank stockholders, and the public. The methodology of these studies has generally gone in one of two directions: (1) tracking the performance of the merging institutions over time or (2) comparing the performance of merging and comparable nonmerging banks, both before and after consummation of the merger transaction. The findings of these studies are interesting but not particularly satisfying or reassuring to either bank owners or to those charged with protecting the public interest.

MERGER MOTIVES AND EFFECTS

One of the earliest studies of the impact of bank mergers was conducted by Edwards (1964) as a doctoral dissertation with the assistance of the Federal Reserve Bank of Boston. Edwards' study of 49 large U.S. metropolitan areas suggested that interest rates on small business loans averaged higher where mergers and other acquisitions led to a more concentrated banking market. For example, rates on small business loans were about six basis points higher for each 10-point rise in the percentage of total metropolitan area deposits held by the three largest banks operating there. Edwards was careful to point out, however, that such a small difference might have been more related to differences in loan production costs than to competition.

Another early study of the bank merger phenomenon was prepared by Bacon (1967) for the Research Department of the Federal Reserve Bank of Chicago. Bacon examined the motives behind bank merger activity in Marion County, Indiana, between 1945 and 1960. Marion County, which includes Indianapolis, was the scene of a large number of bank mergers during this period; in fact, the number of banks serving Marion County declined from 21 in 1945 to only six at year-end 1960 owing principally to mergers. As a result, the percentage of deposits held by the three largest banks in Marion County increased from 67 percent to 96 percent over the 1945-60 period.

Bacon found underlying economic reasons for many of the mergers, such as the rapid growth of suburban areas that required more convenient banking services and the influx of major corporations establishing branch plants and, in some cases, merging with local businesses. Moreover, as a result of postwar economic growth, Marion County banks felt the need for larger lending limits and a wider range of services. As local businesses were absorbed by distant corporations or driven out by franchise operations, many commercial accounts were lost by the local banks, causing some Indianapolis banks to place more emphasis on retail rather than wholesale banking. There was a structural factor too: Indiana permitted branch banking and prohibited entry by outside banks until local banks were absorbed by merger.

Bacon found that the small banks (less than $15 million in deposits) absorbed by merger were as profitable as their larger acquirers, but their salary schedules were significantly *below* the average for the surrounding county. Moreover, their prices—loan rates and demand deposit service charges—were *higher* than those posted by larger metropolitan banks, suggesting competitive problems. The physical facilities of the small banks were often overcrowded and poorly located, and both ownership and management succession problems were present. Finally, generous tender offers (in the form of substantial premiums over cash or book value per share) were generally made by the acquiring banks. In many cases shareholder dividends increased significantly following the mergers, and many officers and employees received substantial salary increases and more generous fringe benefits.

The acquiring banks saw *market penetration* as the principal motivating force behind the mergers. Merger was usually preferred to *de novo* branching because of staffing problems, construction costs, the availability of goodwill from buying an existing bank, lower promotion expenses, and the ready acquisition of market share. Mergers among the largest Marion County banks appeared to arise from a desire to broaden service offerings. Management also hoped for greater operating efficiency and, in one case, resolution of a serious management succession problem. Bacon also detected a desire for increased management prestige as playing a role in these merger decisions, especially among the larger banks.

An equally comprehensive bank merger study was conducted by Smith (1969), serving at the time as a research economist with the Federal Reserve Bank of Cleveland. Smith noted that up to the time of his study, information on the characteristics of acquiring and acquired bank was "virtually nonexistent." He analyzed 239 merging banks (including 139 acquired and 100 acquiring banks) plus an additional 100 nonmerging banks that served as a control group. All were headquartered in the Fourth (Cleveland) Federal Reserve District with the mergers taking place during the 1960–1967 period. Mean-difference tests were employed to compare balance sheet and operating features of acquiring, acquired, and nonmerging banks and to explore the underlying motives for merger.

Predictably, Smith found that most *acquired* institutions were relatively small—only six of 140 held assets exceeding $25 million. Surprisingly, however, the *acquiring* banks were, on average, of only moderate size (half held assets in the $5 to $50 million range). Large banks with assets of more than $100 million represented less than a third of all Fourth District merger combinations, owing, apparently, to fears of antitrust action by the Justice Department and possible regulatory disapproval under provisions of the Bank Merger Act. Smith observed a "ladder pattern" in bank acquisitions with the smallest banks typically absorbed by medium-sized institutions and the medium-sized banks usually acquired by the largest banks in the region. In general, acquiring banks tended to merge with acquired banks different in size and structure (both in organization and portfolio features) from themselves.

From a financial perspective the acquired banks were generally more liquid (in terms of cash assets and U.S. Government securities) and less aggressive in committing assets to loans and municipal bonds than the acquiring institutions. Acquired banks held significantly larger shares of real estate and farm loans, while acquiring institutions were more heavily committed to commercial lending, on average. Deposit structure at the acquired institutions was more heavily tipped toward smaller time and savings accounts. The implication of such differences is that many mergers took place in an effort to grant larger banks access to a greater volume of less expensive deposits to help fund large commercial loans. Most acquired banks were unit institutions, while acquiring banks usually had branches so that the acquired institution generally became a branch office, providing a base to attract additional deposits. In addition, acquiring banks saw substantial unused profit potential in the acquired institutions with the prospect of converting excess liquidity into profitable loans.

In examining motives behind the mergers Smith argued that management succession problems and high prices paid for acquired institutions were more likely facilitators for the mergers rather than basic causes. Nor was there substantial support for the notion that a desire for greater lending limits (and, therefore, the acquisition of additional capital) was a major merger motive. Moreover, there was no significant improvement in ex post profitability of the acquiring institutions following the mergers, though Smith could not rule out the possible role of profit expectations in bringing on the mergers. The average yield on assets rose faster among the merging banks, reflecting a growth in operating revenues, but expenses rose even more rapidly than among nonmerging institutions. Smith suggested that the acquiring banks were assuming the "prospective costs" that the acquired institutions had not met, such as finding replacements for aging management, modernizing plant and equipment, or raising savings deposit rates to competitive levels.

If not profit expectations then what could have motivated the mergers? Smith placed the greatest weight on the desire of the acquiring banks to expand their branch systems more efficiently and cheaply than could be achieved through de novo branching. This suggests that the desire for greater size and/or market power plays a *significant role in bank merger decisions.* Indeed, this conclusion seems to have considerable empirical support in studies by Rhoades and Yeats (1974), Reid (1968), Piper (1971), and Lawrence (1967), which suggest, first of all, that larger U.S. banks have tended to grow more slowly than the industry as a whole and, second, that deposit size maximization (subject to a target profit level) is a common goal among the largest American banking organizations. The problem with choosing the merger route to pursue a size maximization goal, as Moyer (1976) observes, is that the largest banks eventually encounter both significant regulatory and structural constraints as they attempt to grow either through additional mergers or holding-company acquisitions or through *de novo* branching. There are only a limited number of really desirable markets to enter and a limited number of merger and acquisition targets that contribute to growth while still avoiding illegal anticompetitive combinations.

More recently, Phillis and Pavel (1986) in a study of 37 interstate mergers and acquisitions since 1981 found *expansion of retail banking business* to be the "driving force" behind initial interstate acquisitions. Acquiring banks tended to reach across state lines to purchase profitable banks having strong consumer banking operations and extensive retail distribution networks. Moreover, the interstate acquirers tended to be those large banking institutions that already possessed a significant consumer orientation (as reflected in a large number of branch offices) rather than large banks concentrating on commercial clients. Most of the targeted banks were moderate to large in asset size ($400 million or larger), suggesting that really small banks have little to fear from being merged out of existence, at least during the initial phase of the growth of interstate banking.

TERMS OF ACQUISITION

The failure of most merger studies to find gains in profitability probably reflects, among other factors, substantial premiums paid to acquired banks to induce them to sell their shares. For example, a study by Darnell (1973) of bank mergers in Pennsylvania and New Jersey between 1968 and 1972 found that book value premiums paid to shareholders of acquired banks averaged slightly more than 100 percent in Pennsylvania and about one third over book value in New Jersey during this period. On an implied basis of cash to book value, New

Jersey banks selling out received average premiums of 141 percent, while Pennsylvania acquired institutions posted 115-percent average cash-to-book premiums. Moreover, acquiring Pennsylvania banks traded $2.31 in earnings for each $1.00 in acquired-bank earnings over the 1968-1972 period, while the earnings trade-off was $1.40 to $1 in New Jersey.

Darnell found that the larger the size disparity between acquiring and acquired institutions, the greater the merger premiums tended to be. For example, "mergers of large banks with small banks yielded book-to-book premiums roughly twice the size of those paid when the partners were more *comparable in size*—medium/medium banks and small/small banks" (p. 22). Darnell also discovered a tendency for merger premiums to rise as time passed, owing to a dwindling supply of eligible partners and a strong bias toward faster deposit growth at larger banks (often at the expense of short-run returns). Moreover, management of the acquiring banks appeared to place greater present value on the projected earnings of the acquired banks after merger than the acquired banks did, perhaps because acquiring institutions estimate that banks selling out have significantly greater earnings potential, given more aggressive management, improved access to outside capital, and greater efficiency than was true under the original owners. Moreover, the merger may be viewed by the acquiring institution as a cheaper form of market entry than *de novo* charters or *de novo* branches—one that is profitable to begin with instead of having to digest high start-up costs.

MERGERS AND SERVICE AVAILABILITY

A study by Snider (1973) looked at a broader aspect of the bank merger issue—the impact of acquisitions on the composition of credit made available to the public. Using a paired-comparison test Snider examined changes in loan portfolios of formerly independent rural banks in Virginia following their merger into urban branching systems. Comparing merged institutions with nonmerging independent banks of comparable size serving the same county-wide area, this study focused on five loan mix ratios (gross loans to deposits, and rural real estate, farm, business, and consumer loans to total loans) for 36 banks acquired by four different branching systems during the 1962-1968 period. Loan mix data were analyzed three years before and three years after each merger.

Snider could find no statistically significant differences in loan composition between acquired and nonacquired banks before or after the mergers took place. There was no evidence, then, that urban-based branching systems moving via merger into rural areas attempted to "slight" farm borrowers or other rural credit customers. Moreover, the acquired banks, upon conversion to branch offices, experienced faster average deposit growth than comparable nonacquired institutions.

Snider's results were consistent with two earlier studies of mergers in New York and Indiana. The first of these, conducted in the State of New York by Kohn (1964), found no evidence that rural banks absorbed by major branch systems reduced service availability in rural communities. A later study by Kaufman (1969) surveyed bank customers in Elkhart, Indiana, on the quality and convenience of banking services before and after two of the three banks in that moderate-size community had merged. Nearly half the responding businesses and about 40 percent of the households felt that service quality had *improved* after the merger, while less than 10 percent perceived a decline in service quality. However, there seemed to be greater willingness among household customers to consider the use of out-of-town banks two years after the merger had occurred.

MERGERS AND THE PUBLIC INTEREST

In few instances do researchers find any concrete evidence that bank mergers have significantly benefited the public. Indeed, bank merger studies most often point to either neutral effects or, occasionally, even negative effects on the public welfare.

For example, Rhoades (1980) notes an emerging concern during the 1970s on the part of the regulatory agencies and the Department of Justice that at least some bank mergers (principally those of the market extension variety) have adversely impacted statewide banking structures. The roots of this concern appear to be linked to the doctrine of "mutual forbearance," which argues that the expansion of several large, diversified banking institutions into the *same* collection of different local markets creates a mutual awareness among these organizations of their interdependence. Joint exposure in one or more shared markets may lead to retaliation. Thus, mutuality of interest tends to dampen competition and encourage tacit agreements on price and market share. Rhoades analyzed changes in banking structure

among the 48 continental states and the District of Columbia, 1961–
1971. He found that merger activity, whether measured by the number
of mergers or deposits absorbed, tends to significantly increase statewide
banking concentration over time—an effect that probably has been
enhanced by the recent passage of more liberal branching laws.

Rhoades notes, however, that this increased concentration
effect does not *necessarily* mean that bank performance changes over
time in ways that harm the public interest. Indeed, an earlier study by
Rhoades and Yeats (1974) found declining *nationwide* concentration
among the nation's 100 largest banks over the same time period, though
Talley (1974) observed that mergers among the 100 largest banking
organizations between 1968 and 1973 cut the expected decline in
nationwide concentration by half. Yet, in an analysis of *local* banking
markets—areas of greatest relevance for most small borrowers and
depositors—the Alhadeffs (1955) found that a significant number of
bank mergers (29 percent) actually reduced the number of customer
alternatives.

I hasten to note that some research studies find a positive
impact from bank mergers on the public interest. For example, a study
of service prices and service menus by Glassman (1975) identified a
number of favorable merger effects in the late 1960s and early 1970s.
Surveying all commercial banks in Pennsylvania that applied to merge
between 1967 and 1971, she found that five different service prices
changed at acquired banks following their mergers. Passbook savings
rates, time deposit rates, monthly service charges on special checking
accounts, and mortgage loan rates all increased, while charges per
check drawn on regular demand accounts declined. However, at banks
whose merger applications were turned down, only two of these price
changes occurred—mortgage loan rates and time deposit rates rose in
these instances. At the same time the service menu of acquired banks
expanded at a faster rate than among merger-denied institutions. Glassman concluded that the *approved* mergers benefited the public more
than the denied mergers. These results are certainly promising but
require corroboration because of the limited number of banks involved
and the lack of a multivariate model.

Bank mergers may also contribute to the public interest by
reducing the likelihood of failure. Larger banks created via the merger
route tend to be more geographically and service diversified and, therefore, more resistant to adverse changes in economic conditions. This

is the reason often given for the remarkable record of stability among Canada's chartered banks. Not a single Canadian bank closed its doors during the Great Depression of the 1930s. Moreover, until the recent problems of two Canadian banks, one has to go back to 1923 to the Home Bank to find a failure event among Canada's chartered banks. As Jones and Laudadio (1973) observe, a long series of mergers stretching from the mid-nineteenth century to the present had so consolidated the Canadian banking structure that by 1970 only nine domestically chartered full-service banks were in operation—a figure that climbed to just thirteen in the early 1980s. Note, however, that the 1980 revisions in the Canadian Bank Act permitted the issuance of operating licenses to foreign banks. By 1985 almost 60 foreign banks had applied for or secured Canadian operating licenses.

Evaluation of Bank Merger Studies

Overall, it must be said that much serious research work remains to be done in the bank merger field. In fact, it is one of the most neglected areas in the field of bank structure and competition. The majority of studies were completed during the 1960s and early 1970s in the wake of federal merger legislation. Yet, major changes obviously have occurred since that time. Thousands of small (predominantly unit) banks and a fair share of the larger institutions have been absorbed in recent years, accelerating dramatically the growth of branch banking in the American system. In view of the magnitude of the bank merger movement and its profound impact on the spread of branch banking, it is surprising that so few detailed studies have been done.

      The weaknesses present in existing studies are obvious. The acquisition of one bank by another is a *long-term* investment that may not reap substantial positive cash flows for several years; yet, the majority of studies examine a relatively short period following consummation of a bank merger transaction (normally no more than three years). This brief period of postmerger analysis would appear to bias the results toward finding little or no change in performance among the acquiring institutions.

Moreover, some potentially significant effects of a merger, at least on firms whose stock is actively traded, may appear long before the actual consummation of the transaction. For example, in studies of nonbank firms, public announcements of a pending merger, which often occur months before the combination is formalized, have a significant (usually positive) impact on the stock prices of the firms involved (especially for acquired companies). For example, Mandelker (1974) found above-normal stockholder returns averaging about 14 percent for a period of up to seven months before the merger of sampled nonfinancial companies, whereas Elgers and Clark (1980) detected abnormal returns approaching 43 percent for acquired nonbank companies covering a two-year span before legal amalgamation. Similar evidence has been offered for British firms by Franks, Broyles, and Hecht (1977), who found above-normal returns averaging about 26 percent for the businesses acquired over a 4-month time span before the actual acquisition. This research evidence is consistent with an *efficient markets* view of merger transactions.

As we have seen, the majority of merger studies were carried out during the 1960s and early 1970s and, thus, may have little relevance to the environment within which bank mergers occur today. There is heavy emphasis on financial ratio analysis in these studies, grounded in book values from the balance sheet, but little attention is normally paid to the effects of mergers on *market values*—the stock prices of acquired and acquiring banks. And beyond the issue of a merger's impact on the individual bank and its shareholders is the critical question of benefits to the public. Does the public gain from such transactions because smaller, less efficient institutions, many of which face serious management succession problems or may fail, are absorbed by healthier competitors? In other words, is there a net *increase* in competition, rather than a net decrease, that flows from the typical bank merger? On this and the other issues raised in the foregoing pages we find ourselves still wrapped in comparative ignorance.

Policy Implications

Unquestionably, the merger movement has reshaped American banking in the post-World War II period. The result has been significant increases in the concentration of banking resources in many local and statewide markets, particularly in areas where branch banking is permitted. Mergers have contributed substantially to the dramatic, decades-long growth in bank branch offices across the nation—growth that, as we saw in the opening chapter, has resulted in a quadrupling of the number of branch offices since 1960.

Not at all clear, however, is the extent to which the public and the industry have benefited from such a massive merger movement in U.S. banking. The merger regulation process in banking has become excessively costly and time consuming, denials of applications often going well beyond the boundaries of the federal antitrust laws. And in some cases the reverse is true—anticompetitive mergers are sanctioned by the regulators, which, in turn, subsequently insulates most of these combinations from antitrust prosecution. Moreover, an increasing number of depository institution mergers have been approved in recent years to ward off failure, even though an improved deposit insurance system probably could have handled these situations without significant damage to the competitive environment.

There is, however, little evidence that regulation of bank mergers will melt away to play an insignificant role in the industry, even as banking services and various geographic restrictions are deregulated. While competitive standards may be relaxed, there is evidence that the regulators' financial constraints on banking combinations will be as tight (or even tighter) than ever. As Connor (1985) contends, the competitive power of banking institutions in the financial services industry of the future is likely to rest on the amount and continuing availability of "leverageable capital." Many of the largest banking corporations are so thinly capitalized, at least in the view of the regulatory community, if not private investors, that they lack the ability to issue equity or equity-related securities so essential for participating in future industry consolidation at reasonable cost. In short, Connor argues, capital availability will determine the future limits of bank growth, and capital is not only regulated but is also receiving increasing attention in the merger approval process. Unless there is a significant change in regulatory philosophy, inadequate primary capitalization will severely limit future merger activity by leading East and West Coast banks (though it may also be argued that the largest money center banks have more options in raising primary capital and in off-balance-sheet customer accommodation that does not mandate higher capital requirements). The door is open for smaller regional banking organizations, who are better capitalized in regulators' eyes, to capture a larger share of key wholesale and retail markets across the nation and, indeed, they have been doing so.

The foregoing argument that further large-scale consolidation of U.S. banking via mergers and acquisitions will be hampered, if not sidetracked, by financial constraints was further developed recently by Korobow and Budzeika (1985). They argue that a *modest* expansion (of perhaps 5 percent) by any one of the nation's top ten banking organizations may not involve severe financial constraints. However, a more aggressive expansion program by the nation's few largest banking organizations would be unlikely, because of such constraints as: (1) dilution of the stockholders' interests; (2) sharp declines in interest and/or dividend coverage; (3) increases in capital-raising costs due to modest expectations for future bank growth; (4) downward pressure on share prices; (5) significant increases in the required rate of return to investor per-share and retained earnings; and (6) regulatory insistence on minimum capital-to-asset ratios. In the judgement of Korobow and Budzeika current financial constraints on interstate acquisitions clearly favor large, well-managed regional banking firms over the nation's largest banking institutions.

Moreover, there is today the intensely debated but still unresolved question of the proper role of nonbank savings institutions—especially mutual savings banks and savings and loan associations—in analyzing the public interest aspects of bank mergers. Federal and state courts continue to minimize the possible influence of nonbank thrifts in assessing the consequences of a bank merger for local market competition. Yet, with passage of the Depository Institutions Deregulation and Monetary Control Act of 1980 and the Garn-St Germain Depository Institutions Act of 1982 and parallel state legislation (such as Massachusetts' 1982 Banking Reform Act) many nonbank thrifts are or will soon become direct competitors with commercial banks for a full line of credit and deposit services. Moreover, as a recent study by Murphy and Rogers (1984) suggests, there appear to be few demographic differences (in age, education, or income) between customers served by banks and nonbank thrifts. A method must be found that satisfactorily brings these nonbank institutions into the focus of research and public policy analysis of bank merger transactions. Indeed, the FDIC proposed in October 1985 to include thrifts and other financial service companies in determining local bank market shares, as well as to consider potential competition from larger banking organizations poised to enter a new market, and this makes merger approvals more likely for small and medium-size banking organizations. However, this step mandates that we know far more than we do now concerning the impact of financial mergers on the public and on the institutions involved. In the field of bank mergers we have been and still remain perilously close to either blissful ignorance or, if you prefer, a distressing level of uncertainty.

References

Alhadeff, David A. 1954. *Monopoly and Competition in Banking.* Berkeley: University of California Press.

Alhadeff, Charlotte P. and David A. Alhadeff. 1955. "Recent Bank Mergers." *Quarterly Journal of Economics,* 69:503–32.

Bacon, Peter W. 1967. *A Study of Bank Mergers in Marion County, Indiana, 1945– 1966* (October). Staff Memorandum. Research Department, Federal Reserve Bank of Chicago.

CaCace, L. Michael. 1984. "Top 300 Banks Increase Acquisitions in 1st Half." *American Banker* (August), 24:1, 47.

Carey, Roberta Grower. 1975. "Evaluation Under the Bank Merger Act of 1960 of the Competitive Factors Involved in Bank Mergers." *Journal of Monetary Economics,* 1:275–308.

Cohen, Kalman J. and Samuel Richardson Reid. 1967. "Effects of Regulation, Branching and Mergers on Banking Structure and Performance." *Southern Economic Journal* (October), pp. 231–49.

Connor, Michael C. 1985. "The Redirection of Power in American Banking." *Mergers and Acquisitions* (Winter), pp. 48-53.

Darnell, Jerome C. 1973. "Bank Mergers: Prices Paid to Marriage Partners." *Business Review* (July), pp. 16–25. Federal Reserve Bank of Philadelphia.

Di Clemente, John J. and Diana Fortier Alemprese. 1983. "Justice's Merger Guidelines: Implications for 7th District Banking." *Economic Perspectives* (September-October), pp. 14–23. Federal Reserve Bank of Chicago.

Dunham, Constance. 1982. "Thrift Institutions and Commercial Bank Mergers." *New England Economic Review* (November-December), pp. 45–62. Federal Reserve Bank of Boston.

Edwards, Franklin R. 1964. "Bank Competition and Business Loan Rates." *New England Business Review* (March), pp. 2–5. Federal Reserve Bank of Boston.

Eisenbeis, Robert A. 1975. "Differences in Federal Regulatory Agencies' Bank Merger Policies." *Journal of Money, Credit, and Banking* (February), 7:93–104.

Elgers, Pieter T. and John J. Clark. 1980. "Merger Types and Shareholder Returns: Additional Evidence." *Financial Management* (Summer), 9:66–72.

Franks, J. R., J. E. Broyles, and M. J. Hecht. 1977. "An Industry Study of the Profitability of Mergers in the United Kingdom." *Journal of Finance* (December), 32:1513–25.

Gagnon, Joseph E. 1982. "The New Merger Guidelines: Implications for New England Banking Markets." *New England Economic Review* (July-August), pp. 18–26. Federal Reserve Bank of Boston.

Gilbert, Gary G. 1975. "An Analysis of Federal Regulatory Decisions on Market Extension Bank Mergers." *Journal of Money, Credit and Banking*, 7(February):81–92.

Glassman, Cynthia A. 1975. "Pennsylvania Bank Merger Study: Summary of Results." Philadelphia Fed Research Papers (September). Federal Reserve Bank of Philadelphia.

Guerin-Calvert, Margaret E. 1983. "The 1982 Department of Justice Merger Guidelines: Applications to Banking Mergers," *Issues in Bank Regulation*, (Winter), pp. 18–25.

Herman, Edward S. 1964. "The Philadelphia Bank Merger Decision and Its Critics." *National Banking Review* (March), 1(3):391–406.

Jones, J. C. H. and L. Laudadio. 1973. "Canadian Bank Mergers, the Public Interest and Public Policy." *Banca Nazionale del Lavoro*, pp. 109–40.

Kalish, Lionel. 1975. "A Framework for Evaluating Potential Competition as a Factor in Bank Mergers and Acquisitions." *Journal of Money, Credit and Banking*, 7(November):527–30.

Kaufman, George G. 1969. "Customers View a Bank Merger—Before and After Surveys." *Business Conditions* (July), pp. 5–8. Federal Reserve Bank of Chicago.

Kohn, Ernest. 1964. *Branch Banking, Bank Mergers and the Public Interest* (January). New York State Banking Department.

Korobow, Leon and George Budzeika. 1985, "Financial Limits on Interstate Expansion," *Quarterly Review*, Federal Reserve Bank of New York, Summer, pp. 13–27.

Lawrence, Robert J. 1967. *The Performance of Bank Holding Companies*. Washington, D.C.: Federal Reserve Board.

Mandelker, Gershan. 1974. "Risk and Return: The Case of Merging Firms." *Journal of Financial Economics* (December), 2:303–35.

Moyer, R. Charles. 1976. "Growth, Consolidation and Mergers in Banking: Comment." *Journal of Finance* (September), 31(4):1231–32.

Murphy, Neil B. and Ronald C. Rogers. 1984. "The Line of Commerce in Retail Financial Institution Mergers: Some Evidence from Consumer Data in New England." *Journal of Bank Research* (Spring), pp. 21–25.

Phillis, Dave and Christine Pavel. 1986. "Interstate Mergers and Game Plans: Implications for the Midwest." *Economic Perspectives*, Federal Reserve Bank of Chicago (March), pp. 23–35.

Piper, Thomas R. 1971. *The Economics of Bank Acquisitions by Registered Bank Holding Companies* (March), Research Report No. 48. Federal Reserve Bank of Boston.

Reid, Samuel R. 1968. *Mergers, Managers and the Economy*. New York: McGraw-Hill.

Rhoades, Stephen A. 1979. "Aggregate Concentration: An Emerging Issue in Bank Merger Policy." *The Antitrust Bulletin* (Spring), pp. 1–16.

—— 1980. "The Impact of Bank Mergers and Laws on Statewide Banking Structure." *The Antitrust Bulletin* (Summer), pp. 377–90.

—— 1982. "Bank Expansion and Merger Activity by State, 1960–1975." *Journal of Bank Research* (Winter), 12:254–56.

Rhoades, Stephen A. and A. J. Yeats, 1974. "Growth, Consolidation and Mergers in Banking." *Journal of Finance* 29(December): 1397–1405.

Rose, John T. 1976. "Growth, Consolidation and Mergers in Banking: Comment." *The Journal of Finance* (September), 31(4):1233–37.

Rose, Peter S. 1984. "Merger Mania, Banking Style." *The Canadian Banker* (October), 90(5):38–44.

Smith, David L. 1969. *Characteristics of Merging Banks.* Staff Economic Study No. 49 (April). Board of Governors of the Federal Reserve System.

—— 1970. "Motives for Mergers." *The Magazine of Bank Administration* (January), pp. 36–38 and 60.

—— 1971. "The Performance of Merging Banks." *The Journal of Business* (April), pp. 184–92.

Snider, Thomas E. 1973. "The Effect of Merger on the Lending Behavior of Rural Banks in Virginia." *Journal of Bank Research* (Spring), pp. 52–57.

Talley, Samuel H. 1974. *The Impact of Holding-Company Acquisitions on Aggregate Concentration in Banking.* Staff Economic Study No. 80. Board of Governors of the Federal Reserve System.

Velk, Thomas. 1976. "An Estimate of the Federal Reserve Board of Governors' Policy Rule in Merger and Holding Company Cases, 1966–1970." *The Antitrust Bulletin,* pp. 537–58.

Weiss, Steven J. 1980. "Competitive Standards Applied to Foreign and Domestic Acquisitions of U.S. Banks." *The Antitrust Bulletin* (Winter), pp. 701–27.

Welker, Donald L. 1986. "Thrift Competition: Does It Matter?" *Economic Review,* Federal Reserve Bank of Richmond, 72(1):2–10.

Weston, J. Fred and Kwang S. Chung. 1983. "Do Mergers Make Money?" *Mergers and Acquisitions* (Fall), pp. 40–48.

6.

Concentration in the Banking Industry: Theory and Practice

THE CONCEPT of *concentration* focuses on the control of assets, deposits, accounts, sales, or some other measure of business activity by the leading firms in the marketplace. Whether a market is "highly concentrated" or "relatively unconcentrated" depends crucially on how many firms serve that market and how large they are relative to the market's total size. In banking, for example, if the top two or three banks control a majority of local deposits, such a market would normally be considered "concentrated" owing to the uneven distribution of its deposits. In general, the smaller the number of banking organizations or the more unevenly distributed deposits are, the greater the degree of concentration in the financial services marketplace.

Why is the concept of *concentration* important? The basic reason is that concentration is believed to influence the *conduct* of firms serving a given market. Where concentration is high, competitive behavior or rivalry among firms to attract and hold customer accounts may be low. High levels of concentration facilitate collusion among market-leading firms. And, with collusion, instead of competitive rivalry, the prices charged customers for goods or services may be excessively high (above their marginal cost of production) because firms will act jointly, rather than independently, in setting prices. The result can be an inefficient allocation of resources, higher than normal profits, and resistance to using more efficient technology or to offering new and better quality services. As the U.S. Department of Justice (1982) observed:

Other things being equal, concentration affects the likelihood that one firm, or a small group of firms, could successfully exercise market power. The smaller the percentage of total supply that a firm controls, the more generally it must restrict its own output in order to produce a given price increase, and the less likely it is that an output restriction will be profitable.

Thus, greater concentration either makes collusion easier or allows a dominant firm to become a price leader. Moreover, output restrictions usually appear in proportion to the degree of market concentration present.

In summary, the degree of concentration in a given market is believed to influence the *conduct* of firms in serving that market. And the conduct of firms in offering products and services affects the prices charged and the quantity and quality of goods or services available to the public, as well as individual firm size and profitability. In banking there is a longstanding concern on the part of lawmakers, the general public, and the regulatory authorities that the combined effects of regulation and traditional cooperative practices in the industry (such as correspondent relationships) have dampened beneficial competitive rivalry. Indeed, across the United States as a whole the top three banks in each of the nation's urban centers (SMSAs) appear to control about 70 percent of local deposits, on average, and that measure of market concentration averages even higher in many rural areas. Thus, in return for greater safety and reduced risk of bank failures, the public may be receiving higher cost and lower quality financial services than might otherwise be the case with greater ease of market entry and exit and increased competition.

Before investigating various measures of concentration and the proposed linkages between concentration in the banking marketplace and the performance of individual banks, I must note a challenge to this traditional line of reasoning proposed by Demsetz (1973, 1974) and others. The *Demsetz challenge* contends that the relationship and direction of causation implied in the traditional model of concentration for profits and prices is inappropriate. There is, allegedly, too much going on in real-world markets that conventional concentration theory does *not* explain. For example, how is it that many collusive market practices persist despite the fact that individual firms have significant incentives to increase their market shares and profits by entering new product lines, granting substantial price concessions to key customers, and using nonprice competition to skirt around collusive price agreements? There must be a powerful underlying force that allows concentration, collusion, and excess profits to survive in many markets over relatively long periods of time. To Demsetz, that underlying force is *efficiency*. Firms achieving greater efficiency are able to post lower prices and push out inefficient competitors, leading eventually to greater concentration in the markets they serve. Thus, market concentration is more an endogenous *result* of firm conduct rather than an exogenous cause.

To Demsetz, concentration arises from the competitive process itself—a few leading firms eventually rise to the top because of their superior efficiency in production and cost advantage that cannot easily be swept away. We note that both the traditional model and the Demsetz challenge suggest a *positive* correlation between market concentration and individual firm profitability. Indeed, as Clarke, Davies, and Waterson (1984) argue, it may well be true that *both* efficiency and the concentrated market power of certain firms contribute significantly to observed price and profitability differences across industries and markets. However, the public policy implications of the Demsetz challenge and of the traditional market concentration model are quite different. Traditional theory argues for a proactive policy to reduce concentration through prohibition of mergers among leading firms, so that output restrictions will be blunted and prices will fall. The Demsetz challenge, would, however, view such a policy as potentially damaging to the public's welfare because it would prevent the rise of more efficient firms and lower the efficiency level of market leaders. Thus, in the absence of further in-depth research on banking markets that explores the comparative explanatory power of the Demsetz model vis-à-vis the traditional concentration performance model, we must be especially cautious in assessing the policy implications of bank concentration studies.

Alternative Measures of Market Concentration

Measuring the degree of concentration in a given banking market is a complex task. Banks are multiproduct firms, usually serving more than one market and set of customers. One of the markets in which they offer financial services (such as consumer loans) may be highly concentrated, while another market served (such as loans to large corporations) may have low concentration with intense competitive rivalry. As we saw in chapter 2, for many years now, bank regulatory authorities have focused their principal attention on the degree of concentration in the *local market*—county or metropolitan area. This is potentially the "most damaged market" if concentration is high because the local market usually contains smaller businesses and consumers who have few alternative sources of supply for critical financial services. Large corporations and governments, in contrast, seek financial services in markets that are national or international in scope with numerous supply alternatives.

STATIC VERSUS DYNAMIC MEASURES OF MARKET CONCENTRATION

We can measure the degree of concentration of banking resources in the local market in several different ways. One of the most useful distinctions is between *static* and *dynamic* measures. Static measures examine concentration at a single point in time—e.g., how concentrated is a given banking market today? In contrast, dynamic measures focus on *changes* in concentration across time—e.g., is there a trend in the local banking market toward greater or lesser concentration?

STATIC CONCENTRATION MEASURES

The traditional measures of static market concentration are: (1) the number of firms (n) serving the market as of a given date; and (2) the percentage of deposits or financial service accounts controlled by the one, two, . . . , k largest banking organizations represented in the relevant market area. This last measure is known as the

n-firm *concentration ratio.* If there are k largest banks in a given market served by a total of n banks, then the percentage of deposits controlled by the k largest banking organizations is given by

(6.1)
$$_kC_n = \frac{\sum\limits_{i=1}^{k} D_i}{\sum\limits_{i=1}^{n} D_i} \times 100.$$

Presumably, the higher the value of $_kC_n$ or the smaller the total number of financial service firms (n) in the relevant market, the more concentrated it tends to be and the greater the likelihood of damage to customers in the form of excessive prices, lesser quantity and quality of service, and lower levels of efficiency. In banking research the percentages of total market area assets or deposits held by the one, two, three, or five largest banking organizations are the concentration ratios most often used.

These traditional measures of market concentration have a number of obvious shortcomings. For example, merely counting the number of commercial banks in the market overlooks the size distribution of alternative financial-service suppliers. Moreover, as more and more nonbank financial firms come to resemble commercial banks in the services they offer, counting only the number of banks in the market may give a false picture of the true level and intensity of competition. On the other hand, the simple concentration ratio is an arbitrary measure because its value depends on how many of the largest (k) financial firms are selected and the ratio leaves out the residual (smaller) firms that may indeed have a potent impact on the level and intensity of financial service competition.

Several (but not all) of these shortcomings are corrected by focusing on alternative measures of market concentration, such as the Herfindahl-Hirschmann index (HHI) now used by the U.S. Department of Justice to evaluate merger proposals. The HHI is the sum of the *squared* market shares (in percentage terms) of *all* banks or other firms offering services in the relevant market area. That is,

(6.2)
$$HHI = \sum_{i=1}^{n} \left[\frac{D_i}{\sum\limits_{i=1}^{n} D_i} \right] \times 100$$

where, as before, D_i represents the total customer accounts of each bank and financial service firm represented in the relevant financial service marketplace. *HHI* increases with greater variations in bank sizes and with decreases in the number of financial-service competitors. The Herfindahl index gives greater weight to the largest firms and is particularly sensitive to variations in the market shares of larger firms.

The Herfindahl-Hirschmann index was heavily promoted by Stigler (1965) as an appropriate structural index for oligopolistic markets, which, by definition, are served by only a few suppliers. Stigler argued that competition in an oligopolistic market rested on the capacity of each firm therein to attract both new customers entering the market and existing customers away from competitors. He believed that competitive behavior is more probable where there are strong inducements to deviate from established prices and where the enforcement of conformity to established prices is weakened. Such circumstances are more likely to prevail, the larger the number of competitors and the more nearly equal they are in market share—two dimensions reflected in the Herfindahl-Hirschmann index.

An index of market concentration that is conceptually superior to both the concentration ratio and the Herfindahl-Hirschmann index is *entropy*, which measures the probability that a customer choosing banks at random would choose any particular bank. Entropy (*Ent.*) is calculated from the following formula:

$$(6.3) \quad Ent = \sum_{i=1}^{n} \left[\frac{D_i}{\sum\limits_{i=1}^{n} D_i} \right] \times 100 \times \log_2 \left[\frac{1}{D_i \div \sum\limits_{i=1}^{n} D_i} \right] \times 100$$

Thus, entropy is the product of the share of the market represented by each firm multiplied by the logarithm of the reciprocal of that market share. The more banks serving the market, the larger is entropy. Similarly, entropy increases when competing banks approach equality in the size of their operations. A related measure that adjusts for the number of banks in the market is Theil's entropy, discussed by Tschoegel (1982).

A more easily interpretable measure of market concentration based on entropy is the *numbers equivalent* (NE). NE is an index of the number of firms of the same size, as dictated by the value of entropy, that serve a given market. In symbols,

$$Ent = \log_2 NE$$

The larger the value of NE, the more competitive any given market is presumed to be. As NE increases, the customer can secure needed financial services from more potential sources of supply. Competition may also be reflected in the so-called *Lerner index*, which, in banking, is the spread between loan rates and the cost of bank fund-raising.

   An index of market structure not widely used but possessing interesting properties is the Hall-Tideman index (HTIX). This measure counts *all* firms in the market but, like the Herfindahl-Hirschmann index, gives added weight to larger competitors by *ranking* firms by their respective market shares. In mathematical notation the Hall-Tideman index would be

(6.4)
$$HTIX = \left[\frac{1}{2 - \sum_{i=1}^{n} i \times \left(\frac{D_i}{\sum_{i=1}^{n} D_i} \right)} \right] - 1$$

where i represents each of n firms in the relevant market and $D_i \div \Sigma D_i$ captures each firm's market share. In terms of limits, $HTIX$ will assume the value of one in the case of a single (monopoly) bank serving the relevant market and the value of zero in any market where all suppliers hold equal market shares. A related structural measure is the dominance index developed by Kwoka (1977). This is

(6.5)
$$D^2 = \sum_{i=1}^{n} \left[\frac{D_i}{\Sigma D_i} - \frac{D_{i+1}}{\Sigma D_{i+1}} \right]^2$$

where the differential market share between successively chosen firms in the market is ranked by firm size. The dominance index ranges between 0 and 1 with a value of unity denoting a monopoly situation as in the case of the Hall-Tideman index.

DYNAMIC CONCENTRATION MEASURES

   The structure of markets is not static but fluctuates with the entry and exit of suppliers and changes in market shares. Firms that are more successful at meeting customer needs will tend to expand their market shares, while less successful companies will lose ground in the race for shares of the available customer pool. In banking, *both* changes in the number of commercial banks serving the relevant market area and trends in market share are important to the bank regulatory authorities because entry, exit, and relative market shares are all shaped by legislative and regulatory decisions.

The dynamics of bank market structure can be measured in several different ways. Traditionally, economists have looked at *changes* in concentration ratios occurring between two points in time. Thus, we might be interested in the trend in the share of deposits held by the top three banks in the Baltimore, Maryland, banking market over the past decade. Similarly, we could calculate first differences (changes) in any of the other static measures of market structure discussed earlier between a given initial year (t) and any future year ($t + j$). Thus, an approximate measure of the dynamics of bank market structure would be:

$$k\Delta C_n = kC_{n,t+j} - kC_{nt}$$

Where the observed changes are *negative*, concentration in the local banking market would, of course, have *declined* between the beginning and ending years under examination.

Technically superior measures of dynamic market structure include a measure recommended by Prais (1958) called the *share stability index* (SSI) and an indicator developed by Grossack (1965) and Salley (1972) called the *dynamic concentration index*. SSI relates the market share held by a bank in a given base year with its share of the market at the end of the period under study. Prais points out that if individual firms are ranked by their beginning period sizes, and larger firms have grown faster than smaller firms over the study period, this indicates that market concentration has increased. However, if the market's larger firms grow more slowly than average, the interpretation of the trend in concentration is ambiguous—concentration may have either fallen or risen. By similar logic, if firms in the market are ranked by their end-period sizes, and the largest firms have grown more slowly than the rest, market concentration has decreased. However, with this measuring scheme a faster growth rate among the largest firms does not reliably tell us which way market concentration has gone.

A related measure of structural change is the dynamic concentration index, which is obtained through a linear regression of end-of-period market shares for all firms in a given market upon their market shares at the beginning of the study period. New firms entering the market and firms that fail or are voluntarily liquidated are assigned a zero market share for those periods in which they are not operating. When firms merge, only the market share of the largest of the merger partners is included in beginning period market shares, whereas the market shares of all firms involved in the merger are combined at the end of the study period. In essence, the dynamic concentration index assumes a constant population of firms throughtout the period under study. Tschoegel (1982) develops a similar dynamic structural index that considers the first-order serial correlation in bank growth rates in a given market.

A related market share stability index put forward by Hymer and Pashigian (1962) is:

$$(6.7) \qquad MSSI = \sum_{i=1}^{n} \left[\frac{D_{it}}{\sum_i^n D_{it}} - \frac{D_{i,t-j}}{\sum_i^n D_{i,t-j}} \right]$$

Designed to measure stability in market shares, especially among the largest firms, the share stability index is an indirect, proxy measure of interfirm competitive rivalry. $MSSI$ increases with greater changes in market share over the period from point $t - j$ to t. Absolute values are used because both positive and negative fluctuations in market shares indicate lack of stability in existing relationships among firms. The implication is that the more entry and exit activity that occurs and the more extensive the shifts in the market shares of competing firms, the more intense competitive rivalry must be.

Extent of Concentration in Banking Today

Is concentration increasing or decreasing in American banking and in international banking markets today? The answer to that question depends heavily on the definition of the relevent market—the geographic area over which individual banks are presumed to compete—

and on the measure of market concentration used. We must also keep in mind, as Baltesperger (1972) observes, that banks are *multiproduct* firms and each of their products may be sold in different markets. Each market will have its own degree of concentration and its own production cost function, reflecting different economies of scale in the production of each banking service. As Baltesperger states: "in the long run those services with relatively large scale economies become much more concentrated in the hands of a few large banks than those having only insignificant (scale) economies" (p. 475). Moreover, concentration in the provision of banking services appears to vary with the level of risk. High-risk services (such as currency trading) tend to be concentrated among the largest banks, while smaller banks tend to concentrate on low-risk services (such as savings deposits and automobile loans).

INTERNATIONAL BANKING CONCENTRATION

Few studies have attempted to determine the level of concentration or trends in concentration for banking worldwide. And in fact, three studies by Tschoegel (1982), Aliber (1975), and Rhoades (1983) distinctly *conflict* in their findings. The Aliber study calculated concentration ratios—the percentage of the combined deposits held by the world's 100 largest commercial banks accounted for by the 10 largest banks or the 20 largest banks, etc.—and concluded that market concentration among leading international banks remained essentially *unchanged* between 1965 and 1974. Rhoades' (1983) inquiry into banking concentration within and among the world's 100 largest banks over the 1956 to 1980 period, on the other hand, finds a steady *increase* in deposit concentration, though the world market share of U.S. banks has declined. In contrast, by applying more statistically elaborate static and dynamic measures of international market concentration, Tschoegel (1982) concluded that concentration in international banking *decreased* between 1969 and 1979.

Tschoegel defines the international banking market as the area served by the 100 largest international banks (measured by their total assets), including those institutions with at least one office outside the home country plus the top 20 lead managers of medium-term syndicated Eurodollar loans in 1977 and 1979. Three static indices (the Herfindahl-Hirschmann index, entropy, and Kwoka's dominance index) and three dynamic indices (the share stability index and comparative indicators of small-bank versus large-bank growth) are used to measure international market structure. Tschoegel concludes that international banking is "unconcentrated and undominated." Static concentration measures (most notably, the Herfindahl-Hirschmann index and entropy) generally declined between 1969 and 1973 and then tended to stabilize in more recent years.

Tschoegel argues that currency revaluations over the decade of 1970s damaged the market-dominating position of U.S., British, and Italian banks, while aiding more aggressive German, Japanese, and Swiss institutions. New entry into the international banking market (especially the growth of London offices) also substantially altered the market's structure in Tschoegel's view. The same conclusions regarding declining concentration and decreasing dominance by market leaders were recorded when the market shares of the 20 leading Euroloan syndicators were analyzed. Tschoegel believes these trends will continue, owing to increasing international diversification and the rise of many relatively new entrants into the international banking field from Asia, Europe, Japan, Latin America, and the Middle East.

An even more comprehensive review of international banking concentration and competition was prepared by Crane and Hayes (1983), covering more than two decades of international banking trends. These two researchers find that, in the decade of the 1960s, the international banking market was segmented geographically, and this limited competition and any possible reduction in banking concentration. However, in the 1970s and 1980s most geographic barriers were eroded by competition, but revisions in domestic banking regulations did not keep pace. In effect, country-specific regulations over the period limited competition, making governments the principal source of monopoly rents in international banking. Nevertheless, international banking competition, as measured by the number of agencies, branches, and representative offices in foreign countries and by changes in rankings among the world's largest banking organizations, appear to have increased significantly, owing particularly to relative gains made by French, German, and Japanese banks. Indicators of this apparent increase in international banking competition are declining loan rate spreads over the London Interbank Offer Rate (LIBOR) attached to Eurodollar deposits and the partial withdrawal of U.S. multinational banks from European financial centers in the early 1980s.

A handful of studies have appeared in recent years examining the relationship between concentration and bank performance in individual foreign countries. One of the most interesting is a paper by Short (1979) that links the profit rates of 60 banks in Canada, Western Europe, and Japan to concentration in their national banking systems over a three-year period (1972-1974). Bank profitability is measured by ratio of after-tax profits to shareholders' equity. Because of the lack of system-wide profitability or capital scarcity measures, Short chooses the central bank discount rate and the yield on long-term government securities to represent these features of each national economy (though it must be noted that government obligations are traded in an international market). Individual bank profitability is then regressed against variables measuring bank leverage (assets to shareholder equity), bank size, and asset growth, whether or not each bank is privately or publicly owned, and concentration, measured alternately by the Herfindahl-Hirschmann index, its reciprocal, and the concentration ratio. Short finds that government ownership, market concentration, and capital scarcity dominate the regression equations. Concentration is the least important of these three significant variables, and its effect is quantitatively small—one equation indicates that nearly a 30-percent reduction in the three-bank concentration ratio is necessary to reduce the individual bank profit rate by about 1 percent. However, Short observes that "even very small reductions in banks' lending rates or increases in their borrowing rates may in aggregate result in a substantial redistribution of income to bank customers" (p. 214).

NATIONWIDE BANKING CONCENTRATION

While international banking concentration may be both statistically important and declining, what has happened to banking concentration inside the United States? At the national level the findings are mixed, though the consensus is that the concentration of U.S. banking resources in the top 10 and top 100 commercial banks has *declined*. For example, a study by Savage (1982) prepared for the Federal Reserve Board found that the percentage of domestic deposits held by the 100 largest U.S. banks fell from 47.3 percent at year-end 1969 to 45.4 percent at year-end 1980—a result paralleled by declining trends in the 10-bank concentration ratio and the aggregate Herfindahl-Hirschmann index. At the same time the percentage of nationwide industry assets controlled by all billion-dollar banks actually rose (from 46.2 percent to 62.8 percent), but the number of banks in this top asset size group more than tripled from 72 to 240 between 1969 and 1980. Meanwhile, the proportion of nationwide banking assets held by banks ranging in asset size from $100 million to $1 billion declined significantly.

Interestingly enough, this finding of a secular decline in national banking concentration is rejected by Rhoades (1982), who looks at a much longer time period, 1925–1978. He focuses on the percentage of nationwide deposits (both foreign and domestic) held by the 100 largest U.S. banks (though not entire banking organizations including holding-company subsidiaries). Rhoades finds that the 100-bank deposit percentage *increased* substantially from 33.7 percent in 1925 to 51.4 percent in 1978—the latter figure close to the peak 100-bank concentration level reached during the Great Depression of the 1930s. He also finds that the level of concentration in manufacturing often paralleled the level of concentration in banking over the period under study, though some of the time trends were different. Lorenz curves for selected years (1925, 1943, 1963, and 1978) indicate increasing concentration within the top 100 group. For example, the 10 largest U.S. commercial banks held 31 percent of the total deposits controlled by the 100 largest banking institutions in 1925 and 56 percent of this total in 1978. Rhoades finds that *merger activity* among the nation's 10 leading banks over the study period was an important factor in the apparent deepening concentration among the 100 largest banks, though this proved to be much less important a factor during the 1960s and 1970s. Mergers also brought a relatively stable flow of new bank entrants into the top 100 group over time.

In a follow-up study Rhoades (1985) observed two disparate trends in national banking concentration over the 1970–83 period. The percentage of domestic deposits held by the 50 largest commercial banking organizations fell by a full percentage point, but when foreign deposits of U.S. banks were added the 50-bank concentration ratio rose significantly. When concentration is measured by the shares of the 100 largest banking organizations the domestic–deposits ratio rises just slightly (by less than one percentage point), but the 100-bank concentration ratio including *both* foreign and domestic deposits rises more than four percentage points for the 1970–83 period, most of this change occurring during the 1970s.

Rhoades suggests that "equality of opportunity" for U.S. banks to enter the nation's top 100 and compete for major corporate loans probably has decreased. However, this conclusion tends to minimize several other factors that may have heightened interbank competition, such as the rapid growth of the commercial paper market as an alternative source of corporate credit and the growth in foreign bank activity within U.S. borders. The latter factor has become especially significant, with major banks from Australia, Canada, Great Britain, West Germany, and Japan capturing increasing segments of the U.S. corporate loan market. This new foreign competitive factor arises from the greater relative stability and profitability of the U.S. continental market, and the ability of many foreign banks to employ greater financial leverage and, therefore, carry lower profit margins on large loans than can domestic banking institutions.

BANKING CONCENTRATION AT THE STATE LEVEL

The mixed conclusions regarding trends in banking concentration at the national level are amplified at the state level. In the previously cited study prepared by Savage (1982) for the Federal Reserve Board, concentration ratios showing the percentage of commercial bank deposits held by the three and five largest banking organizations (including adjustments for foreign banks and holding-company acquisitions) in each state were calculated for 1960, 1970, and 1980. Overall, there was an *increase* in the proportion of statewide deposits controlled by the five largest banking firms, the average five-firm concentration rising nearly a full percentage point (0.9 percent on an unweighted average basis). In some states the increase was substantial—in Alabama, for example, the five-firm concentration ratio rose nearly 21 points between 1970 and 1980, while Texas and Maine registered gains of about 14 percentage points in their five-bank concentration ratios over the 1970–1980 period. There were some significant (though lesser) *decreases* in concentration in other states, led by Oregon at 14 percent and Louisiana at 8 percent for the 1970–1980 period. Overall, Savage found increasing deposit concentration in 24 states and decreasing concentration in 26 states during the 1970–1980 time period.

It is difficult to reach definitive conclusions regarding these statewide trends because state boundaries do not necessarily coincide with true banking markets. However, the state-level concentration ratios tell us something about the influence of state branching and holding-company laws on banking concentration. For example, in states permitting statewide branching, Savage found that deposit concentration measured by the five-bank ratio rose in 14 states and declined in 10 states over the 1960–1980 period, though increases and decreases in the three-bank concentration ratio were evenly distributed among the states. In contrast, decreases in deposit concentration outweighed increases in both limited branching and unit banking states, especially in the latter. In the 11 unit banking states, for example, concentration measured by the three-bank and five-bank concentration ratios decreased in seven states and rose in four. Unit banking states experiencing increases in concentration generally were those, such as Texas and Colorado, where holding companies have expanded rapidly in recent years.

A later study by Rhoades (1985b) observes that concentration tends to be highest in those states offering the greatest opportunity for geographic expansion by individual banks. Thus, 25 states permitting statewide branching reported an average five-firm deposit concentration ratio of 72 percent in 1983. In contrast, states limiting branching but allowing substantial holding company activity (i.e., where multibank holding companies control at least half of statewide deposits) had an average 1983 concentration ratio of 51 percent. Limited branching states and unit banking states with restricted holding company activity reported 5-bank concentration ratios in the range of 25 to 27 percent. Based on these figures Rhoades predicts that the future expansion of interstate branching will result in a significant *increase* in *national* banking concentration, though he finds no support for arguments that increased nationwide banking concentration would generate adverse economic effects. Moreover, Rhoades (1985c) asserts, the prices charged and services offered by banks in *local* markets will *not* be greatly affected by interstate banking. The application and enforcement of the antitrust laws should have a substantially greater effect on the performance of local banks than whether or not interstate competitors are allowed to enter local markets.

BANKING CONCENTRATION AT THE LOCAL LEVEL

Perhaps the most meaningful index of banking concentration is the structural character of *local* markets serving most households and small businesses. From the point of view, then, of those markets potentially most damaged by high concentration, what has been the trend in banking concentration? Most studies of local market concentration have focused on SMSAs—one or more counties representing a composite urban unit. The Federal Reserve Board study by Savage (1982) cited earlier divided SMSAs in 1970 and 1980 into state branching law categories: statewide branching, limited branching, and unit banking. According to this study five-firm SMSA concentration ratios *declined* in all three state branching law categories as shown in table 6.1.

While the trend suggested by these figures is clearly *downward*, it is also obvious that metropolitan banking concentration levels are higher in states where branching prevails, presumably because large banks are able to branch into rapidly expanding suburbs to protect their market shares. In contrast, larger banks in unit banking states or those where branching is geographically controlled often cannot follow their business and household customers moving to suburban or other outlying areas. The Federal Reserve Board study also analyzed SMSAs in six states where branching laws were liberalized during the 1970s. In these six states statewide concentration rose in four of the six, but concentration declined in all but three of the 45 SMSAs located entirely within those six states.

These findings are confirmed by Rhoades (1985b) who finds a general decrease in both metropolitan area (SMSA) concentration and concentration in larger rural markets between 1966 and 1981. This occurs whether local concentration is measured by the Herfindahl-

Table 6.1. Changes in Banking Concentration in Standard Metropolitan Areas (SMSAs) (Five-Bank Concentration Ratios)

	Percentage of SMSA Deposits in the Five Largest Banks in:	
State Branching Law Categories	1970	1980
1. SMSAs in statewide branching states	88.1%	82.1%
2. SMSAs in limited branching states	85.9	83.7
3. SMSAs in unit banking states	81.8	76.7

SOURCE: Donald T. Savage. 1982. "Developments in Banking Structure, 1970–81." *Federal Reserve Bulletin* (February), p. 85.

Hirschmann index or the three-bank concentration ratio and whether or not nonbank thrifts are included in the market structure measures. Interestingly enough, however, the character of branching and holding company laws in various states do *not* appear to have a significant impact on *local* banking concentration, suggesting that a trend toward further expansion of interstate banking will have little effect on local market concentration.

Thus, in general local metropolitan markets appeared to exhibit *declining* banking concentration. Interesting, too, is an apparent narrowing of the *differences* in the absolute size of metropolitan banking concentration ratios. Thus, in Savage's study (1982) the percentage difference in the average five-bank concentration ratio between SMSAs in statewide branching states and SMSAs in unit banking states was 6.3 percent in 1970 and only 5.4 percent in 1980. Though slight, such a narrowing of differences in metropolitan concentration is likely to continue with improvements in communication and transportation that bridge geographic boundaries and intertwine what were formerly isolated and independent local banking markets.

Research Evidence Bearing
on the Bank Concentration Effect

THE METHODOLOGY OF BANK CONCENTRATION STUDIES
Major changes in banking structure and federal regulation of banking since World War II have resulted in a veritable explosion of research on the linkages between banking market concentration, market conduct, and individual bank performance. The principal methodology of these studies has been to examine a relatively small sample of banking markets (usually approximated by county or SMSA boundaries), often from one state or region of the nation. In those markets, selected measures of bank performance—for example, profitability, availability of financial services, average loan rates charged, mean deposit rates paid, and risk-reducing behavior—have been correlated with measures of market structure—usually either the number of banks serving the local market or a concentration measure or, more likely, *both* structure indicators. Sometimes the mean characteristics of whole

markets are studied with one market area compared with another, while other studies focus principally on the performance of individual banks as that performance is shaped by market forces. In fact, the newer studies have focused more heavily on individual banks rather than on markets in an effort to explore a number of firm-specific issues (such as the impact of market share on individual firm profitability). Most studies use one year as the relevant time frame, but a few compare bank performance differences from one year to the next or across several years, representing different phases of the business cycle or different credit conditions.

There has been a general trend toward greater *variety* in the market structure measures examined in recent research studies. While many early concentration studies tended to focus only on concentration ratios and numbers of banks serving a given collection of markets, later studies ushered in more complex structure variables—such as the Herfindahl-Hirschmann index and entropy—and calculated both dynamic and static structure measures. Moreover, with the growing importance of nonbank institutions offering financial services competitive with banks, more recent studies have frequently tried to capture the impact of credit unions, savings and loans, savings banks, and other nonbank competitors on bank performance. This has been done, for example, by including a dichotomous variable reflecting whether or not such institutions were present in the market or by constructing the ratio of nonbank assets (deposits) to bank assets (deposits). In summary, banking concentration studies have been refined gradually in approach and in design with a general trend toward exploring a wider array of issues and using a wider range of specialized techniques.

PRICE EFFECTS OF BANKING CONCENTRATION

Bank concentration studies have generally focused on three groups of prices for financial services: (1) loan interest rates charged customers, (2) time and saving deposit rates offered, and (3) service charges on checking accounts. Rather than using actual prices posted by individual banks, *average* loan, deposit, and service charge rates measured across the bank's whole portfolio are typically used. Thus, the bank's *mean* loan rate may be formed by dividing its total interest and fees collected on loans during the year by the amount of total loans outstanding at one point (such as year end) or as of several call report dates averaged during the year. Similarly, an *average* time and saving deposit rate is often calculated by dividing total deposit interest paid by a bank by the dollar volume of its time and savings deposits as of a certain date. A service charge ratio, calculated in a similar manner, would compare total service fees collected from checking account customers to the aggregate amount of checkbook deposits outstanding. The obvious problem with these "price" measures is that loan and deposit account mix varies considerably from bank to bank, some banks catering primarily to business customers and others serving principally household clients. A handful of studies have used other data sources such as surveys or Functional Cost Analysis reports from the Federal Reserve banks, which provide cost accounting data.

Whatever method of price measurement is used, the results of bank concentration studies are remarkably consistent in finding a significant *positive* effect of concentration on bank prices. This is particularly true of studies that have looked at whole banking markets (usually a county or SMSA) rather than at individual banks. Examples include studies by Bell and Murphy (1969), Kaufman (1966), Rhoades and Rutz (1979), Rhoades (1981), Whitehead (1977), and Heggestad and Rhoades (1978). These studies used a variety of structural measures, including the three-bank concentration ratio, the number of banks, the Herfindahl-Hirschmann index, and the ratio of nonbank thrift deposits to total commercial bank deposits—all of which proved to be statistically significant in accounting for variations in one price measure or another.

A study by McCall and Peterson (1980) focusing on 155 SMSAs and counties in 14 unit banking and limited branching states is particularly interesting because it employs the numbers-equivalent measure of market structure, focuses on the Lerner index (i.e., the spread between average loan and deposit rates) as a key bank performance indicator, and tests for nonlinearity in the structure-performance relationship. Application of the switching regression technique finds evidence of a critical level of concentration (i.e., a discontinuity in the concentration-performance relationship) in business loan markets. This finding of a threshold level of market concentration above which the market power of leading firms exerts a significant effect on performance supports a similar finding by Rose (1976). The possible existence of threshold concentration levels is pregnant with implications for antitrust policy because it draws our most urgent attention to those banking markets at or near the threshold. More detailed research pointed directly at this threshold issue is needed.

Corroboration for a possible *nonlinear* concentration-bank prices relationship was recently provided by Heggestad and Mingo (1976). They found a curvilinear concentration effect across 69 U.S. metropolitan areas (SMSAs) and 332 banks. Increases in banking concentration appear to have a greater impact on prices charged in markets that are initially *less* concentrated. Thus, antitrust policy should not ignore relatively unconcentrated banking markets.

Another unique study by Rose and Fraser (1976) employs a broad range of static and dynamic measures of market concentration across a sample of 90 county and SMSA banking markets in Texas. Data drawn from the financial reports of 704 banks revealed that the more traditional measures of market structure—the number of banks serving the local market and one-, two-, and three-bank concentration ratios—were rarely statistically significant in accounting for variations in bank loan rates, time deposit rates, or checking account service charges. Dynamic concentration measures—the dynamic concentration index, dynamic Herfindahl index, and share stability index—also were not statistically significant by conventional criteria. Rather, both the Herfindahl-Hirschmann index and the Hall-Tideman index proved to be statistically significant in explaining variations in loan rates and deposit service charges at the 95-percent confidence level, while relative entropy and the Gini coefficient were statistically significant at the 90-percent confidence level. However, the market structure impact was quantitatively small—a 10-percentage point increase in market concentration measured by the Herfindahl index, for example, led to only a 0.10 percent increase in average bank loan rates. This modest concentration effect on bank prices was also reported by Phillips (1964), who found that average bank loan rates rose a scant 0.06 percent for each 10-percentage-point rise in bank market concentration.

When individual banks, instead of banking markets, are used as the unit of observation, the proportion of studies finding significant structural effects on bank prices falls, though a majority of the individual bank studies *do* find statistically significant structure-price links, as Rhoades (1982) has observed. One factor that may intrude in these individual bank studies is *market share*—a variable not often included in the regression models used. Support for a market share effect on bank prices is provided by a recent examination of 147 SMSA and 112 county-wide banking markets by Hanweck and Rhoades (1984) and by Rhoades (1985a) in an analysis of nearly 6,500 banks during the 1970s. The underlying hypothesis of their studies is that some banks may be so large relative to their competitors, possessing markedly superior resources and diversification, that they are able to intimidate smaller banks into adopting the larger institutions' pricing schemes. This predatory pricing thesis is generally supported by Hanweck and Rhoades' regression models, especially for loan interest rates, service charges on deposits, and noninterest operating expenses. Service charges and expenses tend to be higher and interfirm rivalry weaker where a market is dominated by one or a few banks, providing added support for the traditional view of concentration's effects on individual bank behavior.

What is particularly perplexing, however, is the quantitatively *small* impact apparent from structural changes in most banking markets studied. Loan and deposit interest rates are usually found to move by small fractions of a percentage point when market concentration goes through major changes (e.g., 10 to 20 percentage points). This is all the more surprising in light of the findings of sizable price variations across different market structures in the manufacturing and industrial sectors of the economy. Perhaps the service nature of banking, coupled with its extensive regulations, dampens the concentration-price relationship. If so, a greater price impact might be expected as deregulation spreads and affects individual bank management decisions and behavior more significantly.

PROFITABILITY EFFECTS OF CONCENTRATED MARKETS

Conventional economic theory also links concentration to individual firm profitability. Thus, most bank concentration studies have examined interconnections between bank market structure and key profitability ratios, particularly return on assets (i.e., net income after taxes divided by total assets or ROA). Other, less frequently used bank profitability measures include return on equity (i.e., net income after taxes divided by total equity capital or ROE) and operating returns (i.e., net operating income divided by total assets). Most studies (though certainly not all) do find a statistically significant, *positive* relationship between market concentration and individual bank profitability. The most consistent relationship appears to exist between the concentration ratio and ROA.

For example, Heggestad and Rhoades (1976), Rhoades and Rutz (1979), Savage and Rhoades (1979), Glassman and Rhoades (1980), Graddy (1980), Rhoades (1980), Rhoades and Rutz (1982), and Rhoades (1982) all find a significantly *positive* relationship between the three-bank concentration ratio (most commonly) or the one- or two-bank concentration ratio and bank profits. Occasionally the Herfindahl-Hirschmann index is significantly linked to bank profitability as well. Higher levels of concentration are associated with increased bank profitability, as theory would suggest, though the impact is usually of modest proportions.

However, there is no universal agreement on the alleged concentration-profitability connection. For example, an extensive exploration of returns on assets and equity among a structurally homogeneous sample of independent SMSA banks by Wall (1985) finds that neither market concentration nor bank size has a major impact on profits. For his sample banks, which ranged in asset size from $50 to $500 million, Wall finds bank profits to be dominated by asset and funds management strategies and by management's skill in controlling noninterest expenses, not by structure or regulation.

Equally negative results for banking concentration were reported by Smirlock (1985), who argues that the crucial linkage is between market share and profitability, which are positively related. Once the market share effect is controlled for in his regression model, concentration provides no additional explanatory power in accounting for variations in bank profits. Smirlock concludes that Demsetz' efficiency theory is a better explanation of the behavior of banks in the financial marketplace than the traditional structure-conduct-performance (SCP) model is.

Interestingly enough, however, a study of 259 metropolitan and county-wide banking markets by Hanweck and Rhoades (1984) contradicts Smirlock's results when applied to the share of *dominant* banks in each market. They find that the presence of dominating banks significantly affects service prices, but not profits. However, conventional concentration ratios affect *both* profits (measured by ROA) and loan and checking account prices, increased concentration dampening market rivalry.

Actually it may not just be the presence of dominating

firms that significantly affect the level of market performance; the existence of a significant number of "fringe firms"—smaller competitors nipping away at the market leaders—may make the difference in establishing a significant market concentration–profits relationship. At least this is the implication of a study by Rhoades (1985d) of 3777 commercial banks in 372 markets across the U.S. (1976–80). In these markets profits tended to be higher where there were relatively few *fringe banks* (defined to be those ranking 4, 5, and 6 in market share), suggesting that a competitively structured banking fringe stimulates local market competition unless those markets are already highly concentrated in the hands of a few dominant firms. This finding clashes with the conventional argument that mergers among fringe banks should be encouraged in order to create *new* market leaders to challenge the dominant banks.

Support therefore exists for both a price and a profitability impact related to the level of concentration in local banking markets. However, disagreement in this field continues as to the proper index of concentration. The unfolding efficiency theory of market concentration suggests the need for further research across different types of banking markets, organizations, and regions of the country.

OTHER PERFORMANCE MEASURES AND CONCENTRATION

Aside from price and profitability, there appear to be few other significant correlations between market concentration and other aspects of bank performance. Unfortunately, few alternative performance variables have been tested over the years even though market structure can be hypothesized quite rationally to be related to bank risk taking, capital adequacy, quality of services offered, and a number of other important performance dimensions. For example, a few studies during the 1970s and early 1980s investigated the "quiet life" hypothesis promulgated during the 1930s by Hicks (1935). Hicks suggested that "the best of all monopoly profits is a quiet life"; that is, businesses operating in concentrated markets may substitute risk-averse behavior for the pursuit of maximum profitability (p. 8).

A paper by Rhoades and Rutz (1982) draws upon a sample of 6,500 unit banks, operating over the 1969-78 period, to test the Hicksian "quiet life" hypothesis. Drawing upon a return-risk trade-off map developed by Heggestad (1977), Rhoades and Rutz argue that each bank possesses a desired marginal rate of substitution between risk and return and faces an investment opportunity set, expressing how much additional risk must be borne to gain additional return. Presumably, banks with greater market power can secure higher returns for the same level of risk or the same return but a reduced level of risk compared to banks operating in more competitive markets. The "quiet life" hypothesis suggests that a bank endowed with greater market power will display *greater risk aversion* (i.e., a risk-return preference function having a steeper slope) and, thus, will be able to achieve some combination of *both* greater return and lower risk than firms possessing lesser power in the market.

Rhoades and Rutz measure bank risk using the coefficient of variation in profit rates, the ratio of equity to total assets, the ratio of total loan to total assets, and the ratio of net loan losses to total loans. These risk measures are regressed against the three-bank concentration ratio for the SMSA or county in which each bank in the sample is located, along with variables designed to hold bank size, market size, growth, and deposit volatility constant. The regression results indicate a statistically significant concentration-risk relationship: *low bank risk is associated with high market concentration*. Moreover, as the level of market concentration increases, bank profitability (measured by net income to assets) rises while risk falls. Thus, banks with increased market power enjoy *both* excess profits and "quiet life" benefits. Corroborating conceptual and empirical evidence on the banking market concentration-risk relationship is provided by Edwards and Heggestad (1973, 1979), and Heggestad (1977), and Emery (1971).

A study by White (1976) opens up another interesting performance dimension by assessing the linkage between concentration and service quality. White represents quality of service by the number of branch offices in each of 40 SMSAs in statewide branching states on the presumption that more banking offices imply added convenience for customers. The expected *negative* relationship between concentration and number of branches is found to be both statistically significant and quantitatively important (e.g., a decrease of 0.10 percent in the Herfindahl-Hirschmann index is associated with a 14.4-percent average rise in the number of banking offices in each SMSA). White concludes that "more competitive market structures . . . appear to yield higher levels of consumer welfare" (1976, p. 104).

THE ROLE OF NONBANK FINANCIAL INSTITUTIONS

The growing importance of nonbank thrif institutions— particularly credit unions, savings banks, and savings and loan associations—offering financial services competitive with banks has resulted in more concentration studies' including variables reflecting the relative importance of nonbank financial institutions in local markets. However, surprisingly few of the concentration studies have found significant price effects from the market presence of nonbank thrifts. While inclusion of nonbank institutions usually *lowers* local market concentration ratios (as noted by Curry and J. T. Rose (1984) in a study of local mortgage markets), the fit of equations linking market concentration to financial service performance is generally either not affected or only slightly altered by including nonbank intermediaries. (An interesting exception is White's 1976 finding that the number of savings and loans and savings banks is positively associated with the number of branches that banks establish in SMSAs.) Perhaps this result reflects the fact that relatively few of the nonbank institutions have taken full advantage of recent deregulatory actions granting them new service powers—a topic I explore more thoroughly in chapter 10. However, it is likely that greater changes in thrift service offerings will be forthcoming as competition for customer credit and deposit accounts continues to increase.

Evaluation of Concentration Studies and Their Policy Implications

The bank concentration studies tell a reasonably consistent story— perhaps more consistent than any other body of banking research literature. The level or degree of banking concentration in narrowly defined banking markets delineated by county, city, and metropolitan-area (SMSA) boundaries *does* matter in terms of prices charged the public for banking services and usually affects the profitability of individual banks as well. Still, as convincing as the story of concentration and bank performance is, there are shortcomings in the current literature and emerging trends in bank structure that demand further research.

For example, the explanatory power of many of the concentration-performance models (especially those attempting to explain
variations in prices or profitability) is extremely low. Frequently 20
percent or less of the performance variability from bank to bank and
market to market is explained by concentration or other market structure factors. Perhaps this persistence of low explanatory power reflects
the differential impact of fiscal and monetary policies on local markets,
the effects of differing economic conditions not adequately captured
by the various economic proxies usually included by researchers, deficiencies in existing measures of market boundaries and market concentration, improper specification of the form of the concentration
relationship, or other factors. No one has yet developed a convincing
method for sorting out these prospective influences—a fact that is
unsettling to both researchers and those administering public policy. I
cannot help but wonder how our conclusions about bank market
power—its causes and its effects—might change and what new directions public policy might profitably take if our models, methods, and
measures were stronger.

There are important additional *public policy* reasons for
Another unappealing result is the relatively poor showing
of measures of nonbank thrift competition in affecting bank behavior.
This is definitely an area for more intensive study, not only because the
empirical proxies used in the past to represent such competition may
be inappropriate, but also in view of recent federal laws—especially
the Depository Institutions Deregulation and Monetary Control Act
of 1980 and the Garn-St Germain Depository Institutions Act of
1982—that have substantially broadened the powers of nonbank thrift
institutions. Moreover, we know very little as yet about the effects of
bank market concentration on the *quality* of financial services offered
the public. Research in the quality dimension of banking is thin and
faces serious measurement and data availability problems, though these
problems are by no means insurmountable.

There are important additional *public policy* reasons for
carrying out more in-depth research in the bank concentration field.
For one thing, as noted recently by Welch (1983), many local banking
markets are highly concentrated by Department of Justice standards.
Moreover, banking markets have changed dramatically in recent years
and are now far broader in geographic extent than ever before. The
bank concentration studies of the 1960s and 1970s were centered on
relatively narrow markets—counties and SMSAs—which served pri-

marily households and small businesses. But today even the smallest deposit and loan customers are, with the help of dramatic improvements in communications technology, able and willing to access financial services from distant suppliers—a fact proven by the rapid rise of the money market fund. Moreover, as suggested by Heggestad and Rhoades (1978), there is limited evidence that banking markets are sometimes (perhaps often) linked together by geographically diversified banks serving multiple local markets—a factor that may reduce interfirm rivalry. We need to know: (1) to what extent banking market boundaries need to be redefined in light of recent structural and technological changes; (2) how strongly or weakly the structure-conduct-performance relationship holds in the new, broader markets and in markets linked by common competitors; (3) the true impact of the many nonfinancial firms that have chosen recently to invade the financial services market; and (4) to what extent we may need to redefine conventional market concentration measures.

Perhaps the traditional measures of concentration are not as relevant to the more dynamic banking markets of today. This question is all the more important when we consider recent theoretical challenges to traditional market concentration models, such as the Demsetz challenge discussed earlier in this chapter and the developing theory of contestable markets presented briefly in chapter 2. These and other new conceptual models pose a clear challenge to the methodology and policy conclusions of older banking concentration studies. Only further research can satisfactorily blend new and old concepts and perhaps reconcile more recent empirical findings with those reached in the earliest studies of banking market concentration.

References

Aliber, Robert Z. 1975. "International Banking: Growth and Regulation." *Columbia Journal of World Business,* 10(4):9-15.

Bain, Joe S. 1956. *Barriers to New Competition.* Cambridge, Mass.: Harvard University Press.

Baltensperger, Ernst. 1972. "Economies of Scale, Firm Size, and Concentration in Banking." *Journal of Money, Credit and Banking* 4 (August):467–88.

Bell, Frederick W. and Neil B. Murphy. 1969. "Impact of Market Structure on the Price of a Commercial Banking Service." *The Review of Economics and Statistics* (May), 51:210–13.

Benston, George J. 1973. "The Optimal Banking Structure: Theory and Evidence." *Journal of Bank Research* (Winter), pp. 220–37.

Chamberlin, Edward H. 1933. *The Theory of Monopolistic Competition.* London: MacMillan.

Clarke, Roger, Stephen Davies, and Michael Waterson. 1984. "The Profitability-Concentration Relation: Market Power or Efficiency?" *Journal of Industrial Economics,* 32(4):435–50.

Crane, D. B. and S. L. Hayes. 1983. "The Evolution of International Banking Competition and Its Implications for Regulation." *Journal of Bank Research,* (Spring), pp. 39–53.

Curry, Timothy J. and John T. Rose. 1984. "Bank Structure and Mortgage Rates: A Comment." *Journal of Economics and Business,* 36:283–87.

Demsetz, Harold. 1973. "Industry Structure, Market Rivalry and Public Policy." *Journal of Law and Economics,* 16(1):1–9.

—— 1974. "Two Systems of Belief About Monopoly." in H. S. Goldschmid, H. M. Mann, and J. F. Weston (eds.). *Industrial Concentration: The New Learning.* Boston: Little, Brown.

Edwards, Franklin R. and Arnold A. Heggestad. 1973. "Uncertainty, Market Structure and Performance: The Galbraith-Caves Hypothesis and Managerial Motives in Banking." *Quarterly Journal of Economics* (August), 88:455–73.

—— 1979. "Uncertainty, Market Structure and Performance: The Galbraith-Caves Hypothesis Revisited." *Quarterly Journal of Economics,* 93:727–29.

Emery, John T. 1971. "Risk, Return, and the Morphology of Commercial Banking." *Journal of Financial and Quantitative Analysis,* 6:763–81.

Glassman, Cynthia A. and Stephen A. Rhoades. 1980. "Owner vs. Manager Control Effects on Bank Performance." *Review of Economics and Statistics* (May), 62:263–70.

Graddy, Duane B. 1980. "The Measurement of Market Structure and Its Influence on Bank Prices and Profitability." *Nebraska Journal of Economics and Business* (Summer), 19:41–54.

Grossack, Irvin M. 1965. "Towards an Integration of Static and Dynamic Measures of Industry Concentration." *Review of Economics and Statistics,* pp. 301-8.

Hanweck, Gerald A. and Stephen A. Rhoades. 1984. "Dominant Firms, 'Deep Pockets,' and Local Market Competition in Banking." *Journal of Economics and Business,* 36:391–402.

Heggestad, Arnold A. 1977. "Market Structure, Risk and Profitability in Commercial Banking." *Journal of Finance* (September), 32:1207–16.

Heggestad, Arnold A. and John J. Mingo. 1976. "Prices, Nonprices, and Concentration in Commercial Banking." *Journal of Money, Credit and Banking* (February), 8:107–17.

Heggestad, Arnold A. and Stephen A. Rhoades. 1976. "Concentration and Firm Stability in Commercial Banking." *Review of Economics and Statistics* (November), 58:443–52.

Heggestad, Arnold A. and Stephen A. Rhoades. 1978. "Multimarket Interdependence and Local Market Competition in Banking." *Review of Economics and Statistics* (November), pp. 523–32.

Hicks, John R. 1935. "Annual Survey of Economic Theory: The Theory of Monopoly." *Econometrica*, 3:1–20.

Honohan, Patrick, and R. P. Kinsella. 1982. "Comparing Bank Concentration Across Countries." *Journal of Banking and Finance*, 6:255-62.

Hymer, S. and P. Pashigian. 1962. "Turnover of Firms as a Measure of Market Behavior." *Review of Economics and Statistics*, 44(1):82–87.

Kaufman, George G. 1966. "Bank Market Structure and Performance: The Evidence from Iowa." *The Southern Economic Journal* (April), 32(4):429–39.

King, Frank. 1977. *Changes in Seller Concentration in Banking Markets.* Working Paper Series (March). Federal Reserve Bank of Atlanta.

Kwoka, John E., Jr. 1977. "Large-Firm Dominance and Price-Cost Margins in Manufacturing Industries." *Southern Economic Journal*, 44(1):183–89.

McCall, Allan S. and Manfred O. Peterson. 1980. "A Critical Level of Commercial Bank Concentration: An Application of Switching Regressions." *Journal of Banking and Finance* (December), 4:353–69.

Phillips, Almarin. 1964. "Competition, Confusion, and Commercial Banking." *Journal of Finance* (March), 19:32–45.

Prais, S. J. 1958. "The Statistical Conditions for a Change in Business Concentration." *Review of Economics and Statistics*, pp. 268–72.

Rhoades, Stephen A. 1977. *Structure-Performance Studies in Banking: A Summary and Evaluation.* Staff Economic Study No. 92. Washington, D.C.: Board of Governors of the Federal Reserve System.

—— 1982. *Structure-Performance Studies in Banking: An Updated Summary and Evaluation.* Staff Economic Study No. 119. Washington, D.C.: Board of Governors of the Federal Reserve System.

Rhoades, Stephen A. and Roger D. Rutz. 1979. *Impact of Bank Holding Companies on Competition and Performance in Banking Markets.* Staff Economic Study No. 107. Board of Governors of the Federal Reserve System.

—— 1981. "Does Market Structure Matter in Commercial Banking?" *Antitrust Bulletin* (Spring), 26:155–81.

—— 1982. "Size and Bank Stability of the 100 Largest Commercial Banks, 1925–1978." *Journal of Economics and Business*, 34:123–28.

—— 1983. "Concentration of World Banking and The Role of U.S. Banks Among the 100 Largest, 1956–1980." *Journal of Banking and Finance*, 7:427–37.

—— 1985a. "Market Share as a Source of Market Power: Implications and Some Evidence." *Journal of Economics and Business*, 37(4):343–363.

—— 1985b. "National and Local Market Banking Concentration in an Era of Interstate Banking." *Issues in Bank Regulation* (Spring), pp. 29–36.

—— 1985c. "Concentration in Local and National Markets." *Economic Review*, Federal Reserve Bank of Atlanta, March 1985, pp. 28–30.

—— 1985d. "Market Performance and the Nature of a Competitive Fringe." *Journal of Economics and Business*, 37:141–157.

Robinson, Joan. 1933. *The Economics of Imperfect Competition.* London: MacMillan.

Rose, Peter S. 1976. "Threshold Levels of Market Power and the Performance of Commercial Banks." *Vie et Sciences Economiques* (July), pp. 11-23. Paris: Review of the National Economic Association.

Rose, Peter S. and Donald R. Fraser. 1976. "The Relationships Between Stability and Change in Market Structure: An Analysis of Bank Prices." *Journal of Industrial Economics,* (June), 24(4):251–66.

Salley, Charles D. 1972. "Concentration in Banking Markets: Regulatory Numerology or Useful Merger Guideline?" *Monthly Review,* pp. 186–93. Federal Reserve Bank of Atlanta.

Savage, Donald T. and Stephen A. Rhoades. 1979. "The Effect of Branch Banking on Pricing, Profits, and Efficiency of Unit Banks." *Proceedings of a Conference on Bank Structure and Competition,* Federal Reserve Bank of Chicago (May), pp. 187–96.

Savage, Donald T. 1982. "Developments in Banking Structure, 1970–81." *Federal Reserve Bulletin,* pp. 77–85.

Shepherd, William G.. 1972. "The Elements of Market Structure." *Review of Economics and Statistics* (February), 54:25–37.

Sherer, F. M. 1970. *Industrial Market Structure and Economic Performance.* Chicago: Rand McNally.

Short, Brock K. 1979. "The Relation Between Commercial Bank Profit Rates and Banking Concentration in Canada, Western Europe, and Japan." *Journal of Banking and Finance,* 3:209–19.

Smirlock, Michael. 1985. "Evidence on the (Non)Relationship Between Concentration and Profitability in Banking." *Journal of Money, Credit and Banking* (February), 17(1):69–83.

Stigler, George J. 1965. "Theory of Oligopoly." *Journal of Political Economy* (February), pp. 44–61.

Tschoegel, A. E. 1982. "Concentration Among International Banks." *Journal of Banking and Finance,* 6:567–78.

United States Department of Justice. 1982. "Merger Guidelines." *Federal Register* (June 30).

Wall, Larry. 1985. "Why Are Some Banks More Profitable Than Others?" *Journal of Bank Research* (Winter), pp. 240–56.

Welch, Patrick J. 1983. "Concentration in Local Commercial Banking Markets: A Study of the Eighth Federal Reserve District." *Economic Review* (October), pp. 15–21. Federal Reserve Bank of St. Louis.

White, Lawrence J. 1976. "Price Regulation and Quality Rivalry in a Profit-Maximizing Model: The Case of Bank Branching." *Journal of Money, Credit and Banking* (February), 8:97-106.

Whitehead, David D. 1977. *Holding Company Power and Market Performance: A New Index of Market Concentration.* Research Paper No. 5. Federal Reserve Bank of Atlanta.

PART III: MULTIPLE-OFFICE
BANKING ORGANIZATIONS: THEIR CHARACTER
AND PERFORMANCE RECORD

7.

Branch Banking: A Century-Old Issue in American Banking

ONE OF THE oldest controversies in the history of American banking centers on the issue of whether and where banks should be allowed to establish branch offices. Economist and Federal Reserve official Larry R. Mote (1974) once referred to branch banking as "the perennial issue" in American banking, and so it has been for more than a century. Proponents of branching point to the growth and stability of elaborate branch office systems in countries such as Canada and Great Britain and the wide menu of financial services typically available through branch banks. Opponents stress the dangers of branching—real or potential, including concentrated economic power, disregard for local customers' needs, and higher prices for basic financial services. Few topics in the industry have generated as much heat and as little light as the branching issue—a fact reflected in the anguished struggles in recent years in state legislatures across the nation.

In its infinite wisdom (or perhaps incredible lack of foresight) Congress chose more than 50 years ago to leave the branch banking issue to the states. As a result, bitter battles between proponents and opponents of branching have been fought in one state after another with branching forces—buttressed by market-broadening advances in communications technology, population shifts, and soaring bank operating costs—generally gaining ground. However, mute testimony to the past successes of branching's opponents may be found in the crazy quilt of state laws and regulations limiting or restricting full-service branching that blankets the nation.

In Texas, for example, each banking corporation is essentially confined to one main office, though recent legislation permits automated tellers and drive-in windows in more distant locations. In Arizona and California, however, branches can be established statewide without significant barriers, but federal law prohibits full-service branches of Arizona and California banks (or of any state) from reaching into another state's territory unless that state specifically passes enabling legislation. Recently, several states have done so as we observed in chapter 1. For example, the six New England States, as well as Delaware and South Dakota, voted in the early 1980s to permit entry by outside banks with some restrictions. On the horizon is Congressional repeal or at least modification of the half-century-old McFadden Act prohibiting nationwide branch banking, setting in motion an intense competitive rivalry between a handful of the nation's largest money center institutions (principally those in California and New York) and thousands of small locally oriented banks in innumerable cities and towns across America.

Assuming that such legislation will pass, what are the probable effects? Who benefits from branch banking—management? bank stockholders? the public? In this chapter I address "the perennial issue" of branching in light of several decades of serious research.

Brief History of the Controversy Surrounding Branch Banking

Earlier in U.S. history banking services were frequently provided by foreign banks—for example, British banks financed much of the trade in cotton, farm equipment, machinery, and textiles flowing into and out of the eastern and southern states during the nineteenth century. U.S. citizens had little difficulty accepting services from large branch banks abroad, but when it came to the founding of domestically chartered banks, branching was *not* a popular alternative.

To be sure, there were a few branch banks in the early years of the republic. For example, the federally chartered First and Second Banks of the United States, established in 1791 and 1816 respectively, operated branch offices in several states. A handful of state-chartered banks also established branches in the Midwest (mainly in Indiana, Iowa, Missouri, and Ohio) before the Civil War. But most organizers of new banks seemed to prefer either single offices—unit banks—or a small number of limited-service branch facilities.

In fact, as Mote (1974) observes, branch banking was not really a bone of contention among bankers until the early twentieth century. The Comptroller of the Currency, in his capacity as administrator of the nation's federally chartered banks, saw little need for even national banks to establish branch offices. Indeed, in 1900, branchless banks represented 99 percent of all banks in the industry, and two decades later, single-office banks still accounted for about 98 percent of all U.S. commercial banks. Moreover, a strict reading of the National Bank Act of 1863–1864, which created the system of federally chartered or national banks that we have today, implied that national banks were to designate *one* location from which loans would be made and deposits accepted. Some authorities (such as Fischer 1968) believe this was an incorrect interpretation of federal law, however, though there was little debate over such an interpretation for half a century.

The branching issue did not become truly significant until the 1920s and 1930s when consumer-oriented loans became important and a significantly larger group of household (wage-earning) savers began to appear. The spreading industrial revolution, turning out mass-produced automobiles, clothes, and thousands of other consumer goods, created the need for financing household purchases of these items if manufacturers were to find a market for their wares. At the same time the revolution in mass production generated a large and growing class of wage earners who needed an outlet for their savings. This new source of savings was welcome because the new highly capital-intensive industries needed huge amounts of financial capital to construct buildings and assembly lines and to purchase equipment. But who was to provide the needed financial capital? Banks and other financial institutions had to develop new organizational methods and strategies to (1) attract and pool scores of small savings accounts and (2) allocate the pooled funds to those businesses and households in need of financial capital. Consumer credit accounts were a special problem because most banks were not experienced in analyzing and managing small-denomination cash and installment loans.

The rise of the consumer as both a source and a user of bank funds, as noted in the opening chapter, forced a substantial shift in bank marketing strategies. Mass advertising became a necessity, and even more important, banks had to pay more attention to customer *convenience*—making it less costly in time and resources for households to get to the bank's office to transact their business. With the development and mass marketing of the automobile, bank customers became more mobile, requiring American banks to be more flexible in following and holding their customers. Large banks located in states where branch banking was not expressly forbidden by state law had a clear advantage because they were able to set up offices in residential areas. Consumer funds could then be pooled into sizable quantities and funneled into the central cities where both commercial and consumer loan demand was heaviest. In states where branch banking was outlawed or severely restricted, multibank holding companies and chain banking organizations developed in an effort to tie together groups of predominantly small banks so that deposits could be directed more efficiently to the most promising credit markets.

The growth of *multiple-office banking* in both branch and holding-company forms soon generated strong opposition. Several states passed restrictive branching and holding company legislation, including outright prohibitions of either or both multiple-office organizational forms. At the same time, however, many of the larger and more aggressive banks sought wider branching powers at state and federal levels with some success, mainly in the Western States. For example, the California legislature authorized statewide branching in 1909. At the federal level, an attempt was made in 1922 to alter national bank regulations to permit federally chartered institutions to branch by setting up limited-service facilities within the city where their headquarters was located. It was clear from the start, however, that such an initiative would not gather sufficient public and political support unless state-chartered banks were also granted parallel branching powers.

A further step toward liberalization of national bank branching rules was taken in 1927 with passage of the McFadden-Pepper Act. Federally chartered banks were expressly allowed to open full-service branches in their home-office communities provided state law did not expressly prohibit branch banking. However, this so-called "victory" for national banks was a Pyrrhic victory, resulting in severe legal restrictions on the future expansion plans and service offerings of many of the nation's largest banks. McFadden reaffirmed the principle of state control over territorial expansion of *both* state and federally chartered banking institutions. Interstate branching was prohibited except for those few banks that had already crossed state lines or where a state expressly granted out-of-state banks the right to establish offices within its borders. Within each state's boundaries state law would henceforth control whether or not branches could be opened in the same city, county, or district where a commercial bank was headquartered. This fundamental principle of *state* hegemony over the structure of banking firms and the banking industry was further strengthened with passage of the Bank Holding Company Act of 1956, which placed limits similar to McFadden on the holding-company form of group banking.

A further liberalizing step toward branching was taken in 1933 when Congress passed the Banking Act of 1933 (known as Glass-Steagall). National banks were allowed to branch anywhere within a given state, provided state law granted similar powers to state-chartered banking organizations. Perhaps a measure of how strong the opposition to the branch banking movement had become was what compromises were required to win passage of Glass-Steagall's branching provisions. This law reflected the panicky reaction of Congress to the devastating effects of the economic pressures of the 1920s and the Great Depression of the 1930s, which forced the absorption, merger, or closure of nearly half the U.S. bank population in the space of two decades. Many members of Congress saw branching as a way to build larger, more widely diversified, and (hopefully) more viable banking organizations. What is often forgotten, however, is that the large money-center banks probably lost as much as they gained from Glass-Steagall. Many of these leading banks had become involved in the trading of corporate stocks and bonds as an important source of earnings. In what is probably today its most famous provision, the 1933 Banking Act severed the critical links between commercial banking and investment banking, outlawing bank underwriting of corporate securities.

In the years following the Great Depression and into the 1980s the battleground for opponents and proponents of branching moved from the halls of Congress to the state legislatures. There the battle intensified to fever pitch owing to the dramatic growth of branch facilities and of banks with branches. Whereas the ratio of branchless banks to the industry's total population stood at 92 percent at the close of World War II, that ratio had dropped to 74 percent at the end of the 1960s and to just over 50 percent in the mid-1980s. By the early 1970s branch banks held three quarters of all U.S. bank deposits, while the ratio of banking offices to people—a key measure of customer convenience—had risen dramatically.

Buttressed by this dramatic growth trend, branching advocates scored a number of legislative successes beginning in the 1960s and 1970s. For example, New York gradually converted from citywide to districtwide branching and then moved to statewide branching in 1976. New Jersey moved to allow district branching in 1969, along with statewide holding companies, and Arkansas, Florida, Kentucky, Iowa, Maine, Minnesota, New Hampshire, and Virginia made various modifications to state statutes in the 1960s and 1970s to permit branching to play a more prominent role.

As the decade of the 1980s began, the geographic pattern of state laws permitting, prohibiting, or partially allowing bank branching defied both rhyme and reason. Branching had become widespread along the east and west coasts, and significant inroads had been made in the Midwest and South. By 1985 22 states had legalized statewide branching while 20 states permitted at least limited branching activity (and three of these—Florida, Nebraska, and Virginia—allowed statewide branching via mergers). However, mottled forms of unit banking (modified frequently as in Texas by the rapid growth of holding companies) continued entrenched in the nation's midsection, where nine states prohibited full-service branching. It soon became apparent to many bankers bent on interstate expansion that battling for more liberalized rules state by state was costly and time-consuming. As a result, a second front—an effort to pass new federal laws or liberalize federal regulations—was opened as the 1970s drew to a close and the 1980s began.

New Dimension to the Branching Issue: Interstate Branching

The decades-old federal and state laws against interstate branching did not, in fact, prevent the development of a wide array of interstate banking services and institutions. The same may be said for the Douglas Amendment to the 1956 Bank Holding Company Act, which prohibits bank holding companies from owning 5 percent or more of the equity shares of a bank in another state, unless that state expressly approves the acquisition. Nevertheless, bank holding companies through their *nonbank* affiliates—especially through the finance companies, mortgage banking houses, and leasing companies they control—have frequently expanded nationwide. Other vehicles for interstate expansion used by large U.S. banking organizations include loan production office (LPOs) and Edge Act corporations, which may be established without regard to state boundaries provided they do not take domestic deposits and are adequately capitalized. As the 1980s began, many more than one hundred Edge Act offices were in place in the continental states.

As significant as these interstate adventures have been, they have all been subject to an inherent limitation—the legal inability of interstate offices to take *deposits* from the general public. That is, full-service banking across state lines, with limited exceptions, has not been possible legally or even technically until recently. But the barriers to interstate deposit taking *are* falling today as a result of both reciprocal branching and merger agreements between states and advances in electronic transfer techniques. For example, by 1986 more than 27 states had acted to permit some form of entry into their markets by out-of-state banking organizations.

The advent of low-fixed-cost automated teller machines, point-of-sale terminals, and payments by computer tape have severely weakened the artificial barriers against geographic expansion of deposit markets. Both large and small banks have formed regional and national networks centered around strategically placed ATM facilities, offering twenty-four-hour service availability at low cost. Through "financial networking" customers can access their home bank while traveling thousands of miles away and channel funds between their local demand deposit and the distant money market through various types of cash management accounts. Moreover, numerous nonbank financial institutions have developed their own financial networks in defiance of banking regulations, designed especially to attract corporate and household liquid balances.

Recognizing these recent technical developments Congress called for a review of the relevance of the McFadden Act and interstate branching restrictions when the International Banking Act was passed in 1978. The report submitted by the Carter Administration in 1980 recommended major changes in the framework of banking regulation and a gradual phase-down of interstate banking barriers. Proposals to phase in interstate branching with safeguards for local institutions and for the public's deposits were seriously debated in Congress in the mid-1980s. Would such a move be desirable from the public's standpoint? What are the potential benefits and potential costs from further expansion of branch banking?

Advantages Claimed for Branch Banking

Resource Efficiency. Several advantages are usually claimed for branch banking systems. Among the most prominent is the claim that branching increases efficiency in using scarce resources—land, labor, management skills, and capital. This may happen for two reasons: (1) individual banks are able to grow larger through their ability to branch into new markets and take deposits and (2) branch banks can more easily direct incoming funds to areas offering the highest investment returns and thus make possible a more efficient allocation of scarce capital and other resources.

Accelerated Economic Growth Through increased efficiency in allocating scarce capital and by making more credit available, branch banks allegedly contribute to faster economic growth and development in those market areas where they provide financial services.

Improved Availability of Financial Services. Allegedly, branching leads to greater availability of banking services. One line of reasoning in support of this argument contends that branch banks tend to be *larger* than unit banks and those augmented resources make possible a wider range of services. Moreover, the greater average size of branch banks may enable them to better withstand the risks of developing new services. Relatedly, Wacht (1968) argues that increased portfolio diversification attainable through branching may result in more loans because branch banks are less exposed to default risk. He suggests that restricting a bank's access to branching may force the institution to diversify in other ways, such as by reducing funds available to local borrowers and diverting those funds into distant credit markets. Moreover, virtually all the services of a large branch bank are available through each office, even in the smallest local markets. In contrast, the argument runs, a unit bank in a relatively small local market would be unable to offer as wide a range or as much depth of service.

Greater Convenience in Accessing Bank Services. Related to the foregoing claim is one contending that transactions costs are lower for customers of branch banks because branching increases the number of banking offices within a defined geographic area. Moreover, larger branch banks allegedly are able to establish offices in areas where cost and low profit potential prohibit smaller unit banks from entering.

Improved Institutional and Systemic Safety. Averaging larger in size and less dependent on any single local market, branch banks are arguably more stable, especially in periods of economic decline, and less prone to failure than single-office banks. In effect, branch banks are able to diversify more fully, both geographically and in their loan portfolios. And if individual branch banks are more stable, so the argument goes, the entire system of banks is less prone to instability and more likely to engender greater public confidence.

On the other hand, as McCall and Lane (1980) observe, more liberal branching rules may lead to increased numbers of problem and failed banks if barriers to entry are reduced and competition is increased. Branch banks may be more aggressively managed than unit institutions, overriding the stabilizing benefits of their greater diversification. In addition, multiple-office organizations may prove more difficult to examine and regulate, owing, in part, to their greater average size.

Increased Effectiveness for Monetary Policy. The effects of monetary policy on the financial system may be transmitted more quickly through a branching system than through thousands of small unit banks. Thus, the lag between policy implementation and policy impact is reduced, lessening the chances for mistimed and inappropriate policy effects on the economy. Moreover, if branch banks are more stable and less prone to failure, the central bank can be more aggressive in its policy moves to stabilize the economy with less fear of endangering the stability of the banking system.

Disadvantages Often Cited for Branching

As convincing as some of the foregoing arguments may sound, opponents of the further spread of branch banking have some persuasive arguments of their own.

Tendency Toward Concentrated Market Power. Branch banking results in larger banks that have greater potential for overpowering small banks, particularly those that serve a single local market. By undercutting prices in a given market, smaller banks can be driven out of business or forced into mergers. The result, over time, is an increase in the concentration of deposits and loans in the largest banks, reducing competition and ultimately harming the public. The consumer of banking services will have fewer alternative sources of supply in the long run.

Branch Banks Charge Higher Prices for Their Services. Related to the foregoing argument, if greater concentration of banking resources in fewer banks is a consequence of branching, then economic theory would suggest that branch banks charge higher prices for the same services than unit banks do. The logic of such an argument is set out clearly by Gilbert and Longbrake (1974) and by Jacobs (1965).

Increased Danger of Credit Discrimination. Branch banks tend to drain funds from the local area. They attract deposits from local communities and then channel those funds to the central cities where loan demand is heaviest. Frequently, this results in smaller borrowers'—small businesses and households—receiving less credit in total while large corporations and governments receive all the credit they demand. This argument is presented in detail by Guttentag and Herman (1967) and by Gilbert and Longbrake (1974).

Offering Impersonal Service to the Public. People depend on banks for a wide range of essential services, especially as a repository of family savings and as a vital source of credit to sustain living standards and support economic growth. Branch banks allegedly tend to "dehumanize" banking and have little loyalty to the interests of local citizens or to the local community as a whole. The branch manager may or may not be a local resident and, even if he or she is, that manager is not free to make major decisions independent of the organization as a whole. Many credit decisions vitally important to local citizens, for example, must be passed up the organization chart to senior bank officials often unfamiliar with the local community and its unique financial needs.

Research Evidence on Branching's Effects

What does the available evidence have to say concerning these arguments, pro and con? As might be expected, the results are mixed and only a small portion of the principal issues appear to be resolved at this time after nearly four decades of intensive research.

Resource Efficiency. Does branch banking improve the efficiency with which scarce resources are allocated by the banking system? In general, efficiency refers to the ratio of a firm's or system's output to the quantity or cost of resources employed to produce that output. Studies that have attempted to apply such a yardstick to banks have run into serious methodological problems, as noted in chapter 4. For example, how should bank output be measured given that banks are multiproduct firms and each bank has a somewhat different mix of output?

For broad measures of bank output—such as total assets, total deposits, total numbers of customer accounts processed, total revenue, and so on—single-office banks nearly always report lower costs per dollar or per account than branching organizations (as reflected, for example, in the Chicago banking study of Schweiger and McGee 1961). A contrary finding, though, was reported about the same time by Anderson (1964), who found operating costs per capita growing more slowly in Vermont—a branch banking state—compared with New Hampshire—a unit banking state—allegedly because branch systems require fewer management personnel. The problem with such bank output measures, however, is their failure to adequately consider service mix and customer convenience. A few studies have attempted to control for these two factors but with remarkably inconsistent results—some finding branch banks with lower average costs than unit banks of comparable size and structure, others finding the exact opposite, and still others finding no trend either way.

It may be noted, however, that a study of more than 2500 banking organizations by Rhoades and Savage (1981) found that pure bank holding-company systems displayed lower noninterest costs than branching systems. Yet, the branching organizations maintained more offices in each market served, on average, than the holding-company organizations did and, thus, presumably provided more service to the public. One reason for this was suggested recently by Nelson (1985), who finds significant and continuous economies of scale (i.e., monotonically declining average production costs) at the individual branch office level. However, Nelson finds *no* cost savings from simply adding more branches to the banking organizations as a whole.

It is clear that more research work is needed in the area of the *comparative efficiency* of different forms of banking organizations, especially holding companies versus branch systems. What is remarkable, however, is the speed with which state and federal authorities have gone forward with new liberalized rules allowing major structural changes in the industry with only limited (and often inconclusive) evidence upon which to base their decisions.

Credit Discrimination. Research evidence on the issue of whether branch banks discriminate against local borrowers (particularly small ones) in favor of nonlocal borrowers (especially large corporations and governments) is mixed in both direction and quality. First, there appears to be little doubt that large branch banks hold a greater proportion of credits from large business clients outside their local market, as noted, for example, in two extensive Federal Reserve Staff Studies (Board of Governors 1958, 1960). However, a detailed study of Federal Reserve business loan survey data by Eisenbeis (1975) indicated that large banks located in SMSAs where branching was permitted devoted greater proportions of both the number and dollar size of their business loans to *local* firms than comparable-size banks in SMSAs in unit banking states did. Moreover, when banks in unit banking, limited branching, and statewide branching states were compared, the larger banks in states without branching directed a greater fraction of their business credit outside the local area, though these differences narrowed appreciably for small banks with less than $20 million in deposits.

Eisenbeis is quick to note, however, that such evidence does *not* necessarily mean that liberalization of branching will expand the availability of business credit in local markets, because of the importance of other causal elements such as economic conditions and bank size distributions.

Accelerated Economic Growth. Does the banking structure adopted by a state or local community affect the growth of local and state economies? A few studies have addressed this issue for *states* in various regions of the nation. For example, a study by Kreps and Wacht (1970) of three states—North Carolina, Virginia, and West Virginia— and of the entire Southeastern region examined the relationship between several banking variables (including the loan-deposit ratio, deposits and loans per 1000 population, and the number of banks and banking offices) and measures of economic activity (such as nonagricultural employment, personal savings, manufacturing payrolls, and consumer expenditures). Linear regression analysis of data covering the 1947-1965 period convinced the authors that a state's banking structure directly affects its economic and industrial growth. Branching and, where branching is restricted, holding companies were believed to have a favorable effect on both state and (by inference) local economic growth.

The general consensus in the literature, however, appears to be that, if banking structure matters at all, it is of *secondary* importance in shaping growth and living standards in different states and regions. Instances clearly can be found of states with essentially unit banking regimes (such as Colorado and Texas) or holding-company-dominated systems (such as Florida) with per-capita incomes and economic growth as high as branch banking states (such as California and Arizona). As Darnell (1973) concludes, other factors, such as the availability of natural resources, the propensity of local residents to save, and population density, appear to have significantly greater effects on local growth and development than the orgnizational structure of indigenous banking organizations does.

Note, however, that branching activity itself is sensitive to economic forces, especially to growth in cities and local neighborhoods. For example, studies by Booth and Smith (1984), Doyle, Fenwick, and Savage (1981), and Savage alone (1982) find that median income, the distribution of income, and median age of the population of a local area are all *positively* related to the number of branches situated there. Interestingly enough, the first of these studies finds that passage of the Community Reinvestment Act in 1977, which outlawed credit discrimination against selected neighborhoods, tended to increase the cost of deposit raising in low-income neighborhoods and probably resulted in fewer branch offices and poorer banking service in the very neighborhoods intended to be helped by federal antidiscrimination legislation. Caution is called for in accepting this conclusion without further research, however, because it was based on data from a single large metropolitan area.

Improved Availability of Banking Services. There is some evidence that branch banks offer more services than unit banks if bank size is *not* controlled for. Much, if not all, of this service difference disappears, however, when banks of comparable size are compared. Of course, if a branching structure does result in larger size banks, on average, and such banks do offer more services, there is a clear benefit to the customer, especially, as Guttentag points out for a Senate study (Subcommittee on Financial Institutions 1976), in rural areas and small towns. The key issue is, of course, whether there is a *net* benefit to the bank customer if larger banking organizations also reduce competition—a comparative calculus that has, as yet, yielded no definitive conclusions.

Greater Convenience in Accessing Bank Services. To what extent does it appear true that banking services are more conveniently available to the customer under branch as opposed to unit banking? There is some relatively strong evidence that branch banking does increase the number of offices available to the public as compared with unit banking. One prominent example is provided by Anderson's (1964) comparative study of unit banking New Hampshire and branch banking Vermont in the early 1960s. The latter state was found to supply about 50 percent more banking facilities than New Hampshire did before it adopted branching. This conclusion is supported by Seaver and Fraser (1979) in a cluster analysis of more than 200 SMSAs and by a study carried out in the 1960s at the Federal Reserve Bank of Chicago (1970). The latter project suggests that in larger size communities (especially those with more than 25,000 people), the area served by each banking office is approximately twice as large under a unit banking regime as opposed to a branch banking regime. Thus, bank customers must travel greater distances, on average, with a unit banking structure than with branch banking according to these studies.

For smaller size communities, however, the differences in geographic area per banking office are apparently very minor. A study by Seaver and Fraser (1984) finds no evidence that population per banking office is lower in rural counties where branching is allowed than for those rural counties located in unit banking states. Indeed, in terms of raw averages, population per banking office averaged 3273 in randomly selected unit banking counties versus 4417 in branch banking counties. And while both the number of offices and mean bank size tend to increase with more liberalized branching, the number of separately incorporated banks serving a given set of markets tends to decline with branching, as noted by both Jacobs (1965) and Gilbert and Longbrake (1974). Moreover, it may well be that the spread of retail electronic banking, where computer terminals link customer homes and offices directly to banks, will alter the branching customer-convenience relationship if we assume that unit and branch banks will be equally capable of installing and maintaining equipment of this nature.

Improved Institutional and Systemic Safety. There is ample evidence that unit banks fail in much greater numbers than branch banks, as observed by Scott and Rose (1977). The majority of banks that failed during the Great Depression of the 1930s were small unit banks located in rural areas and in relatively small towns. There is, or can be, a diversification effect—spreading of risk—from branch banking related to the ability of branch banks to enter geographically and economically distinct markets. If true diversification is achieved (such that economic conditions are not positively correlated in the set of local markets entered by a branching organization), then a downturn in deposit flows, loan demand, or loan repayments in one market will be offset by an increase in deposit flows, loan demand, and loan repayments in another market. It is more difficult for unit banks, unless they can band together through holding companies or chain banking arrangements, to achieve this degree of diversification. Thus, smaller unit banks are more prone to collapse when economic conditions in the local market deteriorate.

A study by McCall and Lane (1980) argues, however, that "multi-office banking authority and organizational structure have increased the riskiness of banks and the banking system," though, the authors conclude, the increase in risk has not been substantial. Analyzing data on problem and failed banks from FDIC reports during the 1960s and 1970s, they found slight increases in operating risk owing to lower entry barriers, increased competition, and reduced profitability in branch banking areas. Branch banks also appear to be operated more aggressively, as reflected in their higher loan-asset ratios. Moreover, Rhoades and Savage (1981) found that branching systems tended to be more risky (in terms of reduced equity capital and reduced holdings of low-risk assets) than pure holding-company organizations. However, these increased risks have not led to significantly higher percentages of problem or failed banks in branching states—a fact that McCall and Lane attribute to greater geographic and product line diversification and the greater ease with which mergers can be consummated in branching areas.

Another possible explanation for the lack of higher bank failure rates in branching states may be the evidence accumulated in recent years that branch banks can achieve reduced variability in their deposit flows owing to greater diversification. This implies that branching institutions enjoy reduced risk of illiquidity. Wacht (1968), Lauch and Murphy (1970), and Gilbert in a U.S. Senate study (Subcommittee on Financial Institutions 1976) found support for this proposition for demand and savings deposits. However, Anderson, Haslem, and Leonard (1976) analyzed detailed deposit data from one large ($500-million) branch bank with more than 50 branches and found *no* significant reduction in demand-deposit variability from adding more branches. Because of the limited scope of this last study, however, it seems reasonable to place greater weight on the studies that *do* find lower deposit variability in branch banks.

Increased Effectiveness for Monetary Policy. Can monetary policy be carried out more effectively with a smaller number of large branch banks as opposed to a large number of small unit organizations? This is a doubtful proposition about which there is little corroborating evidence. Much seems to depend on the policy tools used by the central bank. Federal Reserve open-market operations, for example, do not depend for their effectiveness on the organizational structure chosen by banks but, rather, on the efficient functioning of the financial markets in reacting to liquidity and interest rate pressures. It might well be argued, however, that heavy use of *moral suasion*—the psychological arm-twisting of bankers and the public by central bank officials—would be more effective with a system composed of a limited number of large branching organizations. It would be far easier for the Chairman of the Federal Reserve Board to communicate his expectations for the growth of bank credit and control of inflation, for example, to the heads of a few large branch banks or bank holding companies than to a highly fractured banking system. It has never, however, been convincingly established that moral suasion is an effective policy tool. There is some evidence, though, that the Federal Reserve has come to use this psychological tool more heavily in recent years owing to the difficulties encountered in managing the U.S. economy with its general credit controls.

Tendency Toward Concentrated Market Power. One of the oldest arguments against branch banking is the fear of concentrated financial power. Branch banking allegedly leads to the concentration of a significant proportion of industry resources under the control of a handful of large banks. Smaller banks, unable to compete, are often driven from the market via merger, absorption, or failure. The result is less competition, excessive profits for the few, and fewer and more expensive alternatives for the bank customer. In a slightly more sophisticated form—the theory of oligopoly—this argument contends that local banking markets soon become dominated by a few firms, each firm recognizing the sensitivity of its profits to actions taken by other firms. Eventually "understandings" develop regarding prices and market shares, and the banks involved seek to optimize their *joint* earnings rather than maintain an aggressive competitive rivalry.

Those who see branching as a catalyst for concentrated banking markets point to recent data on statewide and metropolitan area (SMSA) concentration ratios. For example, states that permit statewide branch banking often report that the three, four, or five largest banks typically control a greater percentage of assets or deposits on a statewide basis (and in most SMSAs as well) compared with states where branching is prohibited or restricted in some way. Most noticeable in this regard are states that liberalized their branching laws in the 1960s and 1970s. Often within the space of a few years a handful of dominant banking organizations emerged in the wake of new and more lenient branching rules, as observed in both New Jersey and New York by Kidder (1971) and Kunreuther, Kidder, and Juncker (1973).

Does the observed increase in concentration mean that there is less competition for the customer's business? Not necessarily. For one thing true competition is not a matter of numbers; it is a matter of *behavior.* The more relevant question is, therefore, whether or not the customer has fewer convenient alternatives or encounters less competitive rivalry among suppliers of financial services under a branching regime as opposed to other forms of bank organization. Here the evidence is much less clear. Several studies (for example: Edwards 1965 and Oldfield and Watson 1972) have found that the number of banking offices increases and concentration tends to decrease in local markets once banks are allowed to branch and, thus, a wider variety of separately owned banks establish their presence in any given local market.

Thus, if statewide branching were permitted in a state previously closed to all branching, we might soon find that each major city would have one or more branches operated by five or six dominant banks in the state, as well as from locally headquartered institutions. As a result, wherever within the state the customer traveled, he or she might find the same five or six leading banks competing against each other with essentially the same services. Moreover, there would be a tendency toward uniform service packages and uniform pricing of individual services across different local markets, as Schweiger and McGee (1961) once observed.

In summary, there is some research evidence that branching promotes bank entry into new markets by lowering barriers to entry. Once entry has occurred, service pricing and packaging becomes more uniform from community to community. One caveat here, as noted by White (1976), is that greater existing concentration in a branching market does discourage growth in new branch offices. However, greater local competition seems to spur growth in new branch offices, sometimes going beyond the profit-maximizing point in an attempt to discourage further entry.

Branch Banks Charge Higher Prices for Their Services. To the extent that branch banks can reduce their costs by growing in size and improving efficiency (also reducing transactions costs for the customer) and lower their own operating and financial risk through diversification, they may be able to charge lower prices for their services. However, if branching results in greater concentration in local markets and that concentration leads to collusion among banks sharing one or more markets, the result might well be higher prices charged the customer, accompanied by a reduction in service quality and, perhaps, an increase in individual bank profits.

What is the evidence on branching's price effects? Considering first the sources-of-funds side, do branch banks pay higher rates on interest-bearing deposits or charge lower service fees on checking accounts? The evidence on this point is mixed and, on the whole, inconclusive.

Most studies (for example, Horvitz and Shull 1964) have found that branch banks charge *higher* average fees to service demand deposit accounts than unit banks situated in the same local market do, though Anderson (1964) finds slightly lower checkbook fees in Vermont under a branching regime than in New Hampshire, which had a unit banking system at the time. Moreover, there is evidence that when branch banks enter a new market, demand deposit service fees tend to *rise*, as reflected, for example, in work by Kohn and Carlo (1969) and Motter and Carson (1964).

What factors may lead branching organizations to levy higher fees on conventional checkbook services? Because service fees tend to cover only a fraction of the true costs of administering demand accounts, it may well be argued that higher service charges at branch banks are a reflection of greater management sophistication and greater capacity to make accurate cost-benefit assessments of each service. Perhaps the simpler explanation that branch banking markets are less competitive and, therefore, result in higher demand account service fees is the best one. Additional research clearly needs to be done in this area to guide us toward convincing conclusions before we move, perhaps irretrievably, toward unrestricted interstate branching.

In the area of interest rates paid on time and savings deposits, research results to date are especially confusing. Comparing rates paid in unit banking states with branch banking states is a futile exercise because of differing market conditions. A few studies have overcome this methodological limitation by examining markets where branch banks and unit banks operate side by side. In these more relevant comparisons there is some evidence that unit banks pay *higher* average rates on time deposits than branch banks do (with bank size, but not account size or deposit mix, held constant). However, an even stronger relationship exists between bank size and interest paid, larger branch banks offering higher average thrift deposit interest rates than smaller unit institutions do. Again, there is the danger here of confounding different background conditions, especially economies of scale, portfolio mix, diversification, regulations, and so on. Then, too, in comparing unit and branch banks of the same size, it would appear that additional factors—especially transactions costs and geographic diversification—enter in, tending to favor branch banks and therefore requiring unit banks to compensate by offering higher interest rates on similar-maturity deposit accounts. Either way, this is another area where further detailed research is needed to qualify the evidence.

When we turn to loan rates, there is considerable variation in the research evidence, depending on the particular kind of loan being discussed. For example, branch banks, on average, seem to charge *lower* rates on consumer installment loans and mortgage loans than unit banks serving the same market areas do, though Anderson (1964) found no significant difference in rates assessed on new auto loans between unit banking New Hampshire and branch banking Vermont. Moreover, when unit banks become branches of larger branching organizations, the few extant studies looking into this issue (for example, Kohn 1964 and Motter and Carson 1964) generally find that rates on these two types of loans are *reduced.*

In the case of business loans, however, the evidence is decidedly mixed. In the field of credit extended to small and medium-size businesses, loan fees levied by branch banks tend to be *lower,* though there are conflicting findings. There is also some evidence that branch banks demand higher average customer deposits as a condition for granting commercial loans. And, as in the case of consumer and mortgage loans, the takeover of a unit bank by a branching organization generally resulted in a business loan rate reduction, as observed by Horvitz and Shull (1964) and Kohn (1964), though Horvitz (1958) found the opposite effect in New England.

Increased Danger of Credit Discrimination. A widely discussed problem with branch banking centers on credit discrimination. Do branch banks discriminate against certain kinds of borrowers—for example, diverting loan funds away from small businesses and consumers in the local community toward large corporate and government borrowers in the nation's money centers? If so, economic growth and development may be reduced in smaller communities while larger cities enjoy accelerated growth. Moreover, such concentrations of financial capital may increase the potential for economic instability.

What can be made of such arguments? There is little question that branch banks move loanable funds from areas of limited loan demand to areas where loan demand is heavy (as discussed, for example, by Edwards 1965, Kohn, Carlo, and Kaye 1973, and, more recently, by Barkley, Mellon, and Potts 1984). However, as the latter study suggests, the primary direction of credit reallocation may be intrarural rather than from rural areas to metropolitan areas. Indeed, Fischer and Davis, reporting to a U.S. Senate subcommittee (Subcommittee on Financial Institutions 1976), found greater funds mobility under multiple-office banking *without* damage to small local markets.

In what sense would such credit reallocation be "bad" or "harmful" to local communities, states, regions, or even the nation as a whole? In general, efficient use of scarce resources demands that land, labor, and capital be allocated by the marketplace to those uses promising the highest expected returns. If branch banking facilitates the flow of scarce financial capital toward those areas promising the greatest expected profitability, then branching produces greater social benefits. On the other hand, if true discrimination occurs in which branch banks as a matter of philosophy and design direct funds away from their potentially most profitable uses or inhibit competition, a solid case can be made against the branching form of organization. However, banking research has not convincingly established such a case to date.

Offering Impersonal Service to the Public. One of the reasons behind the alleged discrimination of branch banks toward small, local customers, it is often argued, is that such banks are coldly impersonal toward many of their clients. Loans allegedly are extended on the sole basis of financial analytics, rather than according to the needs and interests of the local community. Besides, it is claimed, branch managers typically have only limited decisionmaking authority in granting local loans. All but the smallest requests are channeled back to the home office, where credit decisions are far removed from the local environment. Those who make the key decisions in a branch banking organization often do not see the *consequences* of those decisions. In contrast, senior officers in a unit bank usually live in the local area, understand its financial needs, and respond to intangible factors in granting loans, evidencing greater social concern.

The foregoing arguments are difficult, if not impossible,

to evaluate. They rest on normative and not objective criteria. However, if we assume for the moment that they have some validity, then many local areas served exclusively by branch banks would be poorly developed and characterized by less than full employment, inadequate housing, and a relatively low standard of living. Such conditions *can* be measured and evaluated. The interesting point is that no studies have done so, apart from the few studies previously discussed that focus on statewide conditions, *not* local banking markets. Thus, we remain very much in the dark concerning the real-sector effects of branch banking or, for that matter, of the many alternative forms of banking organizations on economic growth and development in rural communities and in cities.

The Financial Effects of Branch Banking

I have focused in the foregoing paragraphs on the potential and observed effects of branch banking on the public and on the conduct of economic policy. But what about the effects of organizational structure on banks themselves? Is there evidence, for example, that branch banks are more profitable or less risky or tend to grow faster than single-office banks?

Interestingly enough, only a handful of research studies touch on this important area, and for the most part, their findings are bloodless. There is little or no support for the notion that branching increases bank profits. Indeed, the cost of brick and mortar and of the personnel to run branch offices is more likely to be a drag upon, rather than a stimulus to, higher profits (as noted, for example, by Greenbaum 1967, Horvitz and Shull 1964, Mullineaux 1973, and Olson and Lord 1979). However, Kunreuther, Kidder, and Juncker (1973) found that rapid branch expansion by New Jersey banks in the early 1970s did *not* adversely affect bank profits even though deposit interest rates tended to rise because of enhanced local competition.

There is some evidence that branching reduces risk, as reflected in bank failure statistics, and results, to some extent, in lesser variability in bank earnings. Moreover, a study by Savage (1982) finds little convincing evidence that the expansion of branching impacts negatively on the growth and profitability of *new* banks, though there is some indication that new banks chartered in statewide branching states recorded significantly lower market shares than new banks chartered in unit banking states did. In theory, the effects of branching on bank growth should be *positive* because branch banks average much larger than unit banking institutions do. More research work is definitely needed, however, in this particular segment of the branch banking issue.

Evaluation of Recent Branch Banking Research

Reading through the branch banking literature is, by and large, a frustrating experience for both practitioners and policymakers. There are few solid conclusions, reflecting perhaps not only the complexity of the issues involved but also variations in local economic and social conditions that undoubtedly (but in some largely unknown way) have affected the research outcomes.

The few conclusions that seem reasonably "safe" are that branching lowers the risk of individual bank failure and results in improved (lower) ratios of population to banking offices and of banking offices per square mile of market area. A wider array of financial services is available through branching organizations, though this effect may be due to bank size as much as or more than it is to branch organization. Operating costs are probably higher, but so are service fees, on average. Some loan rates, especially those attached to small business, consumer installment, and real estate loans, seem to be lower and credit availability in general appears to increase with branching. These gains may be offset in some communities, however, by a transfer of local financial capital through branch banking systems into larger cities. Branching does not appear to significantly raise or lower bank profits but does result in reduced risk and increased statewide and metropolitan area concentration. Whether these changes result in reduced competition, however, remains in doubt. In general, research findings in this field are severely constrained by the severe limitations of existing research methods. A special problem centers on the confounding effects produced by internal factors (such as variations in managerial skills and the quality of other productive resources) and by external factors (such as changes in government policy and the intensity of nonbank financial service competition).

The effects of branch banking on customer convenience and service availability are positive features that promise benefits as interstate branching spreads across the United States. If larger interstate branch banks are able to offer a wider array of financial services with greater convenience, the nation as a whole will presumably benefit. There is, however, little convincing testimony that branching has strong real-sector effects, such as accelerating economic growth and development in the markets it serves. Moreover, the finding in the research literature that branching also contributes to increased concentration of industry resources may be cause for public and regulatory concern. Whereas a more highly concentrated national banking industry may, in the long run, result in greater efficiency in the provision of financial services, it may also result in less responsiveness to the public's abiding interest in an adequate supply of financial services at reasonable cost. However, I cannot help but wonder, given the rapid growth of multiple-office banking over the past three decades, why the concentration of deposits in the nation's handful of multibillion-dollar banks has generally declined rather than risen. This declining trend would seem to suggest that the branching-concentration controversy has been overdrawn.

One obvious gap in existing research literature is its failure to consider the impact of recent technological advances—especially automated teller machines and credit cards equipped with microprocessors ("pocketbook branches")—on the frequency and distribution of bank branches and their competitive implications. Electronic machinery linking the customer directly to the bank's computerized records is now commonplace in shopping centers, retail stores, and other convenient locations. There is evidence that technology of this sort has resulted in substantial economizing in both human and physical resources and, therefore, on the cost of producing financial services, on the number of banks and branches economically feasible in any given market, and on the competitive structure of financial service markets.

A good example is the experimentation of New York's Citibank with in-branch automation where only one or two people, whose chief functions are to supplement machine-delivered services by handling nonroutine customer inquiries and opening new accounts, are needed to operate the branch. This new emphasis on efficient, high-volume service has been studied largely for its impact on unit cost curves, while its full implications for competition and public need remain an open opportunity for serious inquiry.

In summary, as we move increasingly toward interstate banking, there appear to be few concrete fears regarding branching's possible negative effects. At the worst, branching's impact may be regarded as economically neutral—perhaps overwhelmed by much more important determinants of the public's welfare, including industrial mix, the propensity toward saving and capital accumulation, and the level and distribution of incomes and production levels in the economy. And, as Rhoades (1985) observes, interstate banking would not likely bring demonstratable benefits in increased efficiency or enhanced competition, but neither should it generate adverse effects that could not be successfully managed with the effective application of existing laws against anti-competitive mergers and restraint of trade. The controversy over when and where to allow branch banking is by no means "a tempest in a teapot," but the results of three decades and more of serious research suggest that this issue may not be as critical to the pubic welfare as the longevity and depth of the branching controversy would lead us to believe.

References

Anderson, Paul S. 1964. "What Price Branching?" *New England Business Review* (August), pp. 2–8. Federal Reserve Bank of Boston.

Anderson, R. N., John A. Haslem, and John B. Leonard. 1976. "An Empirical Analysis of the Impact of Branching on Demand Deposit Variability." *Journal of Financial and Quantitative Analysis* (September), pp. 455–64.

Barkley, David L., Cindy Mellon, and Glenn T. Potts. 1984. "Effects of Banking Structure on the Allocation of Credit to Nonmetropolitan Communities." *Western Journal of Agricultural Economics*, 9(2):283–92.

Board of Governors of the Federal Reserve System. 1958. "Member Bank Lending to Small Business." *Federal Reserve Bulletin* (April), pp. 393 and 409.

—— 1960. "Banking Concentration and Small Business, 1955–57," Report to the Select Committee on Small Business, House of Representatives. Washington, D.C.

Booth, James R. and Richard L. Smith, II. 1984. "The Impact of the Community Reinvestment Act on Branching Activity of Financial Institutions." *Journal of Bank Research* (Summer), pp. 123–28.

Buynak, Thomas M. 1985. "Interstate Banking: Its Impact on Ohio Banks," *Economic Commentary,* Federal Reserve Bank of Cleveland, September 15, pp. 1–6.

Darnell, Jerome C. 1973. "Banking Structure and Economic Growth." In *Changing Pennsylvania's Branching Laws: An Economic Analysis.* Federal Reserve Bank of Philadelphia.

Doyle, P., I. Fenwick, and G. P. Savage. 1981. "A Model for Evaluating Branch Location and Performance." *Journal of Bank Research* (Summer), 12:90–95.

Edwards, Franklin R. 1965. "The Banking Competition Controversy." *National Banking Review* (September), 3:1–34.

Eisenbeis, Robert A. 1975. "The Allocative Effects of Branch Banking Restrictions on Business Loan Markets." *Journal of Bank Research* (Spring).

Federal Reserve Bank of Chicago. 1970. *Midwest Banking in the Sixties: A Decade of Growth and Change.* Chicago, Illinois.

Fischer, Gerald C. 1968. *American Banking Structure.* New York: Columbia University Press.

Frodin, Joanna H. 1982. "Electronics: The Key to Breaking the Interstate Banking Barriers." *Business Review* (September-October), pp. 3–11. Federal Reserve Bank of Philadelphia.

Gilbert, Gary G. and William A. Longbrake. 1974a. "The Effects of Branching by Financial Institutions on Competition, Productive Efficiency, and Stability: An Examination of the Evidence." *Journal of Bank Research,* part 1 (Spring).

—— 1974b. "The Effects of Branching by Financial Institutions on Competition, Productive Efficiency, and Stability: An Examination of the Evidence." *Journal of Bank Research,* part 2 (Summer).

Greenbaum, Stuart I. 1967. "A Study of Bank Costs." *National Banking Review* (June), 4:415–34.

Guttentag, Jack M. and Edward S. Herman. 1967. "Banking Structure and Performance." *The Bulletin* (February), nos. 41–43. Institute of Finance, New York University.

Horvitz, Paul M. 1958. *Concentration and Competition in New England Banking,* Research Study no. 2, Federal Reserve Bank of Boston.

Horvitz, Paul M. and Bernard Shull. 1964. "The Impact of Branch Banking on Bank Performance." *National Banking Review* (December), 2:143–88.

Jacobs, Donald P. 1965. "The Interaction Effects of Restrictions on Branching and Other Bank Regulations." *Journal of Finance* (May). pp. 332–48.

Kidder, Karen. 1971. "Bank Expansion in New York State: The 1971 Statewide Branching Law." *Monthly Review* (November), pp. 266–71. Federal Reserve Bank of New York.

Kohn, Ernest. 1964. *Branch Banking, Bank Mergers and the Public Interest.* New York State Banking Department.

Kohn, Ernest and Carmen J. Carlo. 1969. *The Competitive Impact of New Branches.* New York State Banking Department.

Kohn, Ernest, Carmen J. Carlo, and Bernard Kaye. 1973. *Meeting Local Credit Needs.* New York State Banking Department.

Kreps, Clifton H. Jr., and Richard F. Wacht. 1970. "State Banking Structure and Economic Growth in the Southeast: A Comparison of Three States and the Region." *Southern Journal of Business,* 5(3):11–20.

Kunreuther, Judith Berry, Karen Kidder, and George Juncker. 1973. "Competition and the Changing Banking Structure in New Jersey." *Monthly Review* (August), pp. 203–10. Federal Reserve Bank of New York.

Lauch, Louis H. and Neil B. Murphy. 1970. "A Test of the Impact of Branching on Deposit Variability." *Journal of Financial and Quantitative Analysis* (September), 5:323–27.

McCall, Alan S. and John T. Lane. 1980. "Multi-Office Banking and the Safety and Soundness of Commercial Banks." *Journal of Bank Research* (Summer), 11:87–94.

McCall, Alan S. and Donald J. Savage. 1980. "Branching Policy: The Options," *Journal of Bank Research,* (Summer), 7:122–126.

Mote, Larry R. 1974. "The Perennial Issue: Branch Banking." *Business Conditions* (February), pp. 3–23.

Motter, David C. and Deane Carson. 1964. "Bank Entry and the Public Interest: A Case Study." *National Banking Review* (June), 1:469–512.

Mullineaux, Donald J. 1973. "Branch Versus Unit Banking: An Analysis of Relative Costs." In *Changing Pennsylvania's Branching Laws: An Economic Analysis.* Federal Reserve Bank of Philadelphia.

Nelson, Richard W. 1985. "Branching, Scale Economies, and Banking Costs." *Journal of Banking and Finance,* 9:177–91.

Oldfield, George S. and Ronald D. Watson, 1973. "Pennsylvania Banking Structure. In *Changing Pennsylvania's Branching Laws: An Economic Analysis.* Federal Reserve Bank of Philadelphia, December.

Olsen, Lola M. and J. Dennis Lord. 1979. "Market Area Characteristics and Branch Bank Performance." *Journal of Bank Research* (Summer), 10:102–10.

Powers, John A. 1969. "Branch Versus Unit Banking: Bank Output and Cost Economies." *Southern Economic Journal* (October), 36:153–64.

Rhoades, Stephen A. and Donald T. Savage. 1981. "The Relative Performance of Bank Holding Companies and Branch Banking Systems." *Journal of Economics and Business* (Winter), 33(2):132–41.

Rhoades, Stephen A. 1985. "Interstate Banking and Product Line Expansion: Implications from Available Evidence," *Loyola of Los Angeles Law Review,* 18(4):1115–1164.

Savage, Donald. 1982. "Branch Banking Laws, Deposits, Market Share and Profitability of New Banks." *Journal of Bank Research* (Winter), 12:200–6.

Schweiger, Irving and John S. McGee. 1961. "Chicago Banking." *Journal of Business* (July), 34:203–366.

Scott, William and Peter S. Rose. 1977. "The Bank Failure Problem Re-examined." *MSU Business Topics* (Winter), pp. 5-10.

Seaver, William L. and Donald R. Fraser, 1979. "Branch Banking and the Availability of Banking Services in Metropolitan Areas." *Journal of Financial and Quantitative Analysis* (March), 14(1):153–60.

——1984. "Branch Banking and the Availability of Banking Offices in Nonmetropolitan Areas." *Atlanta Economic Journal,* pp. 72–78.

Stigler, George. 1964. "A Theory of Oligopoly,." *Journal of Political Economy* (February), pp. 44–61.

Subcommittee on Financial Institutions. 1976. *Compendium of Issues Relating to Branching by Financial Institutions.* Committee on Banking Housing and Urban Affairs, U.S. Senate, 94th Cong., 2nd Sess., October.

Wacht, Richard F. 1968. "Branch Banking and Risk." *Journal of Financial and Quantitative Analysis* (March), 3:97–107.

White, Lawrence J. 1976. "Price Regulation and Quality Rivalry in a Profit-Maximizing Model: The Case of Bank Branching." *Journal of Money, Credit and Banking* (February), pp. 97–106.

8.

Multibank Holding-Company Organizations

TWO MAJOR structural changes have revolutionized the American banking industry in the period since World War II. One is the spread of branch banking; the other is the rise and dominance of the bank holding company. Bank holding companies are simply corporations that own stock in one or more commercial banks. In many cases the stockholding corporation simply maintains an equity (ownership) interest in a bank or group of banks as a pure investment—to earn a suitable rate of return on a relatively low-risk venture. In such instances the holding company is little more than a loose confederation of otherwise independent banks. At the other extreme, the holding company may operate as a substitute for branch banking, particularly in states where branching is prohibited or severely restricted. In this instance the holding corporation and its affiliated banks represent a highly centralized organizational unit in which the company sets portfolio, personnel, and pricing policies for the banks it controls. In between these two extremes are literally hundreds of partly centralized, partly decentralized banking organizations that dot the American land-scape and qualify for regulatory purposes as bank holding companies.

Many advantages are claimed for this uniquely American form of banking organization. It allegedly permits banks to enter finan-cial service markets that normally would be closed to them or be very difficult to enter, including the interstate market. It supposedly leads to a more efficient allocation of economic and financial resources within the banking industry. By welding together diverse units into one large organization certain economies of operation may be achieved—for example, through joint advertising and personnel pro-grams or through centralized investment and tax planning. There may be effective financial economies in that larger banking organizations generally have easier access to the capital market and can sell their securities at lower cost.

To opponents of this century-old form of "group banking" these alleged advantages are either illusory or outweighed by serious disadvantages. They argue that holding companies result in greater concentration within the industry and, therefore, reduce competition and charge higher prices for banking services. Moreover, it is argued, affiliated banks are less responsive to local credit needs than the in-dependent, locally owned and operated commercial bank is. These organizations are allegedly more prone to risk taking and therefore threaten the safety of their affiliated banks and the safety of surrounding institutions.

Whether worthy of praise or deserving of condemnation, bank holding companies have come to dominate the industry as meas-ured by the proportion of banking assets and deposits held by their affiliated institutions. In 1984, for example, holding-company affiliates held more than four-fifths of all U.S. bank assets and operated about half of all full-service bank offices. In all probability their peak growth has passed, largely because holding companies have been so successful at acquiring many of the largest, most rapidly growing, and most profitable banks in the nation. The future of the holding-company movement will depend, more crucially than in the past, on the possible efficiencies that greater size can bring to a banking organization, on the ability of these organizations to attract the best managerial talent available, and on the largess of Congress and the federal regulatory authorities in opening up new financial service lines for them to enter.

Brief History of the Bank Holding Company
in the United States

THE EARLY YEARS

Holding companies began to acquire banks during the first decade of this century. As Fischer (1961) notes, most acquisitions in the early years of the movement centered on the nation's midsection, particularly in states like Minnesota, where branching was prohibited or restricted. The original source of this organizational form was undoubtedly chain banking organizations where one individual or a small group of individuals owned several banks and wanted to create a formal network to expand lending limits, permit easier transfer of funds, open new markets, and reduce overall risk. Later the tax advantages of incorporation became a significant motivating factor in the development of bank holding companies.

The 1920s brought a dramatic acceleration in the growth of the bank holding-company movement. In part, it was a response to the conviction of many bankers and regulatory authorities that the United States was "overbanked." Close to 30,000 banks populated the industry in 1920—many far too small to be operated efficiently and unable to withstand severe economic problems. Unfortunately, in the two decades following World War I, severe economic pressures plagued rural America. Farms and ranches across the nation had geared up their production of crops, meat, and dairy products to answer wartime demands only to watch postwar agricultural prices decline sharply. The market price of farm and ranch land and equipment, often heavily mortgaged, also declined drastically, exposing farmers and ranchers to the threat of foreclosure and unemployment. The rural decline contributed to a massive exodus of people and businesses to the cities—a transition made possible by significant improvements in transportation and communication.

In the wake of these economic pressures many small banks in rural communities became targets for corporate takeovers. Banks threatened with failure readily sold out to holding companies or to branch banks centered in the larger cities. Other, predominantly small, banks used the holding-company form to bind themselves together in what were thought to be more efficient and more stable organizations to withstand competition or acquisition and resist the ravages of a declining agricultural market. Further supporting the expansion of bank holding companies was a lack of state and federal regulation and favorable market reception of their stock during the years preceding the great stock market crash of 1929.

The economic debacle of the 1930s dramatically changed the future of the bank holding-company movement. Deposit runs on banks already laboring under severe loan losses, particularly in their mortgage portfolios, resulted in the collapse of thousands of banks. As noted in chapter 3, the failed institutions tended to be smaller banks located in rural areas and small towns, though some large metropolitan bank closings also occurred. The Great Depression both helped and hurt bank holding companies. Some of the banks they acquired failed, but other new banks were added to holding-company systems, many doing so simply to survive. Depressed bank stock prices created additional opportunities for the expansion of those companies able to maintain good financial strength despite the chaos in the economy.

THE BANKING ACT OF 1933

An ominous note was sounded in 1933, however, when Congress moved to bring bank holding companies under federal regulation, following an attempt at such regulation two decades earlier in the Clayton Act. The Banking Act of 1933 vested the Federal Reserve Board with authority to supervise bank holding companies and limit their voting power when member banks of the Federal Reserve System were involved.

When the stockholders of a member bank controlled by a holding company met to vote on matters affecting the bank as a whole, the holding company could not vote its stock without Federal Reserve approval. Deposit reserve requirements were imposed, and the banks acquired by the company were subject to Federal Reserve supervision and examination. Finally, both commercial banks and bank holding companies were prohibited from serving as underwriters for private security issues, insulating commercial banking from the risks of trading in corporate securities. Thus, the 1933 law represented the first attempt by the federal government to limit the services and products bank holding companies could offer.

Although designed to promote bank safety and restore

public confidence in commercial banks and other depository institutions, it is clear that much of the banking legislation passed during the 1930s was *punitive*. Congress and the public were looking for scapegoats to blame for the enormous debacle of the Great Depression. One of those scapegoats was stock speculators who, in the public consensus, were responsible for both the stock market crash of October 1929 and the unemployment and economic deflation that followed. Thus, *all* holding companies—bank and nonbank—came under closer public scrutiny. Interestingly enough, however, the Banking Act of 1933 was largely ineffective in regulating bank holding-company expansion, for the law applied principally to member banks, which then, as now, represented a minority of all U.S. commercial banks. Moreover, there were no effective limits on the creation of new companies or on the acquisition of additional banks.

Once the economy recovered in the 1940s and 1950s holding companies began to expand their territory once again. Strong credit demands in the post-World War II economy, led by consumers seeking new automobiles, homes, and appliances, created ample profit opportunities for banking organizations willing to offer new services and adapt to changing customer needs. Deposit growth was also strong, particularly in the developing suburbs around the nation's major cities. Branch banking organizations and holding companies moved to take advantage of the developing urban sprawl through selective acquisitions of bank and nonbank businesses.

THE BANK HOLDING COMPANY ACT OF 1956

Rapid holding-company growth during this period proved to be a mixed blessing because it brought these organizations once again into the limelight of public attention and ultimately public action. Congress reacted to the reemergence of holding-company expansionism by passing the most restrictive legislation to date—the Bank Holding Company Act of 1956. This new law codified several popular antidotes to a number of long-standing public fears: (1) concerns of bankers in states prohibiting or limiting branch banking that holding companies were simply an organizational ruse, designed to circumvent antibranching statutes; (2) public fear that bank concentration was increasing in many states, threatening to eliminate competition and raise prices for crucial banking services; and (3) concern on the part of federal regulators and various trade groups that holding companies would use the financial power of their banks to acquire or coerce nonbank businesses and, thus, become a potent competitive force outside the financial field. There was also the prospect that holding companies, striving for increased growth and profits, would weaken the financial condition of their affiliated banks and thus endanger depositors.

Whether these dangers were real or imagined is, of course, irrelevant because the Bank Holding Company Act *was* passed over strong opposition, though opposing groups managed to limit its coverage and weaken its effectiveness. For example, only holding companies controlling *two or more banks* were subject to the Act's provisions, which required them to register with the Federal Reserve Board, submit periodic reports of their condition, and gain the Board's approval before acquiring more than 5 percent of the shares of another bank. Control of two or more banks was legally *presumed* when a company held 25 percent or more of the banks' voting stock or had the capacity to elect a majority of the banks' directors. Companies that controlled only *one* bank were exempt from federal registration and reporting requirements, as were individuals and partnerships, no matter how many banks they controlled.

Under the so-called Douglas Amendment to the Bank Holding Company Act a registered company could not acquire more than 5 percent of the stock of a bank located outside that company's home state unless state law expressly approved the acquisition. Thus, the prohibitions against interstate branching contained in the McFadden Act (1927) were paralleled by similar restrictions against interstate expansion by bank holding companies. The holding companies had one nominal advantage over branching organizations, however: acquisitions of *nonbank* businesses could take place across state lines unless state law expressly prohibited them.

THE 1966 AMENDMENTS

It was feared by many industry observers that the new law would topple or at least severely restrict the expansion of bank holding companies. There *was* a brief period of retrenchment, eight companies altering or reducing their holdings to escape registration requirements. However, group banking proved to be vital and resilient during the decade of the 1960s. By middecade just over 8 percent of all U.S. bank deposits and almost 7 percent of the nation's banking offices were controlled by 53 registered holding companies. At this point Congress intervened again by passing a series of amendments in 1966 that actually *aided* future holding-company expansion.

For example, whereas the new amendments to the Bank Holding Company Act explicitly recognized the right of the Justice Department to bring suit in federal court when an anticompetitive holding-company acquisition was proposed, Justice was generally required to sue no later than 30 days following the Federal Reserve's approval of the proposed acquisition. Voting permits were no longer required for companies controlling member banks as specified in the Banking Act of 1933. Affiliated banks were allowed to engage in interbank lending to other affiliates on the same basis as loans made between downstream and upstream correspondent institutions. Federal tax penalties on holding companies submitting consolidated income tax returns were repealed. Perhaps the most significant victory for the holding-company movement in this new legislation was its failure to bring *one-bank* companies under the same registration requirements as companies controlling two or more banks.

THE 1970 AMENDMENTS

The one-bank company loophole left open by the 1966 amendments to the Bank Holding Company Act proved to be a broad avenue through which scores of both small and large banking organizations marched toward growth and expansion in the late 1960s. Major money center banks, in particular, began to establish one-bank holding-company organizations to enter new fields, mostly but not exclusively in the financial services area. There was evidence of one-bank companies controlling meat packing plants, educational institutions, retail merchandisers, and manufacturing outlets. By 1970 the number of one-bank holding companies believed to exist had climbed well over a thousand, controlling an estimated one third of all insured bank deposits. Congressional fears of a complete breakdown of the traditional walls separating commercial banking from other sectors of the economy prompted passage of a new series of amendments to the Bank Holding Company Act in December 1970.

The new amendments (and subsequent Federal Reserve interpretation of them) proved to be highly restrictive as far as proponents of the bank holding-company movement were concerned. Both corporations and partnerships controlling even one bank were now required to register with the Federal Reserve Board, submit periodic reports of their financial condition, and gain Board approval before proceeding with any further bank or nonbank business acquisitions.

The most restrictive of the new amendments proved to be those dealing with permissible nonbank business activities. The 1970 law imposed two tests on any such acquisitions: (1) the nonbank businesses acquired or begun *de novo* must be "so closely related to banking or managing or controlling banks as to be a proper incident thereto," and (2) the proposed nonbank acquisition must "reasonably be expected to produce benefits to the public. . . that outweigh possible adverse effects." The interpretation of key phrases—"closely related to banking" and "benefits to the public"—were left to the Federal Reserve Board.

STATE REGULATION OF BANK HOLDING-COMPANY EXPANSION

Like the McFadden Act three decades before, the Bank Holding Company Act reserved to the states the power to control bank and nonbank acquisitions within each state's borders. Individual states could outlaw holding-company activity or permit it to the degree that they chose. Section 3(d) of the Bank Holding Company Act requires express state approval before out-of-state companies can cross a state's borders. Under Section 3(b) of the law any proposed acquisition of a state-chartered bank requires the Federal Reserve Board to notify the banking commission of the state involved, permitting state authorities to respond with recommendations within 30 days. If the state opposes the transaction, a federal hearing must be convened.

By the mid-1970s some 35 states had moved to take advantage of their reserved powers to limit, prohibit, supervise, or at least officially monitor bank holding-company activity within their borders (as noted by Rose and Fraser (1974). For example, the states of Arkansas, Georgia, Indiana, Illinois, Kansas, Louisiana, Nebraska, Oklahoma, and Pennsylvania passed legislation outlawing multibank holding companies, though one-bank companies were permitted. A few states—most notably Iowa, New Jersey, and New Hampshire—

acted to limit the overall size of bank holding-company organizations within their borders. For example, New Hampshire established a maximum of statewide deposits under one holding company's control at 20 percent. Some states—for example, Connecticut, Florida, Massachusetts, New York, and South Carolina—demanded their right to approve bank or nonbank acquisitions before they occurred. Many of these state restrictions arose out of fear that state banking structure was now being dictated in Washington through Federal Reserve holding-company decisions. By invoking their reserved powers under the Bank Holding Company Act, the states could exercise at least some measure of control over the future makeup of their banking industry.

The regulatory stance of several states in the late 1970s and early 1980s changed, however, from a restrictive posture to one of positive encouragement of holding-company expansion. By the end of 1985, for example, 42 states permitted multibank holding companies and 7 of the remaining 8 states allowed multibank company activity with restrictions (such as limits on geographic expansion or on the percentage of statewide deposits that could be controlled). While the reasons for this switch in regulatory philosophy varied from state to state, economic factors—especially the desire to encourage local development and create jobs—and anticipation of federal legislation to permit some form of interstate branching seemed to lie at the heart of the changes. In South Dakota, for example, out-of-state companies were allowed to acquire or charter new banks and offer insurance services and thus were provided a loophole around federal restrictions. Similarly, Delaware passed an Economic Development Act that encouraged out-of-state entry by banking organizations. Though piecemeal and probably inefficient from a macroeconomic point of view, these state actions will probably hasten the onset of nationwide retail banking.

Federal Reserve Policies and Decisions
Affecting Holding Companies

The Federal Reserve Board was granted *wide* latitude in approving or denying bank holding-company formation and expansion under the terms of the Bank Holding Act. Only a few general guidelines for the Board were specified in the Act. For example, in considering an application to form a bank holding company or for an existing holding company to acquire a new bank, the law requires the Board to consider:

1. the financial history and financial condition of the holding company and the bank or banks to be acquired.
2. the earnings prospects of the acquired banks and of the holding company
3. the character and quality of management of both the bank(s) and the holding company (including evidence bearing on compliance with banking and consumer credit laws and regulations)
4. the convenience and needs of the public in the relevant banking markets served
5. the preservation of competition in the relevant market areas and in the industry as a whole

If a proposed acquisition has an adverse impact on any of these factors, it must be denied unless offsetting positive effects can be found.

Limited research evidence shows that the Board has not given equal weight to all of the foregoing factors in its decisions. For example, the convenience and needs (public benefits) test does not appear to have received high priority, reflecting some skepticism on the Board's part that holding-company takeovers really lead to new, better quality, or more convenient services, lower prices, or other significant public benefits. Rather, decisions by the Board to approve or deny holding-company acquisitions and formations appear to have stressed the following two factors: (1) the impact of the proposed transaction on either actual or potential *competition* in the relevant market area as reflected in concentration ratios, the behavior of existing firms, the relative size(s) of the business(es) to be acquired, market shares, and the likelihood of entry by outside firms and (2) the *financial condition* of acquiring and acquired institutions. For example, the Board has preferred not to approve a proposed acquisition if there is a significant possibility that a strong potential competitor in the relevant market or markets to be served would be eliminated. Levels of concentration (measured normally by one-, two-, and three-bank concentration ratios or the Herfindahl-Hirschmann index) that appear to be too high or where an unfavorable trend toward greater market concentration is evident are frequently used as the basis for Fed denial of a proposed acquisition. In these cases applications for foothold acquisitions of small banks on the market fringe or *de novo* entry are more likely to win Federal Reserve approval. Also, where approval of a holding-company application would reduce the likelihood that new holding companies would be formed, denial is more likely. Thus, acquisition of a bank having significant size (perhaps $500 million or more in assets) may be denied on grounds that such an institution could form its own holding company and offer significant future competition to the applicant company.

The *financing* of a proposed transaction is generally examined carefully by the Board, especially where large amounts of debt are involved. The Board has argued that, where the level of acquisition debt is high, this endangers future prospects for significant capital growth (and, therefore, increases failure risk) in the holding-company organization. Other financial factors triggering Board denials of holding-company transactions have centered mainly on management fees (such as for consulting or portfolio management) charged acquired firms by the holding company. Where these are excessive, they reduce the net earnings available to affiliated firms to strengthen their capital. Finally, where the proposed transaction would generate excessive premiums for stockholders of the acquired firm, the Board has, on occasion, declined to approve the proposed acquisition. In general, the Federal Reserve expects a holding company to be a source of financial strength for its banks rather than a drain on their vital resources.

Recent Bank Acquisitions—
Characteristics and Growth

Bank holding-company growth has been rapid over the past two decades and has brought these organizations to a dominating position in the industry. Yet, only a handful of studies have looked closely at the types of banks acquired by holding companies and the characteristics of the markets these organizations enter. Still, those studies have yielded some interesting and, at times, unexpected results.

For example, a 1976 study by Peter S. Rose examines the geographic pattern of holding-company acquisitions, the characteristics of acquiring companies, and the features of markets entered by these organizations, 1957–1974. As expected, a majority (60 percent) of holding-company bank acquisitions took place in unit banking states; another 30 percent occurred in limited branching states; and less than 10 percent were consummated in statewide branching states. Moreover, five states—Florida, Missouri, Michigan, Ohio, and Texas—accounted for half (48 to 57 percent) of the bank acquisitions during the years studied. As time passed, Rose found that the average size of holding companies acquiring banks increased, and the mean-size bank acquired rose from just $12 million in 1960 to about $43 million in 1974—substantially larger than the average-size U.S. bank—though the author detected a downward trend in the average size of acquisition targets after 1973 as the Federal Reserve began looking more closely at trends in metropolitan concentration ratios and at potential competition.

Most banks acquired were in SMSAs whose population averaged one million or more and only about one eighth took place in counties of 150,000 population or less. The average population growth rate in targeted markets was 25 to 29 percent, 1970–1974, approximately two times the national norm. Median income levels and proportions of families in upper income strata averaged significantly higher in holding-company-targeted markets than was true of all U.S. metropolitan areas. The author concluded that bank holding companies acquire *not* "typical" or "representative" banks, but those already close to efficient size in rapidly growing, high-income areas. Therefore, holding-company-affiliated banks may display superior performance relative to independent banks simply because they had developed the basis for continuing superior performance *before* they were acquired. Interestingly, there was some evidence that acquired banks possessed "excess" lending capacity with below-average loan-asset ratios, presenting the acquiring companies with opportunities for increasing earnings and attracting new deposits through more aggressive credit management policies.

In 1980 J. T. Rose made a significant contribution to our knowledge of the nature of holding-company acquisitions by examining the *de novo* banks started by holding-company organizations between 1968 and 1977. He found that *de novo* charters secured by holding companies represented about 10 percent of all newly chartered U.S. banks in the most recent year. About two thirds of all *de novo* affiliated banks were nonmember institutions, seeking to avoid the burden of

Federal Reserve membership, and three-quarters were chartered in markets previously entered by their holding companies, indicating a desire to deepen the company's existing market position. Close to half of all affiliated *de novos* appeared in communities where the companies' head office was situated.

J. T. Rose found no case in which a holding company had obtained a charter in a market where its bid to acquire an existing bank had been turned down, providing little support for the legal doctrine of potential competition. The majority of new markets entered were in metropolitan areas, though a surprising two fifths of holding-company *de novos* took place in rural communities. Affiliated *de novos* tended to occur most frequently in states restricting or prohibiting branching and therefore served as a partial substitute for branch banking.

Although the studies reviewed above imply that holding companies tend to acquire banks with unusual or atypical character-istics, this conclusion was rejected by Curry (1981), who examined 91 SMSA banks in unit and limited branching states that were acquired by holding companies over the 1969-72 period. The acquired banks were compared with more than a thousand independent institutions in the same communities in terms of risk orientation, pricing behavior, expenses, and profitability with regression analysis applied to key fi-nancial ratios one year before acquisition. Curry found that none of the acquired banks possessed unique preacquisition operating charac-teristics. As he states: "for the most part, banks acquired by these organizations are typical commercial banks" (p. 89). This finding im-plies that *any* smaller sized independent bank might well serve as a "foothold" entry vehicle for bank holding companies seeking to pen-etrate a new urban market.

The apparent conflict in the conclusions of recent studies suggests the need for further inquiry into exactly how bank holding companies select their acquisition targets. Economic and financial theory suggest that any holding-company acquisition must be regarded as a long-term investment designed to achieve a targeted long-run rate of return at an acceptable level of risk. It seems reasonable to argue that each acquisition will be carefully chosen in terms of its expected return and marginal contribution to overall portfolio risk. I turn now to examine this risk-return theory of what motivates bank holding companies to select particular banks for acquisition.

Motivations for Bank Acquisitions

The reasons behind the continuing acquisition of banks by holding-company organizations remain a subject of controversy and continuing research. From a theoretical vantage point such acquisitions can be viewed as a *capital investment*, which will have a long-term impact on the organization's cash inflows and outflows and the returns to holding-company shareholders. If we assume, as is conventional in finance theory, that a bank acquisition is motivated principally be a desire to maximize the wealth of holding-company shareholders, the company's ultimate target becomes the *per-share price* of its stock in the financial marketplace. The company's stock price will rise if the acquisition of a bank increases the company's expected cash flows, or reduces the perceived level of risk attached to those cash flows, or both.

The relationship between the per-share market value of holding-company stock (P_s), the expected dividends (D) flowing to company shareholders in future periods, and the required yield to equity shareholders (r), given the company's perceived level of risk, is usually written in the following form:

$$(8.1) \quad \text{Stock Price } (P_s) = \frac{\text{Sum of Anticipated Dividend Flows Through the Holding Company}}{\text{Discount Factor Measuring the Required Yield on Stockholders' Equity Capital for Specified Degree of Risk}} = \sum_{t=1}^{\infty} \frac{D_t}{(1+r)^t}$$

This equation defines the *opportunity cost* of any holding-company acquisition. In perfectly efficient and competitive financial markets each business acquired will sell for no less than the seller's opportunity cost—that is, the risk-and time-preference-adjusted present value of the expected stream of future earnings generated by the business as viewed by the seller. The stockholders of the individual bank (or nonbank subsidiary) to be acquired will determine whether or not to sell out to a holding company on the basis of potential optimization of the acquired firm's value as represented by its expected stream of future earnings. An acquisition will be consummated provided the holding company's perception of the acquired firm's present value (i.e., the capitalized value of its expected earnings stream) is at least equal to or greater than the present value of the acquired firm as viewed by its shareholders (i.e., the seller's opportunity cost).

To what extent does the foregoing framework help to explain the practical motivations behind the rapid expansion of bank holding companies over the past several decades? Clearly, this simplistic model suggests that we must consider acquisition motivations that have to do with expanding dividend flows to acquired and acquiring banking organizations, or with decreasing the degree of risk surrounding those flows, or both. Thus, factors leading to expected reductions in operating costs, increases in operating revenue, or decreases in the variability of net cash flows should act as catalysts for holding-company acquisitions.

How is it possible for a holding-company organization to reduce operating or other costs through acquisition? An individual bank may capture economies of scale in a single plant simply through internal growth. However, the acquisition of banks by a holding company literally multiplies plants through which services are produced and does not necessarily reduce the production costs of each separate plant. Are there organization-wide (multiplant) economies of scale in bank holding-company organizations?

One possible source of these economies is through centralization and consolidation of common functions or services offered by more than one bank within the organization. For example, many holding companies have instituted centralized hiring and training of personnel to avoid duplication of human resource departments. Others have centralized advertising programs that avoid hiring duplicate communications and marketing experts and promote a common advertising theme for all affiliated firms. Data processing and trust services also have been centralized for greater efficiency by some companies. These are services that tend to be profitable only in high volume, such that a small or medium-size bank providing trust or data-processing services frequently has difficulty reaching the break-even point for these services, though the group banking organization as a whole may have little difficulty in doing so, as noted by Austin (1973), P.S. Rose (1974), and Rose and Scott (1979). Thus, potential savings in production costs can arise from services supplied internally at a price equal to their marginal cost.

There may also be cost savings in the hiring of scarce managerial talent and in attracting financial capital by combining smaller units into a larger group-banking organization. Managerial skills are limited in extent, but with superior financial resources and wider market contacts, holding companies may be able to identify and locate such talent less expensively and then supply additional training at lower cost through centralized educational facilities. For example, the largest holding companies in the Midwest actively recruit graduates on college campuses throughout the nation. Frequently, career-oriented college graduates will prefer landing a job with a holding company as opposed to a single bank (even at a lower initial salary) owing to the possibility of being promoted to positions of responsibility more rapidly within a larger organization. In contrast, smaller banking organizations with limited access to the market for new managerial talent may avoid paying the *prospective costs* of disposing of incompetent or aging management and, thus, limit their opportunities for profitable expansion, as noted by Jessup (1974) and P.S. Rose (1974).

In addition to possible cost savings from attracting top-flight management, there may be relative cost savings to a holding company in its efforts to attract *financial capital*. The money and capital markets may be more receptive to new issues of stocks, bonds, and notes by holding-company organizations, owing to their larger average size and perceived advantage in strength of resources and lower overall risk. The result is reduced borrowing and equity capital costs that help to increase both net earnings and stockholder returns.

Several possibilities for reducing operating and financing costs through forming a bank holding company and acquiring affiliated businesses were explored above. However, the holding company can also increase its value in the financial marketplace through actions that increase expected revenues (cash flow). For example, a group-banking organization may be able to develop new services (and, therefore, new sources of revenue) more easily and with greater capacity to absorb product development risk than any single banking corporation can. Moreover, it may be easier for a holding company to penetrate new geographic markets such as through the chartering of new banks. Federal and state authorities may be more inclined to approve a new bank charter that is backed by the resources and expertise of a holding-company organization than they would a charter application from a new and untried group of banking entrepreneurs. With higher expected revenues flowing from the development of new services and the penetration of new markets, stockholder earnings should grow more rapidly, *ceteris paribus,* and the company's stock value in the market will rise, increasing shareholder wealth.

Note, however, that the ability of holding companies to charter new banks more easily may not be a significant *practical* advantage. It may be less expensive, for example, to grow via merger with existing banks operating in distant markets than through *de novo* expansion into those same markets. A substantial body of research in corporate finance finds, however, little or no net financial gain via the merger route (for example, Kelly 1967, Gort and Hogarty 1970, Reid 1968, and Lev and Mandelker 1971). Moreover, it may be that in perfectly efficient capital markets a bank targeted for holding-company acquisition will carry a price that fully reflects its expected dividend flows; that is, there are no lasting "bargains" in acquisitions, for no acquisition target will be persistently underpriced.

Can holding-company stockholders benefit from acquisitions through reduction of *risk?* How could a holding company with bank affiliates appear less risky to investors in the money and capital markets? The answer usually given to that question centers on the possibilities for *diversification* within the organization. Holding companies can diversify *geographically* across different markets and by *product line,* offering products with different demand characteristics than their traditional product lines. Either approach to diversification carries the potential for reducing the variability over time of the company's aggregate cash flow and net earnings. If capital market investors perceive less variability in company earnings and assign the holding company's debt and stock offerings a lower risk premium as a result, then the firm should be able to raise financial capital in greater quantity and at lower cost.

As Lewellen (1971) notes, true diversification increases a corporations's borrowing capacity and permits greater use of financial leverage in order to expand stockholder earnings. Note, however, that diversification through holding-company acquisitions is an expensive vehicle for supplying capital, especially when the costs of assimilating new affiliates and the typical premiums paid to shareholders of holding-company-acquired firms in recent years are considered. Moreover, an acquisitions program aimed exclusively at diversification is of questionable social value because capital market investors can achieve diversification benefits through their own purchases of the stock of prospective affiliates, as Evans and Archer (1968) and Westerfield (1970) point out.

To summarize the foregoing analysis, stockholders of a bank or nonbank firm will approve the sale of their stock to a holding company only if the present value of the stockholders' share of the future earnings stream of the holding company (capitalized at a rate that reflects the shareholders' time preference and degree of uncertainty regarding future earnings) exceeds the discounted earnings stream expected from holding stock in the bank as an independent organization. On the holding-company side, as Varvel (1975) observes, if the company's shareholders conclude that acquisition of a bank or nonbank subsidiary will increase the capitalized value of the whole organization, an offer will be made to acquire the proposed subsidiary, rational behavior being assumed.

Holding-company acquisitions occur when *both* the stockholders of proposed bank or nonbank affiliates and holding-company shareholders perceive *differences* between the risk-adjusted present values of their respective organizations. Each organization will have an incentive to bargain when it perceives a possible increase in the net wealth position of its shareholders. The price ultimately settled on for the acquired firm's stock will depend on competitive forces in the market for bank equity securities, the perceived disparity in the capitalized values of acquiring and acquired firms, and the comparative bargaining power of acquiring and acquired firms.

In concluding this discussion of acquisition theory, I should note that recent research has identified reasons other than risk-return considerations for holding-company acquisitions of both bank and nonbank firms. For example, acquisitions may be motivated by expected changes in *market share*. Moyer and Sussna (1973) have put forward a "competitive deposit maximization" hypothesis suggesting that multibank holding companies react to the growth of competing banking groups by acquiring those banks that protect their relative share of deposits in a given state. Piper (1971), on the other hand, suggests that achieving greater *absolute size* in assets, deposits, or lending capacity may be a key acquisitions-motivating factor. And the Alhadeffs (1955) point to an *imitation* factor where many banking organizations follow a lead group of initiating holding companies, imitating their acquisitions purely as a defensive reaction.

Possible Public Benefits
from Holding-Company Acquisitions

While there may be some truth in all of the foregoing explanations for bank holding-company acquisitions, they leave untouched a critical issue: does the *public* benefit from these acquisitions? Over the years a number of public benefits have been claimed by holding-company proponents. I present these alleged benefits below without critical comment, and then in the section that follows I evaluate the available evidence for and against them.

Greater Public Convenience. Allegedly because holding companies give rise to larger and more aggressively managed banking organizations, the public benefits in terms of more and better quality banking services available from more convenient locations.

Increased Competition. Because of their greater average size, superior management, and easier access to capital, holding-company-affiliated banks are aggressive competitors. Morever, the company can usually enter several different markets, raising the level of competition in most markets it enters and leading to more efficient production of financial services at lower prices without excess profits.

Improved Efficiency. By increasing their affiliated banks' opportunity for growth, holding companies allow their banks to achieve more fully the benefits of economies of scale. When an affiliated bank reaches a more efficient size (scale) of operations it can pass those cost savings along to its customers in the form of lower prices for financial services.

Greater Financial Strength. The larger average size and greater name identification of a bank holding-company organization enables it to more easily tap the money and capital markets for funds. Moreover, through the ability of holding companies to expand into more geographically and economically diverse banking markets, as well as to offer new products through nonbank businesses, the aggregate risk level of the whole banking organization can be reduced, minimizing the need for additional equity capital and enabling the company to borrow funds at lower cost. Either way, through easier access to capital, lower cost capital, or through reduced risk, holding-company organizations possess greater financial strength, which makes them less prone to failure and more able to innovate in offering new services to the public.

Stronger Management. Many small banks face serious management succession problems owing to aging management and limited funds to hire competent new management. Through their greater average size, financial strength, and market contacts, bank holding companies have access to superior management talent and the capability of centralizing recruitment, employee training, and personnel management for greater efficiency and greater responsiveness to public demands for more and better quality services.

Research Evidence on the Effects of Bank Acquisitions

After nearly two decades of research on bank holding companies, what can we make of such claims? What are the benefits and costs of holding-company acquisitions of commercial banks? I consider the evidence in the light of three different impacts: (1) on the banks acquired, (2) on the public, and (3) on the holding companies themselves.

IMPACT ON THE BANKS ACQUIRED

Bank Profitability. One of the most enduring controversies in the bank holding-company field is whether the acquisition of a bank by a holding company will improve the bank's profitability. In theory, if holding-company acquisitions result in a lessening of competition, allow increased employment of financial leverage owing to expanded borrowing capacity, or generate economies of scale in production costs, the profitability of holding-company controlled banks will tend to be greater than is true of unaffiliated banks. Moreover, if holding companies are able to achieve true diversification, the resulting decrease in cash flow variability may enable them to pursue more risky, but higher yielding loans and investments.

There is considerable evidence that, on average, affiliated banks do achieve higher ratios of revenue to assets, owing in part, to a shift of assets from more liquid investments in cash and government securities to less liquid and more risky loans and securities (especially commercial, real estate, and consumer loans and municipals). But do these higher revenues filter down into net additions to capital and stockholder dividends? The preponderance of the evidence suggests the answer is *negative*. There are few, if any, differences in net profitability between independent and affiliated institutions, though a large-scale comparison by Rhoades and Savage (1981) found affiliates less profitable (in terms of ROA) than comparable branch banks. Expenses tend to rise significantly following affiliation with a holding company (as noted, for example, by Eisemann 1976, Lawrence 1967, Talley 1971, and Piper 1971), and this offsets the revenue gains. Moreover, even when differences between affiliated and independent bank profitability are compared over longer time frames (such as the six-year span examined by Hobson, Master, and Severiens 1979), a significant profitability edge for either affiliates or independent banks does not generally appear.

However, these findings are not universally shared by all holding-company studies. For example, both Mayne (1977) and Mingo (1975, 1976) find evidence of greater profitability among affiliates, at least in the late 1960s and early 1970s. Mingo concludes that capital-asset ratios are lower at affiliated banks, and this tends to lever up their net earnings to capital, leading to the conclusion that "holding companies are willing to pay premiums for banks, because they expect to raise asset-capital . . . ratios after the takeover" (1975, p. 192). The implication seems clear: holding-company affiliation *can* lead to higher individual bank profitability, but only at the expense of greater risk of insolvency for the individual acquired bank.

Operating Efficiency. Earlier in this chapter I offered several reasons why a holding company may be able to increase its efficiency level relative to a comparable group of independent banks. The ability of a holding-company organization to centralize certain services and operations (such as hiring and training, data processing, advertising, and investment portfolio management) offers the prospect of increased output from the same mix of inputs. It is not clear, however, that gains in operating efficiency for the whole banking organization filter down to the individual banks belonging to that organization. For example, the company may assess stiff charges against its affiliates for such services as data processing and portfolio management, raising their operating costs. Alternatively, because most holding-company organizations appear to be relatively loose confederations of bank and nonbank businesses, there may be few, if any, economies in operating costs either at the macro level of the entire organization or at the micro level represented by each affiliate.

One measure of individual bank operating efficiency commonly used in holding-company studies is the ratio of total operating expenses to total assets. This ratio measures the productivity of dollars expended to augment the firm's total assets, which are a measure of total resources under management control. Generally research studies (in particular Lawrence 1967) suggest there is little difference between affiliates and independent banks in the proportion of operating expenses to assets, though Rhoades and Savage (1981), in a study of more than 2,500 banking organizations, find that noninterest operating costs are lower for holding companies than for branch systems, and Bell and Murphy (1968) find holding-company acquisitions less costly than *de novo* branching.

Mayne (1977) argues that "those banks which maintain their independent status, resisting the overtures of holding companies, are exceptionally well managed" [p. 39]. This would explain the lack of evidence of significantly greater efficiency at affiliated institutions, because surviving independents may be exceptionally efficient. Indeed, recent work on economies of scale by Kalish and Gilbert (1973), Martell and Hooks (1975), and Drum (1978) suggests that affiliated banks display lower operating efficiency (i.e., higher production cost curves) than otherwise comparable independent banks. Moreover, the independents appear to be more successful at preserving any gains in operating efficiency once they are attained. These results may help to explain, in line with Piper's (1971) findings, why holding companies are often forced to pay excessive prices to acquire new banks. Moreover, Lawrence (1967), in a detailed case study for the Federal Reserve Board, found only limited centralization of function practiced by the majority of holding companies that reduced any potential gains in operating efficiency.

Risk. From a regulatory perspective there has been great concern in recent years over the possible increase in financial risk associated with the spread of holding-company organizations. There are logical arguments on both sides. For example, Lamb (1961) and Eisemann (1976) contend that holding companies should be able to enhance the capital adequacy of the banks they acquire owing to their greater capacity to raise equity capital in the open market with lower marginal cost. Moreover, with increased capital, depositors and other creditors of affiliated banks would be *(ceteris paribus)* better protected against loss and, therefore, more willing to commit funds at risk to the organization at lower cost. If an affiliated bank's capital adequacy is increased, it will have superior flexibility in taking on a higher volume of loans and other risky assets.

This is one side of the coin. The counterargument is that, because of greater georgraphic and product line diversification to reduce risk, holding-company banks may require less equity capital than independent banks do. In essence, this argument contends, a holding-company organization functions as a capital insurance fund—a position that seems consistent with the available evidence. A study by Rhoades and Savage (1981) finds that the coefficient of variation in profit rates is progressively lower for multibank holding companies as they add more banks than it is for comparably diversified branch banks. Thus, poor profits at some affiliated banks may be offset by high profits at other affiliates, resulting in a more stable flow of stockholder dividends and more predictable future growth in equity capital as insurance against future risks.

The direct implication is that multibank holding companies can tolerate *lower* capital ratios among their affiliates than is true of independent banks. This conclusion is consistent with a regression study of New York banks by Jessee and Seelig (1977) that finds *lower* ratios of equity capital to risk assets (primarily loans and investments) at affiliated banks than among independently owned institutions. Corroborating evidence is provided by Heggestad and Mingo (1975), who find bank affiliates holding lower capital ratios and displaying slower capital growth than independent banks, even after differences in asset and liability composition and profitability are held constant. Additional support is provided by Kolb (1981), who observes affiliated and independent banks operating under two different behavioral regimes in the management of their capital, dividends, and operating expenses.

Chase and Mingo (1975) argue that regulation may encourage holding companies to minimize the equity capital positions of their banks relative to their nonbank businesses because capital held by nonbank affiliates can be shifted more easily to other affiliates without severe regulatory constraints.

Another important observation is that holding companies more aggressively manage their affiliates, particularly on the asset side of the balance sheet, attempting to boost net earnings by replacing more liquid, relatively low-risk investments with less liquid and more risky loans. Thus, the gain in either greater access to capital or reduced risk through diversification may be partially, wholly, or more than offset by increased risk in the asset portfolio. As Mingo (1976) contends, affiliated banks tend to display greater tolerance for risk, arising perhaps from the preference functions of their management and stockholders or from a desire to recover as quickly as possible the high acquisition premiums frequently paid out for new affiliates. One observation does seem clear, however—the overall long-run failure rate among affiliated banks has averaged substantially *lower* than for independent banks. Moreover, as noted by Lawrence (1971), bank holding companies have made a "positive contribution to financial stability" by absorbing a number of seriously weak banks across the nation (p. 579).

IMPACT ON THE PUBLIC

The *raison d'être* for any and all regulation of holding companies is to protect the public from unsound banking practices and to promote competition in financial services so that more, better quality, and lower cost services are made available. Moreover, Section 3(c) of the Bank Holding Company Act requires the Federal Reserve Board to examine the "convenience, needs, and welfare" of the public most likely to be affected by a proposed bank or nonbank acquisition. Indeed, each application must pass this *public benefits* test even if a proposed holding-company acquisition does not violate the competition standards of the Clayton Act. Is there concrete evidence of benefits to the public from proposed holding-company acquisitions? Is competition affected?

Competition and Concentration. If holding-company activity encourages banks to be more competitive, reduces the concentration of resources in a few dominating banks, and promotes a spirit of intense rivalry among competing financial institutions, the public will certainly benefit in terms of more and better quality services at the lowest resource cost. Do these positive events really happen in real-world markets?

Most of the literature on holding companies and competition has focused on three issues: (1) How does market concentration change after holding companies enter or increase their presence in a given local market? (2) Does holding-company affiliation affect the market shares of individual banks?·and (3) Does the particular vehicle chosen by a holding company to enter a new market affect the way in which market structure changes? The general conclusion that emerges is that holding-company expansion—either within the same market or into new markets—is at least mildly *procompetitive*. Market concentration often declines, rivalry among existing and new competitors increases, and the market shares of entrenched institutions fall.

For example, J. T. Rose and Savage (1981, 1982) examined *de novo* entry by holding companies into new markets in a selected sample of smaller communities. Market concentration (measured by the Herfindahl index) fell substantially over a three-year period after holding-company entry. Moreover, the more concentrated the local market initially, the more powerful the deconcentrating effect from *de novo* entry. Entry by independent banks had a much smaller deconcentrating impact on a given market, according to the authors.

One qualification that needs to be added, however, is that the vehicle used for holding-company entry seems to influence the competitive outcome. When the acquired bank is very small relative to the whole market (i.e., *foothold entry*), the impact on market concentration will be slight, as observed in studies by Rhoades (1977), Rhoades and Schweitzer (1978), and J. T. Rose (1982). Moreover, most acquired banks studied apparently have not significantly expanded their market shares relative to other banks in the same market, according to a collection of studies by Goldberg (1978), Fraser (1978), J. T. Rose (1982), and Savage (1982).

There is evidence that *rivalry* in holding-company-entered markets—measured by changes in market rankings or turnover among the largest banks—does increase, as observed by Rhoades and Rutz (1982). But the competitive behavior of banks in a given local market appears to be more significantly influenced by a *new* holding company entering from the outside than it is by a holding company already present in the market merely making additional acquisitions to strengthen its entrenched position. Moreover, research studies have been notably unsuccessful at linking holding-company-inspired changes in market concentration, market share, and market rivalry to individual-bank performance, particularly to bank pricing policies and profitability.

Public Convenience and Needs. Does the public benefit from holding-company activity in terms of more convenient banking offices and an expanded array of financial services? The evidence here is not all that encouraging. A study of 2,500 branch and holding-company systems by Rhoades and Savage (1981) found that branch banks provide a significantly larger ratio of banking offices relative to size of market than holding companies do. Moreover, the holding-company service record leaves room for doubt. In most applications for bank acquisitions filed with the Federal Reserve Board the applicant company usually claims that one or more services not currently being offered (or not offered conveniently) in the local market will be supplied if their application is approved. Do the applying companies usually carry through on such promises?

A study by Kolari, Rose, and Riener (1983) reports the results of a national survey of 1131 affiliated U.S. banks with regard to any changes that occurred in service offerings following the banks' takeover by a holding company. Responses received from 154 different holding companies controlling these banks revealed that *few* newly affiliated banks made any changes in their service packages. Most of the service changes that did occur were at medium-size ($10-to-$100-million deposit) banks, and the new services offered were predominantly trust services and revolving charge cards. Large banks generally made few changes because they already offered such a broad menu of services, though a few did add leasing, foreign exchange, and overdraft services. Branch banks were more likely to offer new services following affiliation than unit banks were. In general, however, the authors found that bank size was "more closely associated with the availability of bank services than organizational structure" (p. 31). They recommended that holding-company applications be reviewed periodically and that holding companies update the regulatory authorities on a regular basis about their progress in improving public benefits.

Availability of Credit Services. There is substantial evidence that bank holding companies increase the availability of credit to businesses, consumers, and state and local governments. This may be due to more aggressive management policies and a willingness to accept increased risk at the affiliate level because of the risk-reducing benefits of greater diversification at the holding-company level. Whatever the reasons, acquired banks generally experience a decrease in their holdings of cash and U.S. Government securities relative to their total assets, while commercial and industrial loans, consumer installment loans, and holdings of municipal bonds and notes typically increase as a proportion of total assets following affiliation (as reported, for example, by Lawrence 1967 and Talley 1971). Other credit categories— such as real estate or farm loans—usually are little, if at all, affected by holding-company affiliation.

Rhoades and Savage (1981) found that pure holding-company organizations make *fewer* real estate loans than comparable branch banks do. However, a more recent study by Curry and J. T. Rose (1983) finds a strong boost to local bank lending, especially increased real estate lending, resulting from entry into smaller metropolitan markets by outside holding companies, implying, once again, that such outside entry increases local banking competition.

Prices of Bank Services. Most studies of holding companies find few price effects from affiliation, with the possible exception of service charges on checking accounts. For example, studies by Lawrence (1967), Fraas (1974), Mayne (1977), and Graddy and Kyle (1980) find evidence of *higher* demand deposit service charges following a holding-company takeover. This change may be the result of a shift in deposit mix (for example, between commercial and retail accounts), more careful expensing and cost-plus pricing of checking account services, or a reduction in operating efficiency and the impact of diminished competition (including the strengthening of price leadership in local markets). None of these possible causal factors has yet been explored in sufficient depth to assess its individual or joint importance.

A few studies do find higher loan and thrift deposit rates after a holding company moves in (as discussed by Fraas 1974 and Rose and Scott 1979). However, as many or more research studies find *no* loan or deposit interest rate effects at all. On balance, I must conclude that any price effects— pro or con—from holding-company affiliation are slight. Perhaps Lawrence's (1971) observation that holding companies avoid the aggressive implementation of common pricing schemes out of fear (probably ill founded) of antitrust prosecution suggests a reasonable explanation for the absence of strong price effects.

Safety of Public Funds. Although holding-company bank affiliates do appear to make greater use of financial leverage (as found by Johnson and Meinster 1973 and Mayne 1977, for example), no evidence has yet accumulated that failure rates among affiliates have increased, either over time or relative to nonaffiliated institutions. One potentially ominous result has, however, been offered by Mayne (1980) following an analysis of the cash dividend payout policies of more than 12,000 banks (of which 2,735 were affiliated institutions) over the 1973–1976 period. Bank subsidiaries of holding companies paid higher dividends than the average nonaffiliated bank. This is potentially troublesome (as observed also by Gupta and Walker 1975) because retained earnings, historically, have been the principal source of growth in bank equity capital, providing depositors with protection against loss. Mayne (1980) raises the issue of "whether or not the parent companies are using their control over banking subsidiaries to extract from them payments beyond the level that would normally be considered prudent" (p. 479). She calls for close public monitoring of the dividend policies followed by affiliated banks relative to their estimated capital needs.

IMPACT ON BANK HOLDING-COMPANY
ORGANIZATIONS THEMSELVES

The impact of the expansion of bank holding companies on the companies themselves has not been as thoroughly investigated as the impact of those organizations on the banks they acquire and upon the public has. The few studies in this field have focused principally on the profitability and stock prices of individual companies. A second vein of research looks at the risks borne by these firms and the possible benefits from portfolio and geographic diversification.

A handful of studies have looked at rates of return on equity capital and at the stock values of holding companies after their formation and following their acquisition of additional banks. As Varvel (1975) observes, holding companies seek to optimize the value of each company's earnings stream as reflected in the price of its stock. This strategy may or may not be consistent with the maximization of profits for each affiliate. Thus, studies showing that affiliated banks, on average, are no more profitable than independent banks tell us little or nothing about economic benefits for the entire holding company. For example, the company may achieve cost savings and, at the same time, generate fee income by producing and selling services internally to its affiliates—steps that would increase consolidated company earnings but not necessarily the earnings of individual affiliates. Through diversification, the ability to borrow at lower cost may be enhanced for the whole organization, and scarce capital can be directed internally to its most profitable uses, as pointed out by Frieder and Apilado (1983). The result may be to raise the stock values and profitability of holding-company organizations over those of individual banks that have not elected to form a holding company.

Unfortunately, the available studies conflict dramatically on the alleged financial benefits of forming a bank holding company. For example, Piper (1971), in a detailed study conducted for the Federal Reserve Bank of Boston, finds that holding-company profits do *not* compare favorably with other banking organizations, owing largely to the "excessive" premiums paid to the shareholders of acquired banks to encourage them to exchange their shares. This finding is reinforced by Piper and Weiss (1974, 1976) and by Brewer and Dukes (1976), the latter reporting lower stockholder earnings per share, on average, following the conversion of 35 large banks to the holding-company form without a corresponding reduction in market risk (beta). However, these studies considered only the net operating earnings of the acquired institution and of the holding company separately without examining interactions (i.e., intraorganizational transactions) within the consolidated organization, such as fees paid by affiliates to the company for internally supplied services.

The middle ground of research findings on holding-company profitability is represented by Kohers (1977) and Simpson and Kohers (1979). Both studies are unable to reject the null hypothesis of "no significant differences" in profitability and stockholder wealth between holding-company organizations and comparable independent banks. Kohers' analysis of the market performance, systematic risk, and holding-period yields of 84 banking organizations found superior overall financial performance for independent organizations but no difference in mean levels of performance between holding companies and their nonaffiliated counterparts. Simpson and Kohers' study of stockholder returns (including both capital gains and dividend yields) from a stratified sample selected from the 200 largest U.S. banks found no evidence of increased stockholder wealth from the holding-company form between 1970 and 1975. These researchers suggested that management-oriented goals (such as size maximization or management risk reduction) may have been sought by these companies instead of stockholder wealth maximization.

Similarly, DiClemente and Kolari (1986) found no significant benefits from gains in stock prices in 1981 when Illinois' bank holding companies were granted legal permission to acquire other banks in designated regions of that state. Using the Sharpe market model these researchers found *no* effect on shareholder wealth from four large holding companies as a result of the sudden legal authorization of Illinois holding companies to enter new banking markets through acquisition. The authors saw as possible explanations for their findings the potency of the antitrust laws, the possible exhaustion of scale and scope economies by large holding companies, and the high franchise value of existing banks that were possible targets for acquistion. Another possible reason suggested recently by Wall (1985) is the heavy influence of regulation in forcing the larger bank holding companies to maintain high primary capital ratios, placing downward pressure on holding companies' returns to equity.

Earlier Varvel (1975) adopted a valuation approach that considers the discounted stream of future company earnings and the effects of risk on that earnings stream. He contradicts Piper (1971), Piper and Weiss (1976), and Brewer and Dukes (1976) in finding that, over a sufficiently long period of time, holding-company value will exceed the value of comparable-size nonholding-company banking organizations. Reviewing financial data from the 1962–1969 period, Varvel observes an apparent negative impact on earnings the first year after holding-company formation. Thereafter, however, holding-company earnings appeared to steadily increase relative to nonholding-company earnings, and income risk was reduced. This result is supported by Upson and Jessup (1972), who find higher stockholder returns (owing to more rapid growth of dividends) from 28 major holding companies relative to large independent banks over the 1957–1971 period.

More recently, Frieder and Apilado (1983) empirically tested a valuation model that views the holding company as a consolidated entity. Their approach considers intraorganizational effects, service fees, overall debt capacity, and adjustments in equity shares. They find that bank acquisitions *do* have a positive impact on the profitability of acquiring holding companies. Moreover, holding companies do gain financial strength from bank acquisitions and, through that added strength, are better able to assist financially troubled affiliates.

Supporting the Frieder-Apilado conclusions is a more recent study by Lobue (1984) that employs the capital asset-pricing model to examine bank and nonbank acquisitions by 37 of the largest U.S. banking organizations. Positive acquisition returns were found for bank holding companies listed on the New York Stock Exchange and in those instances where the seller-to-buyer asset ratio is relatively large, while limited branching laws were found to significantly *reduce* holding-company returns. Additional confirmation has been provided by Desai and Stover (1985), who detected positive abnormal returns to holding-company stockholders from the stock market's reaction to the announcement and completion of an acquisition bid. Moreover, additional positive abnormal returns appear to accrue to holding-company shareholders when the Federal Reserve publicly announces approval of an acquisition request.

The higher profitability and increased financial strength of holding companies as revealed by the more recent studies may be due to greater use of financial leverage by these organizations. For example, a study by Karna and Graddy (1982) suggests that large bank holding companies are able to make effective use of financial leverage to raise their rate of return on net worth. Their quadratic-regression study of 40 of the nation's largest bank holding companies, 1970–77, grouped by the range of consolidated leverage (total liabilities to book value of stockholders' equity) employed, showed that an optimum level for each organization's consolidated leverage (debt-to-equity) ratio was about 18.4 to 1. Below that ratio the company's return on net worth was less, and beyond that leverage ratio, earnings rates declined. Unfortuately, there is anything but universal agreement on this conclusion. For example, Hagamen and Chamberlain (1975) and Megen (1971), the latter looking at the nation's 50 largest banks, found *no* positive leverage effect on bank stockholders' equity. However, Martin, Keown, and Scott (1977), as well as Karna (1979), found evidence of favorable leverage effects, especially when debt-equity ratios remained below 50 percent.

Only a few studies have examined the growth pattern of bank holding companies and the determinants of that growth. Probably the most complete of these studies was performed by Boczar (1980), who tracked external growth in bank acquisitions, offices, and deposits for 64 multibank holding companies between 1970 and 1973. His predictive equations included variables measuring the characteristics of the banking organization (in terms of size, age, internal growth, capital adequacy, and prior acquisition activity), the demand for banking services, the tendency for holding companies to imitate other market-leading companies (the "snowball" or "bandwagon" effect), the supply of independent banks, state branching laws, and control variables to adjust for unusually large acquisitions and individual state effects. The results of Boczar's multivariate tobit analysis indicted that the external growth of a holding company will be faster if (1) its lead bank has a larger share of statewide deposits, (2) it experiences rapid internal growth, (3) it has engaged in prior acquisitions, (4) it has a higher capital-to-asset ratio, (5) it faces a larger supply of independent banks as potential acquisition candidates, and (6) it is located in a region experiencing rapid increases in per-capita personal income. However, company age, deposit size, and the character of state branching laws did not appear to significantly affect a bank holding company's rate of external expansion.

Evaluation of Research Studies Dealing with Holding Companies

The research literature dealing with the impact of bank holding companies on the companies themselves, the public, and the businesses they acquire has virtually exploded since the early 1960s. Unfortunately, the volume of definitive conclusions is far more limited than the volume of studies. This deficiency may be due to the diversity of economic conditions in areas served by the companies and to variations in managerial talent and philosophy. In fact, during the 1970s and early 1980s several studies appeared—most notably those by Fraas (1974), Mayne (1976), Rose and Scott (1984), and Whalen (1981–82)—suggesting that lumping all holding-company banks into a single group for performance analysis was a mistake. Holding companies allegedly are so diverse in the degree of centralized control over their affiliate banks and so different in management philosophy and objectives that any generalizations made about the holding-company sector as a whole are likely to be misleading. Indeed, these studies produced at least some evidence that the particular company an affiliated bank belonged to was far more significant in shaping its performance than the bank's membership in the holding-company sector as a whole.

Equally likely in explaining the paucity of consistent conclusions is the problem of deficiencies in *methodology*. Many of the research studies used paired comparisons between affiliated and independent banks and the pairings are often questionable, due especially to differences in bank size and levels of operating efficiency. Most studies failed to allow sufficient time for holding-company management to have an impact on recently acquired banks or to allow for competitive interactions between affiliates and independent banks. There is a clear need for new studies that analyze the relative degree of competitive rivalry displayed by markets characterized by extensive holding-company activity compared with those where such activity is minimal or nonexistent.

Many studies of banking companies have clearly looked in the wrong places for relevant conclusions. For example, until recently most studies exploring the influence of holding companies on profitability examined only the affiliated banks, not the holding companies themselves. Fortunately, within the past decade correction of this error has established quite convincingly that the formation of bank holding companies can contribute significantly to stockholders' equity returns, overall growth, and improved access to the capital markets.

Implications for Public Policy

It seems clear that bank holding companies have neither completely fulfilled the exotic dreams of their organizers nor given rise to the disasters often predicted by their opponents. Concrete benefits to the public are probably limited and certainly much less than claimed in applications for holding-company growth and expansion filed with the Federal Reserve System. It is unfortunate that the Federal Reserve has only half-heartedly followed up on such claims to ensure that the public receives what it has been promised. If the "public benefits" test prescribed in the Bank Holding Company Act is to have any meaning at all, it would appear to require closer regulatory supervision than has been the case in the past. Moreover, it is now apparent that simply comparing affiliated and independent banks to assess the impact of the holding-company movement is too myopic an approach. Bank affiliates of a larger holding-company organization are best viewed in an overall investment portfolio context in which intracompany flows of resources and functions are taken into account.

Whatever their benefits and costs, however, the bank holding company has literally transformed the American banking structure. Holding less than 10 percent of nationwide bank deposits in 1960, these organizations today account for more than three quarters of the industry's deposit total and close to half of the nation's full-service banking offices. Unfortunately, neither regulation nor research has kept pace with the rapidity of change in the bank holding-company sector. After more than two decades of detailed research few conclusions concerning the public costs and benefits of the spread of these organizations can be confidently maintained. Credit availability appears to increase in local communities, though financial risk also rises, and there appear to be no net reductions in service prices. Given the state of our knowledge today, venturing beyond those simple and innocuous observations seems hazardous at best.

References

Alhadeff, Charlotte and David Alhadeff. 1955. "Recent Bank Mergers." *Quarterly Journal of Economics* (November), pp. 503–532.

Austin, Douglas V. 1973. "Who Needs A Holding Company?" *The Magazine of Bank Administration* (January), pp. 46-48.

Bell, R. W. and Neil Murphy. 1968. *Costs in Commercial Banking: A Quantitative Analysis of Bank Behavior and Its Relation to Bank Regulation.* Research Report no. 41. Federal Reserve Bank of Boston.

Boczar, Gregory E. 1975. "The Determinants of Multibank Holding Company Formations." *Southern Economic Journal* (July), pp. 120–129.

——1980. "The External Growth of Multibank Holding Companies." *Journal of Bank Research* (Autumn), pp. 147–58.

Brewer, Virgil and William P. Dukes. 1976. "Empirical Evidence on the Risk-Return Relationship Between Banks and Related Bank Holding Companies." *Review of Business and Economic Research* (Spring), pp. 56–65.

Chase, Samuel Jr. and John Mingo. 1975. "The Regulation of Bank Holding Companies." *Journal of Finance,* 30:281–92.

Curry, Timothy J. 1981. "The Pre-Acquisition Characteristics of Banks Acquired by Multibank Holding Companies." *Journal of Bank Research* (Summer), pp. 82–89.

Curry, Timothy J. and John T. Rose. 1983. "Multibank Holding Companies: Recent Evidence on Competition and Performance in Banking Markets." *Journal of Bank Research* (Autumn), 14:212–20.

Desai, Anand S. and Roger D. Stover. 1985. "Bank Holding Company Acquisitions, Stockholder Returns, and Regulatory Uncertainty." *The Journal of Financial Research* (Summer), 8(2):145–56.

DiClemente, John J. and James Kolari. 1986. "Wealth Effect of Geographical Deregulation: The Case of Illinois," *Economic Perspectives,* Federal Reserve Bank of Chicago, March, pp. 13–17.

Drum, Dale S. 1978. "Relative Costs of Affiliated Versus Independent Banks." Occasional Paper 78–3. Federal Reserve Bank of Chicago.

Eisemann, Peter. 1976. "Diversification and the Congeneric Bank Holding Company." *Journal of Bank Research,* 7:68–77.

Evans, J. L. and S. H. Archer. 1968. "Diversification and the Reduction of Dispersion: An Empirical Analysis." *Journal of Finance* (December), 23:761–68.

Fischer, Gerald C. 1961. *Bank Holding Companies.* New York: Columbia University Press.

Fraas, Arthur G. 1974. *The Performance of Individual Bank Holding Companies.* Staff Economic Studies no. 84. Board of Governors of the Federal Reserve System.

Fraser, Donald R. 1978. "Holding Company Affiliation and Commercial Bank Market Share." *Antitrust Bulletin* (Winter), 33:825–34.

Fraser, Donald R. and Peter S. Rose. 1973. "Holding Company Expansion: When the Fed Says No." *The Magazine of Bank Administration* (December), pp. 36–44.

Frieder, Larry A. and Vincent P. Apilado. 1982. "Bank Holding Company Research: Classification, Synthesis and New Directions." *Journal of Bank Research* (Summer), pp. 80–95.

——1983. "Bank Holding Company Expansion: A Refocus on its Financial Rationale." *Journal of Financial Research* (Spring), 6(1):67–81.

Goldberg, Lawrence G. 1976. "Bank Holding Company Acquisitions and Their Impact on Market Shares." *Journal of Money, Credit and Banking,* 8(1):127–30.

Gort, M. and T. F. Hogarty. 1970. "New Evidence on Mergers." *Journal of Law and Economics* (April), 13:167–84.

Graddy, Duane B. and Reuben Kyle, III. 1980. "Affiliated Bank Performance and the Simultaneity of Financial Decision-Making." *Journal of Finance* (September), pp. 951–57.

Gupta, Manak C. and David A. Walker. 1975. "Dividend Disbursal Practices in Commercial Banking." *Journal of Financial and Quantitative Analysis* (September), 10:515–29.

Hagamen, T. C. and P. K. Chamberlain. 1975. "Bank Leverage Doesn't Pay." *Bankers Magazine* (Spring), pp. 25–30.

Heggestad, Arnold and John Mingo. 1975. "Capital Management by Holding Company Banks." *Journal of Business,* 48:500–5.

Hobson, Hugh A., John T. Masten, and Jacobus T. Severiens. 1978. "Holding Company Acquisitions and Bank Performance: A Comparative Study." *Journal of Bank Research* (Summer), 9:116–120.

Holland, Robert C. 1975. "Bank Holding Companies and Financial Stability." *Journal of Financial and Quantitative Analysis* (November), pp. 577–87.

Jessee, Michael A. and Steven A. Seelig. 1977. *Bank Holding Companies and The Public Interest*. Lexington, Mass: Lexington Books.

Jessup, Paul F. 1974. "Acquisitions by Bank Holding Companies: Promise, Performance, Potential," *Proceedings of a Conference on Bank Structure and Competition*, Federal Reserve Bank of Chicago May, pp. 15–28.

Johnson, Rodney D. and David R. Meinster. 1973. "An Analysis of Bank Holding Company Acquisitions: Some Methodological Issues," *Journal of Bank Research* (Spring), pp. 58–61.

Kalish, L. and R. A. Gilbert. 1973. "An Analysis of Efficiency of Scale and Organizational Form in Commercial Banking." *Journal of Industrial Economics* (July), 21:293-307.

Karna, Adi S. 1979. "Bank Holding Company Profitability: Nonbank Subsidiaries and Financial Leverage." *Journal of Bank Research* (Spring), pp. 28–35.

Karna, Adi s. and Duane B. Graddy. 1982. "Bank Holding Company Leverage and the Return on Stockholders' Equity." *Journal of Bank Research* (Spring), 13:42–48.

Kelly, E. M. 1967. *The Profitability of Growth Through Mergers*. University Park: The Pennsylvania State University.

Kohers, Theodor. 1977. "Commercial Banks and Bank Holding Companies: A Financial Performance Comparison." *University of Michigan Business Review*(July), pp. 6–10.

Kolari, James W., Peter S. Rose, and Kenneth W. Riener. 1983. "Convenience and Needs: A Survey of Holding Company Bank Services." *Issues in Bank Regulation* (Winter), pp. 21–31.

Kolb, Robert W. 1981. "Affiliated and Independent Banks." *Journal of Banking and Finance*, 5:523–37.

Lamb, W. Ralph. 1961. *Group Banking*. New Brunswick, N.J.: Rutgers University Press.

Lawrence, Robert J. 1967. *The Performance of Bank Holding Companies*. Board of Governors of the Federal Reserve System.

Lawrence, Robert J. 1971. *Operating Policies of Bank Holding Companies: Part I*, Staff Economic Studies 69, Board of Governors of the Federal Reserve System.

Lev, Baruch and Gershon Mandelker. 1972. "The Microeconomic Consequences of Corporate Mergers." *Journal of Business*, pp. 85–104.

Levy, Haim and Marshall Sarnat. 1970. "Diversification, Portfolio Analysis and the Uneasy Case for Conglomerate Mergers." *Journal of Finance* (September), 26:795–802.

Lewellen, Wilbur G. 1971. "A Pure Financial Rationale for the Conglomerate Merger," *Journal of Finance* (May), 26:521–37.

Lobue, Marie. 1984. "Categorical Bank Acquisitions." *Journal of Bank Research* (Winter), pp. 274–82.

Martell, Terrence and Donald Hooks. 1975. "Holding-Company Affiliation and Economies of Scale," *Midwest Finance Association Proceedings,* pp. 59–71.

Martin, J. D., A. J. Keown, and D. F. Scott. 1977. "Bank Leverage Really Does Pay." *Bankers Magazine* (Spring), pp. 70–76.

Mayne, Lucille S. 1976. "Management Policies of Bank Holding Companies and Bank Performance." *Journal of Bank Research,* 7(1):37–48.

—— 1977. "A Comparative Study of Bank Holding Company Affiliates and Independent Banks, 1969–1972." *Journal of Finance* (March), pp. 147–58.

—— 1980. "Bank Dividend Policy and Holding-Company Affiliation." *Journal of Financial and Quantitative Analysis* (June), 15(2):469–80.

Magen, S. D. 1971. "Cost of Capital and Dividend Policies in Commercial Banks." *Journal of Financial and Quantitative Analysis* (March), pp. 733–46.

Mingo, John J. 1975. "Capital Management and Profitability of Prospective Holding Company Banks." *Journal of Financial and Quantitative Analysis* (June), pp. 191–203.

—— 1976. "Managerial Motives, Market Structures, and the Performance of Holding Company Banks." *Economic Inquiry* (September), pp. 411–24.

Moyer, Charles R. and Edward Sussna. 1973. "Registered Bank Holding Company Acquisitions: A Cross-Section Analysis." *Journal of Financial and Quantitative Analysis* (September).

Mueller, Dennis C. 1969. "A Theory of Conglomerate Mergers." *Quarterly Journal of Economics* (November), 83:643–59.

Piper, Thomas. 1971. *The Economics of Bank Acquisitions by Registered Bank Companies.* Research Report no. 48 (March). Federal Reserve Bank of Boston.

Piper, Thomas and Steven J. Weiss. 1971. "The Profitability of Bank Acquisitions by Multibank Holding Companies." *New England Economic Review* (September-October), pp. 2–12. Federal Reserve Bank of Boston.

—— 1974. "The Profitability of Bank Acquisitions by Multibank Holding Company Acquisitions," *Journal of Finance* (March), 29:163–74.

Reid, Samuel R. 1968. *Mergers, Managers, and the Economy.* New York: McGraw-Hill.

Rhoades, Stephen A. 1977. "The Impact of Foothold Acquisitions on Bank Market Structures." *Antitrust Bulletin* (Spring), 22:119–128.

Rhoades, Stephen A. and Roger D. Rutz. 1982. "The Impact of Bank Holding Companies on Local Market Rivalry and Performance." *Journal of Economics and Business,* 34(4):355–365.

Rhoades, Stephen A. and Donald T. Savage. 1981. "The Relative Performance of Bank Holding Companies and Branch Banking Systems." *Journal of Economics and Business,* (Winter), 33(2):132–41.

Rhoades, Stephen A. and Paul Schweitzer. 1978. *Foothold Acquisitions and Bank Market Structure.* Staff Economic Studies no. 8. Board of Governors of the Federal Reserve System.

Rose, John T. 1980. "Multibank Holding Company Expansion via De Novo Banks." *The Magazine of Bank Administration* (February), pp. 47–51.

—— 1982. "Bank Holding Company Affiliation and Market Share Performance." *Journal of Monetary Economics* (January), 9:109–19.

Rose, John T. and Donald T. Savage. 1982. "Bank Holding Company *De Novo* Entry and Banking Market Deconcentration." *Journal of Bank Research* (Summer), 13:96–100.

—— 1981. "Bank Holding Company *De Novo* Entry and Market Share Accumulation." *Antitrust Bulletin* (Winter), 26:753–67.

Rose, Peter S. 1976. "The Pattern of Bank Holding Company Acquisitions." *Journal of Bank Research* (Autumn).

—— 1974. "What Can A Holding Company Do for Its Banks?" *The Southern Banker* (December).

Rose, Peter S. and Donald R. Fraser. 1974. "State Regulation of Bank Holding Companies." *The Bankers Magazine* (Winter), 157(1)42–48.

Rose, Peter S. and William L. Scott. 1979. "The Performance of Banks Acquired by Holding Companies." *Review of Business and Economic Research* (Spring), 14(3):18–37.

—— 1984. "Heterogeneity in Performance Within the Bank Holding Company Sector." *Journal of Economics and Business* (February), pp. 1–14.

Savage, Donald T. 1982. "Branch Banking Laws, Deposits, Market Share, and Profitability of New Banks." *Journal of Bank Research* (Winter), 12:200–6.

Simpson, W. Gary and Theodor Kohers. 1979. "The Market Performance of Large Commercial Banks and Bank Holding Companies." *Review of Business and Economic Research* (Spring), 14(3):38–48.

Talley, Samuel H. 1971. *The Effect of Holding Company Acquisitions on Bank Performance.* Staff Economic Study no. 67. Board of Governors of the Federal Reserve System.

Upson, Roger B. and Paul F. Jessup. 1972. "Returns from Bank Holding Companies." *Bankers Magazine* (Spring), pp. 59–62.

Varvel, Walter A. 1975. "A Valuation Approach to Bank Holding Company Acquisitions." *Economic Review* (July-August), pp. 9–15. Federal Reserve Bank of Richmond.

Wall, Larry D. 1985. "The Effect of Capital Adequacy Guidelines on Large Bank Holding Companies," *Working Paper* 85–3, Federal Reserve Bank of Atlanta (December).

Westerfield, R. 1970. "A Note on the Measurement of Conglomerate Diversification." *Journal of Finance* (September), 25:909–14.

Whalen, Gary. 1981-82. "Operational Policies of Multibank Holding Companies." *Economic Review* (Winter), pp. 20–31. Federal Reserve Bank of Cleveland.

9.

The Conglomerate Bank
Holding Company

THE TRADITIONAL boundaries of American banking have been reasonably well defined for a century or more. Under federal statutes a commercial bank is distinguished by the offering of two services—the extension or granting of commercial credit and the acceptance of deposits payable on demand. Other closely related services, such as making consumer and real estate loans, purchasing securities, and offering savings accounts, are also understood to be consistent with banking practice and tradition.

For an industry heavily rooted in tradition, however, many bankers have become *innovators* in recent years, testing the legal and economic boundaries of their marketplace. To be sure, new services have developed within *existing* bank markets, essentially variations on the traditional banking products of credit, thrift, and payments. Well-known examples of such variations on traditional banking products include NOW accounts, variable-rate loans and deposits, financial counseling, and market making. New services of this sort have provided the basis for continuing growth in banking resources, market shares, and earnings.

Unfortunately, the development of still more variations on traditional banking products inevitably runs into two formidable barriers. First, further development of existing service lines and markets is subject to essentially the same regulatory restrictions that inhibit the offering of traditional services. For example, bankers can develop new forms of demand deposits or CDs, but the terms and the offices from which those new deposit plans can be offered are subject to the same state and federal laws as before.

A second barrier to simply offering new variations on traditional banking products is the lack of diversification benefits. Proliferation of similar services results, perhaps, in a larger cash flow through the bank, but the variability of bank cash flow patterns over time probably changes very little. Thus, if a recession in local economic conditions weakens the market for loans, demand for both old and new types of loans may decline, leading to a drop in aggregate bank earnings. Raising funds by offering new types of deposits will probably *not* insulate the bank from declining growth when a rise in local unemployment causes all or most deposit balances to fall. If the individual bank is to reduce the risk of fluctuations in its aggregate cash flow, it needs to find new services and new markets that generate cash flows whose timing and distribution differ significantly from those emanating from its traditional product lines.

Brief History of the Conglomerate Bank Holding Company

These two behavioral forces—the desire to avoid long-standing regu-latory restrictions and to diversify sources of cash flow in order to reduce risk—have been key motivators in the movement of American banks toward nontraditional products and services. And that movement out-side banking's traditional product lines is by no means new. In the nineteenth and early twentieth centuries and on into the Great Depres-sion of the 1930s, many U.S. banks, particularly larger money center institutions, were active in a broad range of financial and nonfinancial activities. Probably the most conspicuous example was the heavy in-volvement of domestic banks in stock loans and stock investments—a common practice abroad and one that allegedly contributed to the stock market debacle of the late 1920s and early 1930s and to the ultimate failure of many commercial banks. Seeking a remedy, Congress passed the Banking Act of 1933, which precluded commercial banks from stock ownership and underwriting and from interlocking relationships with securities firms.

In more recent history, one-bank holding companies during the 1960s—several centered around the nation's leading banks—moved to acquire or start businesses offering products or services far removed from traditional credit, thrift, and payments accounts. These banks took advantage of a glaring loophole in the Bank Holding Company Act that left one-bank holding company organizations unregulated. The growth of these loopholed one-bank organizations was phenomenal. By year-end 1970 there were 1,352 one-bank holding companies operating in the United States, accounting for more than a third of the industry's deposits. The one-bank companies owned subsidiaries or engaged directly in nonbank business activities from 276 different three-digit SIC code industries, as reported in a Federal Reserve Board study (Board of Governors 1972). While the bulk of nonbank ventures controlled by one-bank companies were confined to finance, insurance, and real estate, a substantial number of companies entered livestock raising and processing, became subdividers and developers, entered market research and management consulting, or offered auditing and bookkeeping services. And there were a small number that drifted well away from financially oriented areas into manufacturing and retailing.

Regulation of Permissible Nonbank Services

Concern over the safety of depositor funds committed directly or indirectly to such ventures, as well as concern for the competitive implications of bank ownership of nonbank firms, led to passage of the 1970 Amendments to the Bank Holding Company Act. *All* bank holding companies controlling one or more commercial banks were brought under the examination, supervision, and regulation of the Federal Reserve Board. Subsequent Federal Reserve rulings dictated that most large bank holding companies and smaller companies holding substantial *nonbank* assets would be examined at least once every eighteen months, and other holding companies were subject to examination at least once every three years. As a rule, these examinations would center on the operations of the parent company and its *nonbank* subsidiaries, while the bank affiliates of these same holding companies would be examined by their respective federal regulatory agencies.

Permissible nonbank business ventures were expanded under the new law, in part recognizing how far afield many holding companies already had strayed. But any future acquisitions of nonbank firms and those already acquired but not grandfathered by the law had to conform to two primary tests expressed in Section 4(c)(8) of the amended Bank Holding Company Act: (1) the *closely related* test, requiring that any acquisitions of nonbank firms be in fields "so closely related to banking or managing or controlling banks as to be a proper incident thereto" and (2) the *public benefits* test, requiring applicant companies to demonstrate either that competition or efficiency will increase or that the public will receive financial services that are more conveniently located and more responsive to their needs, to an extent that outweighs "possible adverse effects," such as undue concentration, decreased or unfair competition, conflicts of interest, or unsound banking practices. Bank holding companies that acquired nonbank businesses not fitting these tests and not covered by grandfather provisions were required by the 1970 Amendments to divest themselves of those businesses no later than December 31, 1980. In its 1977 *Annual Report* (p. 404) the Board reported that three hundred and fifty holding companies were involved in approximately seven hundred and seventy nonbank activities subject to the divestiture rule.

Though pressed repeatedly to do so, Congress declined to define what activities were "closely related" to commercial banking, leaving that politically sensitive issue to the Federal Reserve Board. Beginning in 1971 the Board began a series of public hearings on the nature of nonbank businesses acquired and, shortly thereafter, published an initial list of approved nonbank 4(c)(8) business activities. What was most interesting about the Board's nonbank activities list was the *absence of geographic limits* on such ventures. The original Bank Holding Company Act passed in 1956 contained no explicit mention of geographic restraints on nonbank business expansion, leaving the matter open to interpretation. However, as noted by Frodin (1982), the abbreviated list of permissible nonbank ventures included mainly *locally* oriented financial services with limited potential for geographic expansion. In addition, the Board seemed hesitant to run counter to the underlying philosophy of the McFadden Act and the Douglas

Amendment, which, as we have seen, militated against interstate expansion by banking organizations. Thus, holding companies were often geographically limited by the Board *prior* to the 1970 Amendments. However, the Board acknowledged that the Bank Holding Company Act imposed no express geographic boundaries on nonbank 4(c)(8) ventures and, thus, the Fed declined to impose any of its own.

The predictable result of the Federal Reserve Board's liberalized attitude toward nonbank business growth was a substantial increase in interstate operations through selected nonbank ventures—these centered mainly around consumer finance companies, investment advisory services, industrial banks, leasing companies, management consulting firms, mortgage banking houses, reinsurance firms, and trust companies. A study by Whitehead (1982) found 5500 offices of nonbank subsidiaries operating outside the holding companies' home states, including 4442 finance company offices, 584 mortgage banking offices, 105 industrial banks, 98 leasing-company offices, 58 trust company facilities, and 56 offices related to the underwriting of credit life insurance. Leading states with bank-holding-company-controlled nonbank business (4(c)(8)) offices included California (521 offices), Florida (372), Pennsylvania (320), Illinois (310), and Texas (289).

Nonbank business activities allowed by the Federal Reserve Board have expanded considerably since 1971 when the first list of permissible activities was published. Table 9.1 is a list of the most important currently permitted activities. Requests to enter new 4(c)(8) business activities must be filed with the Federal Reserve bank serving the applicant banking organization's section of the country. Approval or denial by the Fed normally occurs within thirty days after the application and all other requested information has been filed. However, approval is *not* needed for acquisitions of less than 5 percent of the voting shares of any nonbank firm or for setting up new branch offices of an already approved nonbank subsidiary. Acquisition of small (up to $15 million in assets) nonbank businesses offering products on the Fed's permitted list is normally permitted automatically, provided the holding company gives the Fed a minimum of 15 days' notice. In general, nonbank applications not involving "significant issues" may be approved at the level of the individual Reserve Bank without the necessity of a Federal Reserve Board hearing in Washington, D.C.

In a broad sense the allowable 4(c)(8) business activities listed in table 9.1 appear to group themselves into a relatively short list of permitted *functions*. The area of greatest holding-company growth

Table 9.1. Nonbank Business Activities Permitted to Bank Holding Companies Under Section 4(C)(8) of the Bank Holding Company Act and Federal Reserve Board Regulations:

Management consulting for unaffiliated depository institutions

Full-payout leasing of personal and real property

Mortgage banking, including servicing loans and other credit extensions

Consumer credit and operating an industrial bank, Morris Plan bank, or industrial loan company

Commercial and sales finance and factoring operations

Acting as insurance agent or broker primarily in connection with the extension of credit and in small communities

Underwriting of credit life, accident, and health insurance directly related to credit extensions by the holding company system

Trust or fiduciary services

Acting as investment or financial advisor to trusts, mutual funds, individuals, and state and local governments

Debt or equity investments in community welfare or rehabilitation projects

Providing data processing, transmission, and bookkeeping services to subsidiaries and to selected other customers

Agency brokerage services for credit-related insurance in small communities (populations of less than 5,000)

Providing armored car and courier services for explicit fees and involving information that must be transmitted on a timely basis

Operating a discount brokerage company as agent and providing related margin lending for customers

Investments in export trading companies (under provisions of the 1982 Bank Export Services Act)

Providing economic information and advisory services

Check verification on a case-by-case arrangement

Appraising real property

Underwriting and dealing in government and selected money market securities

Acting as a futures commission merchant for selected contracts

Acquiring a troubled or failing savings and loan institution in another state

Operating a credit card company

Selling selected payments and savings instruments (e.g., travelers' checks, money orders, and U.S. savings bonds)

Arranging equity financing for income-producing (commercial) property

Providing foreign exchange advisory and transactions services

Establishment by order of bank service corporations (under the Bank Service Corporation Act)

and expansion has centered on the extension of credit—the *credit-granting function.* Included here are full-payout leasing, consumer credit, commercial finance and factoring operations, mortgage banking, investments in community welfare projects, operating a credit card company, and loan servicing. In addition, the Export Trading Company Act of 1982 permits bank holding companies to invest up to 5 percent of their capital and surplus in an export trading company that can be jointly owned with other firms and may engage in export trade financing and other related services.

Still another growing area is the provision and transfer of financial information—the *information function*. This function is represented by management consulting for depository institutions, acting as an investment or financial advisor, providing data processing and bookkeeping services, supplying economic information and advisory services, and performing real-property appraisals.

A third important role is facilitating the making of payments—the *payments function*. In this role bank holding companies are permitted to provide fee-basis armored car and courier services, conduct check verifications, sell selected payments and savings instruments (such as travelers' checks and money orders), and provide foreign exchange and advisory transactions services.

Increasingly, bank holding companies are penetrating the securities' brokerage and underwriting field—the *securities' function*, illustrated by selling trust or fiduciary services, underwriting and dealing in government and selected money market securities, acting as a futures commission merchant, marketing savings bonds, arranging equity financing for income-producing property, operating a discount brokerage company, and executing orders for the purchase of shares in mutual funds.

Finally, a developing area that is still tightly constrained by law and regulation is the marketing and underwriting of insurance services—the *insurance function*, represented today by the underwriting of credit life, accident, and health insurance and the offering of insurance agency and brokerage services in smaller communities. Future growth of the insurance function is likely to be treacherous and unpredictable owing to the presence of strong political opposition from insurance lobbies and because of the volatile earnings-risk environment in the insurance industry today.

None of these functions and service powers is immutable. Proposals from several members of Congress, the administration, and the regulatory community, if adopted, would give banks and bank holding companies greater latitude to compete with security brokers and dealers, insurance companies, and real estate firms. Key issues in the future extension of banking organizations into nontraditional service fields are to what extent banks play a special and unique role in the economy because of their offering of credit, payments, and thrift services and how this unique role will be affected by service extension. Can we successfully isolate banks from the misfortunes of nonbank business ventures operated by their parent holding companies? Would further expansion of bank holding companies into new service fields lead to excessive concentration of power in the financial sector? Will the public lose confidence in banks as repositories of savings if they are increasingly allied with more risky insurance, securities, and real estate ventures?

This last issue of public confidence in the safety of banks and how that confidence might be damaged by nonbank business activities and by the misfortunes of nonbank firms within the same holding company has been a concern of the Congress of the United States for more than 50 years. The Glass-Steagall Act (1933) contained provisions restricting financial transactions between member banks and their holding companies—restrictions that subsequently were amended to encompass *all* federally insured banks. Still, these legal barriers to intracompany transactions were apparently not formidable enough, for as J. T. Rose and Talley (1982) observe, several large banks were weakened by intracompany financial transfers during the 1970s. The failure of Hamilton National Bank of Chattanooga, for example, was attributed to its acquisition of low-quality mortgages from its troubled mortgage-banking affiliate.

Congress responded to these recent developments with further tightening of the limits on intracompany transactions in the Garn-St Germain Depository Institutions Act of 1982. That law broadens the definition of bank "affiliates" to include any company determined by the Federal Reserve Board to have such a close relationship with a banking organization that transactions involving the company and its affiliated banks could have an adverse impact on the banks involved. Transactions between a holding-company bank and a single affiliated company cannot exceed 10 percent of the bank's capital stock and surplus. Covered transactions with all affiliates combined cannot exceed 20 percent of the bank's capital and surplus. Loans must be collateralized up to 120 percent of this amount if the lowest quality debt instruments are used as backing and up to 130 percent if real or personal property or leases are the designated collateral.

Thus, as reported by J. T. Rose and Talley (1982) and discussed by Whalen (1981–82), the Garn bill recognizes that bank affiliates in a holding company are similar to branch offices in a branch banking organization. As such, affiliated banks are potentially vulnerable to the misfortunes of the lead company or any of its component business enterprises. Intraconglomerate dealings involving bank and nonbank businesses must therefore be carried out in ways that are consistent with safe and sound banking practice.

Motivations for Nonbank Business Acquisitions

As noted at the outset of this chapter, several major factors have contributed to the rise of conglomerate bank-holding-company organizations. These motivating factors are now briefly summarized.

INCREASING EXPECTED EARNINGS
FROM NEW MARKETS AND NEW SERVICES

Acquiring a nonbank business is a long-term capital investment from which the holding company hopes to recover its costs plus an acceptable rate of return on owners' capital. If earnings do increase as expected, the company's stock price will rise and its capacity to carry additional debt for future growth and expansion, including additional acquisitions, will grow as well. When one-bank holding companies first began to expand outside traditional banking fields they were undoubtedly encouraged by the fact that average rates of return on net worth in manufacturing, trade, nonfinancial services, and commercial finance exceeded banking's return on equity, often by a substantial margin. In addition, the rapidly rising cost of deposits encouraged banks to reach farther afield for higher expected returns to offset their escalating costs.

Of course, it is by no means certain that higher expected returns will be achieved. The acquisition process can be expensive for a holding company, owing to required Federal Reserve reports, frequent examinations, and the redemption of promises frequently made to the Fed to increase capital or to offer new services. In addition, there is ample evidence that holding companies frequently pay excessive premiums for the nonbank businesses they acquire. Perhaps reflective of disappointed earnings expectations, a substantial number of nonbank businesses were sold off by bank holding companies (especially mortgage banking and finance-company affiliates). Most occurred after 1979.

REDUCING RISK THROUGH DIVERSIFICATION

As noted at the beginning of this chapter, many nonbank acquisitions have been motivated by a desire to increase the stability of cash and net earnings flowing through the holding-company organization. This can be achieved by choosing nonbank subsidiaries whose cash flow and net earnings stream are negatively correlated with the cash earnings stream of the holding-company organization itself. For example, suppose that interest rates begin rising and come to exceed the maximum legal rate that the finance company affiliate of a holding company can charge its customers on cash loans. The finance company's profitability declines, but the profitability of commercial banks belonging to the same company may increase when it makes or renews loans at higher and higher interest rates. The net result is that earnings at the aggregate level of the holding company are stabilized, one source of profitability offsetting another.

The diversification effect may arise from differences in the nature of services offered or from differences in the economic characteristics of the markets served by the holding company and its new subsidiary. Thus, the holding company may benefit from product line diversification, geographic diversification, or both. Either way, the net result is to reduce earnings risk through the diversification (portfolio) effect. And if earnings risk is reduced without a significant decline in the expected rate of return, the value of the holding company's stock will rise, creating potential for future growth and further diversification.

Of course, there is no guarantee that significant diversification benefits will materialize. For one thing it is not clear that U.S. holding companies have, in the main, acquired nonbank subsidiaries whose earnings are negatively correlated with their banks' earnings. Moreover, as noted in chapter 8, financial theory suggests that the value of the firm will *not* rise from the merger of diversified companies if capital markets are perfect. Thus, the diversification argument does *not* appear to have overwhelming support from either a theoretical or an empirical point of view.

AVOIDING REGULATORY RESTRICTIONS

Nonbank business activities have allowed many banking organizations to make an "end run" around federal and state banking laws and regulations. These restrictions range from limits on commercial bank branching within the home state to prohibitions against interstate branch banking and the pursuit of controlling acquisitions of banks across state lines. With recent improvements in electronic communications it is becoming more economically attractive to have or be a part of nationwide electronic funds transfer (EFT) systems, permitting greater speed and convenience in serving customers. However, there are other restrictions, such as state usury laws, that pose barriers not easily bridged by electronic means. The legal restrictions that banking has operated under for generations can often be more effectively avoided via nonbank business ventures than through the agency of conventional banking organizations and facilities.

ACHIEVING GREATER EFFICIENCY IN USING RESOURCES

Expansion into nonbank businesses may permit a banking organization to make more efficient use of its real and financial resources. For example, the management of a bank holding company may be pushed to maximum efficiency when it is handed the responsibility of directing and supervising additional affiliates—a *synergistic* effect. Similarly, the company may have excess computer capacity available that affiliated firms can tap with little additional drain on other resources. Where a lending-type business such as a finance or leasing company is acquired that serves many of the same customers as bank affiliates, credit analysis and recordkeeping can often be done more efficiently through the elimination of unnecessary duplication.

There may also be cross-selling of services through several different affiliates to the same customer. Joint selling of services and shared information may lower production costs and increase the aggregate efficiency of the whole organization. For example, profitable investments identified by an affiliated bank's bond department can be pursued through an affiliated nonbank business. Some of these investment opportunities will be unavailable to banks within the holding company owing to funding limitations or to legal restrictions (such as the requirement that banks purchase only investment grade bonds).

Marketing programs and product distribution channels established by one affiliate may be useful sales vehicles for another affiliate.

REDUCING FINANCING COSTS

Because of its potentially greater size and diversification across different markets and products, a conglomerate holding company may be able to borrow funds at lower cost. With cheaper funding the potential for financial leverage is increased and thus offers company shareholders the possibility of greater returns on their investment. Moreover, freeing up more cash from the burden of debt service should provide additional capital for future growth. And a portion of lower financing costs may be passed through to customers in the form of lower prices or better quality services.

Lower financing costs presumably arise from the superior credit ratings of bank holding companies (often a result of the "halo effect" surrounding banking itself) and their access to the highly competitive commercial paper market. In addition, there may be less risk of failure for affiliated firms, compared with unaffiliated businesses, because the holding company may use the resources of other affiliates to rescue a troubled member firm. This benefit is limited, however, because the Federal Reserve Board closely monitors intracompany transactions and insists that bank affiliates of a holding company not be drained of resources in order to strengthen a troubled subsidiary.

Impact of Nonbank Acquisitions

Whereas a number of motivational factors have been at work spurring nonbank business acquisitions, it is not clear that all of the hoped-for objectives have been achieved. Indeed, the track record of conglomerate firms in general is *not* exemplary. For example, a 1970 study of industrial mergers by Gort and Hogarty concluded that "mergers, on the average, have an approximately neutral effect on the aggregate worth of firms that participate in them; the owners of acquiring firms lose on the average; and the owners of acquired firms gain on the average" (p. 175).

On balance, the principal beneficiaries of many corporate combinations appear to be shareholders of the *acquired* companies—a finding reminiscent of the bank merger literature reviewed in chapter 5. However, a study by Melicher and Rush (1973) finds that the non-bank conglomerate companies performed at about the same level as nonconglomerates, though the conglomerates' performance was described as "not at all outstanding" (p. 387). Other studies in the bank holding-company field by Jessup (1974) and Piper (1970) find, as we saw in the previous chapter, that many acquisitions of *banks* have been unprofitable because many of the acquired institutions had already reached efficient size, abrogating any gains from potential economies of scale, or because excessive premiums were paid to shareholders of the acquired banks. What evidence is there of similar results from bank holding-company acquisitions of *nonbank* businesses?

EFFECTS ON PROFITABILITY AND SHAREHOLDER RETURNS

Unfortunately, the available evidence on the impact of nonbank acquisitions is limited to only a handful of studies. Many of the most important issues and alleged benefits of conglomerate holding companies remain to be investigated, largely because of a lack of data in a number of nonbank fields.

One study that *does* find evidence of added returns from nonbank acquisitions was published by Swary in 1983. He looks at the impact of the *announcement* of nonbank acquisitions on the profitability and riskiness of the acquiring holding companies as reflected in the behavior of their stock prices. Using a market index model in which individual stock returns for the 1971–1976 period were linked to the New York Stock Exchange Common Stock Index, Swary found that stockholders of acquiring holding companies scored above-normal returns around the earliest announcement date of the proposed nonbank acquisition. However, announcements of Federal Reserve *approval* of a proposed acquisition did not appear to affect the perceived investment risk or result in higher than normal realized returns for stockholders of the acquiring holding companies. But when an acquisition was *denied* by the Board, shareholders of the affected holding company appeared to sustain significant losses in stock values over a five-week period following the announced decision.

Swary believes that capital market investors interpret a denial decision as evidence the Federal Reserve Board regards a holding company as excessively risky. A similar conclusion is reached by M. Lindahl-Stevens (1976), who found that the announcement of nonbank acquisitions produced a measurable market reaction only when the Federal Reserve Board denied the proposed acquisition or in a bear market. Often in such cases the company is subsequently asked to increase its equity capital, which, other factors held constant, lowers its realized rate of return.

A related study by Martin and Keown (1981) examines the question of whether the mere *formation* of a one-bank holding company affects the observed distribution of bank shareholder returns. They test whether differences exist between average market-adjusted returns for bank stock versus holding-company stock and whether the formation of a one-bank company leads to greater stability in a banking organization's market-adjusted returns. The company formation date (rather than the announcement date) was used as the basis for analysis because that date was available for all banks in a sample of 25 one-bank companies formed between July 5, 1968, and July 7, 1974. The capital-asset pricing model (CAPM) was used to analyze the behavior of individual company returns measured against month-end stock prices for the Standard & Poor's 500-stock index over a 72-month period surrounding the formation date. Martin and Keown found visual evidence of a *favorable* market reaction (i.e., above-normal returns) over a nine-month period following the announcement of company formation. However, company formation did *not* appear to have statistically measurable effects on the volatility of residual returns for the affected banks or on the return-generating mechanism for bank equity values.

The Martin and Keown study was criticized subsequently by Billingsley and Lamy (1984), who argued that the earlier work had failed to consider the impact of the 1970 Amendments to the Bank Holding Company Act on the return-generating process. Because the 1970 amendments restricted one-bank holding companies to acquisitions "closely related to banking," the amended law appears to have substantially attenuated the set of investment opportunities for these firms, while simultaneously expanding the set of investment opportunities for multibank companies. Billingsley and Lamy, using a sample of 12 one-bank companies formed before and after the 1970 amendments and a regression scheme based on the capital-asset-pricing model, found that stock market investors reacted favorably to the formation of one-bank companies before 1970 and unfavorably to one-bank company formations after 1970. They conclude that *both* one-bank holding company formations and passage of the 1970 Amendments have affected the return-generating process for one-bank financial conglomerates.

A contrary result was recorded by Aharony and Swary (1981), however, who concluded that the 1970 Bank Holding Company Act Amendments had *no* differential impact on the risk-return position of one-bank holding companies, multibank holding companies, or independent banks. Unfortunately, it is not clear that Aharony and Swary successfully bracketed the time period during which important legislative and regulatory changes were being made. Correcting for this problem, Eisenbeis, Harris, and Lakonishok (1984) found results that were in essential agreement with Billingsley and Lamy. For the 1968–74 period, announcements of the formation of one-bank companies coincided with statistically significant positive abnormal returns to stockholders. The authors concluded that these banking organizations were upvalued in the market owing to investor perceptions of greater opportunities for expansion through the one-bank holding company form. However, abnormal returns tended to cluster in the few weeks around a company formation announcement date; moreover, formation announcements did *not* produce abnormal stockholder returns after passage of the 1970 Bank Holding Company Act Amendments.

The principal long-run benefit gleaned by stock investors from bank holding-company penetration into nonbank fields appears to be the ability of a holding-company conglomerate to branch into markets closed to banks themselves and not strictly from being able to offer nonbank product lines. Eisenbeis et al. (1984) believe that product line and geographic diversification *are* perceived by stockholders as raising a firm's market value but that geographic diversification and customer segmentation dominate other possible gains from nonbank activities.

A somewhat older study by Karna (1979) finds little net benefit from nonbank expansion, however. Examining 109 bank holding companies nationwide, each with aggregate assets exceeding $1 billion, he finds that average returns on investments in nonbank activities averaged 6.5 percent in 1976—little more than half the return on bank investments (12%). Unfortunately, these findings are limited because they apply only to a single year and do not adjust for differences in starting points or for holding-company expansion via *de novo* businesses versus acquired firms. However, they are corroborated by Nader and Brown (1976), who find that unprofitable nonbank activities reported by 23 holding companies had weakened the financial position of their affiliated banks during the 1974–75 period. Additional pessimistic findings have been reported by Whalen (1984), who found that a substantial number of nonbank affiliated firms were unprofitable in one or more years over the 1978–82 period with generally negligible dividends flowing to their parent companies. Often greater risks and limited diversification benefits plagued the nonbank acquisitions examined.

But contrary findings are reported by Heggestad (1975), who concluded that, for the 1953–67 period, risk-adjusted returns in nonbank product lines were greater than in banking activities. Similarly, Jacobs, Beighley, and Boyd (1975) found nonbank asset returns higher than bank asset returns over the 1970–73 period, though more recent research suggests that these added returns proved far more difficult to attain in the 1980s.

THE BENEFITS OF DIVERSIFICATION AND REDUCTION OF RISK
The mixed findings in these studies raise doubts about the long-run value of diversification by bank holding companies. Indeed, studies by Mayne (1977) and Silverberg (1975) imply that nonbank diversification may have a tendency to raise the probability of organizational failure. One possible reason for the limited and mixed benefits observed from past holding-company diversification is tied up in Congressional and Federal Reserve entry restrictions. Congress, as we have seen, mandated that any nonbank acquisitions must be "closely related to banking," and the Federal Reserve has adopted a relatively strict posture on what *is* "closely related" to banking. This narrow construction of the law is grounded in the fear that holding companies ranging far afield would weaken their affiliated banks and threaten the safety of the public's deposits.

Stover (1982) investigates the hypothesis that holding companies are still able to maximize their equity market values in the face of the Fed's nonbank business entry restrictions. He examines six allowable, three possible, and five nonallowable nonbank business activities, including among the possible and allowable activities commercial finance, small loans, credit card operations, leasing, the management of mutual funds, sales finance, business forms, small business investment companies, and title insurance. Nonallowable activities included savings and loan associations, life and property-casualty insurance, investment banking, and land development. Stover calculates the mean and standard deviation of annual operating income for each of these industries over the 1959–68 period. Correlation coefficients and equity-capital costs based on the capital asset pricing model were also derived.

Stover concludes that regulation has effectively limited the profitable expansion of bank holding companies into nonbank fields. He argues that permission to enter the savings and loan field would be beneficial in net-present-value terms to bank holding companies, along with entry into the sales finance and mutual fund industries. Ranging farther afield, leasing, title insurance, and life insurance would have offered additional diversification benefits to bank holding companies. This finding that regulation has limited the potential benefits of risk-reducing diversification by bank holding companies is perhaps all the more serious given Booth and Officer's (1985) recent observation that both bank and holding-company stocks show extra-market sensitivity to actual, anticipated, and unanticipated changes in interest rates—an interest rate sensitivity not found among nonfinancial firms. If this is correct, then existing legal limits on nonbank expansion prevent banking organizations from effectively buffering themselves against interest rate risk through product line diversification.

An earlier study by Talley (1976) looked at profitability and the use of leverage by consumer finance companies and mortgage banks affiliated with bank holding companies in 1973 and 1974. He found significantly greater use of leverage by holding-company-affiliated firms than was true of the industry average. Yet, both consumer finance and mortgage banking affiliates were significantly *less* profitable (measured by return on equity) than the average profit rate in their respective industries. For example, in 1973, affiliated mortgage companies reported an 8-percent return on equity compared with an 11-percent average for the industry as a whole, while finance company affiliates tallied a 4.9-percent equity return compared with an average of 9.3 percent for the entire industry. On balance, then, affiliated companies carried greater risk and achieved lower profitability, though they did report a lower average cost of funds. Many, however, sharply expanded their new service offerings and increased their office facilities to better position themselves in interstate markets—long-run investments that may have dampened their near-term profitability.

PUBLIC BENEFITS

The Talley study is interesting not only from a financial point of view but also from its raising the critical question of *public benefits*. Does the public really benefit in terms of more and better services, more conveniently provided, at lower cost because of holding-company penetration of nonbank fields? Talley (1976) finds *some* positive gains in service offerings and new office facilities in the consumer finance and mortgage banking fields. Unfortunately, a study of the consumer finance field by Rhoades and Boczar (1976) appearing at about the same time provides *no* support for this conclusion. Analysis of groups of affiliated and independent finance companies one year after one of the groups had been acquired by holding companies did not find evidence of new offices, lower operating expenses, or diminished losses. In brief, Rhoades and Boczar could find no evidence of "numerous public benefits," and the profits of affiliated finance companies averaged *below* those of independent finance companies. In general, their findings were consistent with an earlier investigation of the mortgage banking industry by Rhoades (1975), which, again, found no support for the notion that affiliation of nonbank firms with a bank holding company generates significant and tangible public benefits.

MANAGEMENT POLICIES AND CENTRALIZATION

In a unique study Lawrence (1974) examined the operating policies of 27 of the largest U.S. bank holding companies with regard to their methods and procedures for managing nonbank subsidiaries. Conducting personal interviews with senior officials of each organization, Lawrence found that the lead banks in conglomerate holding-company organizations displayed considerable influence over the operations of their nonbank subsidiaries. For example, in a majority of companies surveyed by Lawrence the chief executive officer of the holding company and of the lead bank in the organization were one and the same person. Moreover, important services—especially accounting, auditing, and personnel services—were extended from the lead bank or banks to the nonbank affiliates.

Nevertheless, Lawrence predicted that affiliated banks' role in the operations of nonbank subsidiaries would diminish, resulting in the holding company's becoming "a more distinct entity than it is today" [p. 42]. He suggested that nonbanking activities were generally growing more rapidly than banking activities and that a majority of the companies examined were moving toward having separate staffs of officers for their holding company as opposed to their principal subsidiary banks. Nonbank subsidiaries were viewed as *profit centers,* and their profitability, capital structures, and fund-raising activities were closely monitored and often controlled. Lawrence observes that "in most cases, the holding company raises virtually all the funds for its subsidiaries, including bank loans" [p. 44]. Lawrence saw this fund-raising control as "the greatest contribution" that holding-company organizations were making to the operations of their nonbank subsidiaries.

DEBT CAPITAL EXPANSION AND LEVERAGE

One benefit from the formation of conglomerate holding companies about which there is some measure of agreement is a societal one—the market for long-term bank capital has expanded and deepened tremendously over the past two decades. Both bank and nonbank acquisitions have been financed by increasing amounts of long-term borrowing (in many cases with double leveraging by both the parent company and its affiliates) and equity offerings. As Jacobs, Beighley, and Boyd (1975) have pointed out, the volume of bank stock trades has expanded dramatically since the early 1970s and bank stock prices appear to have adopted broad price movements in line with overall trends in the stock market as a whole. Moreover these developments have dramatically improved the science ("art") of analyzing bank financial statements and contributed to the growth of research on bank behavior and performance.

A growing body of literature has emerged over the past decade concerned with the causes and effects of heavy long-term borrowings in the capital markets by bank holding companies. One interesting study by Beighley (1977) looked at the characteristics of holders of bank holding-company debt. In particular, Beighley wished to determine if the long-term creditors of holding companies viewed firm size, financial structure, and loan losses as relevant measures of perceived risk—factors that previous research (for example, Beighley, Boyd, and Jacobs 1975 and Jacobs, Beighley, and Boyd 1975) had indicated bank stockholders look at in judging bank investment risk. Applying regression analysis to 56 publicly held capital note and debenture issues from 42 parent holding companies and their leading subsidiaries, 1972–74, Beighley found that size of company, realized loan losses, and financial structure *were* important determinants of the risk perceptions of holding-company debt holders. More recently, Billingsley and Fraser (1984) found that these same factors appear to influence the credit ratings assigned to holding-company debt.

Beighley's sample did show indifference on the part of debt holders, however, about whether the debt issued was the responsibility of the parent firm or of the lead bank in the holding company. But over the period examined, creditors did appear to respond to differences in financial structure between lead banks in different holding companies and to size differences, smaller holding companies having to pay investors higher yields to hold their equity and debt securities. Beighley argues that his findings provide useful information to the regulatory authorities, though they may not aid in controlling the use of financial leverage by holding companies. In particular, he was not certain that the financial marketplace could be relied on in the future as an effective regulator of the use of financial leverage by bank holding companies.

There is some evidence of an *optimal leverage position* (i.e., debt-to-equity ratio) for banking organizations that minimizes their cost of raising capital. For example, Karna and Graddy (1979) studied 40 large bank holding companies, 1969–76, each classified by the size of their leverage ratio. They found a significant relationship between average capital costs (measured by before-tax-and-interest earnings relative to the market value of the consolidated organization) and degree of leverage. An optimum leverage ratio of about 15 to 1 appeared to minimize average capital costs, while the market value of a holding-company organization appeared to be sensitive to the proportion of long-term debt outstanding. The optimal ratio of long-term debt to total permanent capital was found to be in the vicinity of 16 percent; thereafter, holding-company valuation declined.

Not all recent studies agree, however, that such a predictable leverage relationship exists. For example, examining a cross-section of 50 large banks over the 1970–75 period, Humphrey and Talley (1977) found no significant link between the amount of leverage employed and the ratio of holding-company equity values to earnings per share (i.e., the P/E ratio) or to weighted-average debt costs. In general, when the cost of fund raising increased, holding companies tended to increase their use of leverage. Humphrey and Talley saw little chance that the financial marketplace could be relied on to regulate the use of leverage by bank holding companies because there was no evidence that these organizations reacted to investor risk perceptions.

More recently, Scott, Hempel, and Peavy (1985) find that *leverage reduction* in the form of stock-for-debt swaps by holding companies may have positive benefits in contrast to nonfinancial companies, where such swaps have been found to reduce average returns. Analysis of the impact on stockholder returns from 22 bank holding companies announcing stock-for-debt swaps found *no* significant reduction in abnormal returns. The authors believe that such leverage reductions lower the potential costs of regulatory interference because they allow bank holding companies to more closely conform with the tougher capital standards imposed by the Federal Reserve as the 1980s began.

Frequently, holding companies borrow capital in the open market in order to funnel loanable funds to their banking subsidiaries. J. T. Rose and Talley (1984) examined the nature and implications of such financial transactions within holding-company organizations. These researchers developed an abbreviated theory of financial transactions within holding companies which posits that interaffiliate transactions will take place and funds will flow from one holding-company affiliate to another until the difference between the marginal cost of funds raised and the marginal revenue of funds invested is eliminated. Profits of a consolidated conglomerate banking organization can, in theory, be increased by having affiliates with relatively low marginal funds costs transfer these funds to affiliates with relatively high marginal investment returns.

Examining funds flows between bank and nonbank affiliates for 224 bank holding companies, 1976–80, J. T. Rose and Talley found that, increasingly over time, credit extensions and transfers to assets tended to flow from nonbank affiliates toward banks in the same organization. Conversely, upstream extensions of credit from banking affiliates to nonbank affiliates were small relative to each bank's equity capital and *below* the amount permitted by law. Thus, provisions in the Bank Holding Company Act and, more recently, in the Garn-St Germain Depository Institutions Act, that limit bank lending to affiliates within the same organization appear to have effectively constrained such activity. Moreover, these findings suggest that banks tend to have lower marginal cost functions than their companion nonbank affiliates and higher marginal revenue functions. Thus the observed tendency for funds to flow toward those banks locked inside a conglomerate organization is explained.

Conclusions and Implications

Overall, the research evidence supporting the wisdom of conglomerate expansion by bank holding companies is not especially convincing. Few, if any, concrete benefits—such as more services, greater convenience, improved efficiency, greater safety, or lower prices—seem to accrue to the public. Yet, "public benefits" is one of the tests imposed by law upon the regulatory approval process. In defense of the companies and the regulators, however, we must note that limited availability of data and serious methodological problems have severely hampered research in this area. These problems must be dealt with more adequately in future research if we are to confidently resolve the critical issue of whether the public interest is truly being served by conglomerate banking organizations.

There is disputed evidence that the acquisition of nonbank business ventures improves holding-company profitability or lowers company risk beyond possible temporary benefits around the date that new nonbank ventures are announced. Reflecting these disputes and, in some instances, real financial distress, nonbank business divestitures by U.S. holding companies recently have increased. Moreover, there is evidence as noted by Whalen (1986) that divestiture announcements generally have been viewed *favorably* in the capital markets and led to short-term increases in shareholder wealth. Nor can it be argued convincingly, on the basis of the research to date, that affiliated nonbank businesses outperform other firms in their own industries. Rather, nonfinancial objectives—especially achieving geographic penetration of new financial service markets—appear to have been the key motivators of conglomerate expansion by bank holding companies.

This last observation carries an interesting implication for the future growth and development of nonbank companies. If interstate banking eventually is legalized over wider areas, the demand for non-bank business entities as vehicles for interstate expansion is likely to decline and divestitures of nonbank affiliates will increase. The con-glomerate movement in the bank holding-company field may well fade as more of the services that formerly were offered through nonbank offices are marketed through banking offices. Of course, the willingness of the Congress and the Federal Reserve to broaden the list of permis-sible nonbank business activities will be, as it has been in the past, a key determinant of the future expansion of conglomerate bank holding-company organizations.

References

Aharony, J. and I. Swary. 1981. "Effects of the 1970 Bank Holding Company Act: Evidence from Capital Markets." *Journal of Finance* (September), 36:841–53.

Beighley, H. Prescott. 1972. "The Risk Perception of Bank Holding Company Debt-holders." *Journal of Bank Research* (Summer), 9:85–93.

Beighley, H. P., J. H. Boyd, and D. P. Jacobs. 1975. "Bank Equities and Investor Risk Perceptions: Some Entailments for Capital Adequacy Regulation." *Journal of Bank Research* (Autumn), pp. 190–201.

Billingsley, Randall S. and Donald R. Fraser. 1984. "Determinants of Bank Holding Company Debt Ratings." *Journal of Financial Research*, pp. 55–56.

Billingsley, Randall S. and Robert E. Lamy. 1984. "Market Reaction to the Formation of One-Bank Holding Companies and the 1970 Bank Holding Company Act Amendments." *Journal of Banking and Finance*, 8:21–33.

Board of Governors of the Federal Reserve System. 1971–1982. *Annual Report*, various annual editions.

——1972. "One-Bank Holding Companies Before the 1970 Amendments." *Federal Reserve Bulletin* (December), pp. 999–1008.

Booth, James R. and Dennis T. Officer. 1985. "Expectations, Interest Rates, and Com-mercial Bank Stocks." *The Journal of Financial Research* (Spring), 8(1):51–58.

Buynack, Thomas M. 1983. "Banking and Commerce: To Mix or Not To Mix?" *Economic Commentary* (December 5), Federal Reserve Bank of Cleveland.

Chase, Samuel B., Jr. 1971. "The Bank Holding Company as a Device for Sheltering Banks from Risk" (October 19). Board of Governors of the Federal Reserve System.

Childs, Bradley D. 1975. "Bank Holding Company Acquisitions: The Role of Non-Banking Finance Affiliates." *The Magazine of Bank Administration* (August), pp. 30–33.

Drum, Dale. 1977. "Nonbanking Activities of Bank Holding Companies." *Economic Perspectives* (March-April), pp. 12–21. Federal Reserve Bank of Chicago.

Eisemann, Peter. 1976. "Diversification and the Congeneric Bank Holding Company." *Journal of Bank Research* (Spring), pp. 68–77.

Eisenbeis, Robert A., Robert S. Harris, and Josef Lakonishok. 1984. "Benefits of Bank Diversification: The Evidence from Shareholder Returns." *The Journal of Finance* (July), 39(3):881–94.

Frodin, Joanna H. 1982. "Electronics: The Key to Breaking the Interstate Banking Barrier." *Business Review* (September/October), pp. 3–11. Federal Reserve Bank of Philadelphia.

Gendreau, B. and D. B. Humphrey. 1978. "Feedback Effects in the Market Regulation of Bank Leverage: A Time-Series and Cross-Section Analysis." *Research Papers in Banking and Financial Economics.* Board of Governors of the Federal Reserve System.

Gort, Michael and J. F. Hogarty. 1970. "New Evidence on Mergers." *Journal of Law and Economics* (April), 8:167–84.

Heggestad, Arnold. 1975. "Riskiness of Investments in Nonbank Activities by Bank Holding Companies." *Journal of Economics and Business* (Spring), pp. 219–23.

Humphrey, D. B. and S. H. Talley. 1977. "Market Regulation of Bank Leverage." *Research Papers in Banking and Financial Economics.* Board of Governors of the Federal Reserve System.

Jacobs, P. P., H. P. Beighley, and J. H. Boyd. 1975. *The Financial Structure of Bank Holding Companies.* Association of Reserve City Bankers.

Jessup, Paul F. 1974. "Analyzing Acquisitions by Bank Holding Companies." *Journal of Bank Research* (Spring), 5:55–63.

Johnson, Robert W. 1974. "The Rationale for Acquisitions of Finance Companies by Bank Holding Companies" (September). Institute for Research in the Behavioral, Economic and Management Sciences. Paper no. 481. Purdue University.

Karna, Adi. 1979. "Bank Holding Company Profitability: Nonbanking Subsidiaries and Financial Leverage." *Journal of Bank Research* (Spring), 10:28–35.

Karna, Adi and Duane B. Graddy. 1979. "Bank Holding Company Leverage, Risk Perception, and Cost of Capital." *Review of Business and Economic Research.*

Lawrence, Robert J. 1974. *Operating Policies of Bank Holding Companies—part 2: Non-Banking Subsidiaries.* Board of Governors of the Federal Reserve System.

Lawrence, Robert J. 1976. *Operating Policies of Bank Holding Companies—part 2: Nonbank Holding Company Subsidiaries.* Staff Economic Studies, no. 81. Board of Governors of the Federal Reserve System.

Levy, H. and M. Sarnat. 1970. "Diversification, Portfolio Analysis and the Uneasy Case for Conglomerate Mergers." *Journal of Finance* (September), 26:795–802.

Lewellen, W. 1971. "A Pure Financial Rationale for the Conglomerate Merger." *Journal of Finance* (May), pp. 521–37.

Lindahl-Stevenson. 1976. "The Market Effect of Diversification Mergers by Bank Holding Companies." Paper Presented to the Financial Management Association, October 14–16.

Martin, John D. and Arthur J. Keown. 1981. "Market Reaction to the Formation of One-Bank Holding Companies." *Journal of Banking and Finance,* 5:383–93.

Mayne, Lucille S. 1977. "A Comparative Study of Bank Holding Company Affiliates and Independent Banks, 1969–1972." *Journal of Finance,* 32:147–58.

Meinster, D. and R. Johnson. 1979. "Bank Holding Company Diversification and the

Risk of Capital Impairment." *Bell Journal of Economics* (Autumn), pp. 683–94.

Melicher, Ronald W. and D. F. Rush. 1973. "The Performance of Conglomerate Firms: Recent Risks and Return Experience." *Journal of Finance* (May), 28:381–88.

Mote, Larry R. 1970. "The One-Bank Holding Company—History, Issues, and Pending Legislation." *Business Conditions* (July), pp. 2–16. Federal Reserve Bank of Chicago.

Nader, Ralph and Jonathan Brown. 1976. *Disclosure and Bank Soundness—Nonbank Activities of Bank Holding Companies.* Nader Report (June 30).

Peavy, John W., III and S. Michael Edgar. 1983. "A Multiple Discriminant Analysis of BHC Commercial Paper Ratings." *Journal of Banking and Finance,* 7:161–73.

Piper, Thomas R. 1970. *The Economics of Bank Holding Company Acquisitions.* Federal Reserve Bank of Boston.

Rhoades, Stephen A. 1975. "The Effect of Bank Holding Company Acquisitions of Mortgage Bankers on Mortgage Lending Activity." *Journal of Business* (July), pp. 344–58.

Rhoades, Stephen A. and Gregory E. Boczar. 1976. *The Performance of Bank Holding Company-Affiliated Finance Companies.* Staff Economic Studies no. 90. Washington, D.C.: Board of Governors of the Federal Reserve System.

Rose, John T. and Samuel H. Talley. 1982. "The Banking Affiliates Act of 1982: Amendments to Section 23A." *Federal Reserve Bulletin* (November), pp. 693–99.

—— 1984. "Financial Transactions Within Bank Holding Companies." *The Journal of Financial Research* (Fall), 7(3):209–17.

Mote, Larry R. 1970. "The One-Bank Holding Company—History, Issues, and Pending Legislation." *Business Conditions* (July). Federal Reserve Bank of Chicago.

Scott, Jonathan A., George H. Hempel, and John W. Peavy, III. 1985. "The Effect of Stock-for-Debt Swaps on Bank Holding Companies." *Journal of Banking and Finance,* 9:233–51.

Silverberg, Stanley C. 1975. "Bank Holding Companies and Capital Adequacy." *Journal of Bank Research,* 6:202–7.

Stover, Roger D. 1982. "A Re-Examination of Bank Holding Company Acquisitions." *Journal of Bank Research* (Summer), 13:101–8.

Swary, Itzhak. 1983. "Bank Acquisition of Nonbank Firms." *Journal of Banking and Finance,* 7:213–30.

Talley, Samuel H. 1976. "Bank Holding Company Performance In Consumer Finance and Mortgage Banking." *The Magazine of Bank Administration* (July), pp. 42–44.

Whalen, Gary. 1981–1982. "The Operational Policies of Multibank Holding Companies." *Economic Review* (Winter), pp. 20–31. Federal Reserve Bank of Cleveland.

Whalen, Gary. 1984. "The Nonbanking Operations of Bank Holding Companies," *Economic Review,* Federal Reserve Bank of Cleveland, Spring.

Whalen, Gary. 1986. "Bank Holding Company Voluntary Nonbanking Asset Divestitures," *Economic Commentary,* Federal Reserve Bank of Cleveland, January 15, pp. 1–4.

Whitehead, David D. 1982. "Interstate Banking: Taking Inventory." Staff Study. Federal Reserve Bank of Atlanta.

Whitesill, William E. 1969. "The Economics of the One-Bank Holding Company." *The Bankers' Magazine* (Winter), pp. 28–34.

PART IV: INTERINDUSTRY COMPETITION AND STRUCTURAL CHANGE IN BANKING

10.

Competition from Nonbank Thrift Institutions:

Credit Unions, Savings and Loans, Savings Banks, and Money Market Funds

BANKERS GENERALLY paid little attention to their competitors outside the industry until after World War II. Indeed, until the decade of the 1960s competition from neighboring depository institutions—the credit unions, savings and loans, and mutual savings banks—was viewed more as a nuisance than as a real threat. True, these nonbank depository institutions frequently advertised in the same local newspapers and offered their deposit rates and loans through convenient offices in the same neighborhoods as commercial banks. Moreover, the thrifts were often the first in their local markets with new consumer-oriented innovations—weekend hours, "free" transactions via telephone and by mail, financial counseling services, loan rebates, and insurance and mutual fund sales, to cite just a few examples. But commercial banks dominated the commercial loan and checkable deposit markets—services for which the nonbank thrifts offered few effective substitutes. For their part, savings and loans and mutual savings banks concentrated heavily on residential mortgage loans and fixed-rate passbook savings accounts, while credit unions devoted their efforts to household installment credit and dividend-paying customer share accounts. Moreover, federal and state regulations erected strong barriers against the thrifts' making significant inroads in financial service markets outside the consumer field.

As we saw in chapter 1, the long history of commercial banking is one of heavy emphasis on *business* lending and *business* transactions services. As Herzog (1928) notes, consumer deposit and loan accounts were often regarded by bankers as excessively volatile, expensive to analyze and monitor, and generally unprofitable. Indeed, with restrictive state usury laws and the extremely small dollar size of most consumer credit requests—loans as small as $5, $10, or $50 were common only a few decades ago—there was some basis for the banker's hesitation to aggressively pursue consumer accounts.

So strong was the banker's aversion to consumer accounts that even when industrialization spread across the nation, swelling the ranks of middle-income wage earners who had rapidly growing needs for credit and attractive outlets for their savings, commercial banks still largely ignored these demands. Personal loans extended by commercial banks were generally confined to their wealthier customers who already held commercial accounts or sizable deposits. Bankers generally expected that such credit requests would be short-term and occasional. Indeed, as Rogers (1974) notes, it was not until 1928, when National City Bank of New York established a personal loan department, that major banks began to take consumer accounts seriously. Nugent (1937) estimates that in 1920, when the nation had 30,000 commercial banks, only about 30 were consistently offering consumer installment loans.

Predictably, where there is a financial vacuum, enterprising institutions will move in to fill that need. Mutual savings banks and savings and loan associations first appeared in the 1830s in response to the demand for small savings deposit programs and an even more pressing demand for home mortgage credit. The growing demand for consumer installment loans gave rise to credit unions, which first appeared in New England in 1909 and spread westward, followed by Morris Plan and industrial banks, which began along the eastern seaboard. These sources of consumer financial services were supplemented by a potpourri of financial and nonfinancial companies entering the consumer field to finance the growing volume of consumer durables— furniture, home appliances, and automobiles. Included in this list were manufacturing companies setting up sales finance affiliates to handle consumer installment paper, retailers offering time payment plans, pawn brokers, and small loan companies. In this chapter I look in some detail at the most important of these consumer-oriented financial institutions—credit unions, savings and loans, savings banks, and money market funds. With the sweeping changes in federal law and regulation during the 1980s, these institutions are becoming significant competitors with commercial banks in both commercial and consumer loan and deposit markets in thousands of local markets across the nation. For example, market share calculations by Nathan (1980) suggest that, for most of the period since World War II, commercial banking's share of the total assets of all private-sector financial institutions has increased only slightly, while savings and loan associations significantly expanded their asset share, and both credit unions and money market funds saw their asset shares rising at least twice as rapidly as those of commercial banks. Many of these gains in market share by the nonbank thrifts could be traced to their broader legal powers for geographic expansion (particularly branching) than those possessed by most commercial banking institutions.

Origins of the Nonbank Thrifts

MUTUAL SAVINGS BANKS
        The first nonbank thrift institution—the mutual savings bank—appeared in Scotland in 1810. The basic idea was to create a financial institution operated exclusively for the benefit of small savers whose funds would be channeled into relatively safe investments— commercial and residential mortgages, government bonds, and high-quality stocks. Virtually all the income from these investments (less relatively small amounts earmarked for reserves) would be returned to the depositors—the legal owners—as dividends. The idea rapidly caught on in the United States and in Western Europe. In fact, six years after Reverend Henry Duncan founded the first mutual in Scotland, two savings banks opened in Boston and Philadelphia—the Philadelphia Savings Fund Society and the Provident Institution of Boston, which still rank among the top mutuals in the United States.

They have since been joined by more than 600 other savings banks in 45 states, holding total assets of nearly $220 billion at year-end 1985. In the five states where mutuals are most prominent—Connecticut, Massachusetts, New Jersey, New York, and Pennsylvania—they are the leading institutional holders of small-denomination savings deposits.

A key trend in mutual savings banking today, as it is among all the nonbank thrifts, is *service diversification*. Mutuals are among the most aggressive and innovative of the nonbank thrifts. It was a mutual savings bank in Worcester, Massachusetts, for example, that developed NOW interest-bearing checking accounts. Mutuals seized early upon recently legalized opportunities to offer over-the-counter life insurance, shares in mutual funds, discount brokerage, retirement plans, travel agency services, and family financial planning. One key advantage over the years has been the mutuals' exemption from federal regulation because of their state charters. An option for federal chartering of savings banks was created by Congress in 1978, however, and the Garn-St Germain Depository Institutions Act of 1982 permitted easier conversion of mutuals into federal savings banks and free convertibility between savings and loans and federal savings banks. Thus, in future years the historic distinction between mutual savings banks, which predominate along the eastern seaboard, and savings and loan associations, dominant in the Midwest and West, should become less and less relevant.

Like the savings and loans to be discussed later in the chapter, the concentration of mutuals upon a narrow range of investment assets—a specialization enforced by regulations designed to promote the safety of their deposits—has been the Achilles' heel of many firms in the industry in an era of volatile interest rates. Half of mutuals' assets consist of residential and commercial mortgages. In 1985, for example, of the industry's $219 billion in total assets, $110 billion was represented by mortgage loans. Most of these loans carried either fixed interest rates or faced government restrictions on the speed with which contract loan rates could be changed. Nevertheless, the cost of attracting deposits, as well as the cost of innovation through offering new services, continued to spiral upward, putting intense pressure on savings bank profit margins and net earnings. With rising costs and decreasing margins the number of mutuals began to decline through failure, merger, and consolidation. However, today's survivors are both larger and more aggressive in seeking new and more profitable services and markets.

SAVINGS AND LOAN ASSOCIATIONS

The mutuals were joined in the small-saver and home mortgage markets by the savings and loan association as far back as 1831. In that year the Oxford Provident Building Association was established in Philadelphia County, Pennsylvania. The basic idea was to bring together a group of local citizens who would be willing to pool their savings so that, periodically, home mortgage loans could be made to certain members of the group. Once all members of the participating group had their homes constructed the savings and loan association could be closed. However, many associations sought permanent charters under either state or federal law.

The number of savings and loans (S&Ls) expanded rapidly, particularly in the years immediately after World War II when the public had substantial pent-up savings, as well as a strong demand for new homes. In addition, the S&Ls were quick to take advantage of the shifting demographics of the nation and establish themselves in growing urban centers of the South, West, and Midwest. By year-end 1960 the industry's population reached an all-time high of more than 6300 associations and then began to decline rapidly. At year-end 1984 there were 3391 S&Ls operating, with 1913 carrying state charters and 1478 with federal charters. The industry reported book value assets of over $1 trillion in 1985, ranking second in the financial services industry to commercial banks which held more than $2 trillion in assets.

The decline in S&L numbers reflects the influence of powerful economic forces redefining the fundamental character of the industry. One potent force was external competition from commercial banks, money market funds, and other intermediaries offering consumer financial services, which combined with soaring operating and capital costs to bring on a rash of mergers. Encouraged by a relatively lenient Federal Home Loan Bank policy toward these combinations, scores of smaller S&Ls were absorbed by larger associations during the 1970s and early 1980s. These mergers may have resulted in significant gains in operating efficiency and risk-reducing diversification—an outcome detected in earlier S&L mergers by Bradford (1975).

Certainly the savings and loans' most serious problem in recent years has been an inflexible asset portfolio ranged against flexible-term deposits. In 1985, for example, about three fifths (61 percent) of S&L assets were devoted to mortgage loans, many of which carried fixed interest rates or contract loan rates that could be changed only on a limited basis. As Daly (1971) and Weber (1966) observe, rising interest rates have a differential impact on savings and loan costs and revenues; rising mortgage rates affect revenue flows on *new* loans only, while rising deposit rates soon affect virtually *all* S&L deposits. During the 1970s and early 1980s, deposit interest rates—under the combined influence of rapid inflation, economic expansion, and deregulation— were repeatedly pushed to record levels, drastically reducing the industry's net profit margin. Changing regulations permitted new deposit plans, such as money market certificates, whose interest rates more accurately reflected prevailing market conditions. As the industry's deposit mix shifted toward these higher rate and more flexible accounts, its interest costs spiraled upward.

The inability of operating revenues to match the fast-track growth in S&L operating expenses was reflected in the industry's eroding after-tax income (especially relative to its assets and equity). As reported by the United States League of Savings Institutions (1985), S&Ls' return on average assets was 0.57 percent in 1970, but only 0.13 percent in 1980, before turning negative in both 1981 and 1982. Although the industry had returned to positive profitability by the mid 1980s, its return on assets compared unfavorably with the profit levels achieved by banks and other competing intermediaries.

Factors other than a low-velocity asset portfolio were also at work in worsening the industry's earnings picture. There has been a continuing shortage of qualified management, particularly as S&Ls have grown larger and established extensive branching and holding company systems offering many new services. Federal tax laws and tradition strongly favored the industry's steadfast commitment to residential mortgage lending. Yet, housing construction is one of the most cyclically sensitive and economically vulnerable of all industries. Whereas S&Ls generally won the battle for savings deposits over commercial banks in the 1950s and 1960s, they clearly lost the battle for deposit market shares in the 1970s and early 1980s as banks and other financial institutions with more flexible asset portfolios widened their own shares.

The specter of hundreds of S&L failures and the potential insolvency of the federal deposit insurance fund prompted a double-barreled response from Congress. In 1980 the Depository Institutions Deregulation and Monetary Control Act (DIDMCA) was passed, authorizing S&Ls to invest up to 20 percent of their assets in consumer loans and corporate debt securities, including commercial paper. In addition, S&Ls were granted authority to issue credit cards, offer trust services, and make increased investments in service corporations, and thus open up new and more flexible sources of revenue. A temporary federal override on state usury ceilings against mortgages was extended, offering greater flexibility for new mortgage loans. More options in deposit plans were also instituted with a gradual phaseout of Regulation Q time and savings deposit interest rate ceilings (completed in 1986), increased deposit insurance from $40,000 to $100,000, and nationwide legalization of checkable NOW accounts.

Not fully satisfied with the results of these innovations, Congress made a second pass at the problem in October 1982 with passage of the Garn-St Germain Depository Institutions Act. Federal associations received further expanded authority to invest in consumer, commercial, and agricultural loans; were permitted higher loan value ratios on new mortgage loans; and were allowed to invest in tangible personal property for sale or lease up to 10 percent of their total assets. On the deposit side new thrift deposits were authorized to carry interest rates adjustable with money market conditions, allowing S&Ls to compete more effectively with money market mutual funds. For troubled S&Ls a "rescue plan" was instituted, empowering the FDIC and the FSLIC to assist beleaguered depository institutions with an infusion of net worth through the issuance of insurance corporation notes to be traded for net worth certificates issued by the troubled thrifts.

These sweeping changes have certainly aided the industry but appear to have fallen short of their principal objective—to solidify S&Ls and other thrifts against failure by encouraging them to acquire more flexible asset and deposit portfolios similar to those held by commercial banks. While many S&Ls have firmly committed themselves to becoming "financial department stores," offering a broad range of new services, others have resisted making significant changes in their service menus. This is surprising to many observers because there is evidence that adoption of *selected* new deregulated services might aid S&L profitability. For example, a study conducted by Crockett and King (1982) of Texas' state-chartered S&Ls, which already possessed asset powers similar to those in DIDMCA and the Garn bill, found that the new asset powers enabled associations in that state to reduce their exposure to interest rate risk while improving their average net returns on assets (particularly for those becoming active in real estate development). Paralleling this result, a study by Benston (1985) of 202 savings and loans failing over the 1981–85 period finds evidence that federal and state permission granted to S & Ls to offer consumer and commercial loans and to make direct investments in real estate development projects and service corporations did *not* contribute significantly to those failures. Rather, expanded loan and investment opportunities appear to have strengthened the financial condition of thrifts by increasing their profit potential and reducing their exposure to interest-rate risk. Over-specialization and portfolio imbalances appeared to Benston to be more probable causes of savings and loan bankruptcies than did deregulation of service powers. However, one serious flaw in recent legislation is its failure to consider reasons other than regulation for the S&Ls' heavy emphasis on residential mortgages. Tradition, management expertise, mispriced deposit insurance with no adjustments for portfolio risk, and the significant tax shelters associated with residential mortgage lending have encouraged the persistence of a "business almost as usual" attitude among many savings associations.

CREDIT UNIONS

The unsettling problems that racked the savings and loans and mutuals in the 1970s and early 1980s were also visited upon the credit unions, though with somewhat less virulence and somewhat less damaging results. Credit union asset portfolios proved to be more flexible and deposit regulations were relaxed earlier than in the savings bank industry, permitting a more rapid adjustment to prevailing market conditions. Moreover, credit unions deal with a unique group of customers compared with other thrift institutions—a factor that goes to the very roots of the credit union movement. Credit unions are non-profit cooperative associations, composed of groups of people who pool their savings and make loans to each other. To belong to the group credit union members must share a common bond, such as the same employer, labor union, church, fraternal organization, or residential area. This common-bond requirement however, has been significantly liberalized in recent years, giving the industry an expanded membership base. A member may make deposits in return for ownership shares that earn dividends and entitle the member to vote on all matters affecting the organization as a whole, including the election of officers. Loans, which make up approximately three quarters of the industry's assets, are made only to members of the association. Credit unions are tax exempt because all their net earnings (minus relatively small allocations to reserves) flow to the members. Charters for new credit unions can be issued by either the states or the National Credit Union Administration (NCUA), their federal supervisory agency.

The first credit union was organized in New Hampshire in 1909. The movement spread rapidly across private industry and government in the wake of growing industrialization and a spreading government bureaucracy. With small, less interest sensitive savings deposits accounting for 80 percent or more of total funds sources plus tax-free status, volunteer help, and sponsor subsidies, the industry has been able to offer its borrowing members below-average interest rates on consumer loans. Although deposits and loans are restricted to qualified members, each credit union must compete with commercial banks, savings and loans, and other financial institutions in its local market for both deposit and credit accounts. This competitive pressure has stimulated deregulation of the industry and service innovation to attract and hold membership. The industry's success in doing so is indicated by recent growth figures: in 1970 there were 22.8 million credit union members in the United States and the industry held $15.5 billion in deposits; by 1984, 50.4 million members had signed on with deposit shares totaling $103.1 billion and total assets of more than $113 billion, as reported by the Credit Union National Association (1984).

Credit unions have not been totally immune, however, to the troublesome events plaguing savings banking in recent years. One indication is recent changes in the total population of credit unions. The number of credit unions tripled during the Great Depression of the 1930s, the federal government strongly encouraging their growth, and savers desperately seeking a *safe* outlet for their funds. The industry's rapid growth continued after World War II, the number of associations nearly doubling during the 1950s. The higher interest rates and more volatile economy of the 1960s slowed their growth dramatically, and by 1969 their numbers had reached a plateau at nearly 24,000 associations. Since then, a decline in numbers has taken place fueled by economic problems, a more liberal federal merger policy, and a phasing out of federal deposit rate ceilings that previously granted credit unions a significant deposit rate advantage. In 1975 there were 22,678 U.S. credit unions; in 1980, 21,467, and in 1984 industry rolls listed 18,515. On the positive side, however, the average-size association has expanded significantly, perhaps positioning the industry for greater stability in the period ahead.

Credit unions continue to offer a challenge to commercial banks in developing new services. The industry was among the pioneers in developing payroll deduction plans, interest-bearing checking (share drafts), low-cost money orders, debit and credit cards, and loan insurance protection without added cost to members. Beginning in 1978 credit union mortgage lending was gradually deregulated to the point that today federally supervised associations can make residential mortgage loans of any size and maturity plus sell their mortgages in the secondary market. More recently, IRA plans, discount brokerage, money market share accounts, and a national network for customer access to automated teller machines (ATMs) have been under development. With access to a large industrial base of workers (particularly through payroll savings programs), a tradition of "loyalty" on the part of its members, and continued liberalization of regulations by its chief federal supervisor (NCUA), the credit union is likely to continue to be an effective innovator of new services and, therefore, a significant competitive factor in urban financial markets for the foreseeable future.

MONEY MARKET MUTUAL FUNDS

Money market funds first appeared in 1972 as a vehicle for channeling the short-term, liquid savings of individuals and corporations into the unregulated money market. The initial impetus to the growth of money funds was the record high interest rates of the late 1960s and early 1970s coupled with federal (Regulation Q) interest rate ceilings and reserve requirements on deposits offered by banks and thrifts. Mutual funds' management saw an opportunity to offer more interest-sensitive individual and institutional savers higher returns on liquid balances for very little additional risk by selling shares in a pool of money market securities and passing the earnings from that pool (less administrative costs) on to the investor.

Money market funds are technically *open-end investment companies* because they sell as many shares as the public demands, offering the subscribing investor not only flexible returns but also professional management of liquid funds. Moreover, operating costs are held to a minimum by setting a low initial investment to get into the fund—usually $500 to $5,000, though some funds selling shares to institutions require an initial deposit of at least $50,000. Access to investor shares may be made via check, telephone, or wire with the funds remitted either to the investor or directly into his or her bank account. The check-writing option has been particularly attractive to the small investor who can continue to earn interest until the check clears, though the usual $500 minimum on any checks written has discouraged the smallest accounts. The majority of money fund investments are in U.S. Treasury bills, domestic and Eurodollar CDs, commercial paper, bankers' acceptances, and federal agency securities. Generally, investment maturities are shorter than four months, thus ensuring a high degree of flexibility in responding to short-run changes in market conditions.

Money funds have proved advantageous to large brokerage houses and families of mutual funds because they expand the line of available services, bringing in more customers who may then be sold other investment services. The prospect of additional sales encouraged most money funds to adopt "no load" policies whereby the customer can purchase or redeem shares without paying a commission. Any fund expenses are deducted from gross earnings before investors receive their dividends. Once a fund reaches efficient size (perhaps $50 to $100 million in assets under management) the ratio of expenses to total assets becomes quite low—in most years, this ratio has averaged well under 1 percent for the industry.

Initially, money funds grew modestly with one in operation at year-end 1972, four at the end of 1973, and 15 by year-end 1974. Then in 1978 their growth rate accelerated dramatically, paralleling a dramatic run up in open-market interest rates. By year-end 1979, money-fund assets totaled $45 billion and then spiraled upward to exceed $200 billion in 1982. Their rapid growth spawned a welter of product line innovations, particularly in the form of specialized funds. For example, money funds devoted exclusively to U.S. Government securities were created to lure those investors particularly sensitive to default risk. Tax-exempt funds were launched in 1977 to provide a channel for investors in top tax brackets to invest in shorter term tax-exempt municipal bonds and notes, gaining tax shelter benefits while avoiding significant market risk. Broker-oriented short-term investment trusts were resurrected in 1978 to give investors access to the higher yields available on foreign bank or U.S. foreign-branch CDs.

Whereas many financial analysts believe the heyday of money market funds has passed, especially after the appearance in 1983 of bank money market deposits (MMDAs and Super NOWs), others are not so sure. Money fund assets did decline significantly with the appearance of the new flexible-rate, money market deposits but appeared to reach a floor in the $160 to $170 billion range by 1983. The funds have regained some lost ground since then, however. It is important not to overlook the fact that money funds reflect the potent capacity of security brokers and dealers to develop new financial products without the burden of regulation in response to changing public needs. Because further significant banking deregulation is by no means assured, the unregulated funds continue to hold an important competitive edge for the future.

Effects of Nonbank Thrifts on the Competition for Banking Services

In theory at least, the presence of nonbank thrift institutions in banking markets, offering bank-like services, *should* have a strong competitive impact on bank behavior. In particular, bank prices should be closer to competitive norms, excess bank profits should be eliminated, the quality of banking services should be higher, the availability of banking services should approach the level of public demand more closely, and resource efficiency should be greater in markets where nonbank thrifts offer competition for either credit or deposit customers or both. The problem with these conclusions is they are not always supported convincingly by the available research evidence.

Moreover, for more than two decades since the Philadelphia National Bank case, discussed in chapter 5, commercial banking has been defined legally as a "distinct line of commerce" separate from the nonbank thrifts—a position still maintained in many quarters despite recent federal legislation granting the thrifts many bank-like powers. In fact in the Connecticut National Bank case decided in 1974, the Supreme Court ruled that nonbank thrifts must (1) offer enough bank services so that customers view them as alternative sources of supply and (2) "significantly participate" in any bank service lines they choose to offer before they could be considered part of commercial banking's line of commerce. Because most thrifts have not chosen to "significantly participate" in the commercial services field, they would, as Dunham (1982) observes, have great difficulty meeting these two legal conditions. However, despite these court decisions, what is the *reality* of the competitive situation between banks and thrifts? Do nonbank thrifts really represent a potent competitive force in commercial banking markets? As we will see, past research studies provide decidedly mixed answers to those questions.

There is an interesting dichotomy in past research studies on bank vs. thrift competition. One set of studies focuses on the *portfolio substitutability* between bank services and those offered by the nonbank thrifts, especially for time and savings deposits. These studies may be labeled *national market studies* because they focus principally on the responsiveness of bank and thrift deposits to changes in their relative yields and to changes in interest rates in the national money and capital markets. One important motivation for such a study is to define more precisely the makeup of the nation's money supply, which depends crucially on the degree of substitutability among different financial assets. A second set of studies, generally of more recent vintage, examines whether the presence of nonbank thrifts in local counties, cities, or SMSA markets affects bank behavior in some significant way. I label these research projects *local market studies*. As we will see, the findings of these two sets of studies are often quite different.

NATIONAL MARKET STUDIES

One of the earliest national market studies, by Hamburger (1968), examined the substitutability in household investment portfolios of four liquid assets—marketable bonds (including U.S. Treasury bills and notes, municipals, and corporate and foreign bonds), time and savings deposits at commercial banks, life insurance reserves, and savings accounts at nonbank thrifts. Hamburger employed household investment data from the Federal Reserve's Flow of Funds Accounts and a collection of open-market bond and bill rates, along with national averages for rates paid on bank and nonbank time and savings accounts, 1952–62. He found that households do *not* treat time and savings deposits at commercial banks as if they were substantially different from thrifts' savings accounts or from bonds sold in the open market. Changes in national average interest rates offered by nonbank thrifts appeared to significantly alter household purchases of bank-offered time and savings accounts. Hamburger estimates that an increase of one quarter of a percentage point in the average savings rate paid across the nation by nonbank thrifts resulted in bank-held personal time and savings deposits' falling by nearly $1.9 billion (measured in constant purchasing power dollars). Kardouche (1969), Silber (1970), Vernon (1966), and Cohen and Kaufman (1965) achieved qualitatively similar results in finding savings and loan share accounts a close substitute for commercial bank time and savings deposits.

Vernon's results are particularly interesting because of a finding that a yield spread of 0.75 percent in favor of S&L share accounts over bank time and savings deposits appeared to be a point of *indifference* between the two institutions in the minds of household savers. A spread of this magnitude would be sufficient to preserve banking's share of the household savings market, roughly indicating the relative value to consumers of the complete financial service package offered by commercial banks. Of course, with recent moves toward deregulation of savings and loans and other depository institutions, I would expect to see the magnitude of that indifference yield spread declining.

Indeed, Kardouche (1969) finds *increasing* responsiveness of bank deposits to thrift bank yield spreads over time and considerable sensitivity in the relative attractiveness of bank versus nonbank thrift deposits to thrift institution advertising. Moreover, there is evidence of significant competitive interaction between commercial bank and mutual savings bank deposits and between similar accounts offered by mutuals and savings and loans, though such interactions appear to be greater in metropolitan areas than in rural communities. Finally, we now have evidence (from Kwon and Thornton 1983) that sales of notes and bonds by federal credit agencies—especially those designed to aid the savings and loan industry—significantly affect thrift deposit flows.

These national time series findings are not universally confirmed by all researchers, however. For example, studies by Fiege (1964) and Stevens (1966) reached conflicting results concerning the substitutability of commercial bank time deposits and savings and loan shares, 1949–59. Moreover, Hartley (1966) found a *complementary* relationship between S&L share accounts and bank-held time accounts, suggesting that an increase in thrift-offered deposit rates would cause the public to increase its holdings of *both* bank and nonbank savings deposits. However, more recent national studies have tended to confirm the bank-nonbank deposit *substitutability* thesis, even when money market funds are included. For example, access to high money market yields has been a significant inducement to many bank and thrift depositors to disintermediate their funds and send them by mail or by wire into money market fund share accounts. A study by Cook and Duffield (1979) confirms this interest sensitivity phenomenon, at least for the 1975–79 period. These researchers compared the yield to maturity on the security portfolios held by five major money funds with the bank passbook savings rate. As expected, they found that when money market fund yields were below the passbook deposit rate (as occurred between October 1975 and July 1977), assets held by money funds decreased but then rose when this yield spread favored the money funds.

Of course, this latest evidence, while interesting, leaves open the question of whether yield differentials between money funds and banks are any longer really significant in the minds of depositors now that *both* commercial banks and nonbank thrifts can offer ceiling-free MMDAs and Super NOWs. There is also an interesting side issue of whether money fund share accounts are more competitive with bank checking accounts or with bank time and savings deposits. Limited evidence (primarily a study by Dotsey, Englander, and Portlan 1981–82) suggests that money fund accounts are more like savings balances rather than checkbook deposits. The velocity of share accounts has proved to be substantially less, for example, than regular checking accounts.

Either way, it seems clear that the success of money market funds during the 1970s and early 1980s was a major factor in accelerating the deregulation movement in banking. Indeed, now that deposit deregulation has made such significant strides since 1980, some observers predict the eventual demise of the money market fund, at least as a potent, market-share-stealing competitor for banks and other nonbank thrift institutions. This is improbable, however, for, as Cook and Duffield (1979b) have observed, money market funds appeal to a wide range of clientele with a diverse set of financial needs. Money funds are perhaps less attractive now to the average individual investor because that customer has another route of access—the local bank or thrift—to high money market yields. However, institutional depositors in money funds, particularly nonfinancial corporations, still find the nonrate terms and professional management services of money fund share accounts highly attractive. There are significant scale economies for a corporation turning over the task of portfolio investment decisionmaking to a professional money fund.

Moreover, there is evidence, in studies by Davis (1982) and Shawky, Forbes, and Frankle (1983), that money fund managers have been able to score excess returns over and above what is normal for the market at their level of risk. Ferri and Oberhelman (1981) found evidence that fund managers have a better track record of interest rate forecasting than the average market forecaster. Examining monthly changes in the average maturity of money fund portfolios, they found a significant *negative* correlation between money market interest rates and money fund maturities. Maturities generally shortened just before interest rates rose and lengthened just before interest rates declined. Of course, these findings may be logically related—money fund managers may score excess returns because they are better than average interest rate forecasters. Owing to inconsistencies with efficient-markets research, however, additional studies are needed to give these research findings stronger credibility.

LOCAL MARKET STUDIES

The generally positive findings for bank versus nonbank competition in the national market studies are often contradicted by studies of local county and city markets. And there is ample evidence (provided, for example, by Lapp 1978) that the market for the services offered by nonbank thrifts is predominantly *local,* rather than regional or national.

As we saw in chapter 2, economic theory argues for a significant relationship between the structure of local banking markets—the number and relative sizes of competitors serving counties, SMSAs, or other geographic areas—and the performance of banks in terms of their prices, costs, service quantity and quality, and profitability. Rhoades (1977, 1982) reviewed 65 banking studies exploring this relationship that were published during the 1960–82 period. Do any of these local market studies examine whether the presence of thrifts influences local bank behavior and performance? Actually, of the 65 banking studies examined by Rhoades, only 25 studies included a measure of competition from nonbank thrift institutions. This measure ranged from the number of nonbank thrift offices present in local markets to the ratio of nonbank thrift deposits to commercial bank deposits in each market area. Slightly over half (13) of these studies found a statistically significant impact from nonbank thrift competition on bank behavior and performance.

As we might expect, when we turn this research question around and ask, "does the presence of commercial banks in a local market affect the behavior and performance of thrifts?" the findings do *not* point to a consistently strong and powerful bank competition effect. For example, Verbrugge and Shick (1974) explored the determinants of profitability (both return on assets or ROA and return on equity or ROE) for 104 savings and loans operating in both rural and urban markets during 1971 and 1972. Their structure-performance models included variables measuring the financial and managerial characteristics of S&Ls, the economic and demographic character of their local markets, and proxies for competition between banks and savings and loans. While S&L profitability was most strongly affected by operating efficiency and growth variables, the degree of S&L market concentration and the numbers of savings associations present in local markets were also statistically significant in the theoretically expected direction. However, commercial bank activity (as measured by the number of banks in the local area) was *not* a statistically significant determinant of S&L profitability. Only when the number of banks was *combined* with the number of S&Ls did the expected *negative* relationship between numbers of competing institutions and profitability appear. Verbrugge and Shick suggest refining the measure of local bank activity in future research (perhaps by focusing only on the local market for savings deposits). It may well be that the character of bank-thrift competition is far more complicated than we have supposed.

A follow-up S&L study by Shick, Thygerson, and Verbrugge (1976) considers S&L *service mix* as a profitability determinant, along with the more conventional economic and market structure variables. The authors find that higher risk mortgages (other than single-family home loans), mortgage trading, and mortgage loan servicing increase S&L revenues but also increase operating expenses. The average interest return on mortgages, the ratio of S&L fee income to aggregate revenue, individual association size, branching activity, and the number of S&Ls and mutual savings banks present in the local market proved to be the most significant factors influencing individual S&L profitability. Once again, the presence or absence of commercial banks in local markets did *not* emerge as a significant S&L profit factor, though the period chosen for study was characterized by a stronger economic environment with heavier regulation than now prevails. Similarly, Lapp (1978) found no evidence of commercial bank influence on S&L growth or posted deposit rates.

One factor that may hamper *both* commercial bank and thrift studies of competition and profitability is the developing evidence of *expense preference* behavior (as opposed to profit-maximizing behavior) among depository institutions. If the management of such institutions tends to seek greater personal utility (e.g., higher salaries, more workers to supervise, plush offices, etc.) at the expense of higher profits, employment of resources may be pushed beyond the optimal production point, reducing both operating efficiency and profitability. Support for the presence of such behavior in S&Ls is provided by Verbrugge and Jahera (1981) and in commercial banks by Edwards (1977) and Hannan (1979). Further research by Verburgge and Goldstein (1981) suggests that expense preference behavior and operating inefficiencies, as well as strong aversion to risk taking, is more characteristic of mutual (i.e., depositor-owned) associations—the category to which most of the thrifts belong—than those adopting the corporate (stock) form of ownership, which includes all commercial banks and about a fifth of all savings and loans. Stigum (1976) finds that S&Ls entrepreneurs display increasing absolute risk aversion, and the smaller the S&L, the more unlikely it is to pursue profit maximization as a primary goal.

Some research studies *do* find a persuasively strong impact on banks from nonbank thrift competition. For example, Hannan (1984) analyzed the behavior of 412 banks operating primarily in local markets in Pennsylvania during 1971. Using market areas carefully defined from demographic and service area information, Hannan measures bank performance by passbook savings rates offered and the number of hours per week each bank's headquarters is open for business. Herfindahl indices of market structure, first defined separately for each type of bank and nonbank thrift present in the local market and then combining bank-nonbank market shares, are tested for their effects on bank performance. Applying tobit maximum likelihood and ordinary least-squares regression analysis, Hannan finds that "the level of statistical significance of the coefficients of market structure increases considerably when thrift institutions are included in the analysis" (p. 12). This relationship is strongest for the passbook savings rate and when savings and loans are included with commercial banks in indices of local market structure. The presence of mutual savings banks and credit unions appeared, however, to add little to the explanation of variations in local bank hours or savings rates. Hannan's findings are particularly interesting because they are based on data gathered well *before* the major deregulation moves of the late 1970s and early 1980s that allowed thrifts to become even more like commercial banks.

Because the majority of these earlier local market studies did *not* include credit unions or money market funds, would the results perhaps have been different if the latter institutions had been considered? Limited evidence suggests the answer is "no." For example, an econometric study by Koot (1976) of the volume of share accounts held by 260 large U.S. credit unions at year-end 1965 found that neither the ratio of commercial bank savings deposit rates to credit union savings yields nor the ratio of savings and loan deposit rates to credit union savings yields had a statistically significant impact on credit union deposits. Koot also found no effect on the volume of credit union deposits from adding additional commercial banking offices in the local area. This may be a reflection of Taylor's earlier findings (1972) that the *nonprice* terms surrounding deposits—e.g., convenience and institutional image—are important factors in the customer's choice of a nonbank thrift (in this case, a credit union), perhaps even more important than when customers choose a commercial bank. Yet, there are shreds of evidence that credit unions and commercial banks may not be that far apart and certainly are moving closer in their behavioral and portfolio characteristics. For example, Koot and Walker (1980) find bank and credit union patterns of lending behavior and speed of response over time to changes in monetary policy "remarkably similar."

Implications of the Nonbank Thrift Studies

Most nonbank thrift institutions appear to have weathered the financial storms of the late 1970s and early 1980s when record high market interest rates and an inverted yield curve threatened many with bankruptcy and indeed pushed some over the brink. More recently, the thrifts have faced severe crises of customer confidence, generating in some instances massive deposit runs, as in Ohio and Maryland where state-sponsored insurance systems appeared to be inadequate, and in the wake of public concerns over the long-run viability of the FSLIC. But history is a fickle storyteller, for it has also spun out periods of great success—rapid growth and strong profitability—for many thrift institutions. Examples include the spectacular performance of most savings and loans in the 1950s and 1960s, mutual savings banks in the 1960s and 1970s, and money market funds in the decade following their birth in 1972.

Whether blessed by success or beleaguered by distress, however, the thrifts have displayed two characteristics that may promote their long-run survival: (1) the capacity for creativity and innovation, especially in invading the service lines and markets of other financial institutions, and (2) the ability to win major legislative and regulatory concessions, though often belatedly. For example, when the future growth of thrifts depended crucially on their getting into the nation's payments system (including the spreading EFTS network), mutual savings banks developed the NOW account, and credit unions, the share draft. When survival of savings and loans required greater diversification and more flexibility in the cash flows generated by earning assets, S&Ls eventually won Congressional and federal agency approval to offer a wide range of customer and commercial loans and security investments, as well as the authority to offer credit cards and trust services on a par with commercial banks.

These two elements of long-run survival are the same ones that have challenged the competitive capabilities of commercial banks, threatening them with an erosion of market share and a narrowing margin of profitability. But one must ask: how strong is the competitive challenge to banking posed by the nonbank thrifts? To what extent have they actually affected the behavior and performance of commercial banking institutions in thousands of local markets across the United States? Is there evidence of significant differences in loan charges, yields offered on deposits, profitability, etc., among those banks confronted with substantial numbers of nonbank thrifts serving their local markets compared with banks not faced with significant nonbank competition? Thus far, the answer to these questions must be listed as either "inconclusive" or "negative."

Indeed, many observers would argue that the challenge to banking posed by the thrifts has been overrated. In the minds of most businesses and consumers, they suggest, the thrifts are viewed as separate institutions, offering a *differentiated* rather than a pure substitute product. If true, this statement supports the bias in federal court antitrust rulings, which have tended either to ignore or to minimize the impact of nonbank thrifts and to emphasize the number and relative sizes of commercial banks alone in assessing concentration and competition in local markets. Yet *national* market studies generally suggest significant bank-nonbank competitive interaction and argue for the inclusion of thrift market shares in assessing competition and concentration in financial service markets. And, the Federal Reserve Board recently began to include 50 percent of thrift deposits as a component of relevant local banking markets in selected cases—a practice followed by the Department of Justice, which, according to Welker (1986), may elect to include up to 100 percent of thrift deposits in defining retail financial service markets.

If such regulatory practices become widespread and are accepted firmly by courts of justice, this step would obviously have profound implications for merger and holding-company acquisition activity among commercial banks. If the services offered by nonbank thrifts are encompassed in banking's line of commerce, more bank acquisitions will qualify under federal antitrust laws. Presumably, larger numbers of small and medium-size banks will disappear as independent competitors, where market demand justifies their acquisition.

If research to date fails to fully support the bank/thrift substitution hypothesis in *local* financial markets, as we have argued in this chapter, the future *may* provide that support because of significant new bank-like powers granted to credit unions, savings banks, and savings and loans by Congressional action in 1980 and 1982 and through regulatory changes reaching back to the mid-1970s. In virtually all the important bank service areas—commercial, consumer, and real estate lending, credit card operations, business checking accounts, time and payments accounts, and trust services—nonbank depository institutions have received broad new powers to compete with commercial banks. However, the *receipt* of power is only part of the story, for effective competition depends on the *use* of newly won power. Will the thrifts really use the newly granted powers to become effective competitors in the thousands of local financial service markets that span the nation? The evidence thus far is *not* encouraging.

For example, a study by Eisenbeis (1983) finds that a substantial proportion of savings and loans had not ventured into the newly legalized service areas some three years after passage of the enabling Depository Institutions Deregulation Act in 1980. A similar conclusion was reached by Baker (1982) in a study of Florida savings and loans. However, Crockett and King (1982) found that Texas' state-chartered S&Ls moved aggressively to offer consumer loans after they were authorized by that state's legislature, but only a minority (especially among smaller S&Ls) adopted other liberalized services, such as business loans and real estate development. Finally, Dunham (1982) observes continuing significant differences in portfolio composition and relative shares of bank-like service markets between mutual savings banks and commercial banks in New England—the "cradle" of the financial deregulation movement.

It is interesting to speculate on the reasons for the thrifts' reluctance to use their newly gained financial service powers. Lack of experience and trained management undoubtedly have been important factors. Moreover, as noted by Eisenbeis and McCall (1972), long-standing affiliations between banks and nonbank thrifts prevail in many markets, particularly in New England, and there is a tendency for one depository institution to avoid aggressively offering those financial services supplied by a sister institution. Also, Congress did not eliminate some of the most significant tax advantages associated with the services traditionally offered by thrifts, especially home mortgages.

Perhaps, too, many of the new services are not as potentially profitable as was first anticipated, owing to changing customer demands and intensifying competition. For example, a recent study by Joffrion and Rose (1986) finds that savings and loan profitability was *not* significantly influenced by the proportion of nontraditional loans and investments (such as consumer and auto installment loans, junior mortgages, land holdings, and security trading) held by a random sample of more than 300 S&Ls, stratified by size and region of the nation. Rather, the most profitable S&Ls were those that managed to control their operating expenses (especially interest and advertising costs) most successfully. Finally, the weakened financial condition of many thrifts has dampened their enthusiasm for the significant risks involved in offering new services, most of which must be sold in markets already intensely competitive. Whether the future will bring a reduction in the thrifts' hesitation to enter these new service lines is problematic. As has been the case for decades, the strength of the competitive challenge posed for banks by the nonbank thrifts will depend crucially on Congress' willingness to make still more concessions to bankers and to the thrift industry.

References

Baker, Robert. 1982. "Florida S&Ls' Use of Expanded Powers." *Economic Review* (July), pp. 7–15. Federal Reserve Bank of Atlanta.

Benston, George J. 1985. "Investments by and the Failure of Savings and Loan Associations: An Analysis with Particular Concern for Direct Investments and Non-mortgage Loans," Presented to the U.S. House of Representatives Subcommittee on Financial Institutions, Supervision, Regulation, and Insurance of the Committee on Banking, Finance and Urban Affairs, October 2nd.

Bradford, William D. 1975. *Mergers in the Savings and Loan Industry, 1969–1974: Structural Changes and Financial Comparisons.* Working Paper no. 58. Washington, D.C.: Federal Home Loan Bank Board.

Chase, Samuel B. Jr. 1969. "Household Demand for Savings Deposits, 1921–1965." *Journal of Finance* (September), 24:643–58.

Cohen, Bruce C. and George G. Kaufman. 1965. "Factors Determining Bank Deposit Growth By State: An Empirical Analysis." *Journal of Finance* (March), 20:59–70.

Cook, Timothy Q. and Jeremy G. Duffield. 1979a. "Money Market Mutual Funds: A Reaction to Government Regulation or A Lasting Financial Innovation?" *Economic Review* (July–August), pp. 15–31. Federal Reserve Bank of Richmond.

—— 1979b. "Average Cost of Money Market Mutual Funds." *Economic Review* (July–August), pp. 32–39. Federal Reserve Bank of Richmond.

—— 1980. "Short-Term Investment Pools." *Economic Review* (September–October), 66(5):3–23. Federal Reserve Bank of Richmond.

Credit Union National Association, Inc. 1984. *Credit Union Report.* Madison, Wisconsin.

Crockett, John and A. Thomas King. 1982. "The Contribution of New Asset Powers to S&L Earnings: A Comparison of Federal- and State-Chartered Associations in Texas." Research Working Paper No. 110 (July). Federal Home Loan Bank Board.

Daly, George G. 1971. "Financial Intermediation and the Theory of the Firm: An Analysis of Savings and Loan Association Behavior." *Southern Economic Journal* (January), 37:283–95.

Davis, Carolyn Dubose. 1982. "Money Market Mutual Funds: An Arbitrage Pricing Theory of Performance Evaluation." *Staff Papers.* Washington, D.C.: Comptroller of the Currency.

Dotsey, Michael, Steven Englander, and John C. Portlan. 1981–1982. "Money Market Mutual Funds and Monetary Control." *Quarterly Review* (Winter), pp. 9–17. Federal Reserve Bank of New York.

Dunham, Constance. 1982. "Mutual Savings Banks: Are They Now or Will They Ever Be Commercial Banks?" *New England Economic Review* (May/June), pp. 51–72. Federal Reserve Bank of Boston.

Dunham, Constance and Margaret Guerin-Calvert. 1983. "How Quickly Can Thrifts Move Into Commercial Lending?" *New England Economic Review* (November–December), pp. 42–54. Federal Reserve Bank of Boston.

Edwards, Franklin R. 1977. "Managerial Objectives in Regulated Industries: Expense Preference Behavior in Banking." *Journal of Political Economy* (February), 85:147–62.

Eisenbeis, Robert A. 1983. "New Investment Powers for S&Ls: Diversification or Specialization?" *Economic Review,* (July), pp. 53–62. Federal Reserve Bank of Atlanta.

Eisenbeis, Robert A. and Alan S. McCall. 1972. "Some Effects of Affiliations Among Mutual Savings and Commercial Banks." *Journal of Finance,* pp. 865–77.

Fiege, Edgar L. 1964. *The Demand for Liquid Assets: A Temporal Cross-Section Analysis.* Englewood Cliffs, N.J.: Prentice-Hall.

Ferri, Michael and H. Dennis Oberhelman. 1981. "A Study of the Management of Money Market Mutual Funds: 1975–1980." *Financial Management* (Autumn), pp. 24–29.

Gilbert, Gary G. and Neil B. Murphy. 1971. *Competition Between Thrift Institutions and Commercial Banks: An Examination of the Evidence.* Working Paper no. 71–18. Division of Research. Federal Deposit Insurance Corporation.

Hamburger, Michael J. 1968. "Household Demand for Financial Assets." *Econometrica* (January), 36(1):97–118.

Hannan, Timothy H. 1979. "Expense-Preference Behavior in Banking: A Reexamination." *Journal of Political Economy* (August), 37:891–95.

—— 1984. "Competition Between Commercial Banks and Thrift Institutions: An Empirical Examination." *Journal of Bank Research* (Spring), pp. 8–14.

Hartley, Philip Bovary. 1966. *The Demand Function for Liquid Assets.* Unpublished doctoral dissertation. University of Washington—Seattle.

Herzog, Peter W. 1928. *The Morris Plan of Industrial Banking.* Chicago: A. W. Shaw.

Joffrion, Theresa and Peter S. Rose. 1986. "Savings and Loans' Response to Deregulation: Survey and Analysis." *Housing Finance Review,* forthcoming.

Kardouche, George K. 1969. *The Competition for Savings.* New York: National Industrial Conference Board.

Koot, Ronald S. 1976. "The Demand for Credit Union Shares." *Journal of Financial and Quantitative Analysis* (March), pp. 133–41.

Koot, Ronald S. and David A. Walker. 1980. "A Statistical Analysis of the Impact of Monetary Policy on Credit Union Lending." *Journal of Banking and Finance,* 4:301–11.

Kwon, Jene K. and Richard M. Thornton. 1971. "An Evaluation of the Competitive Effect of FHLB Open Market Operations on Savings Inflows at Savings and Loan Associations." *Journal of Finance,* pp. 699–712.

Langrehr, Fredrick W. 1982. "Money Market Mutual Fund Investors' Savings Account Holdings and Demographic Profile." *Journal of Bank Research* (Autumn), pp. 202–6.

Lapp, John S. 1978. "The Determination of Savings and Loan Association Deposit Rates in the Absence of Rate Ceilings: A Cross-Section Approach." *Journal of Finance* (March), 33(1):215–30.

Lee, Tong Hun. 1966. "Substitutability of Nonbank Intermediary Liabilities for Money: The Empirical Evidence." *Journal of Finance* (September), 21(3):441–57.

Motley, Brian. 1970. "Household Demand for Assets: A Model of Short-Run Adjustments." *Review of Economics and Statistics* (August), 52:236–41.

Nathan, Harold C. 1980. "Nonbank Organizations and the McFadden Act." *Journal of Bank Research* (Summer), 7:80–86.

Nugent, Rolf. 1937. "A Census of Personal Loan Departments." *Banking* (November), 30:28–29.

Pearce, Douglas K. 1984. "Recent Developments in the Credit Union Industry." *Economic Review* (June), pp. 3–19. Federal Reserve Bank of Kansas City.

Rhoades, Stephen A. 1977. *Structure-Performance Studies in Banking: Summary and Evaluation.* Staff Economic Studies (December). Board of Governors of the Federal Reserve System.

—— 1979. "Nonbank Thrift Institutions as Determinants of Performance In Banking Markets." *Journal of Economics and Business* (Fall), 32(1):66–78.

—— 1982. *Structure-Performance Studies in Banking: An Updated Summary and Evaluation.* Staff Economic Studies (August). Board of Governors of the Federal Reserve System.

Rogers, David H. 1974. *Consumer Banking in New York.* New York: Trustees of Columbia University.

Shawky, Hany, Ronald Forbes, and Alan Frankle. 1983. "Liquidity Services and Capital Market Equilibrium: The Case for Money Market Mutual Funds." *The Journal of Financial Research* (Summer), pp. 141–52.

Shick, Richard A., Kenneth J. Thygerson, and James A. Verbrugge. 1976. "An Analysis of Savings and Loan Profit Performance." *Journal of Finance* (December), pp. 1427–42.

Silber, William L. 1970. *Portfolio Behavior of Financial Institutions.* New York: Holt, Rinehart and Winston.

Stevens, Edward J. 1966. "Deposits at Savings and Loan Associations." *Yale Economic Essays* (Fall), 6(2).

Stigum, Marcia L. 1976. "Some Future Implications of Profit Maximization by a Savings and Loan Association." *Journal of Finance* (December), 31(5):1405–26.

Taylor, Ryland A. 1972. "The Demand for Credit Union Shares: A Cross-Sectional Analysis." *Journal of Financial and Quantitative Analysis* (June), pp. 1749–56.

United States League of Savings Institutions. 1985 *'85 Savings Institutions Sourcebook.* Chicago, Ill.

Verbrugge, James A. and Richard A. Shick. 1976. "Market Structure and Savings and Loan Profitability." *Quarterly Review of Economics and Business,* 16(2):79–90.

Verbrugge, James A. and John S. Jahera, Jr. 1981. "Expense-Preference Behavior in the Savings and Loan Industry." *Journal of Money, Credit and Banking* (November), 13(4):465–76.

Verbrugge, James A. and Steven J. Goldstein. 1981. "Risk, Return, and Managerial Objectives: Some Evidence from the Savings and Loan Industry." *The Journal of Financial Research* (Spring), 4(1):45–58.

Vernon, Jack R. 1966. "Competition for Savings Deposits: The Recent Evidence." *National Banking Review* (December), 4(2), pp. 183–92.

Walker, David A. 1983. "Effects of Deregulation on the Savings and Loan Industry." *Financial Review* (Spring), pp. 94–110.

Weber, Gerald S. 1966. "Interest Rates on Mortgages and Dividend Rates on Savings and Loan Shares." *Journal of Finance* (September), 21:515–21.

Welker, Donald L. 1986. "Thrift Competition: Does It Matter?" *Economic Review,* Federal Reserve Bank of Richmond, January–February 1986, 72(1):2–10.

11.

The Rise of Nonbank
Financial Conglomerates

IN THE 1960s bank holding companies penetrated deeply into non-bank business ventures in search of new markets and less regulation. In the 1970s and early 1980s leading nonbank companies, including automobile and steel manufacturers, discount houses, insurance and credit card companies, and security brokers and dealers, penetrated the banking services field in unprecedented numbers. For some, such as Sears, Roebuck & Company and American Express, the development of bank-like services was simply the extension of a beachhead estab-lished in the financial services field many years before. For others, such as Parker Pen Company and American Can Company, it represented a sudden awareness of the growth and profit opportunities offered by a rapidly expanding sector of the economy. As we will soon see, for many of the new nonbank conglomerates the deep and turbulent waters of the new financial services marketplace proved far more treacherous and unforgiving than they had anticipated and several pulled back. For the survivors formidable management control and customer acceptance problems, along with new opportunities for profit, waited to greet the unwary.

Portions of this chapter are based on the author's earlier article (1982) in the *Canadian Banker* and are used with permission from the publisher.

Services Offered by Nonbank
Financial Conglomerates

A new label, borrowed from the science of biology, was developed to describe these financial service-oriented nonbank companies—*symbiotics*. Paralleling its biological origins, the concept of "financial symbiosis" suggested that these new conglomerate entities could successfully merge and manage such diverse products as insurance, cash management, security brokerage, mutual funds, mortgage banking, retail dry goods, automobiles, and industrial hardware. How difficult and challenging this task could prove to be and how "nonsymbiotic" the intracompany relationships could become time would soon amply testify.

Whereas the symbiotics have tended to spread themselves over many different financial services, their most notable gains have been in the field of *consumer credit*—an area deemphasized by commercial banks until after World War II. For example, as pointed out by Cleveland Christophe (1974) over a decade ago, the volume of actively used Sears credit cards exceeded that of the two national *bank* card systems, Master Card and Visa. Sears' Allstate Insurance Company, begun in 1931 with an auto insurance program, became one of the nation's leading property-casualty insurers by capitalizing on mail order sales in order to reduce marketing costs. In the early 1970s Sears after-tax income from a variety of financial services ranging from personal finance and insurance through mortgage banking, management and sales of open-end mutual funds, management of business and residential properties, construction of residential housing, and the operation of an auto club and travel bureau came to exceed that of any U.S. banking organization and accounted for a third of Sears' net earnings. Christophe also observed that when the consumer credit accounts held by J. C. Penney and Montgomery Ward were combined with those of Sears, the volume of such credit was more than half again as large as total consumer installment credit held by BankAmerica, Citicorp, and Chase Manhattan combined—the three largest U.S. banking organizations. Broaddus (1985) points out that by year-end 1981 the financial service units of three leading manufacturers—General Electric, Ford, and General Motors—held $45.8 billion in consumer installment credit, while Citicorp, BankAmerica, and Chase Manhattan reported worldwide consumer installment loans of just $27.7 billion. Rosenblum and Siegel (1983) found that during the same period 32 lending non-bank financial conglomerates held more than $100 billion in total business credit, which represented a third of all business credit extended by the nation's 15 largest bank holding companies.

Even more substantial was the volume of *consumer* install-ment loans reported by General Motors Acceptance Corporation (GMAC), which inaugurated auto lending in 1919. GMAC is one representative of a potent group of competitors for banks whose history covers more than three-score decades—the captive finance company. Other leading captive finance companies with substantial consumer lending programs include General Electric Credit Corporation, which recently acquired an industrial loan company that accepts savings deposits; Ford Motor Credit Company; Motorola Credit Corporation; and Westinghouse Credit Corporation, offering revolving charge and installment credit to consumers, as well as life and casualty insurance.

The captive finance companies also constituted a formi-dable foe in a second bank service line—*commercial lending*. Organized to promote sales of their sponsored company's manufactured products to businesses in an era when most banks preferred not to loan money on costly durable goods, many financial subsidiaries and divisions of leading manufacturers became potent competitors in the market for commercial equipment loans and leases. Prominent examples include General Electric Credit Corporation, previously mentioned as active in the consumer credit field; Westinghouse Credit Corporation; Borg-Warner Acceptance Corporation; and Control Data Corporation (CDC). General Electric also entered the fire and casualty insurance business as the 1970s began. Ford Motor Credit Company, in addition to its consumer loan activities, launched short- and long-term com-mercial credit programs in 1960, inventory financing and property-casualty insurance the year before, and in later years entered the real estate development, credit life insurance, and equipment/personal property leasing fields. A number of these companies, seeking to be-come profit centers, reached far afield in their financing operations to include commercial and sales finance for products other than those produced by the sponsoring manufacturer.

The early symbiotics, then, were concentrated mainly in

the fields of consumer and commercial credit, tied principally to sales of manufactured products. Their "symbiotic" relationship was not primarily with other financial services and financial companies but was a bridge between financial and manufacturing activities. Until the 1980s the nonbank company most closely resembling a true financial symbiotic—offering a broad range of different, but essentially complementary, financial services—was Sears Roebuck, the nation's largest retail chain, with its interests in consumer credit, insurance, and real estate. In contrast, other nonbank companies tended to be more narrowly focused into a few financial service lines. But the decade of the 1980s changed all that with the appearance of highly diversified financial firms expressly targeted to the "financial department store" model. This decade was marked by the acquisitions of Bache securities by Prudential Insurance Company, one of the world's insurance leaders; of Salomon Brothers, one of the largest private investment banks and bond traders, by Philbro Corporation, at the time the world's largest publicly held commodity trader; of Shearson, Loeb Rhoades Inc. by credit card leader American Express, in a $1 billion stock swap, followed later by Express' acquisition of leading investment banker Lehman Brothers Kuhn Loeb, Inc. and Investors Diversified Services, a mutual fund. Sears Roebuck, not to be outdone, moved to acquire Dean Witter Reynolds, a leading investment bank, and Coldwell Banker, the top U.S. real estate finance company.

　　　　Many of the largest nonbank companies offered a wider menu of financial services than commercial banks competing in the same markets did. The major nonbank symbiotic financial firm of the 1980s had become (or certainly had the potential to become) a conglomerate offering any or all of the following financial services:

Credit Services	*Real Property Investments and Services*
Consumer installment credit and cash loans	Commercial and residential real-estate brokerage
Commercial finance	Real property development
Sales finance	Property leasing
Equipment and auto leasing	Mortgage servicing
Credit card operations	
Commercial and residential mortgage loans	
Venture capital	

*Securities' Brokerage and
Investment Services*
Brokering stocks, bonds, and other
  securities
Sales of mutual fund shares
Corporate and personal cash man-
  agement services

Securities' Underwriting Services
Underwriting new security issues
Advising on new security offerings
Mortgage banking

Insurance Services
Insurance agencies
Life insurance underwriting
Property-casualty insurance
  underwriting

Financial Counseling Services
Investment advice
Tax advice and preparation of returns
Travel planning and reservations
Executive relocation
Corporate trust services

Miscellaneous Services
Data processing
Telecommunications
Funds transfer
Foreign exchange and deposits

Although no conglomerate either has or perhaps could offer *all* of these service lines, conglomerates such as Merrill Lynch, Sears, Prudential-Bache, and Shearson-American Express come uncomfortably close for many bankers.

Moreover, as the decade of the 1980s opened, several of the leading financial conglomerates, as well as some manufacturing firms, acquired commercial banks and other depository institutions to permit the offering of both deposits and direct cash loans. Because the acquisition of commercial banks exposed them to regulation as bank holding companies, they began to strip any acquired banks of their commercial loans or of deposits payable on demand, creating "nonbank banks." For example, Gulf and Western, a manufacturing concern, acquired a federally chartered commercial bank in 1980 devoid of commercial loans. In April 1983 Prudential-Bache acquired a small Georgia bank that eventually became Prudential Bank and Trust Company, stripped of its commercial credits. Presumably, the services offered by the bank—such as money market deposits, CDs, and loans against the equity built up in clients' homes—would be sold through brokers and agents working for Prudential-Bache, as reported by Carrington (1983). Not to be outdone, National Steel Corporation, which already owned Citizen's Federal Savings and Loan Association of San Francisco, moved into the interstate deposit and loan market through the merger of Citizen's with West Side Federal Savings and Loan of New York and Washington Savings and Loan Association of Miami Beach. The result was the creation of a congeneric depository institution with a substantial presence on both coasts and holding combined assets of nearly $7 billion.

A new trend was launched by Merrill Lynch & Company, which acquired an Edge Act bank in 1983 and, in 1984, established a new unit called Merrill Lynch Bank International to offer foreign-exchange and correspondent services. Not to be outdone, American Express International Banking Corporation, New York, acquired ownership shares in European-American Bank International, Los Angeles, to expand its international service offerings. These acquisitions of Edge Act corporations by major symbiotics have taken place through a loophole in federal banking legislation that allows domestic bank and nonbank firms to acquire the shares of an existing Edge Act corporation without federal regulatory approval. Because Edge Act corporations must confine the majority of their lending and deposit-taking activities to international markets, they escape many domestic banking regulations, such as those related to branching and holding-company activities.

Motivations for Conglomerate Expansion into Financial Services

What factors have motivated the rapid expansion of nonbank conglomerates into the financial services field and especially into banking services? This is a particularly interesting question in view of the fact that elsewhere in private industry the trend in recent years has been away from large conglomerates, many companies selling off divisions and subsidiaries ("down-sizing"), often in the wake of leveraged buyouts. The expanding bank-like activities of many nonbank conglomerates appear to be influenced by some or all of the following factors.

Impressive Track Record of Bank Profits. Bank profitability is impressive, not in size relative to other industries, but rather in its *stability.* Banking is a moderately profitable industry, the industry's return on equity averaging in the range of 10 to 13 percent in recent years. But the industry has experienced very few declines in annual after-tax net earnings over all costs. Or on overall basis, banking's after-tax net income has increased at a long-term growth rate faster than inflation, with a particularly significant acceleration in the late 1970s. Generally, bank earnings have been much more stable than those experienced by any of the nonbank conglomerates, motivating the latter firms to move in banking's direction.

Banking's Consistent Asset Growth Record. Year in and year out banks have experienced a healthy growth rate through recessions, energy crises, tight credit conditions, and other impediments that have often had damaging effects on the growth of other industries, such as steel and autos. To the nonbank conglomerates this growth record is an attractive bulwark against the decline or stagnation they have frequently experienced in their own traditional product lines.

Weaknesses in Sales of Traditional Products and Services. Some analysts (most notably, Ford 1982) have seen in the nonbank financial conglomerate movement a "defensive," rather than an "offensive," effort designed to protect these firms against declining sales and decreasing earnings. Life insurance companies, for example, witnessed growing public dissatisfaction with their traditional insurance offerings in an environment of inflation, high interest rates, and tax law changes. As pointed out by Edmister (1982), life insurance companies represented the second largest financial institution in terms of their market share of financial assets over the 1950–70 period but had lost their second-place ranking to savings and loan associations by 1980.

A similar trend occurred among U.S. security brokers and dealers, whose 1980 share of total financial assets in the American financial system was less than half as large as in 1950, related to securities' deregulation in 1975 and to customers' increased emphasis on convenience and one-stop financial transactions. This trend in traditional brokerage and security services helps to explain, for example, an announcement by Merrill Lynch in 1985 of plans to enter the small-business market—a traditional banking specialty—first with investment services and later with small-business loans. Squeezed by growing expenses and declining sales of conventional service lines, the symbiotics' deeper penetration into the securities, credit, and cash management fields represents potentially attractive solutions to serious problems. Similar problems have motivated nonbank conglomerates offering such traditional products as automobiles, retail dry goods, and property-casualty insurance.

Benefits of Diversification. As noted in chapter 9, investments in unrelated lines of business increase the probability of stabilizing cash flows for the conglomerate organization as a whole. This occurs when the cash flows from various product lines are *negatively* correlated with each other; declining sales in one product line, for example, can be offset by rising sales in another product line. The firms that would appear to reap the largest potential gain from this diversification effect would be those in manufacturing and retailing (such as Sears, GM, GE, etc.) whose traditional product lines differ markedly from financial services. Diversification combined with growth in size can reduce the cost of raising capital in the financial markets and make more economically feasible the introduction of new products and services and of capital-intensive production technologies. The offsetting problem is, however, that such highly disparate services and products are more difficult to manage and control.

Taking Advantage of Branch Networks and Established Customer Relationships. To conglomerates like Sears, Prudential, and Merrill Lynch with elaborate branch office networks, the marketing of bank-like services offers the prospect of more fully using existing brick-and-mortar facilities with very little additional capital. Locational convenience has always been a key factor in marketing banking services; people generally bank near their home, place of work, or along frequent routes of travel to work or to shopping (i.e., adjacent to their daily *errand cycle*). Indeed, as Kareken (1981) notes, establishing numerous branch offices is a way of overcoming geographic distance. Through their extensive branch systems symbiotics like Sears can reach into virtually all geographic markets in the nation. Moreover, by offering a broad menu of financial services and perhaps nonfinancial products as well, these firms can offer "one-stop" shopping convenience—a significant advantage where transportation and other transactions costs are significant.

Synergistic Marketing and Production Benefits. By bringing several different firms under the same corporate umbrella, presumably one subsidiary can sell the products and services of another. For example, as pointed out by Hilder and Metz (1984), the Shearson unit of American Express offers its customers brokerage services linked to the American Express gold card, while travel insurance sold to American Express' credit card holders is underwritten by its affiliated Firemen's Fund unit. The possibility of successful cross-sales, improved access to stronger managerial talent, and full utilization of managerial resources suggests potential gains in operating efficiency (i.e., synergy) from combining corporate resources more effectively.

Tax Advantages. Federal taxation has encouraged the recent upsurge in corporate mergers of all types, offering a tax-sheltered form of capital investment. Because of rising effective personal tax rates during the 1970s and early 1980s—in part the result of inflation—many corporations were encouraged to retain their earnings for future expansion rather than pay out heavily taxed current dividends to their shareholders. Moreover, as Benston (1980) notes, this potent combination of higher personal and corporate taxes coupled with inflation often reduced the market price of companies targeted for acquisition below the replacement value of their assets. Many symbiotic acquisitions appeared to be real "bargains" to expansion-minded management.

New Communications Technology. Even for those conglomerates without extensive branch networks the developing technology of electronic funds transfer systems (EFTS) offers the prospect of reaching into distant markets across the nation and around the globe. Transmissions by satellite and microwave and the increasing use of home and office computer terminals, along with networking, make possible the delivery of financial services to remote locations with high volume and low production costs. In effect, the nonbank financial conglomerates may be able to outmanuever commercial banking organizations such as BankAmerica, Citicorp, etc., which invested heavily in extensive brick-and-mortar facilities in the pre-EFTS era.

Competitive Advantages
of Nonbank Conglomerates

Nonbank conglomerates possess some important competitive advantages that cannot be ignored by bankers.

Less Regulation. For one thing, they face fewer regulations than American banks do. In most cases they do not need to seek approval for the development of new funds-raising or funds-using services as a bank or bank holding company would have to do under current federal law. As Greer and Rhoades (1975) observe, this regulatory hurdle increases the cost of product innovation for banks and may lead to premature disclosure of their new product ideas to competitors. Moreover, there are no regulatory impediments to the number or geographic placement of symbiotic branch offices or other customer-convenient facilities, even across state lines. The Department of Justice or the Federal Trade Commission, under the provisions of the Clayton Act (1914) or the Celler-Kefauver Act (1950), may attempt to block a symbiotic merger where antitrust or anticompetitive issues appear to be significant, but this is not frequently done where businesses are not clearly related to or do not trade with each other. Moreover, antitrust factors are of little moment in the case of *de novo* ventures. Funds can be raised without reserve requirements or legal interest rate ceilings that increase their cost. In brief, with few exceptions, the nonbank financial conglomerates have an advantage over commercial banks in the greater *flexibility* of what they can do stemming from lower regulatory compliance costs.

One-Stop Convenience. With greater flexibility in service offerings and in where office facilities can be established, the symbiotics have the option of offering a complete menu of financial services—insurance, savings plans, credit, security and real estate brokerage, transactions accounts, and financial counseling—through each and every office. The menu of services each conglomerate ultimately offers will depend, of course, on the intensity of public demand, the conglomerate's own resources, and its ability to attract and retain qualified management.

Adaptable Physical Facilities. In some instances the non-bank symbiotics already have in place an elaborate branching system to serve customer needs. Sears, for example, has more than 800 retail store outlets nationwide, while its All-State Insurance affiliate operates more than a thousand offices. Merrill Lynch has in excess of 300 offices across the United States, each of which can offer a significant portion of that security firm's service package. In the future this will probably be less of an advantage with the spread of electronic communications equipment. Indeed, at some point in the future physical transportation to and from financial service outlets will be unnecessary, and the distance between customer and financial service office will be of little or no practical significance. Yet, here, too, many of the nonbank conglomerates have an advantage in not having to carry the cost burdens of an existing brick-and-mortar branch system. Sears, for example, has an extensive system of on-line terminals and more than 24 million credit card holders capable of using those cards to access electronic terminals for bank-like services. Sears was one of the retail pioneers, as Christophe (1974) observes, in developing electronic cash register systems that store large volumes of customer information and permit on-line credit verification. Similar facilities are either in place or are being planned by Penneys, Wards, and other major retail merchants.

Other Competitive Advantages. Owing to the restrictions imposed by the Bank Holding Company Act Amendments of 1970 and the Federal Reserve Board's Regulation Y, banking organizations can innovate over a narrower range of services than is available to the nonbank conglomerates. In contrast, the symbiotics can serve a nationwide, even international, market for retail and commercial accounts, unrestrained by such banking barriers as state home-office protection laws, the Douglas Amendment, the McFadden Act, or the Glass-Steagall Act. Financial capital can be raised in form and amount subject only to the discipline of the financial marketplace without regard to capital-adequacy tests imposed by federal and state regulatory authorities. In summary, the symbiotics' growth and earnings potential *is* significant. Whether or not they will be able to fully achieve that potential, however, is questionable because of a number of problems that stand in their way.

Problems Faced by Nonbank Financial Conglomerates

Span of Management Control. Many of the conglomerates hope to stretch existing management over an expanding menu of products and services. This runs the obvious risk of poor management decisions founded on inadequate knowledge of how the company's product lines are produced and delivered and of customer needs. Inexperience with many financial services can be costly in a highly competitive environment. And those symbiotics that have attempted to hire new management skilled in managing their diverse products have frequently found the available stock of managerial talent scarce and expensive. As Rhoades (1983) observes in the case of industrial conglomerates, real *diseconomies* of scale may exist after a conglomerate reaches a given size, owing to the difficulties of controlling a large and diverse organization. Indeed, the recent increase in leveraged buyouts of corporations, following which subsidiaries and divisions are frequently spun off, suggests some inherent problems associated with great size and diversity.

There is also the issue of whether affiliated companies with diverse management styles and approaches really can ever be welded into a single, efficiently run business organization. Differences in employee benefit programs, methods of internal communication, and organizational goals can wreak havoc with conglomerate planning systems. On the basis of the recent experience of American Express, symbiotics may pass through an evolutionary growth process in which initial acquisitions tend to be diverse, aimed at securing the benefits of diversification and increased size. Later, when many of the hoped-for benefits turn out to be illusory and the management process becomes unwieldy, these organizations begin to refine and narrow the thrust of their operations to one or a few primary facets of the financial services market. For example, as Hilder (1985) notes, American Express now appears to have narrowed its focus to a group of related, mainly consumer-oriented financial services.

Customer Acceptance of Related Products. It is not clear that one of the hoped-for advantages of the conglomerate financial service firm—the ability to offer a broad range of services conveniently from a single location—will be appreciated and used by the customer. There is, for one thing, the intangible issue of *trust.* A symbiotic's liabilities are not federally insured, and there is usually no banking subsidiary of the conglomerate important enough to reassure skeptical customers that the firm will be able to back up its products and services with financial strength. A customer concerned about risk may be inclined to spread his business across several different institutions to minimize the risk of loss from imprudent management. Commercial banks have a reputation for stability and experienced money management that other financial service firms generally do not have and may not be able to acquire. Moreover, in a more competitive, deregulated financial marketplace, the public is more likely to "shop" for financial services and seek the best terms on each individual service offered.

Thus, the symbiotics face serious problems of inexperience, management control, public image, and public acceptance. An added problem appeared in the late 1970s and early 1980s as major bank holding companies responded to the conglomerates' challenge by diversifying into many of the *same* financial service areas.

Banking's Counterattack with Competing Services

Predictably, major U.S. bank holding companies began to penetrate the symbiotics' principal service areas in the wake of the latter's invasion of the banking field. In part, the move was "defensive" but was also an attempt to diversify both by product line and geographically. I look at these two trends—the proliferation of new services and geographic expansion—among major banking organizations in the following paragraphs.

PROLIFERATION OF NEW SERVICES

In May 1981, Seattle–First National Bank extended security brokerage services to its customers through any branch office with orders executed through a third party. Six months later, in November 1981, BankAmerica Corporation announced plans to acquire Charles Schwab & Company, the largest discount security broker in the United States. The following January, Crocker National Bank and Security Pacific National Bank announced joint ventures with brokerage companies to offer discount security trading to their customers. In the case of Security Pacific this was later changed to a bank subsidiary instead of a holding-company affiliate. In August 1983 the Chase Manhattan Corporation received Federal Reserve Board approval to acquire Rose & Company Investment Brokers of Chicago, a retail discount securities broker and margin lender.

Soon a number of other major banking corporations— Citicorp, J. P. Morgan & Co., North Carolina National, First National Bank of Chicago, Bankers Trust, National City Bank–Minneapolis, and BankAmerica Corp.—announced the offering of buy-sell services for futures contracts or, in the case of United Jersey Banks and Union Planters National of Memphis, new discount brokerage services, either through bank subsidiaries or holding-company affiliates. In November 1982 Rainier Bancorporation entered a joint arrangement to provide venture capital funds with Hambrecht & Quist, an investment banking firm, and was soon joined in the venture capital field by Continental Illinois of Chicago. Then, in July 1983 Norwest Corporation, a Minneapolis-based bank holding company, received approval from the Federal Reserve Board to offer through its wholly owned subsidiary Norwest Mortgage, Inc. the arranging of equity financing for commercial and industrial income-producing property on behalf of institutional investors.

The 1980s have also been marked by a strong effort by leading money center banks to develop investment banking services. For example, J. P. Morgan & Company has scored notable successes in arranging corporate security offerings in foreign markets. In June 1985 Security Pacific Corporation launched a merchant banking group to expand its operations in the fields of corporate financing, investment banking, and security trading. The major legal barrier to further bank expansion in this field is the Glass-Steagall Act, which prohibits bank underwriting of corporate securities and, therefore, limits bank contact with corporate security investments and with professionals in the investment banking field. Major banks undoubtedly will continue to push for more freedom from regulation in the investment banking field owing to the substantial profit potential it offers.

It seems clear that commercial banks with adequate capital and borrowing capacity will continue to seek out new service ventures as quickly as regulatory standards are relaxed to expand their fee income as an offset to loan quality problems and rising operating expenses. To the extent that banking organizations can borrow less expensively than nonbank competitors, they will be able to leverage more effectively and probably widen their market share against competing nonbank firms in most new service fields they choose to enter. The key uncertainty here is the capacity of bank management to control and direct a conglomerate's resources effectively over a widening menu of increasingly dissimilar services. On that issue we must await the verdict of time and future research.

Moreover, not everyone agrees that commercial bank penetration of nonbank financial service lines is a wise move. Edmister (1982), for example, refers to bank conglomerate expansion as a "strategic error" on grounds that demand is increasing less rapidly in nonbank service markets than it is in banking markets. In addition, he argues, such markets are generally smaller and offer less potential for future growth. Edmister observes:

depository institutions are already engaged in the fastest growing financial markets . . . banking advances in transactions, credit, currency exchange, and other services are significant in capturing market shares. Therefore, maintaining dominance in these advances would appear to be of greater importance than entering the slower growing insurance and broker/dealer markets (p. 12).

GEOGRAPHIC EXPANSION

The rise of one-bank holding companies in the late 1960s, as we saw in chapter 9, launched a rapid expansion of interstate banking operations. While interstate deposit taking remained prohibited by federal law in the 1970s and early 1980s, interstate lending and investing activities by banking organizations expanded at a rapid pace through finance company, mortgage banking, and leasing affiliates of major holding companies. But the 1980s opened up a new front—finding ways to invade distant *local* markets to take deposits, make loans, and offer selected nonbank services. In some cases, where state law expressly permitted outside entry, this was done by immediate acquisition or through the chartering of new banking units. In other cases, especially where state law still effectively barred entry, conditional and foothold acquisitions were made in anticipation of the day when full-service interstate banking would be legally sanctioned. The chronology of events during this period suggests the major trends.

For example, in 1980, both Citicorp and Provident National Corporation, through one of their subsidiaries, acquired minority interests in out-of-state banks and bank holding companies. Citicorp purchased nonvoting preferred shares in Central National Chicago Corporation with warrants to acquire $12 million of Central's common equity if interstate banking legislation were enacted. Although this Citicorp purchase option was subsequently dropped, it set the stage for similar ventures in the months that followed. Provident National purchased a 5-percent equity share in three out-of-state banks in May 1980—the maximum equity percentage allowed an out-of-state bank under the Douglas Amendment to the Bank Holding Company Act. The following year Citibank–South Dakota, NA was opened in Sioux Falls to conduct credit card operations, pursuant to a South Dakota law passed in 1980 allowing outside entry for this purpose.

Delaware followed South Dakota's lead and enacted an economic development bill in February 1981 that invited money center banks into the state under specified conditions. The response of leading out-of-state banking organizations to Delaware's initiative was swift. Before the year ended, J. P. Morgan & Company announced the chartering of Morgan Bank–Delaware to market wholesale banking services. In February 1982, Chase Manhattan Corporation opened a consumer-oriented bank in Delaware, just ahead of Chemical New York Corporation, which launched its own consumer banking firm. The following month Maryland National Bank announced the transfer of its credit card operations to that state, and Provident National Corporation chartered Provident of Delaware to carry on wholesale banking activities. Philadelphia National Corporation and Equitable Bancorporation followed Maryland National's lead, its credit card operations also moving to Delaware. Both Citicorp and Manufacturers Hanover Corporation acted to charter Delaware banks in 1982, the former primarily to service existing commercial customers in need of cash management services and the latter to offer a menu of wholesale banking services.

As the 1980s began, much attention was focused on New England, especially Massachusetts and Connecticut, where state laws were enacted permitting bank mergers across state lines provided the banks involved were headquartered in New England. Soon after the enabling state legislation was passed, several large-scale New England bank mergers were announced—for example, Bank of New England Corporation of Boston moved to ally itself with CBT Corporation in Hartford, Connecticut, while Bank of Boston Corporation announced a proposed merger with Colonial Bancorp of Waterbury, Connecticut. Because these state laws excluded the entry by merger of major New York banks into New England, the regional compacts were attacked in federal court and the issue ultimately reached the Supreme Court. In a unanimous decision reached in June 1985 the high court upheld the Connecticut and Massachusetts laws, literally tossing the interstate banking issue into the lap of Congress for ultimate resolution. Both the House and the Senate passed various bills providing for a gradual transition toward full-service banking across state lines, as well as eliminating or at least limiting the creation of nonbank banks. However, sharp disagreements soon emerged on the permissible scope of interstate banking activities, the speed with which entry into the interstate market should be allowed, and the degree of nationwide deposit concentration that would be permitted.

A wave of interstate bank and thrift takeovers occurred early in the decade of the 1980s, many encouraged by the regulatory authorities because of financial troubles. The Garn-St Germain Depository Institutions Act of 1982 granted the federal insurance agencies power to promote depository institution mergers across state lines where a failing institution is involved. Good examples include the Federal Reserve Board's approval of Citicorp's acquisition of First Federal Savings and Loan Association of Chicago in 1984 and BankAmerica Corporation's acquisition of Seafirst Corporation of Seattle in 1983.

Other bank acquisitions have been contingent on the eventual legalization of interstate banking. Examples included the contingent interstate holding-company merger of three companies headquartered in Alabama, South Carolina, and Georgia; Marine Midland's purchase of warrants for the common stock of Centran Corporation of Cleveland in March 1982; and more recently, First Bank System, Inc. of Minneapolis' contingent acquisition of Banks of Iowa, Inc. In March 1982 Girard Company of Philadelphia purchased capital notes in two New Jersey banking organizations with the option to convert to equity shares in the advent of interstate banking. Subsequently, Alaska opened the door to out-of-state bank acquisitions, which brought in Rainier Bancorporation of Seattle through acquisition of a controlling interest in Peoples Bank & Trust Company of Anchorage. Arizona, Maine, and New York also approved entry by out-of-state banking organizations.

Florida's rapidly growing cities have been eyed by East Coast banks and banking organizations in neighboring states for many years. Not surprisingly, then, 1982 ushered in a flurry of attempts, some successful, to penetrate Florida's metropolitan markets. For example, in August 1982, North Carolina Bank Corporation was granted permission by the Federal Reserve Board to acquire Gulfstream Banks, Inc. of Boca Raton. Acquisition of another Florida holding company, Exchange Bancorporation, Inc., by North Carolina National followed in December 1982. These acquisition moves were preceded in 1981 by several acquisition agreements in which large out-of-state holding companies laid claim to Florida banking organizations in the event interstate banking became legal. For example, Chemical New York Corporation reached such an agreement with Florida National Banks, Inc. in November 1981. Meanwhile, several large savings and loan associations and S&L holding companies announced mergers involving Florida S&Ls. Examples included the consolidation of Glendale Federal Savings of California with First Federal of Fort Lauderdale; Boca Raton Federal Savings with City Federal Savings of New Jersey; Palmetto Federal Savings with Buffalo Savings Bank of New York. Subsequently, the Florida legislature agreed to permit mergers and acquisitions among banking organizations headquartered in states of the southeastern region—a move that accelerated attempts at entry into rapidly growing Florida cities, principally by large Georgia and North Carolina banking organizations.

Thus, the nation's major banks refused to sit back and watch while the interstate financial services market became completely dominated by nonbank financial conglomerates. They sought out loopholes in current law, such as the failing-firm doctrine, for setting up interstate depository facilities and began to position themselves for out-of-state, full-service branch offices if and when federal or reciprocal state laws would allow such branching. While these moves certainly opened up avenues for future growth, they also created more complex management problems for growth-oriented, expansion-minded banking organizations during a period when the true economic benefits of increased size and conglomeration still have not been convincingly established.

Summary and Implications for Bank Management

There is little question that the nonbank symbiotics pose a formidable challenge to banks, especially to the market shares of the nation's leading banking organizations. And the regulatory restraints on permissible nonbank business ventures by bank holding companies are currently, as noted in chapter 9, major barriers to true service line diversification by U.S. bank holding companies. From an overall perspective, however, banking organizations may not be as severely disadvantaged as the Christophe (1974) study and other recent analyses of the symbiotic phenomenon might have us believe.

For example, an article by Ford (1982) argues that the nonbank conglomerates are by no means an "irresistible force." Many of the conglomerates have diversified into financial services "out of weakness rather than strength, weakness that might well limit their ability to threaten banks" [p. 2]. Insurance companies are a notable example; their earnings margins have been eroded by unexpected underwriting losses, lagging rates of return on long-term investments, and rising sales expenses. Further, banking has a strong earnings record, and some of its most important services have gained market share at the expense of the symbiotics. Commercial banks' share of all financial assets and of the household credit market in particular stopped declining in the 1960s and began to grow again during the 1970s. For example, bank credit card balances have grown significantly faster (on an annual rate basis) than Sears' credit card sales. In the credit card business, Ford (1982) observes, "Sears is playing defense, not offense" [p. 4].

Ford *is* concerned about the ability of Sears and, by implication, of the other highly diversified nonbank conglomerates to successfully merge the management styles of very different affiliated companies. To be sure, one conglomerate service—the money market fund—presented strong competition to banks and savings and loan associations during the 1970s. Bank and S&L deposit costs rose sharply owing to competitive pressures to offer accounts with flexible money-market yields. However, much of the money attracted out of deposit accounts by money market funds has flowed back into the banking industry through money fund purchases of negotiable CDs, Eurodollar deposits, commercial paper, and bankers' acceptance.

Laws and regulations *do* pose a problem for banks trying

to compete with the symbiotics, especially the Glass-Steagall Act (1933), which limits banks themselves to a narrow range of services centered on deposit taking and lending. Moreover, the spirit of Glass-Steagall is reflected in the Bank Holding Company Act, which narrowly confines permissible nonbank business ventures to those "closely related to banking." Today these laws represent major barriers to greater bank involvement in insurance and the securities business. Thus, as reflected in the so-called "level playing field" issue, commercial banks are legally constrained from entering some potentially profitable areas, while the symbiotics face few legal barriers to offering competing financial services (save, of course, the remote danger of being designated "commercial banks" by the regulatory authorities and having to divest themselves of prohibited nonbank activities).

In the symbiotics we have a clear demonstration that geography—the physical location of brick-and-mortar offices—is far less relevant to today's bank customer than may have been true in an environment where communications costs were far more significant, the majority of customers financially unsophisticated, and economic conditions more favorable to passive "savers" rather than active "investors." The dramatic growth of the money market funds in the late 1970s and early 1980s demonstrated convincingly that even small accounts were essentially unconstrained by geographic boundaries. Improvements in the flow of market information and the rapid communication of financial transactions, coupled with attractive, unregulated market yields, were sufficient to erode the advantages of local savings institutions vis-à-vis national savings institutions. And, judged by the success of Merrill Lynch's Cash Management Account (CMA), which expanded from ground zero in 1977 to a million customers in 1983, what was true of small savings accounts is also likely to be true of cash management services and cash loans.

The neighborhood convenience of a brick-and-mortar branch office may quickly become irrelevant to many customers. And even for those individuals and business firms for whom such convenience still matters, the spread of home and office banking via computer and video screen may pose an effective substitute. Moreover, there are no apparent technical barriers to the nonbank conglomerates' offering insurance and securities services through the same home or office electronic banking system that conveys deposit and credit transactions. All this presumably can be accomplished without the costly overhead of extensive brick-and-mortar facilities—a burden that may well hamper the flexibility of branch banks and large holding-company systems in responding to the changing demands of a dynamic financial marketplace. Not the least of these demands is for more explicit pricing of financial services so that the customer can realistically compare competing service alternatives.

In this kind of environment the survival of commercial banks as we know them will certainly depend on their ability to be flexible and efficient in managing resources and controlling expenses. One positive note, contributed by Rhoades (1983a), is that banks do not *have* to become "financial supermarkets" themselves in order to survive; *specialization* in selected financial services and selected financial markets appears to be a viable alternative. Strategic management research suggests that most industries, banking included, are broad enough to allow many firms to specialize and find their own niche. Yet, admittedly, research on the issue of the comparative benefits of the conglomerate approach versus specialization in producing and marketing financial services is limited. Much more serious research work is needed in this crucial and dynamic aspect of the unfolding financial services marketplace.

Equally important for the industry, bankers must be more effective in the political arena in pursuing further deregulation of services and fewer restrictions on their geographic expansion. Although significant strides toward deregulation were made in the early 1980s, much remains to be done both in terms of greater latitude for interstate banking and in the range of permissible financial services. Recent bank failures and the financial troubles of major money center banks have made the political side of deregulation more treacherous and uncertain. In a serious political clash between the potential economic benefits of deregulation and the specter of weakening public confidence in the banking system, it is by no means clear that deregulation would win. To that important issue I now turn in the two concluding chapters of this book.

References

Benston, George J. 1980. *Conglomerate Mergers: Causes, Consequences, and Remedies.* Washington, D.C.: American Enterprise Institute for Public Policy Research.

Broaddus, Alfred. 1985. "Financial Innovation in the United States—Background, Current Status and Prospects." *Economic Review* (January-February), 71(1):2–22. Federal Reserve Bank of Atlanta.

Carrington, Tim. 1983. "Prudential Names Ex-Im Bank Official To Co-ordinate Expansion Into Banking." *The Wall Street Journal* (September 13), p. 7.

Christophe, Cleveland A. 1974. *Competition in Financial Services*. New York: First National City Corporation.

—— 1975. "Evaluation of 'Competition in Financial Services': A Reply," *Journal of Bank Research* (Spring), pp. 66–69.

Di Clemente, John J. 1983. "What Is a Bank?" *Economic Perspectives* (January-February), pp. 20–31. Federal Reserve Bank of Chicago.

Edmister, Robert O. 1982. "Commercial Bank Market Share of the Financial Services Industry: A Value Added Approach." Paper Presented at the Conference on Bank Structure and Competition (April 13). Federal Reserve Bank of Chicago.

Emmet, Boris and John E. Jeuck. 1950. *Catalogues and Counters*. Chicago: The University of Chicago Press.

Ford, William F. 1982. "Banking's New Competition: Myths and Realities." *Economic Review* (January), pp. 4–11. Federal Reserve Bank of Atlanta.

Greer, Douglas F. and Stephen A. Rhoades. 1975. "Evaluation of a Study on Competition in Financial Services." *Journal of Bank Research,* (Spring), pp. 61–65.

Hilder, David B. 1985. "American Express Chief Keeps Tight Grip." *The Wall street Journal* (June 28), p. 6.

Hilder, David B. and Tim Metz. 1984. "A Spate of Acquisition Puts American Express in Management Bind." *The Wall Street Journal* (August 15), pp. 1 and 18.

Kareken, John H. 1981. "Technical Change and the Future of Banking: One Man's View." *Memorandum*. Washington, D.C.: Golembe Associates, Inc.

Loomis, Carol J. 1981. "The Fight for Financial Turf." *Fortune* (December 28), pp. 54–65.

Luckett, Charles. 1982. "Recent Developments in the Mortgage and Consumer Credit Markets." *Federal Reserve Bulletin* (May), pp. 281–90.

Rhoades, Stephen A. 1983a. "The Implications of Financial Deregulation, Interstate Banking and Financial Supermarkets for Bank Merger Policy." *The Magazine of Bank Administration* (November), pp. 48–52.

—— 1983b. *Power, Empire Building and Mergers*. Lexington, Mass.: Lexington Books.

Rose, Peter S. 1982. "Symbiotics: Financial Supermarkets in the Making." *Canadian Banker & ICB Review* (April), 89(2):54–59.

Rosenblum, Harvey and Diane Siegel. 1983. *Competition in Financial Services: The Impact of Nonbank Entry*. Staff Study 83–1. Federal Reserve Bank of Chicago.

Rosenblum, Harvey and Christine Pavel. 1984. *Financial Services in Transition: The Effects of Nonbank Competitors*. Staff Memoranda 84–1. Federal Reserve Bank of Chicago. (Prepared for *The Banking Handbook*. Richard C. Aspinwall and Robert A. Eisenbeis, eds. New York: Wiley.)

12.

Regulation and Deregulation of the Banking Structure and Bank Services: The Causes and the Scope

IN EARLIER chapters I have spent considerable time focusing on two major structural trends that have characterized American banking for a century or more—*consolidation* of resources into larger, multiple-office banks and growing *diversification* of financial services offered to the public. In this chapter and the next I focus on a third major structural trend now having a profound impact on the industry—*deregulation*. As we will see, the roots of this major structural change are not buried deep in past history as is true of the consolidation and diversification trends. Today's trend toward deregulation of bank services and operations really began in the 1970s, arising out of growing public dissatisfaction with the performance of financial institutions in meeting business and household demands for financial services. My purpose in this chapter is to explore both the causes and the content of the bank deregulation movement.

The Regulatory Burden in Banking

For decades in the United States and for centuries in Western Europe commercial banking has been one of the most heavily regulated of all industries. Only in the public utility field, especially in the provision of electric power, water, and telephone services, is regulation more pervasive. The price and makeup of many banking services, the location of branch offices, the internal growth and external expansion of the banking organization, the quantity and quality of loans and investments, the volume and constituency of owners' capital, and even the scope and content of bank advertising messages have come under government scrutiny at one time or another.

BRIEF HISTORY OF BANKING REGULATION

Both the extent and the intensity of banking regulation have varied over time. Before the Great Depression of the 1930s banking regulation on a global scale, especially in Western Europe and the United States, was limited primarily to control over the outward expansion of the industry—the chartering of new banks, the admission of foreign competitors, and branching powers at home and abroad—and less involved with internal bank policies regarding prices, public service, the granting of loans, and the maintenance of capital. In one massive stroke, however, the Great Depression of the 1930s changed all that and left the industry and the public it serves with a legacy not yet outlived. The collapse of thousands of commercial banks and nonbank thrift institutions, one upon another in domino fashion, led to a three-day banking holiday declared by President Franklin D. Roosevelt on March 3, 1933, in an effort to restore a measure of public confidence in the viability of the nation's banking system.

In the ensuing weeks and months an elaborate structure of government agencies emerged, with two primary objectives in mind: (1) protection of the solvency and stability of individual banks to protect the public's deposits and (2) isolation of the business of banking from other forms of commerce, most notably investment banking and manufacturing. This was to be achieved essentially by substituting regulation for competition, expanding the range of the former and limiting the intensity of the latter. It was hoped that a delicate *balance* could be achieved that reaped the benefits of competition in providing the public with efficient, low-cost financial services, while preserving the liquidity and integrity of the banking system through deposit insurance, emergency credit, surveillance of bank financial dealings, and isolation from outside competition.

Whereas *in theory* a delicate balance was sought between competition and regulation, there seemed little doubt during the 1930s and for years thereafter that Congress and the President preferred to err on the side of close banking regulation as a proxy for greater safety rather than on the side of competition. And placing ourselves in the financial marketplace of a half century ago, we can understand *why* the pendulum swung so drastically in favor of regulation and away from competition. In 1920 there were 30,000 banks in the United States; by 1940 that number had been cut in half to less than 15,000—a result of the prolonged agricultural depression of the 1920s and the industrial depression of the 1930s. In one year, 1933, 3840 banks failed; over the 1930–33 period there were 9096 bank suspensions, as noted by Benston (1983). Mergers and holding-company acquisitions absorbed thousands of smaller financial institutions in order to head off imminent collapse.

The economic statistics of the 1930s seem appalling even today. Unemployment nationwide was variously estimated at 15 to 20 million persons—a quarter to a third of the nation's labor force. In 1934, when the Federal Housing Administration was created to insure home mortgage loans, an estimated 5 million home loans were either delinquent or in default. Measured in dollar terms the nation's gross national product (GNP) dropped from $90 billion in 1929 to an estimated $45 billion in 1933. Commercial enterprises ranging from retail shops to automobile manufacturers found themselves with bulging bank-financed inventories of unsold goods in an era when bank financing of inventories rested heavily on the "self-liquidation" principle. However, no commercial loan is self-liquidating when there is little or no demand for a business's products and services. Bank loan losses far exceeded the reserves built up to protect against foreseeable defaults. Thus, the nation's banks were squeezed between rapidly depreciating assets and growing deposit withdrawals.

Overriding all these economic and financial factors was a climate of fear and suspicion. President Roosevelt had reassured the nation in his 1932 Inaugural Address that "we have nothing to fear but fear itself." But in banking, fear has very real financial consequences.

Recent experience has shown that even a hint of trouble regarding the financial viability of a bank can result in substantial deposit erosion, especially among large uninsured depositors. Because they offer immediately withdrawable deposits, banks face more risk of damage from swings in public opinion than any other business enterprise does. And as a bank begins to contract in size from deposit withdrawals, there are several potentially destructive effects: (1) liquidity problems increase because most of the funds left on deposit have already been loaned out, often in relatively illiquid securities, forcing the bank to borrow heavily in the money market; (2) service production becomes increasingly inefficient if the bank drops below optimum size; (3) earnings deteriorate because the additional liquidity needed must often be borrowed at higher interest rates, and operating costs have increased; and (4) with declining earnings the infusion of new capital becomes more difficult and expensive, restricting the bank's opportunity to strengthen its financial position and provide a base for future growth. During the 1930s the simple *fear* of bank collapse, often unjustified, was translated into grim reality as hundreds of otherwise sound banks simply could not satisfy all the demands of their panic-stricken depositors.

THE SCOPE OF BANKING REGULATION TODAY

Out of the cataclysmic experience of the 1930s emerged an elaborate framework of rules and regulations that literally spanned bank operations "from cradle to grave." As Kane (1981) notes, most of the regulatory rules focused on an individual bank's capacity for deposit taking and for taking over other businesses. The era of *free banking* in which any group of organizers could start a bank as long as a minimum amount of equity capital was pledged and other banking regulations were adhered to came to an abrupt end during the Great Depression. Both federal and state banking agencies now required substantive evidence of public need and evidence that banking operations would be profitable before a bank would be chartered or a branch certified. In addition, it was now incumbent upon the new bank's organizers to convincingly demonstrate that banks already operating in the same market area would not be damaged by the appearance of new competition.

Once the bank was chartered, unannounced bank examinations were to be conducted by federal and/or state authorities at least once each year, subjecting individual loans, security investments, and operating rules and procedures to detailed scrutiny. Banks could not own the stock of other corporations, acquire significant amounts of real estate, or liberally value leases. Limits placed on bank territorial expansion were clarified and tightened with passage of the McFadden-Pepper Act of 1927, which forbade branching across state lines, and the Banking Act of 1933, which broadened McFadden's provisions and granted the Federal Reserve Board regulatory authority over bank holding companies. Interest rates paid on bank deposits were subject to legal interest rate ceilings set by the Federal Reserve Board for member banks and by the Federal Deposit Insurance Corporation for nonmember insured banking institutions (see table 12.1). This step was aimed at preventing "destructive rate competition" for deposits, alleged to be a material factor in the collapse of many banks during the 1930s, and also at protecting savings and loan associations and mutual savings banks so they could raise sufficient funds to support the housing market.

Set in place, then, was an elaborate *dual regulatory system* of federal and state controls on both internal bank operations and external bank growth. The states and the federal government were to be "co-equal" partners in insuring a sound and stable banking system. To be sure, the dual banking system was not created in the 1930s; it was a legacy from the Civil War era when the Office of the Comptroller of the Currency was created. However, the troubles of the 1930s resulted in a proliferation of *both* federal and state banking regulations plus an elaborate regulatory structure at the federal level centered around three principal agencies—the Federal Reserve System, Federal Deposit Insurance Corporation, and Comptroller of the Currency (Administrator of National Banks)—paralleled by banking commissions in each state. Savings and loans and credit unions were subsequently placed under a similar dual regimen of federal and state supervision (see table 12.2). Each agency's powers overlapped the others to some extent, creating a system of "checks and balances."

It was hoped that with government agencies literally watching each other, the result would be a more stable banking system. An unfortunate by-product was competition and conflict over jurisdictional boundaries, at times leading to what has come to be known as "competition in laxity." Moreover, the focus of U.S. bank regulation changed as the decades passed. During the depression years the focus was on penalizing or prohibiting unsafe banking practices and promoting public confidence in the banking system. In recent years regulation has aimed at protecting various groups—small banks, thrifts, small businesses, consumers, and agriculture—and in promoting greater efficiency in supplying financial services to the public.

Table 12.1. Landmark Federal Legislation Affecting U.S. Bank Expansion

National Bank Act (1863–1864)	Authorized the chartering of national banks by the Comptroller of the Currency.
Federal Reserve Act (1913)	Established the Federal Reserve System.
McFadden-Pepper Act (1927)	Blocked interstate branching, leaving state laws to regulate intrastate branching.
Banking Act of 1933 (Glass-Steagall Act)	Launched the FDIC and federal deposit rate ceilings while prohibiting bank underwriting of corporate bonds and stocks.
Bank Holding Company Act (1956)	Brought multibank holding companies under Federal Reserve supervision.
Bank Merger Act (1960)	Required federal banking agencies to rule on proposed bank mergers.
Bank Merger Act and Bank Holding Company Act Amendments (1966)	Contributions to public need and public convenience could be used to justify bank acquisitions and offset loss of competition.
Bank Holding Company Act Amendments (1970)	Brought one-bank holding companies and their nonbank business ventures under federal supervision.
Consumer Credit Protection Act (1968)	Institutional providers of consumer credit required to disclose finance charges and other pertinent credit information.
Community Reinvestment Act (1977)	Depository institutions must serve all segments of a community without discrimination.
Depository Institutions Deregulation and Monetary Control Act (1980)	Conferred expanded credit and deposit services upon thrift institutions and set in motion the elimination of interest rate ceilings on deposit accounts.
Garn-St Germain Depository	Approved deposit accounts competitive with money market mutual fund share accounts, permitted thrifts expanded services, and strengthened the role of deposit insurance agencies in dealing with failing banks and thrifts.

SOURCE: Federal Reserve Bank of Dallas.

THE RATIONALE FOR BANK REGULATION

Why have commercial banks always been so heavily regulated? A wide variety of reasons may be offered, some of dubious quality and others having some justification.

Banks Create Money. "Money is what money does" is an old saying that also happens to be true. Any asset or object that is used by the public as a medium to purchase goods and services and is generally accepted for that purpose is money. Since the seventeenth century, when deposits against which checks could be written were developed into an important financial service, checkable bank deposits have been the major ingredient of the nation's money supply. In the United States today checking accounts (demand deposits) represent about 70 percent of the nation's narrowly defined money stock (M1). The majority of demand deposit balances in existence arise from bank lending and investing—the extension of credit.

What does it cost to create demand deposits? More precisely, what is the marginal cost of production to a bank of turning out one more dollar of demand deposit money? The marginal cost of money production is *negligible*, which implies that, in the absence of regulation, the quantity of spendable bank deposits could expand virtually without limit. And because there is a high correlation between the growth of the money stock and the volume of production, employment, and the price level in the economy, the regulatory authorities, especially the Federal Reserve, maintain a close watch on the growth of bank-held demand deposits. As Boyd and Kwast (1979) observe, "extreme fluctuations in the aggregate level of the money supply could impose massive external costs on society as a whole" (p. 37).

A great preponderance of the regulations that restrict bank activity relate to the quantity of lending—and, therefore, deposit creation—that individual banks are permitted to do. In a sense, these regulations are designed to make government monetary policy function more effectively in achieving the nation's economic goals. Examples of monetary control regulations include capital adequacy rules, which require the volume of loans and other risky assets to be maintained at a satisfactory ratio to equity capital, and liquidity (reserve) requirements, which attempt to maintain a satisfactory balance among loans, security investments, and cash reserves. Limiting entry into the banking industry is also a means of controlling money growth by restricting

Table 12.2. Federal and State Regulatory Agencies for Banks and Nonbank Thrifts

Categories of Bank or Nonbank Thrift Institutions	Chartering a Licensing Agency	Agency Granting Approvals for Branches:		Agency Granting Approval of Mergers and Acquisitions:		Deposit Insurance Agency	Agency Supervising and Examining Institutions
		Intrastate	Interstate	Intrastate	Interstate		
Commercial Banking Organizations							
National Banks	Comptroller of the Currency	Comptroller of the Currency	[a]	Comptroller of the Currency	[c]	Federal Deposit Insurance Corporation	Comptroller of the Currency
State-chartered member banks of the Federal Reserve System	State banking department	Federal Reserve/ state banking department	[a]	Federal Reserve/ state banking department	[c]	Federal Deposit Insurance Corporation	Federal Reserve/ state banking department
State-chartered non-member banks	State banking department	State banking department	[a]	State banking department	[c]	Federal Deposit Insurance Corporation or state insurance agency or none	State banking department
Bank holding companies	Federal Reserve System			Federal Reserve/ state banking department	Federal Reserve/ state banking department		Federal Reserve

Nonbank Thrift Institutions

Federal- and state-chartered savings and loan associations	Federal Home Loan Bank Board/state banking department	Federal Home Loan Bank Board/Federal Savings and Loan Insurance Corp./state banking department	[b]	Federal Home Loan Bank Board/state banking department	Federal Savings and Loan Insurance Corporation	Federal Savings and Loan Insurance Corporation/state insurance funds	Federal Home Loan Bank Board/state banking department
Federal- and state-chartered credit unions	National Credit Union Administration/state banking department	No approval required	National Credit Union Administration/state banking department	National Credit Union Administration/state banking department[c]	National Credit Union Administration/state banking department	National Credit Union Share Insurance Fund/state insurance funds	National Credit Union Administration/state banking department

SOURCE: Adapted from Federal Reserve Bank of New York, *Depository Institutions and Their Regulators*.
[a]Not applicable. Interstate branching prohibited unless specifically authorized by state law.
[b]Prohibited generally for federal thrifts.
[c]Federal insurance agencies may arrange interstate mergers of closed or failing institutions.

potential sources of credit and deposit creation. However, because the Federal Reserve can control the size and rate of growth of the nation's money supply regardless of how many banks there are, this rationale for bank entry restrictions seems very weak today.

Banks Support Economic Growth. Closely related to the money creation function of banks is their essential role in supporting the economy's growth. By providing credit for commercial projects that offer the highest expected profits, banks aid in directing resources toward investments that increase the economy's ability to produce more goods and services in the future. To accomplish this, however, the public must be offered attractive savings instruments to generate the investment funds needed. Here, banks have played a vital role in the savings investment process, offering safe deposits that offer at least a moderate rate of return to the saver and are available in affordable denominations.

One of the most important features of savings instruments offered by commercial banks over the years has been *convenience.* By setting up numerous offices and automated teller machines in convenient locations the saver's transactions and search costs are reduced. As Boyd and Kwast (1979) point out, banks and other intermediaries reduce search and transactions costs for both creditors and debtors, and this "lowers the net interest rate paid investors and raises the net rate of return of lenders, thereby increasing the real level of investment and savings" (p. 37).

Whereas banks have functioned reasonably well, particularly in this century, in providing a conduit for the flow of savings into investment, society has virtually from its inception closely regulated the savings-investment process. Recognizing that a breakdown in the flow of savings toward the highest return investment projects would slow the nation's economic growth and lead to an inefficient use of scarce resources, regulation has for decades acted to protect the public's savings from undue risk, promote competition in offering savings instruments, and ensure that loans are made on a sound and equitable basis. Moreover, banking regulation has sought to ensure that loanable funds will flow to their most socially productive uses.

A host of existing federal and state regulations, then, can be attributed to public concern over the safety, efficiency, and direction of the savings-investment process—e.g., federal regulations that insure commercial bank, credit union, and savings and loan deposits; deposit interest rate controls; registration requirements on new security offerings; restrictions on bank entry; and periodic examinations of bank loans and net worth requirements carried out by federal and state supervisory authorities. All arise ultimately from concern over the reliability and stability of the sources of financial capital, the manner in which that capital is employed, and the linkages between capital flows and the nation's economic growth.

Banks Provide Credit for Governments. From the earliest history of banking there has been a close relationship between banks and government. It is interesting that the first commercial bank in the modern form, the Bank of Venice, chartered in 1157, was created in part to assist the City of Venice in war and preparation for war. The first major bank in the United States, the Bank of North America, chartered in 1781, was chartered to assist in financing colonial government activities and the Revolutionary War. The National Bank Act of 1863–64, which set up the present system of federally chartered national banks, was tailored to meet the federal government's pressing need to finance the construction of ships and the raising of armies to fight the Civil War.

Today U.S. banks play a vital role in the buying, selling, and refunding of U.S. Government securities, both as security dealers and as lenders to both dealers and some of their customers. Many existing regulations are aimed at ensuring government access to an adequate supply of bank credit, especially in times of national emergency. Examples of this regulatory rationale include liquidity requirements, which encourage banks to invest in substantial quantities of U.S. government bills, notes, and bonds; and pledging requirements behind government deposits, which require banks to purchase and hold reserves of U.S. government and municipal bonds to "back" the deposit of public funds. Moreover, all U.S. banks chartered today must be corporations and, as such, are subject to federal income taxation as corporations, providing an important source of government revenue. As Benston (1983) observes, deposit reserve requirements are also a form of federal taxation of money users that boosts the net income of the Federal Reserve banks, 90 percent of which ultimately flows to the U.S. Treasury.

Banks Possess Great Financial Power and Influence. No explanation of the rationale for bank regulation would be complete without consideration of the fear and suspicion that the public has

long held about banks and their activities. In an earlier era a number
of banks were burned to the ground by irate mobs, partly for religious
reasons and partly out of fear of the financial power that banks seem
to possess. Many states that prohibited or restricted bank branching
were located in the Midwest (e.g., Kansas, Minnesota, Missouri, Oklahoma, Texas, and Wisconsin), where conflicts arose between farming
and ranching interests and commercial banks. Some banks and railroads pursued anticompetitive policies that resulted in scarce and expensive credit and excessive charges for transporting farm products to
market. Thus, antibranching laws were passed in an effort to limit the
size of individual banks and promote localized banking competition.
In an era characterized by limited mobility of funds and relatively poor
transportation and communication facilities, branching restrictions
generally *were* effective in restraining the growth of small banks into
larger ones. The result was to make each banking institution more
heavily dependent on its own local community for deposits and loans
and, presumably, more responsive to the needs of those same local
communities for an ample supply of credit at low cost.

Legislation passed during the 1930s to aid, protect, and
restrict the nonbank thrifts can also be viewed as exemplifying the fear
of banking's power and influence. Whereas many of these rules limited
the ability of nonbanks to enter banking markets (such as the Banking
Act of 1933's rule confining checking account powers to commercial
banks), other laws (such as maximum deposit rate ceilings) were passed
to ensure that critical sectors of the economy long ignored by commercial banks and bereft of resources—especially households and the
housing market—would no longer be ignored. And when commercial
banks invaded consumer markets in great numbers after World War II,
legislation appeared in the 1960s and 1970s in an effort to protect the
consumer from credit discrimination (e.g., the Equal Credit Opportunity Act of 1974 and the Community Reinvestment Act of 1977), from
usurious and undisclosed credit costs (e.g., the Truth in Lending Law
of 1968 and the Truth in Leasing Act of 1976), and from the consequences of error and negligence (e.g., the Fair Credit Billing and Fair
Credit Reporting Acts of 1974). If banks stand astride the vital lifeline
of credit to consumers, it was argued, their power must be limited so
that consumers will be assured of fair and equitable treatment.

The alleged capability of banks to take over private industry because of their financial power has been a key regulatory issue for

more than 50 years. In 1933 Congress passed the Glass-Steagall Act, which isolates commercial banking from investment banking, prohibiting banks themselves from investing in corporate stock and from underwriting corporate debt and equity securities. Congress was motivated to enact Glass-Steagall's restrictive provisions because of the alleged risky practices of banks in speculating in corporate stock, which allegedly fueled the stock market crash of 1929. More recently, fear has been expressed that banks, if left unchecked in their dealings with industrial corporations, would significantly increase concentration in American industry through their service on corporate boards of directors and their control over corporate credit.

Similar fears were at work when Congress passed the 1970 Amendments to the Bank Holding Company Act. As discussed in chapter 9, this law prohibited banks from acquiring equity interests in businesses not "closely related" to commercial banking as defined by the Federal Reserve Board. Moreover, even acquisitions of banking-related businesses, such as finance and leasing companies and mortgage banking concerns, had to result in benefits for the public in the form of greater convenience, lower prices, or other important advantages. The intense public debate that has surrounded recently proposed revisions in federal banking laws that would allow banks greater freedom to invest in real estate ventures, municipal revenue projects, and security brokerage services is further testimony to the widespread fear of bank power and influence. In the main, the current trend toward deregulation of banking represents an effort to open the floodgates of competition so that the marketplace, not regulation, limits the great financial power banks seem to possess.

What Is Being Deregulated?

Deregulation of banking may be taken to have begun in the mid-1970s with the advent of NOW (negotiable order of withdrawal) accounts—interest-bearing checkbook plans—in New England. Mutual savings banks, first in Massachusetts and a short time later in New Hampshire, began offering this hybrid form of savings-checking account in 1970. Attacked by the banking community as a violation of the Banking Act of 1933, which allowed only commercial banks to offer checkbook deposits and also specified that such deposits could not bear interest, Massachusetts savings banks pleaded their cause in court, arguing that federal banking laws did not apply to state-chartered nonbank thrift institutions. The Massachusetts Supreme Court upheld this argument in 1972, and the new payments service spread in the ensuing years throughout New England. Not to be competitively disadvantaged, commercial banks in that region sought Congressional approval to offer NOWs, which was granted in 1974 to all federally supervised depository institutions in Massachusetts and New Hampshire. In 1976 banks and thrifts in Connecticut, Maine, Rhode Island, and Vermont were added to the NOW-approved list. Passage of the Depository Institutions Deregulation and Monetary Control Act in 1980 permitted the offering of NOWs nationwide beginning in January 1981.

This brief history of the NOW suggests that deregulation really began on the *deposit* side of the banking business. Indeed, as reflected in table 12.3, the principal steps toward deregulation of commercial banks (as opposed to nonbank thrifts) have centered on liberalization of *deposit* powers. It is the nonbank thrifts—principally savings and loan associations and savings banks—that have scored the greatest gains in *asset* deregulation. And as table 12.3 also shows, the most important deregulation actions were set in motion with passage of the Depository Institutions Deregulation and Monetary Control Act of 1980 ("DIDMCA") and the Garn-St Germain Depository Institutions Act of 1982 ("the Garn bill"). What were the major provisions of these two laws?

PRINCIPAL PROVISIONS OF DIDMCA

DIDMCA authorized commercial banks to sell NOW accounts to individuals and nonprofit associations nationwide and to market automatic transfer services (ATS), permitting the movement of funds between checking and savings deposits to cover overdrafts and to earn interest on working balances. This step was a major blow to the prohibition of interest payments on demand accounts, set in place originally by the National Bank Act of 1933 (Glass-Steagall). Thus, it was no surprise when in June 30, 1983, the Depository Institutions Deregulation Committee (DIDC) voted to recommend to Congress that federal rules prohibiting payment of interest on regular demand deposits be repealed.

Table 12.3. Recent Federal Deregulation Legislation and Regulatory Decisions Affecting Banks

Year	Legislation or Regulatory Decision
1973	Regulation Q deposit rate ceilings are suspended for all $100,000 + CDs.
1974	NOW (interest-bearing checkable) accounts approved for federally supervised banks and thrifts in Massachusetts and New Hampshire. Banks allowed to offer six-year investment certificates.
1975	Federal Reserve Board allows preauthorized transfers from savings accounts for paying bills and allows member banks to offer corporate savings accounts up to $150,000.
1976	Banks and thrifts in Connecticut, Maine, New Hampshire, and Vermont are permitted to offer NOW accounts.
1977	Savings and loans are permitted to hold savings accounts at commercial banks. Federal credit unions were granted new loan powers, and permissible maturities on their mortgage loans were extended out to 30 years.
1978	Federal Reserve Board approves automatic transfers from savings to checking accounts. Money market CDs authorized with 26-week maturities, $10,000 minimum denominations, and ceiling rates based on T-bill rates.
1979	Four-year CDs and 2½-year small-saver CDs with no minimum denomination and rates tied to yields on Treasury bonds are permitted.
1980	Depository Institutions Deregulation and Monetary Control Act equalizes reserve requirements for all depository institutions and grants them access to the discount window. NOW accounts are authorized nationwide and interest rate ceilings on time and savings deposits are to be phased out over a six-year period. Thrift institutions can offer such new services as consumer and commercial loans, credit cards, and trust services. Deposit insurance is increased to $100,000.
1981	Ceiling-free IRA and Keogh accounts authorized.
1982	Garn-St Germain Depository Institutions Act requires differences in the maximum legal deposit rates offered by federally supervised institutions to be phased out no later than January 1, 1984. National bank loan limits are raised and borrowing limits are removed. National banks are permitted to broker real property loans. Larger bank holding companies are prohibited from acting as agent, broker, or underwriter for insurance services, except for credit life, disability, or involuntary unemployment insurance. Federally regulated nonbank thrifts may offer demand deposits to commercial or agricultural customers. Federal savings and loans may issue capital stock, and both savings and loans and savings banks are eligible for membership in the Federal Home Loan Bank System and may convert from mutual to stock form or vice versa. Federal savings associations are granted expanded asset portfolio powers for nonresidential real estate loans, municipal bonds, and consumer loans. State laws restricting enforcement of due-on-sale clauses in mortgage loans are preempted (with some loans grandfathered or exempted). Federal credit unions may grant first mortgage loans with maturities exceeding 30 years and second mortgages out to 15 years, and legal price ceilings on such loans are eliminated. Federal credit unions may offer travelers checks and money orders, issue mortgage-backed securities, hold deposits in any federally insured state bank, and invest in municipal bonds. Commercial banks and federal nonbank thrifts may offer deposit accounts "directly equivalent to and competitive with" share accounts offered by money market mutual funds with terms to be set by the Depository Institu-

Table 12.3. *Continued*

tions Deregulation Committee. The FDIC and FSLIC may make loans to or assume
the liabilities of any federally insured depository institution to prevent its closing or
reduce risk to the insurance agency.

1983   All interest rate ceilings are eliminated except those on passbook savings deposits and
        regular NOWs. Super NOWs are created with unlimited third-party transfer and no
        rate ceiling.

1984   The rate differential between commercial bank and thrift passbook savings accounts
        and short-term CDs under $2,500 is eliminated.

1985   The minimum denominations for MMDAs, Super NOWs, and short-term CDs that
        are rate ceiling free are reduced to $1,000.

1986   The Depository Institutions Deregulation Commission moved to eliminate the required
        minimum denominations on MMDAs, Super NOWs, and short-term ceiling-free CDs
        and the legal rate ceilings on passbook savings accounts.

SOURCES: Federal Reserve Bank of Chicago, *Economic Perspectives* (November-December),
1983; and R. Alton Gilbert and A. Steven Holland, "Has the Deregulation of Deposit Interest
Rates Raised Mortgage Rates?" *Review*, Federal Reserve Bank of St. Louis, May 1984, pp. 5–15;
and Federal Reserve Board.

In order to calm public fears of increased banking problems
in the wake of deregulation and also to "catch up" with the effects of
inflation on the nominal size of deposits, federal insurance of deposits
was increased to $100,000 from the $40,000 figure set in 1978. Unfortunately, this move toward expanded deposit insurance coverage represented only a partial remedy for the economic and financial
distortions engendered by the federal deposit insurance system. As
Boyd and Kwast (1979) testify, the combination of the depression-
spawned deposit insurance system along with other long-standing regulatory standards

has given banks an incentive to hold riskier portfolios than they would in the
absence of regulation. It has reduced the effectiveness of the self-regulating
powers of the market. It has generated a dynamic interaction of response-
counter-response between regulator and regulated. All these factors stimulate
the need for more and more regulations and standards. . . . This environment
unnecessarily obstructs the flow of funds through financial intermediaries,
wastes real resources, distorts financial innovation, and may make the system
more subject to financial panic (pp. 38–39).

As these researchers correctly observe, these distortions are magnified
by an insurance system that does not exact higher casualty premiums
on those banks that willingly accept greater risk.

Perhaps the most important step taken in DIDMCA was to begin the gradual dismanteling of federal deposit interest rate ceilings. These maximum permissible demand, time, and savings deposit rates had been set for commercial banks in 1933 with enforcement for member banks left to the Federal Reserve Board and, for nonmember banks, to the Federal Deposit Insurance Corporation. Nonbank thrifts were exempted from these rate ceilings until 1966. The rationale for the new deposit rate limits was a familiar one in banking history: *promote safety by restricting price competition.* Confronted by thousands of banks in trouble or collapsing, Congress concluded that aggressive price competition encouraged banks to offer higher and higher deposit interest rates that weakened their earnings margins, making them more susceptible to failure. The solution was to encourage the setting of *uniform* deposit rates that supposedly would create greater stability and predictability for bank deposit costs and earnings margins.

One obvious effect of the rate ceilings was to encourage competitive banks to substitute nonprice competition for price competition. Banks would strive to offer greater convenience to their customers such as through the construction of additional branch offices and subsidizing checkbook deposits by charging user fees below actual production costs. The result was to build into the system a heavier fixed-cost burden that would reduce the industry's flexibility in adapting to a new and more intensely competitive environment.

Whereas deposit rate ceilings *may* have brought additional stability to the banking industry (though this is debatable because they also encourage disintermediation of deposits), the ceilings penalized savers, especially those whose small volume of savings and strong liquidity needs prevented them from finding other attractive and viable investment outlets for their funds. More interest-sensitive, large-volume savers were able to escape the negative effects of the ceilings by diverting their funds into money market securities, taxable and tax-exempt bonds, stocks, and real property investments. The small saver with limited investment alternatives was consigned to promote bank viability by accepting submarket yields on savings deposits when open-market yields increased. Equally significant, research evidence has suggested that the underlying rationale for the ceilings—the prevention of "destructive" deposit interest rate competition—was largely without empirical validity. Bank failures in the 1930s, Cox (1966) finds, could be traced more directly to problems on the *asset* side of the industry's ledger and to the failure of government economic policy to respond in timely fashion to the banking system's liquidity needs.

DIDMCA called for a phaseout of deposit rate ceilings by 1986. The phaseout was to be implemented by a new federal commission—the Depository Institutions Deregulation Commission (DIDC), composed of the Secretary of the Treasury, the Comptroller of the Currency (the only nonvoting member), and the chairmen of the Federal Reserve Board, Federal Deposit Insurance Corporation, Federal Home Loan Bank Board, and National Credit Union Administration. DIDC began its most significant work dismanteling the rate ceilings approximately 16 months after DIDMCA was signed into law by President Jimmy Carter on March 31, 1980. In August 1981 interest rate ceilings on the longest term CDs, with maturities of four years or more, were eliminated. Nine months later, in May 1982, all federal rate ceilings on deposits with maturities of 3 ½ years or longer were removed and a new 91-day variable rate CD was permitted—a step followed in September by the legalization of even shorter term (7 to 31-day) variable-rate deposits.

One of the most significant of all deregulation steps taken by DIDC occurred as 1982 was drawing to a close. On the heels of the Garn-St Germain Depository Institutions Act passed in October 1982, DIDC authorized money market deposit accounts (MMDAs) designed to be "directly equivalent to and competitive with" share accounts sold by money market mutual funds. The interest rate on MMDAs was left to the discretion of the offering institution; there was to be no legal maximum rate, provided an average balance of no less than $2500 was maintained (a requirement that subsequently was eliminated). The new account was eligible for FDIC insurance coverage and, if offered to nonpersonal deposit holders, carried the same reserve requirements as other business-type time deposits. MMDAs could be used for third-party payments—up to six preauthorized transfers per month (no more than three by check) were permitted. The success of MMDAs was phenomenal. By May 1983, approximately six months after their inauguration, MMDA volume exceeded $300 billion—roughly half the size of the nation's narrowly defined (M1) money supply.

In January 1983 DIDC surprised the industry by coming forward with still another flexible-rate deposit instrument, the Super NOW. Like MMDAs, Super NOWs' yield to the customer was left to the financial marketplace and the discretion of the offering institution.

Unlike MMDAs, however, institutions were permitted to offer unlimited third-party payment powers on Super NOWs. These higher yielding NOWs have not been as popular as MMDAs, perhaps because the latter, along with money market mutual fund accounts, have already drained off most of the liquid savings balances previously held by the public in transactions balances, leaving only checkable deposits that turn over rapidly with low average balances. Subsequently, DIDC ruled that any existing minimum denominations on MMDAs, Super NOWs, and short-term (7 to 31-day) ceiling-free CDs would be eliminated in 1986.

NEW LOAN AND INVESTMENT POWERS
FOR BANKING ORGANIZATIONS

Whereas the 1980 DIDMCA law granted new loan and investment powers almost exclusively to banking's major competitors— the thrift institutions, the 1982 Garn-St Germain bill did grant commercial banks more latitude in making loans. As table 12.3 indicates, the historic 10-percent-of-capital limit on national bank loans to a single borrower was increased to 15 percent and further expanded to 25 percent of unimpaired capital and surplus for fully secured loans. Loans to foreign governments and government agencies were brought under this percentage-of-capital limitation. National banks were also permitted by the Garn bill to more freely broker real estate loans and to use residential and farm construction loans as collateral for borrowings from the Federal Reserve's discount window. In addition, "bankers' banks"—subsidiary corporations—could be set up to offer many of the services formerly provided by holding-company organizations. Among the most important of these are the offering of discount brokerage services, further supporting the public image of banks as one-stop financial department stores.

STRUCTURAL REFORMS IN THE GARN-ST GERMAIN BILL

One of the most significant changes ushered in with passage of the Garn bill in 1982 was an opening of the door to formal interstate deposit banking. Garn-St Germain is often referred to as the "Regulators' Bill" because it granted broad new powers to the federal insurance agencies—particularly the FDIC and the FSLIC—to deal

with troubled banks and thrifts. In order to eliminate or reduce potential depositor claims on federal insurance funds, the Garn bill provides
for interstate mergers under a form of the "failing-firm doctrine." A
troubled commercial or savings bank whose assets exceed $500 million
may, with the approval and assistance of the FDIC, be merged with
the lowest bidding depository institution within the same state and
industry—the preferred solution—or with an out-of-state institution
not necessarily in the same industry. Thus, in 1983 a Minneapolis
commercial bank was permitted to acquire a problem bank in Oregon.
Even before the Garn bill became law a major acquisition across both
state and industry lines was allowed when Citicorp of New York, then
the second largest bank holding company, was permitted to acquire
troubled Fidelity Savings of San Francisco. Mergers of this sort further
hasten the advent of de facto interstate branch banking even if Congress
continues to avoid the politically sensitive issue of federally sanctioned
interstate branching for all banks willing and able to expand into
national and regional deposit markets.

The Why of Deregulation

What factors led to the deregulation movement? As Silber (1983)
notes, *inflation*, by sharply increasing operating costs, drove the financial industry toward service innovation and increased efficiency. Therefore, much of the pressure for deregulation has come from financial
institutions themselves (especially the nonbank thrifts) seeking greater
latitude in responding to severe economic and financial pressures. This
form of internal industry pressure is mindful of Kane's (1977) *regulatory
dialectic*—the cyclical interaction between political and economic
pressures in regulated markets, regulators and regulatees each seeking
to maximize their own performance objectives.

Inflation's impact on financial services has also been felt
through a tight Federal Reserve monetary policy and in certain years
both *high and volatile interest rates*. When interest rates rose rapidly in
some years the change frequently led to severe disintermediation of
funds from depository institutions because they increased the opportunity cost to the customer of holding money in regulated deposits.

Banks and other financial institutions were forced to seek out new fund sources and new markets. This brought about not only the development of new services but also pressure on legislatures and regulatory authorities to allow greater geographic expansion through branching, mergers, and holding-company acquisitions.

As Colton (1980) observes, pressure for change has come from *federal and state legislative and regulatory authorities* as well, reflecting public concern over the safety and viability of financial institutions and the level of competition in financial services. Inflation and volatile interest rates exposed depository institutions to increased risk of fluctuating earnings and increased bankruptcy risk. This problem became most evident among savings and loan associations and savings banks. Rising interest rates not only squeezed the thrifts' operating returns as deposit costs rose faster than operating revenue but also frequently generated a negatively sloped yield curve in which deposit interest rates substantially exceeded the average rate of return on institutional asset portfolios, reducing the thrifts' net worth cushion against failure. Commercial banks also felt these net worth pressures, as reflected in their rising failure rate in the late 1970s and early 1980s. Thus, the additional flexibility in dealing with depository institution failures granted in the Garn-St Germain bill, as well as the increase in deposit insurance mandated by DIDMCA, reflected public, legislative, and regulatory concern over the safety of the public's savings held by depository institutions. The same is true of the added asset and liability powers granted banks and thrifts in DIDMCA and the Garn bill, which permitted greater diversification and perhaps promoted increased stability for federally supervised depository institutions.

There is also public and regulatory concern over the *level of competition* in providing key financial services, such as residential mortgage credit and savings deposits. When inflation began to drive home mortgage interest rates to record levels, the public and the Congress began to raise questions about the intensity of financial services competition in thousands of local markets across the nation. If high interest rates could not be brought down with conventional fiscal and monetary policy tools, additional competition from expanding the service powers of depository institutions and a more liberal chartering policy to create new competitors might well serve to bring the cost of credit down and improve the ability and convenience of services provided. That added competition might also spur financial innovation in critical areas, such as in the development of alternative residential mortgage instruments and savings plans.

Public and industry concern over *regulatory equity*—the "level playing field" issue—has also stimulated many recent legislative changes. Until the 1960s and 1970s regulation imposed relatively few costs on the banking industry as a whole, though the few largest U.S. banking organizations keenly felt the product and geographic restrictions imposed by the Glass-Steagall Act and the McFadden and Bank Holding Company Acts. Indeed, some regulations, such as those providing for access to Federal Reserve loans and federal deposit insurance, conferred positive benefits that roughly neutralized the industry's regulatory burden. Then, in 1966, Congress mandated a deposit rate advantage for nonbank thrifts over commercial banks, designed to protect the flow of loanable funds into home mortgages. Thrift institutions' ability to offer deposits at higher maximum legal rates imposed an almost devastating burden on banking in the 1970s. Soaring inflation drove market interest rates far above regulatory limits and severely constrained banks' ability to attract loanable funds. Bankers, the Congress, and public-interest groups came to view federally enforced deposit rate limits as inconsistent with the drive to promote greater financial services competition in the late 1970s and early 1980s.

And there were several other key regulatory-equity issues that supported the trend toward banking deregulation, especially the dramatic growth of unregulated money market mutual funds, whose assets exceeded $200 billion by the early 1980s. The money funds offer of high, market-sensitive yields on low-denomination, checkable share accounts pulled billions of dollars from commercial bank deposits but were especially telling competition for nonbank thrifts. The Garn bill's authorization of money market deposit accounts in October 1982 represented a belated Congressional response to this decade-old regulatory inequity. Many observers feel that Congress finally responded to the issue of the unregulated money market funds because of the explosion in the numbers of unregulated financial service firms during the middle and late 1970s. The success of Merrill Lynch's Cash Management Account program (which eventually signed well over a million customers), the Sears' Financial Network, and the marketing initiatives of Shearson-American Express and Prudential-Bache Securities made it clear that the regulatory-equity issue was not going away, even as the growth of the money market mutual funds slowed and then reversed itself in the early 1980s.

Moreover, as various banking groups pointed out, the equity issue not only encompassed the fact that unregulated firms were offering bank-like services such as savings accounts and installment credit, but also that such firms were able to develop new financial services that commercial banks legally could not offer, such as insurance underwriting and investment banking. Unregulated financial firms literally could offer any new service they wished as long as the method of offering it to the public conformed with federal disclosure requirements. Other factors held equal, customers would shift from regulated to unregulated financial firms, distorting the allocation of resources within the financial sector and creating additional regulatory problems.

What is noteworthy about the Garn bill is that it dealt primarily with the older equity issue of the unregulated money market fund but not with the newer (and today more potent) challenge posed by nonbank financial conglomerates such as Sears, Merrill Lynch, and Prudential-Bache. This regulatory lag is consistent with Kane's (1981) observation that, confronted with the same environmental changes, "the adaptive efficiency shown on average by deposit-institution managers is greater than that shown by managers of the several competing banking agencies" (p. 356).

Still another aspect of the regulatory equity issue centered on the failure of Congress to fully recognize that the *regulatory structure* itself must be changed, along with changes in the service powers of regulated financial institutions. For example, if nonbank thrifts are to be granted broader deposit and loan powers commensurate with those possessed by commercial banks, then there is a strong rationale to impose liquidity and capital requirements on the thrifts similar to those faced by commercial banks. Comparably, if nonmember banks were subject to less rigid rules (particularly in the form of deposit reserve requirements) than member banks of the Federal Reserve System but both possessed essentially the same service powers, it should have been no surprise that hundreds of member banks left the Fed and (as the Board of Governors viewed the matter) weakened the Federal Reserve's monetary control powers. As we saw earlier in this chapter, Congress dealt with key aspects of this problem in DIDMCA (1980) by requiring all depository institutions offering payments accounts and nonpersonal time deposits to hold the *same* reserve requirements. Unfortunately, little was done to alleviate other serious regulatory differences related to such issues as taxation of earnings, capital requirements, branching powers, and peripheral service offerings. Presumably these regulatory differences will be dealt with in future federal and state legislation when a stronger political consensus is achieved.

Finally, *technological innovation* has also proved to be a major force for deregulation of banking and the thrift business. Indeed, just as the invention of the automobile encouraged the growth of branch banking in the United States, recent advances in communications technology have broadened today's financial markets and the scope and deliverability of financial services, bringing distant financial institutions into direct competition with one another. Legal limits on bank geographic expansion became a growing and costly regulatory burden for banks to shoulder in an era when states and regions were becoming increasingly interdependent. Indeed, rapid technological change made many regulatory restrictions virtually irrelevant to real-world choices and problems. Antibranching statutes prevent the location of full-service brick-and-mortar facilities in distant markets but cannot shut out the electronic movement of funds via computer and wire over great distances. Decades-old regulatory rules that distinguish between payments accounts and liquid savings balances become irrelevant and burdensome when new technology permits the immediate movement of funds between these accounts by customers increasingly aware of the importance of close management of their daily cash positions.

As Eisenbeis (1980) observes, the electronic movement of financial data is converting banking from a local and regional industry to a national and international industry. The new technology is eliminating differences between bank and nonbank financial functions and, at the same time, multiplying the operative levels of regulatory supervision. Although the changing technology of information transfer has outmoded may geographic restrictions (and, as Kane 1981 contends, probably lowered the marginal cost to banks seeking ways of avoiding regulatory burdens), those changes may also have altered the fundamentals of production economics in banking, conferring on those institutions able to achieve a high volume of sales significantly lower production costs. Smaller financial institutions less capable of upgrading their facilities with the latest technology may have difficulty surviving in the changing financial marketplace. Thus, technological innovation has not only been a cause of deregulation but also offers the potential for a major restructuring of competition and service delivery in the financial institutions' field. Perhaps, in the words of Benston (1983), "it is time that we recognize that financial institutions are simply businesses with only a few special features that require regulation" (p. 218).

Epilogue

It seems clear, then, that the current trend toward financial deregulation springs from *multiple causes*—inflation; high and volatile interest rates in a number of earlier years; public and regulatory concern over the safety, viability, and competitiveness of depository financial institutions; long-standing regulatory inequities; the appearance of unregulated financial firms; and technological innovation in communications and service delivery. Thus, the causes of financial deregulation are not simple but complex, and it is likely that the *effects* of deregulation on banks and nonbank institutions and on the public they serve will also be complex. Adding to that complexity are the many unresolved deregulation issues: interstate branching, insurance and investment banking powers for depository institutions, the status of unregulated financial conglomerates, the centralization of remaining regulatory powers, a new formula for federal deposit insurance that reflects variations in bankruptcy risk among individual banks in a deregulated environment, etc. I turn now to analyzing a number of these critically important issues—deregulation's effects and its uncertain future direction—in the next and concluding chapter of this book.

References

Benston, George J. 1964. "Interest Payments on Demand Deposits and Bank Investment Behavior." *Journal of Political Economy,* 72:431–49.
—— 1983. "Federal Regulation of Banking: Analysis and Policy Recommendations." *Journal of Bank Research* (Winter), 13(4):216–44.
—— 1983. "Deposit Insurance and Bank Failures." *Economic Review* (March), pp. 4–17. Federal Reserve Bank of Atlanta.
Boyd, John H. and Myron L. Kwast. 1979. *Bank Regulation and the Efficiency of Financial Intermediation* (April). Financial Studies Section. Board of Governors of the Federal Reserve System.

Carson, Andrews S. 1982. *The Plight of the Thrift Institutions.* Washington, D.C.: The Brookings Institution.

Colton, Kent W. 1980. *Financial Reforms: A Review of the Past and Prospects for the Future* (September). Washington, D.C.: Office of Policy and Economic Research. Federal Home Loan Bank Board.

Cox, Albert. 1966. *Regulation of Interest Rates on Bank Deposits.* Ann Arbor: Bureau of Business Research. University of Michigan.

Eisenbeis, Robert A. 1980. *Financial Innovation and the Role of Regulation; Implications for Banking Organization, Structure, and Regulation* (February). Washington, D.C.: Board of Governors of the Federal Reserve System.

Flannery, Mark J. 1982. "Deposit Insurance Creates a Need for Bank Regulation." *Business Review* (January–February), pp. 17–24. Federal Reserve Bank of Philadelphia.

Gambs, Carl. 1977. "Bank Failures—An Historical Perspective." *Monthly Review* (June), pp. 10–20. Federal Reserve Bank of Kansas City.

Guffey, Roger. 1983. "After Deregulation: The Regulatory Role of the Federal Reserve." *Economic Review* (June), pp. 3–7. Federal Reserve Bank of Kansas City.

Kane, Edward J. 1981. "Accelerating Inflation, Technological Innovation, and the Decreasing Effectiveness of Banking Regulation." *The Journal of Finance* (May), 36(2):355–67.

—— 1977. "Good Intentions and Unintended Evil: The Case Against Selective Credit Allocation." *Journal of Money, Credit and Banking* (February), 9:55–69.

Rockoff, Hugh. 1974. "The Free Banking Era: A Reexamination." *Journal of Money, Credit and Banking* (May), 6:141–67.

Silber, William L. 1983. "The Process of Financial Innovation." *American Economic Review* (May), pp. 89–95.

13.

Probable Effects
and Future Course
of Banking Deregulation

THE PROCESS of deregulating American banking began more than a decade ago with the suspension of federal interest rate ceilings on money market CDs and the approval of interest-bearing payments accounts (NOWs) in New England. Since then each new year has brought new deregulatory initiatives at either state or federal levels and often both. The result is that we now have had enough time and experience to begin to see, at least in broad outline, how deregulation is likely to affect the banking industry—its profitability, growth, pricing policies, risk, and services offered.

   Of course, no one knows *for sure* what will happen in the wake of deregulation, but strong hints are provided from at least three different sources: (1) the economic theory of individual firm behavior in competitive markets; (2) the few financial institutions' deregulation studies available to date; and (3) the experience of firms in other industries that have been deregulated in recent years—for example, the airlines, trucking, and security brokerage industries. In this chapter I examine five critical areas of bank performance—profitability, growth and market share, pricing policies, risk, and services offered to the public—and the evidence offered in each performance area by economic theory, recent financial deregulation studies, and the experience of other deregulated industries.

Bank Profitability

The primary concern of most bankers is the possible or probable impact of deregulation on their profitability or net margin overall costs. Because deregulation calls for the replacing of fixed, legal interest rates on deposits with flexible market rates, economic theory would imply that bank profits would become more sensitive to interest rate fluctuations and credit market conditions. In particular, a period of rising interest rates would squeeze net bank profits because deposit costs would rise faster than yields on earning assets (relatively low asset portfolio velocity being assumed). Moreover, deregulation brings in more competition from nonbank thrift institutions, which, with passage of the 1980 Depository Institutions Deregulation Act and the 1982 Garn-St Germain Depository Institutions Act, can offer competing financial services on both the credit and deposit side of the banking business.

Economic theory would imply that prices charged for some financial services would be driven below the break-even point in the short run, driving some financial institutions from the market with unacceptable losses. Over the long run bank profits would be driven to no more than a *normal* level in which net returns per production unit equaled long-run average cost. In summary, we would expect *lower* average profitability across the industry, reflecting significant decreases in the average earnings rate for banks in markets previously sheltered by regulation.

EVIDENCE FROM STUDIES OF FINANCIAL INSTITUTIONS
A study by Flannery (1983) suggests that such theoretical arguments may be much too simplified. In particular, the dire predictions for bank profitability following the complete removal of federal deposit rate ceilings assume that the ceilings really have been effective in holding down bank fund-raising costs. If those ceilings *have* been

effective in reducing bank costs, then an increase in the interest cost on those same deposit balances up to market levels would, *ceteris paribus*, reduce bank profits dollar for dollar. On the basis of this naive assumption Flannery shows that bank profits would have fallen nearly 80 percent in 1982 if fully competitive interest rates were paid on retail demand and savings deposits.

But what if deposit rate ceilings have *not* been totally effective in restraining bank deposit costs? For example, many banks have attempted to compensate for below-market deposit rates by lowering the customer's search and transactions costs through the heavy advertising of hours and services, the building of convenient branch offices and remote teller windows, and the provision of bank-by-mail and wire-transfer facilities and by offering prizes to customers opening a new account or adding funds to an existing account.

An early study by Benston (1964) found that during the 1920s, when demand-deposit interest was legal, banks choosing not to pay interest on these accounts substituted other services and, interestingly enough, displayed a higher failure rate due perhaps to their less flexible deposit costs. The result, as noted by Flannery, is that processing costs for checking accounts (especially small consumer-type accounts) usually far exceed bank service charges.

As deposit interest rates have risen with gradual deregulation banks have compensated for those higher deposit costs in at least two ways: (1) noninterest operating costs (particularly labor costs) have been reduced per account through greater efficiency, leaner staffs, more selective hiring of new employees, reduced use of brick-and-mortar facilities, etc.; and (2) service charges have been increased and/or explicitly assessed on what were formerly "free" services. Thus, as Flannery (1983) observes, many bank depositors have benefited from higher gross interest earnings on their deposited funds but have also faced higher service fees for individual transactions and for other bank services they use. Thus, the *net* benefit to the deposit customer from a deregulated environment is not necessarily significantly greater than before; much depends on the particular bank services the customer uses and the activity levels in individual accounts. However, it is arguably better for bank customers to possess unconstrained choices rather than artificially limited options.

We must not lose sight too of the significant "drag" on bank profitability represented by the rapid growth of brick-and-mortar branches over the past several decades. As noted in chapter 1, the number of branches of U.S. commercial banks virtually quadrupled over the 1960–1980 period—from about 10,000 full-service banking offices to just over 40,000. Petersen (1981) estimates that close to one third of commercial bank branches across the nation can be attributed to the era of federally controlled deposit rates, and Chase (1981) finds that nearly two fifths of savings and loan branches are traceable to the deposit rate regulations.

Thus, the legal rate ceilings resulted in a substantial increase in both explicit operating costs and fixed costs to branching banks, though a substantial reduction in customer search and transactions costs also occurred. With the advent of electronic banking many financial institutions are faced with much larger physical facilities than they need to have in order to conveniently and competitively offer their services. Meyer and Tye (1985) argue that the presence of these "sunk costs" limits management's options until those costs are recovered, resulting in a transition phase for deregulation that may bear little resemblance to the long-run equilibrium quantity of bank services, prices, and profits that will prevail when all or most current sunk costs are no longer relevant. We may question this argument, however, on grounds that if these previously incurred costs are truly "sunk" they cannot rationally influence a banker's competitive options today.

In a curious twist of fate, unit banks, most of which are in the Midwest and South, may possess a significant advantage in the race for customer deposits because they have no full-service branches. Of course, many of these institutions have banded together in holding-company organizations and, therefore, have created a "quasi-branching" system that could create problems in trying to dispose of smaller, less profitable affiliated banks. It may be difficult (if not impossible) to obtain regulatory permission to close small unit bank offices and replace them with automated remote-service teller units on grounds of public need.

A number of arguments have been advanced to date on why bank profitability might *not* be adversely affected in the long run, once short-run adjustments to deregulation are completed. These positive arguments include the following:

1. *The Cost Reduction Argument.* Savings from a reduction in costly nonprice incentives (such as free services

and numerous branch offices) will offset a substantial share of any projected increase in deposit interest costs.

2. *The Customer Acceptance Argument.* Relatedly, in an environment of open price competition, customers will more readily accept higher explicit prices for bank services reflective of the true production costs of those services.

3. *The Economies-of-Scale Argument.* With banks freer to compete aggressively for deposits, the volume of deposits (that is, average bank size) will rise because bank deposits will become more attractive compared with alternative financial instruments; therefore, the profit margin on each unit of service may fall, but larger total profits could result from a greater overall volume of deposit production with lower unit costs of production. This argument has recently lost some of its luster, however, due to recent findings (as noted by Benston, Hanweck, and Humphrey [1982]) that small branch and unit banks are more cost-efficient than larger banks, at least for the most important banking services.

4. *The Leverage Argument.* Bank profits are not affected solely by deposit costs; other adjustments in operating and portfolio policies can be made to offset higher deposit costs. For example, banks can prevent a squeeze on their equity returns through greater use of financial leverage (i.e., less equity capital and more debt to fund their assets).

5. *The Flexible Rates Argument.* Bank profits need not be adversely affected by flexible deposit interest rates because those flexible rates may *fall* as well as rise, depending on market conditions; thus, the net long-run impact of freely adjustable deposit rates on banks' net profit margin depends on management's ability to control both asset and liability portfolios in such a way as to benefit from (or at least not be hurt by) interest rate fluctuations.

6. *The Maneuverability Argument.* For large banks whose stock is actively traded, the market may react positively to deregulation announcements because deregulation implies greater freedom for management decisionmak-

ing, realizing that commercial banks have the distinct
advantage of greater maneuverability owing to their
more flexible asset portfolios as compared with nonbank
thrifts; thus, investors in the financial marketplace may
place a higher value on bank stock because the banks'
greater maneuverability will enable them to grasp a
larger share of deposit and credit markets.

7. *The Differential-Impact Argument.* Whatever its effects, deregulation will not impact all banks the same
way; banks with superior management, less overhead to
carry in the form of extensive branch systems and large
payrolls, and a smaller volume of retail deposits—the
service most directly affected by the lifting of federal
interest rate ceilings—or located in less competitive
suburban or rural markets will probably be the *least*
impacted by deregulation and, in fact, may benefit in
terms of market share and profits over those institutions
not so fortuitously situated.

It is difficult not to be persuaded by at least *some* of the
foregoing arguments. Indeed, though limited in number and scope, the
few deregulation studies currently available are generally consistent
with a number of the points made here. For example, industry profitability measured principally by return on equity remained remarkably
buoyant during the 1970s despite significant steps to expand the powers
of competing nonbank financial institutions and increasingly aggressive
competition from symbiotic financial firms such as Merrill Lynch and
Sears Roebuck. Moreover, a comprehensive theoretical and empirical
analysis by Kilcollin and Hanweck (1981) reaches the hopeful conclusion that deposit rate ceilings have neither increased nor decreased
bank profitability (measured by return on assets) over the long run. In
the short run, these researchers find that even a full percentage point
increase in deposit rate ceilings reduced the industry's net income-to-
asset ratio only by an estimated five one-hundredths of a percent, on
average, over the 1960–1980 period. This modest change occurred
because nonprice competition under the rate ceilings drove up bank
noninterest costs by roughly the same amount as interest expenses
would have increased in a deregulated deposit market. Although short-
run profit deterioration seems likely during the transition period from

regulated interest rates to unregulated ones, Kilcollin and Hanweck expect no significant long-run effects on either bank profitability or soundness.

Industry-wide equity returns also appear to have weathered the recent introduction of more costly deposit plans, such as the suspension of short-term money market CD ceiling rates in 1970, the introduction of consumer-type money market CDs in 1978, and the launching of Super NOWs and Money Market Deposit Accounts (MMDAs) in 1983. Much of the potentially negative impact on bank profitability of these developments was absorbed by greater use of financial leverage. Moreover, Spellman (1980), in a study of savings and loans, and Taggart (1978), viewing New England savings banks, found substantial room for further expense reduction in banking, especially from closing full-service branch offices. Following this same line of reasoning, Petersen (1981) projects a decline of "at least 25 percent" in the number of bank offices in the decade following the phaseout of rate ceilings on savings deposits. This conclusion is based on the application of a regression model that takes population, income, and state branching law differences into account.

Even the recent behavior of bank stock prices provides a hopeful augury concerning the possible consequences of deregulation. For example, a study by James (1983) of prices attached to common stock issued by some of the nation's largest banks indicates investors reacted in a generally *positive* fashion to announcements of the relaxation of deposit rate ceilings on short-term $100,000 + CDs in 1970. James argues that many investors anticipated strong gains in bank deposit volume that would more than offset higher deposit interest costs.

Nevertheless, the evidence on recent changes in bank profitability is not all that favorable. For example, a study by Rose (1985) calculates average profitability ratios for banks in 240 U.S. SMSAs whose geographic boundaries were fixed over the 1970–83 period. Examining data for the years 1970, 1972, 1974, 1976, 1978, 1980, 1982, and 1983, Rose finds evidence of sharp urban bank profitability *declines* after 1980. For example, he observes that the average return on assets (ROA) for banks in these metropolitan areas peaked in 1970 at 0.85 percent, remained relatively stable in the 0.77 to 0.78 percent range until 1980, and then rose to 0.82 percent in 1980. However, despite a recovering economy, urban-bank ROA declined, with the most significant decreases occurring in unit banking states and in communities over 1 million in population. Return on equity (ROE) displayed a similar pattern in these 240 urban markets.

Unit banking states generally recorded the sharpest deterioration in bank profitability ratios, suggesting perhaps that the overhead cost burdens of large branching systems may be overstated. Whereas Rose finds that banks in all size communities reported declining average profitability, the steepest declines occurred in the largest communities so that the spread in bank profitability between small and large communities widened. Of course, these findings must be tempered with caution in view of the significant changes in economic and financial conditions that occurred during the 1970s and 80s, especially energy and farm financing problems that had a serious impact on a substantial number of both urban and rural markets.

EVIDENCE FROM OTHER DEREGULATED INDUSTRIES

What has been the profitability experience of other industries facing deregulation? A study by McKinsey & Company reported by one of its directors, Donald C. Waite III, in *The Bankers Magazine* (1982) looks at five industries—air travel, railroads, security brokers, trucking, and business telephone equipment—recently deregulated by the federal government. Waite (1982) finds that profits are, at least initially, squeezed by deregulation, spurring aggressive individual-firm efforts to reduce costs. Moreover, profit performance (measured either by return on sales or return on assets) became more variable from firm to firm. He finds that the firms most successfully adjusting to deregulation were those with (1) substantial capital and price flexibility (including relatively low debt-to-equity ratios); (2) superior cost measurement, cost control, and information systems; (3) strong information-oriented marketing and new product development programs; (4) effective planning systems; and (5) selective business acquisitions and hiring of key personnel. The implication is that individual firms need not passively accept the possible negative consequences of deregulation for their profitability. Proactive management can actually benefit from a more openly competitive market environment.

Actually as we look across the spectrum of recent nonbank deregulation studies, the research findings on profitability are often confusing and defy simple, unqualified conclusions. There is some evidence of gains immediately following deregulation announcements and events, but these immediate gains are often erased as a confluence of other factors begins to intrude. For example, Michel and Shaked (1984) found that actual stockholder returns in the U.S. airline industry significantly exceeded expected returns during the middle and late 1970s once deregulation plans were announced but before any regulatory changes actually occurred. However, most of these gains were erased for the largest air carriers once deregulation was underway, though smaller regional carriers continued to report increased returns to their shareholders. This differential impact of airline deregulation appeared to be related to energy price changes. Michel and Shaked contend that deregulation contributed to a differential impact from energy price movements on airline profits because it allowed greater flexibility in each firm's response to the energy crisis.

This generally promising assessment of airline deregulation is supported by Gomez-Ibanez, Oster, and Pickrell (1983). They reviewed the tumultuous period of 1979–1982 when airline traffic and net earnings declined precipitously and the first declared bankruptcy of a major air carrier (Braniff) took place. These researchers found deregulation *not* the principal cause of these disruptive developments but instead placed primary emphasis on business recessions and sharp energy price increases. Gomez-Ibanez et al. conclude that deregulation helped, rather than hurt, airline earnings by permitting the carriers greater flexibility in adjusting to adverse environmental changes. For example, the airlines were able to discount fares in order to fill empty seats, and this move cushioned the impact of falling demand and rising fuel prices.

In contrast to the generally positive profitability effects reported by Michel and Shaked (1984) and Gomez-Ibanez et al. (1983), Davidson, Chandy, and Walker (1984a) found that airline stockholders suffered windfall losses in the wake of deregulation. Their analysis of daily stock returns for 32 air carriers detected a downward drift in stockholder returns around the time the Airline Deregulation Act was signed into law by President Carter in October 1978. Davidson et al. argue that the stock market fully and correctly anticipated a negative impact on airline financial performance. These same researchers found, however, that not all deregulated industries experienced the same negative earnings results. Indeed, their analysis of trucking deregulation (1984c) found positive gains, while their study of natural gas deregulation (1984b) implies a neutral deregulation impact on industry financial performance. In summary, the impact of deregulation on industry profitability may be positive, negative, or neutral depending on industry production characteristics, the nature of economic developments occurring around deregulation events, and the extent to which deregulation changes the deregulated firms' exposure to market forces.

Bank Growth and Market Share

Various theoretical and conceptual arguments have been offered regarding the probable impact of deregulation on the growth of individual banks. The conventional wisdom to date has predicted dire consequences for the future growth rate of the majority of banks, especially smaller ones. Faced with more competitors from outside the industry and with the prospect of large banking organizations reaching nationwide for deposits even at the retail level, smaller banks will likely be fighting for a smaller and smaller share of the available market. Depositors—particularly the more interest-sensitive and convenience-oriented customers—will move toward the point of highest return and toward the most attractive packages of financial services. In theory, the most efficient producers of financial services will attract the accounts held by inefficient financial firms. Moreover, whereas commercial banks have possessed a distinct advantage in attracting customers because of their extensive branch systems, the advent of electronic equipment and automated tellers offers nonbank financial companies the opportunity to compete for and service the same customer accounts. In the long run inefficient banks will leave the industry, usually by merger or through holding-company acquisition.

One problem with this projected scenario is its exclusive emphasis on technological and price factors. It deemphasizes the role of innovative bank management in adopting new policies to take advantage of a deregulated environment. Moreover, it ignores the *personal* side of the financial services business. Banking services are not selected by all customers solely on the basis of price or efficiency. Institutions unable to reach the minimum cost point in a deregulated market may still survive and profit by serving customers willing to "pay extra" for personalized treatment, locational convenience, or unique service packages. Some analysts believe, for example, that the financial institutions' sector of the future will comfortably accommodate two very different kinds of financial intermediaries: (1) *full-service institutions* that seek to offer a broad range of transactions, investment, insurance, and credit services—all quite similar to their competitors and highly price competitive and (2) *financial boutiques* that focus essentially on a limited range of specialized services (such as meeting the funds management and financial counseling needs of attorneys, physicians, and other professional clients) and are characterized by tailored packaging of services to meet each customer's specific financial need. To some extent the specialized financial firm may be insulated from broader market forces, provided management can successfully differentiate its services and achieve strong customer loyalty. Thus, financial boutiques should be less affected by future deregulation than full-service financial firms.

EVIDENCE FROM STUDIES OF FINANCIAL INSTITUTIONS
    Among the most useful studies of the effects of deregulation on bank growth and market share are those conducted when NOWs were first legalized in New England during the mid-1970s. For example, Paulus (1976) studied changes in bank net income following the introduction of NOWs by Massachusetts and New Hampshire mutual savings banks. He found that net earnings and deposit growth rates were significantly reduced in the short-run period immediately following the introduction of NOWs. Initially many institutions were uncertain about the appropriate pricing schedule for the new accounts and some simply elected not to compete. The result is that bank deposit growth rates tended to fall at first but then recovered as banks learned more about pricing NOWs and about service features that were important to customers. In the long run, economic theory suggests, prices and costs for a new financial service tend to move toward an equilibrium level in which quantities offered clear the market at prevailing prices and all production costs (including a normal profit) are fully covered. Thus, if there is an initial negative impact on growth traceable to deregulation, the NOW studies suggest it may be only *temporary*. Banks determined to aggressively pursue a larger share of the available market by adjusting prices, nonprice credit and deposit terms, and advertising

programs to more closely conform to the needs of their customers should continue to grow at an acceptable rate.

One additional lesson emerging from the NOW studies is the important competitive advantage banks historically have had because of their extensive branch office systems. For example, whereas mutual savings banks gained initially in market share and in relative deposit growth rates after the introduction of NOWs, the greater convenience of commercial bank branch offices eventually brought a large proportion of NOW customers to commercial banks. Of course, a key issue for the 1980s and beyond is whether greater availability and use of automated teller machines, especially in the form of remote service units (RSUs) in retail stores, homes, and offices, will substantially reduce the convenience advantage of bank branch systems. In this event there would obviously be a more significant growth and market share impact from deregulation. Much depends, of course, on how aggressively commercial banks expand their own remote electronic facilities relative to nonbank financial institutions.

EVIDENCE FROM OTHER DEREGULATED INDUSTRIES

Clues about the growth and market share effects of deregulation on individual firms and industries are provided by studies of such industries as security brokerage, deregulated in May 1975. For example, Waite (1982) reports a tendency of "second-tier" brokerage firms to *consolidate* their market position, primarily by merger and acquisition, in the two- to three-year period proximate to deregulation. During this same early period the top ten brokerage companies added to their market share by growth from within. However, over the longer time frame of a second postderegulation phase, the ten leading securities firms appeared to increase their market share substantially by eroding the market share of second-tier firms.

A third and final phase beginning several years after formal deregulation is allegedly marked by diversification. The leading deregulated companies reach outside their industry to acquire businesses that may or may not be in related product lines. For example, deregulated airline companies may acquire ownership interests in trucking firms. Also, leading firms in other industries may invade the deregulated industry, acquiring top-tier companies, making foothold acquisitions, or launching new firms.

To the extent that realistic and relevant parallels to bank-ing can be drawn from other recently deregulated industries, the im-plications seem clear enough.

1. The top tier of leading banking organizations may not only survive but also grow in market share essentially within their existing organizational structure and re-sources, at least for a short time following deregulation; smaller and weaker banks are also able to expand their market shares, but principally through merger and ac-quisition in an effort to increase their efficiency and provide a base for future expansion.

2. Later (perhaps three to five years in the wake of dereg-ulation), growth among the banking industry's leaders can continue, but largely by the same route as second-tier firms—merger and acquisition, reducing the mar-ket shares of smaller and weaker companies.

3. Ultimately, banking deregulation is likely to invite en-try by strong outsiders who have greater latitude for external acquisition and tend to take advantage of the newfound freedom by acquiring leading firms offering different products or by serving new customer groups who seem to offer gains in profitability, risk reduction, or both.

Pricing Policies

One of the most frequently discussed effects of deregulation is its possible or probable impact on prices charged for bank services, espe-cially loan rates and deposit rates. Recent structural changes in the economy and financial system appear to have increased the volatility of interest rates. The phasing out of federal deposit rate ceilings has apparently made and will continue to make bank deposit rates even more sensitive to changes in general economic and financial condi-tions. The same should be true for deposit rates offered by savings and loans and other major nonbank competitors, as noted by Walker (1982).

Perhaps more important, deregulation, coupled with invasion of traditional bank product lines by nonbank firms, will increase competition for both deposit and credit customers. Thus, individual-bank offer rates on both loans and deposits should become more sensitive to changes in interest rate schedules offered by competitors. And with greater use of "electronic shopping" by bank customers, even small price differences or slight variations in other service terms may result in frequent customer switching to other financial firms to find the best combination of service availability and price. Therefore, the setting of competitive prices and the flexibility to make frequent price adjustments will be crucial in a deregulated environment. There should be less room under deregulation for setting prices without regard to the true cost of providing financial services. Many customers used to "free" or "low-cost" services will find banks adjusting their fee schedules *upward* in order to more fully cover long-run service production and delivery costs, consistent with economic theory.

EVIDENCE FROM STUDIES OF FINANCIAL INSTITUTIONS
Although not numerous, a number of studies in recent years have focused on deregulation of financial service prices. Most center on the impact of eliminating federal deposit rate ceilings or on the development and spread of NOW accounts in New England.

One useful study by Dann and James (1982) finds a significant effect on the price of common stock issued by savings and loan associations stemming from removal of deposit rate ceilings on selected small-saver CDs. Dann and James studied the performance of common stock prices at 34 S&Ls around the calendar dates when the regulatory authorities announced changes in legal deposit rates during the 1973–78 period. The authors' findings may be summarized in their own words:

The major finding is that stockholder-owned thrift institutions have experienced statistically significant declines in value at the announcement of the removal of ceilings on certain consumer (small-saver) certificate accounts and the introduction of short-term, variable-rate money market certificates. No decline in value was experienced following the removal of ceilings on certificates of deposit of over $100,000. For none of the regulatory changes that we examined did prices of S&L shares show a statistically significant increase. Our findings are consistent with the hypothesis that thrifts have earned rents on consumer accounts because of the existence of deposit rate ceilings (p. 1260).

The most direct evidence on the effects of deregulation on financial service pricing comes from New England, where NOWs were first introduced in 1972 and authorized for federally supervised banks and thrifts in Massachusetts and New Hampshire in 1974 and Connecticut, Maine, Rhode Island, and Vermont in 1976. Studies conducted at the Federal Reserve Board and the Federal Reserve Bank of Boston suggest that commercial banks approached the NOW market very cautiously following legalization of this service. As the studies by Basche (1976), Kimball (1976), and Paulus (1976) observe, many banks delayed either introducing or aggressively advertising NOWs until forced to do so by aggressive thrifts. A major fear among New England bankers was that their customers would simply trade in conventional checking accounts for the more costly NOWs, resulting in severe damage to bank earnings.

The majority of thrifts and a few commercial banks rushed early and eagerly into the NOW market with liberal pricing and numerous "free" services. As Paulus (1976) notes, however, these institutions often suffered significant declines in net earnings even as their market shares increased. Commercial banks with only marginal earnings to begin with seemed to suffer the most from the cost pressures associated with the introduction of a new service. On the other hand, banks entering the market later priced the new service more conservatively to encourage the maintenance of high balances and limited account activity. Latecomers seemed to learn from the early adopters and used explicit, full-cost pricing. As Dunham (1983) observes, "over the past decade, NOW account pricing has developed from the very simple, often free or highly promotional levels to complicated, conditional price schedules set at increasingly realistic, sustainable levels" (p. 30). As might be expected with such diverse strategies there were, initially, wide disparities in NOW service quality, pricing schedules, and market shares achieved. Over the longer run, however, bank deposit pricing appeared to become more conservative, market shares stabilized, and bank earnings generally recovered.

EVIDENCE FROM OTHER DEREGULATED INDUSTRIES

Studies of deregulation in other industries conclude that firms are soon forced to pay closer attention to *both* their prices and their costs. Companies that are more aware of their own cost structures and the true costs of offering each service possess a significant advantage in responding to an environment of more wide-open price competition. The importance of having an adequate cost measurement system is also imperative because of another characteristic of recently deregulated industries—the tendency to continually introduce new services and accelerate marketing and advertising activities. For example, Waite (1982) finds that following deregulation of the airlines, railroads, and trucking, prices were quickly adjusted to reflect service costs, and services previously provided without charge were often switched to a fee basis.

In a deregulated environment, the *bundling* together of groups of services in one package without attempting to price each service according to its individual production cost schedule should occur less frequently. Bundling of services has, of course, been accepted practice in commercial banking for decades. Banks often underprice checking account services on the theory that the full costs of providing those services would be made up through higher prices on loans and other services used by the checking account customer. However, the trend in other deregulated industries clearly has been to *unbundle* groups of related products with each product line priced *individually* based on its own cost structure.

The exception to this rule of greater attention to production costs usually occurs very *early* in the deregulation process when pricing terms are often overly generous. The apparent purpose is to capture a large market share before later adopters of the new service enter the competition. Advertising tends to emphasize price rather than quality, convenience, or other features of newly deregulated services. Firms not choosing to compete on price seek out those services and market segments where there is less customer sensitivity to price, offer services that cannot easily be unbundled, or use information-oriented advertising.

The Riskiness of Banks

Deregulation implies increased risk for banks—both increased risk of earnings losses and increased risk of ultimate failure. It destroys the old regulatory equilibrium in which some services and suppliers are subsidized and protected in order to maintain stable relationships. The new hazards to both bank earnings and financial viability spring from a number of sources:

1. Risks posed by new competition from nonbank entities (especially from revitalized savings and loan associations and financial conglomerates)
2. Risks posed by more aggressive banks fighting for survival in a more competitive environment
3. Risks posed by the introduction of new financial services, some of which will not be well received by the public
4. Risks posed by the accelerated pace of technological change in service delivery and information processing
5. Risks posed by political factors—changes in laws and regulations reshaping the permissible scope of banking activities

Such risks imply that inefficient providers of financial services, those institutions serving declining markets, and those unwilling or unable to adjust to the rapidly changing financial marketplace face increased earnings risk, probable absorption by more successful institutions, and in some cases ultimate collapse.

This problem is exacerbated by recent deterioration in bank equity capital positions—the ultimate source of protection for depositors. The period since World War II has witnessed a steady and cumulative decline in standard measures of bank capital adequacy. For example, the ratio of equity capital to total assets for all U.S. insured banks combined declined from approximately 8 percent in 1960 to about 6 percent in 1984. At the largest American banks the decline in this standard measure of capital adequacy has been even more significant. For example, U.S. banks with more than $10 billion in assets reported a ratio of equity capital to total assets in 1960 of more than 6 percent; however, by year-end 1984 this measure of the net worth cushion against asset depreciation had fallen to about 4 percent. Thus, at the very time that deregulation is posing substantially greater risk for banks, the safety cushion to depositors and other creditors offered by equity capital is at a historically low ebb as a proportion of bank assets and deposits. The risk of loss to bank stockholders, large (uninsured) depositors and the FDIC has increased and should grow even larger in the wake of a trend toward more deregulation, other factors held constant. One factor that *cannot* be held constant, however, is capital regulation by the bank regulatory agencies, which has recently stiffened in the wake of large numbers of bank failures and can be a major tool in limiting the acceptance of risk by bankers in the future.

Accompanying increased bankruptcy risk is likely to be increased *earnings risk,* even for banks that do not fail. Deregulation widens the possible outcomes for bank earnings performance. It offers the potential for greater earnings because the management of individual banks is less constrained in its options for maximizing revenues, minimizing costs, and adapting to new market environments. Concomitantly, however, deregulation exposes management more openly to the consequences of its weaknesses and mistakes. For these reasons we might expect the variance of bank earnings to gradually rise as deregulation proceeds.

EVIDENCE FROM STUDIES OF FINANCIAL INSTITUTIONS

The advent of deregulation in the 1970s and early 1980s corresponded with a substantial increase in the U.S. bank failure rate, including a marked increase in the number of large ($100-million-plus) banks collapsing. As Scott and Rose (1979) note, the mean number of U.S. bank failures from the end of World War II through 1976 was just 5.5 banks per year. In 1976, however, a postwar record of sixteen commercial banks closed. The bank failure rate then dropped through 1979, averaging only seven bank closings per year over the 1977–79 period. However, the 1980s ushered in a sharp acceleration in total numbers of banks closing and in the average deposit size of failing institutions. The increased average size of recent bank failures is indicated by a telling statistic: *of the ten largest failures in U.S. banking history, all occurred during the 1970s and 1980s.*

Is the correspondence between an upsurge in bank failures and deregulation a mere coincidence? That is unlikely. Deregulation exposes banks to the full fury of unexpected changes in the demand for and supply of loanable funds and in market interest rates. As Kaufman, Mote, and Rosenblum (1982) note, during the 1940s, 1950s, and 1960s, interest rate changes were usually gradual, related to Federal Reserve pegging of Government security prices early in the 1950s and the Fed's emphasis on a money market strategy and the absence of severe inflation until the 1970s. However, the decade of the 1970s ushered in rapid inflation, supported by rapid growth in the money supply and spiraling energy price increases. As inflationary pressures and money growth ebbed and flowed, interest rates moved through wider ranges—far wider than commercial banks and other financial intermediaries had come to expect. Then, in 1979, the Fed adopted its reserve-targeting procedure for controlling the money supply, which allowed interest rates to float more freely. Though the Fed moderated its operating strategies in 1982 in an effort to dampen interest rate movements, the net result was still increasing strain between the reality of increased financial market volatility and banking regulations designed for an earlier and more stable environment. Banks encouraged in the past to take on added portfolio risk owing to the backing of federal insurance now found that added risk was more likely to lead to ultimate failure.

Not all the research evidence points, however, to increased risk of bankruptcy from banking deregulation. For example, Smirlock (1984) explores the impact of deposit rate regulation and deregulation on bank solvency through a model of stock price movements linked to systematic and nonsystematic risk. He finds that "deposit rate ceilings do not affect bank risk and that elimination of these ceilings will not decrease the soundness of the banking system" (p. 208). Smirlock finds *no* selective deregulation impact by bank size, so that small banks, in his view, will *not* bear a differential burden beyond that carried by large banks following removal of deposit rate ceilings. These conclusions are supported by Koehn and Stangle (1980), who, using the capital-asset pricing model, find no significant link between deposit rate ceilings and bank systematic risk. And Mingo (1978) contends that, by encouraging nonprice competition, the deposit ceilings made banks less adaptable to changing interest rates and limited their hedging capacity and thus increased the variance of earnings and the risk of bankruptcy. By implication, then, removal of deposit rate ceilings should allow banks to be more adaptable to changing interest rates and, therefore, reduce both earnings risk and bankruptcy risk (unless, of course, banks received significant economic rents while the ceilings were in force).

Moreover, some portion (probably a significant share) of the recent acceleration in bank failures is attributable not to deregulation, but to the regulatory structure of deposit insurance. As Benston (1985) notes in recent Congressional testimony, deposit insurance

increases the propensity of depository institutions to accept risk, including both credit risk and interest-rate risk. He finds, for example,
that most savings and loans failing during the 1981–85 period did not
collapse principally due to the offering of newly deregulated services,
but rather because of over-specialization and interest-rate risk. As
Benston (1984) observes elsewhere, with the present system of federal
deposit insurance the *complete* lifting of rate ceilings on demand deposits would probably be unwise due to excessive bank risk-taking
because today's insurance system subsidizes riskier banks at the expense
of less risky ones. If the current restriction against demand deposit
interest is repealed eventually, he argues, deposit insurance coverage
should either be restricted to discipline risky banks or, if 100-percent
deposit insurance is adopted, interest rates on demand deposits should
probably carry some interest-rate ceiling (tied perhaps to Treasury bill
rates).

Developing both one-period and multiperiod models of the
banking firm, Marcus (1984) introduces the "charter effect" into the
analysis of deregulation's impact on bankruptcy risk. He criticizes earlier
studies of current FDIC deposit insurance programs that conclude that
these programs have encouraged banks to take on additional risk because deposit insurance premiums are not adjusted for bank risk levels.
Marcus points out that, because bank charters have a positive market
value owing to entry restrictions, owners and management have a
significant incentive to be averse to risk in order to avoid loss of their
charter. His model demonstrates that, under the current insurance
plan, a value-maximizing bank will tend to choose either extreme high-
risk or low-risk strategies. All midrange risk strategies will be suboptimal. Nevertheless, Marcus emerges with a conclusion similar to earlier
deregulation studies: *if deregulation lowers entry barriers, economic rents
accruing to bank charters will fall, encouraging greater risk taking, and
the incidence of bank failure should increase.*

In addition to evidence of increased bankruptcy risk there
is also some evidence of increased bank *earnings risk.* In the study of
240 U.S. metropolitan areas cited earlier, Rose (1985) finds that the
variance of bank returns on assets (ROA) averaged significantly higher
in 1982 and 1983 than in any earlier year back through 1970. Moreover,
this result held true for all size categories of communities (with the
exception of SMSAs having 250,000 to 500,000 population) and for
all types of state branching law environments, though metropolitan

banks in unit banking states displayed less of an increase in ROA variance than banks in branch banking states did. Rose found a similar escalating pattern beginning most markedly in 1980 in the variances around the yield spread between average loan and deposit rates, the net operating margin (i.e., operating revenues minus operating expenses), and the net interest margin (i.e., interest income from loans and investments less interest expenses on deposits and other borrowed funds).

Using a general linear model with class input variables, Rose found that the largest increases in earnings variance were experienced by statewide branching states and there was a tendency for this variance to increase most markedly among larger SMSAs (particularly those over half a million in total population). All three class effects—state branching law, population size category, and year—were statistically significant at the 99-percent confidence level. While intriguing, these results must be regarded as only suggestive. Indeed, there were numerous economic changes over the tumultous 1970–83 period, and further research is needed to separate the impact of deregulation versus other exogenous and endogenous factors that affected bank behavior during this period.

Of course, the foregoing studies do not consider the possibility that banking deregulation may eventually open up new product lines sufficiently dissimilar to traditional banking services that true diversification will be possible in the industry. For example, a recent study of the variability of asset returns from selected nonbank product lines and their correlation with banking industry earnings showed that the returns to savings and loans, personal credit agencies, security brokers and dealers, life insurers, and general merchandising firms are not only more risky then banking but also are negatively correlated with bank asset returns. These earnings results by Wall and Eisenbeis (1984), covering the 1970–80 period, suggest the possibility of beneficial risk-reducing diversification for banking through selective product line deregulation.

EVIDENCE FROM OTHER DEREGULATED INDUSTRIES

Peltzman (1976) argues that regulation reduces the risk of regulated firms by shielding them, at least partially, from market forces. The evidence on risk effects from recently deregulated nonbank industries is not extensive but, thus far, tends to support Peltzman's claim. For example, Cavarra, Stover, and Allen (1981) found higher average systematic risk among a small sample of deregulated air carriers, while Davidson, Chandy, and Walker (1984a) observed a third of their airline company sample undergoing changes in systematic risk during the period that a major deregulation bill was passed, though the firms involved split about evenly between increasing and decreasing systematic risk. On balance, most studies do find greater bankruptcy risk in the post-deregulation era; however, increased earnings and stock price risk is a less well-supported conclusion from recent research on deregulation.

Services Offered

One of the prime arguments for deregulation, cited repeatedly in Congressional hearings and by deregulation's proponents, is that it will result in more and better services for the public. Service availability should increase, presumably, for three reasons: (1) regulatory approval would no longer be required when new services are introduced; (2) the force of competition would encourage suppliers of financial services to expand and improve service offerings in order to retain their market shares; and (3) the introduction of new services produces new cash flow streams that may be uncorrelated or negatively correlated with cash flows from existing services and thereby produce a diversification effect. If existing financial firms choose not to improve existing services or innovate with new ones, new firms more attuned to the public's financial service needs would presumably enter the marketplace and capture a significant share of both old and new accounts. A good example is the success of unregulated money market funds during the 1970s in attracting small-saver deposits and the success of New England savings banks in attracting interest-bearing NOW deposits during the same period.

In theory, deregulation should affect bank financial service offerings in at least three different ways. First, lifting or weakening of restrictions against bank geographic expansion will permit deposit taking and lending even to small borrowers over wider geographic areas, bringing banks of all sizes into closer competition with one another. Thus, deregulation should contribute to a broadening of the markets for individual services. Second, the pace of service innovation—both new types of services and service delivery methods—should accelerate. Third, service quality is likely to improve to the extent that competition increases, owing to market broadening and to the entry of new firms into the financial services industry.

EVIDENCE FROM STUDIES OF FINANCIAL INSTITUTIONS

What evidence is there from the financial institutions' sector that service offerings and service quality have responded to deregulation? One body of evidence emerges again from changes in federal law during the 1970s permitting the offering of NOW accounts in New England. The introduction of NOWs resulted in numerous new nonbank institutions' offering the new service. Banks refusing to join in the competitive race for NOWs experienced a slowing in growth and banks already financially weak found that earnings declined, as observed by Paulus (1976). Whereas *service competition* (stressing free gifts, location, longer hours, etc.) had been the chief method of attracting new payments account customers previously, *price competition* was used more heavily in the wake of deregulation to differentiate one institution's NOW services from those of another. These findings are of interest but are certainly not conclusive.

One route taken recently by a few studies of bank service offerings is to go abroad and examine the service behavior of banks in less regulated market systems or, better yet, to study how foreign bank service offerings changed when regulatory restraints were loosened. For example, the Bank of England's relaxation of restraints against the combining of commercial and merchant banking in 1971 led to the offering of investment portfolio management and securities underwriting services by major British banks. The implication is obvious: *U.S. banks would reach farther afield in their service offerings if deregulation provides the opportunity to do so.* However, the problem with such foreign evidence is equally obvious—tradition, public attitudes, economic forces, and competitive factors have combined in many countries to produce a foreign operating environment that is different from the United States. Whether all but the largest U.S. banks would offer the same expanded list of services in *domestic* markets is at least doubtful.

Moreover, the evidence on depository institutions actually offering the new financial services that deregulation already has granted them is not all that encouraging. A substantial proportion of affected institutions seem to adopt a "wait and see" attitude, allowing a few innovators to precede them into newly opened markets, perhaps to see if the new services will be profitable or contribute positively to other institutional goals. For example, following deregulation legislation in Maine during the early 1970s, a substantial proportion of state-chartered thrift institutions (mainly mutual savings banks and savings and loans) declined to offer the new auto loans and unsecured consumer installment loans they were then permitted to make. Hayssen (1977) found that nearly one quarter of Maine's mutual savings banks and about half the savings and loans declined to offer auto loans. The Maine experience with deregulation of entry into the installment loan market was a little better, however; only 10 percent of the state-chartered mutuals and 42 percent of the state-chartered S&LS chose not to grant unsecured consumer installment credit after they were legally permitted to do so.

As Eisenbeis (1983) observes, there are powerful forces related to the business cycle, service production economies, and remaining legislative impediments that explain why the speed of adoption of new service packages by thrift institutions has been relatively slow to date. These same factors also argue against any significant acceleration in the pace at which service diversification will proceed in the foreseeable future. And at least some of those economic and regulatory factors apply as well to proposed new *banking* services like corporate securities' underwriting, mutual funds sales, and insurance marketing.

EVIDENCE FROM OTHER DEREGULATED INDUSTRIES

Have other recently deregulated industries responded in the same way? Waite's analysis (1982) of the airline, trucking, railroad, security brokerage, and business telephone equipment industries generally finds a proliferation of new services on the heels of deregulation. Particularly in the airline business, he finds a wider range of prices and service quality with customers offered significant price-quality trade-offs—i.e., limited service and less quality at lower prices or full service with better quality at substantially elevated prices. Other firms respond by narrowing their service or product lines and competing aggressively for a smaller segment of the market.

Morrison and Winston (1984) have contributed an innovative study of the passenger welfare effects of airline deregulation. Drawing on a sample of passenger trips covering more than 800 different routes, they found a substantial welfare gain due to fare reductions and improvements in the availability of air service (especially departure frequencies). Airline deregulation was, thus, judged to have lifted entry restrictions and provided incentives for a major restructuring of carrier networks. However, Morrison and Winston, in a later article (1985), point out that such gains resulted, in large measure, from economies of scope, which deregulation allowed air carriers to utilize more fully. They do not foresee such favorable deregulation results for service availability in the railroad and intercity bus industries, however, because of a lack of significant economies of scope. This last conclusion is pregnant with importance for banking, where scale economies for most individual services appear to be limited. But economies of scope from the simultaneous production of several related and often jointly demanded financial services may be substantial. If true, the bank customer would probably benefit from deregulation in terms of increased service availability (including increased service to smaller, outlying markets) even if the pricing of bank services is unaffected.

Finally, studies of other deregulated industries suggest that *marketing* activity tends to increase with deregulation. This happens because of constant pressure to develop new product or service lines, the need to strengthen marketing channels, and greater pressure for market research on customer needs. Advertising budgets generally expand, some firms choosing to more intensively promote lower prices, others stressing image, and still others engaging in information advertising that makes consumers better informed of market opportunities.

Other Possible Deregulation Effects

If deregulation increases bankruptcy and earnings risk, commercial banks, in theory, will strive to reduce their risk exposure relative to a given targeted level of earnings. Thus, deregulation may give rise to a *diversification effect* designed to minimize risk exposure. This may be accomplished through greater use of geographic diversification or through greater use of product line diversification, redirecting funds into alternative financial instruments and services. Deregulation appears to have been a causal element in the recent upsurge in financial innovation, and, as noted by Simpson and Parkinson (1984), the innovation trend has tended to integrate the financial system, ensuring that shifts in market conditions are transmitted more rapidly throughout the system with wider swings in interest rates. This, in turn, has encouraged *both* geographic and product line diversification in order to bring greater stability to the banking environment.

To the extent that deregulation results in increased competition and narrower profit margins, there should be a strong incentive to increase operating efficiency. This *efficiency effect* may appear in the guise of greater productivity in generating increased dollars of assets, revenues, and net income per employee and lower ratios of operating expenses relative to operating revenue.

The drive to seek greater efficiency may accentuate a third trend characteristic of American banking for at least half a century— *consolidation*. Fewer, but larger, independent banking organizations may continue to emerge—some analysts expect no more than 10,000 independent banking organizations to be in operation when various interstate branching arrangements are fully activated—as bankers try to achieve an optimum size institution to promote cost savings. There is a perception in the industry that increasing use of automated equipment plus the need to borrow at reasonable cost in the capital markets demand a much larger average-size banking organization than currently prevails in the industry. If this is true (and there is evidence to the contrary), consolidation of the industry into fewer, but larger, organizations should be reflected in increasing concentration ratios in key banking markets.

RESEARCH EVIDENCE ON OTHER DEREGULATION EFFECTS

Little detailed research evidence has been amassed as of yet on the diversification, efficiency, and consolidation effects of the current deregulation movement in the industry. Most of what has been done has concentrated upon the potential *negative* effects of diversification by nonbank thrifts on the availability of loanable funds in the residential mortgage market. Will the thrifts, particularly savings and loans, freed from their mandatory devotion to home and apartment mortgages, provide enough funds to support the nation's pressing need for housing? For example, both Jaffee (1972) and Hendershott (1975) carried out simulations of the impact on the home financing market of various reform proposals. Jaffee found that deregulated deposits would rise enough to offset other potentially negative effects on the volume of mortgage credit, and thrift mortgage loans would actually increase rather than decline. A later study by Jaffee and K. T. Rose (1979) reached similar conclusions following the introduction of high-yield money market CDs in 1978. Hendershott's study of the combined effects of savings and loans offering transactions deposits and consumer loans and purchasing corporate debt suggested that mortgage credit extended by S&Ls would decrease; however, commercial banks and mutual savings banks presumably would move in to take up the slack. Thus, the majority of existing studies do *not* support the often-expressed fear that financial deregulation would significantly harm the residential mortgage market.

The Rose (1985) study of 240 metropolitan areas alluded to earlier provides at least some suggestive findings regarding the diversification, efficiency, and consolidation effects. He finds a growing commitment to mortgage loans among urban commercial banks in all size communities in the late 1970s and early 1980s, despite increases in the volatility and cost of bank funds. In contrast, the commitment of bank-loaned funds to consumer installment loans generally went down in bank portfolios in all sizes of metropolitan areas, especially after 1979. These changes are consistent with the notion that banks deemphasized consumer installment credit as nonbank thrifts took advantage of deregulation and moved in to capture a larger share of the consumer credit market. Similarly, as thrifts diversified away from their historically heavy reliance on real-property loans, commercial banks moved in to corner a larger share of the real estate financing activity.

Whereas banks may have *sought* greater efficiency, Rose found that certain efficiency measures, such as the ratio of operating expenses to operating revenue, declined between 1970 and 1983, though most of the deterioration occurred before 1978 and therefore before major deregulatory actions were taken. Net operating margins declined sharply after 1980, which damaged earnings and reflected adversely on efforts at increasing bank efficiency. However, employee productivity in generating assets, revenues, and net income rose dramatically throughout the 1970–1983 period and helped to soften the blow against bank earnings from rising deposit costs. In part, this gain in average employee efficiency was less a response to deregulation and more a result of increasing use of automation, which not only made existing labor more productive but also resulted in some substitution of labor for capital. Rose also found evidence consistent with the *consolidation* thesis. For example, the average number of banks per SMSA (adjusted for common holding-company affiliations) declined after 1980.

Other research evidence bearing on the likelihood of significant consolidation of the banking structure is in serious conflict because different authors have examined different possible sources of consolidation, such as efficiency and the value of greater convenience and geographic diversification. On the basis of operating efficiency *alone* there is little support for significant consolidation of the U.S. banking structure. As discussed in chapter 4, recent studies of plant and organizational economies find little evidence of cost savings from bank expansion beyond roughly $100 to $150 million in deposits. As Nelson (1983) observes, by itself this finding suggests consolidation among the very smallest U.S. banks but not among moderate and large banking institutions.

Yet, as Kaufman, Mote, and Rosenblum (1984) have argued, to the extent that the public effectively demands the convenience of multiple-office banking and investors demand bank risk reduction through geographic diversification, these market forces may lead to substantial industry consolidation even if gains in operating efficiency are absent or perhaps even moderately negative (except that bank cost curves tend to be relatively flat beyond the point of optimal size). Perhaps, too, future electronics-oriented production and delivery systems will bring significant size economies, though (as Metzker 1982 notes) recent findings on banking automation do not offer much hope for such savings.

There may be, however, significant economies of scale today in some financial services not yet thoroughly researched, such as in correspondent banking, agency functions, or cash positions. On balance, the seeds of industry consolidation are there—only the magnitude remains in dispute.

Future Directions for Banking Deregulation

Will the banking deregulation trend continue? What aspects of banking will be deregulated next? Crystal-ball gazing is always dangerous—even more so when it comes to predicting the future course of a political process. Indeed, as I observed in the preceding chapter, the history of bank regulation resembles a swinging pendulum—moving to and fro, from letting the market solve the basic economic questions of what and how much to produce and what prices should be charged, to placing some or all of those decisions in the hands of the regulatory authorities. Whereas the pendulum swung strongly in the late 1970s and early 1980s toward market solutions, economic and financial developments in the mid–1980s appeared to slow the regulatory pendulum's swing in that direction.

The most notable change was increasing public and Congressional fear over the solvency of several major money center banks on the one extreme and, on the other, the survivability of hundreds of small rural banks with heavy commitments to the troubled farming sector—fears that approached near-panic proportions with the $4.5-billion federal bailout of Continental Illinois in August 1984 and President Reagan's veto of a farm support bill in March 1985 (though subsequently a new farm bill was passed). Congressional proposals that would have granted banks expanded powers to sell insurance, offer broader securities brokerage and underwriting services, and participate more fully in real-property ventures stalled out of fear that recent deregulation moves had encouraged banks to take on excessive risk, as well as out of continuing concern over the quality of international loans.

Despite these deregulation-retarding developments many analysts believe that additional deregulation moves are on the near horizon. These future deregulatory actions are likely to fall into three areas: (1) new service powers, (2) organizational changes, and (3) regulatory reforms.

NEW SERVICE POWERS
Among the new developments most likely in the area of expanded service offerings are:

1. Further erosion (if not complete destruction) of the legal barriers between commercial banking and investment banking set up by the 1933 Glass-Steagall Act, allowing banks to underwrite at least investment grade private debt securities and municipal revenue bonds; one impetus for this move is the concern of some members of Congress that competition is not high in some phases of the securities' underwriting field, so that bank entry would promote lower borrowing costs.
2. Expanded power for banks in the direct selling of insurance, real estate, management consulting, travel agency, and security investment services.
3. An eventual lifting of the remaining restrictions on federal savings and loans, savings banks, and perhaps credit unions, which prevent them from achieving a complete commercial-bank-like menu of financial services—a development particularly probable if the financial viability of many large savings and loans does not materially improve in the period ahead.

ORGANIZATIONAL CHANGES

The most likely legalized changes in banking structure include:

1. Gradual lifting of restrictions against *intrastate* expansion of branch or holding-company banking organizations still imposed by several states.
2. Full or nearly full legalization of interstate branching and holding-company acquisitions preceded by further expansion of regional reciprocal compacts between individual states; thus, major provisions of the McFadden and Bank Holding Company Acts pertaining to interstate banking will be substantially modified.
3. Increased freedom for banking conglomerates to acquire financial institutions in neighboring financial industries, such as bank holding companies' routinely acquiring savings and loans, insurance agency and underwriting firms, mutual funds, real estate development companies, and security brokers.

REGULATORY REFORMS

Along with the expanded powers of depository institutions there should be concomitant changes in the structure and policies of the regulatory agencies, such as the following:

1. Revisions in federal deposit insurance programs that allow higher insurance fees to be assessed against more risky institutions in order to protect the insurance funds against excessive drawings and encourage more prudent management practices in the industry. Indeed, in September 1985, the FDIC proposed a risk premium penalty schedule that would force risky banks to pay an insurance rate four times larger than banks judged to be safe, though such a proposed risk premium would probably be too small to be really effective.

2. Eventual merging of federal insurance funds—the FDIC, FSLIC, and NCUSIF—as the functions and services offered by commercial banks, savings banks, savings and loans, and credit unions become more and more alike.

3. Consolidation of regulatory and supervisory functions of the federal agencies regulating depository institutions (including the Comptroller of the Currency, Federal Deposit Insurance Corporation, Federal Reserve Board, Federal Home Loan Bank Board, and National Credit Union Administration) into a single federal agency and a redistribution of bank regulatory power to establish a stronger federal leadership role.

It is impossible at this stage to assign probabilities to any of these future deregulation moves. Each proposed change has powerful opponents, either in the industries affected or within the regulatory community. One lesson from the recent past, however, comes through clearly: *if federal and state authorities do not find a way to politically sanction new service offerings or changes in bank organizational structure and there are strong economic incentives behind these changes, the banking industry will find a way to meet the demands of the financial marketplace.* New services will be offered either directly through banks or indirectly through joint ventures and leasing arrangements provided there is sufficient public demand for them. Organizational affiliations will occur where economically justifiable, though less efficiently and more burdensome to the bank customer than if the marketplace alone were allowed to shape the character of change in financial services and financial institutions.

References

Anderson, Gerald H., Thomas Buynk, and James Balazsy Jr. 1984. "Regional Interstate Banking." *Economic Commentary* (June 18), pp. 1–4. Federal Reserve Bank of Cleveland.

Basche, Donald. 1976. "The Diffusion of NOW Accounts in Massachusetts." *New England Economic Review* (November–December), pp. 20–30.

Benston, George J. 1964. "Interest Payments on Demand Deposits and Bank Investment Behavior." *Journal of Political Economy*, 72:432–49.

Benston, George J. 1984. "Interest on Deposits and the Survival of Chartered Depository Institutions." *Economic Review*, Federal Reserve Bank of Atlanta, October, pp. 42–56.

Benston, George J. 1985. "Investments by and the Failure of Savings and Loan Associations: An Analysis With Particular Concern for Direct Investments and Non-mortgage Loans." U.S. House of Representatives, Committee on Banking, Finance and Urban Affairs, Subcommittee on Financial Institutions, October 2nd.

Benston, George J., Gerald A. Hanweck, and David B. Humphrey. 1982. "Operating Costs in Commercial Banking." *Economic Review*, Federal Reserve Bank of Atlanta, November, pp. 6–21.

Chase, Kristine L. 1981. "Interest Rate Deregulation, Branching, and Competition in the Savings and Loan Industry." *Federal Home Loan Bank Board Journal* (November), pp. 2–6.

Corporate Planning Division. 1983. "New Dimensions in Banking: Managing the Strategic Position." *Bank Planning News* (October), pp. 1–3. American Bankers Association.

Dann, Larry Y. and Christopher M. James. 1982. "An Analysis of the Impact of Deposit Rate Ceilings on the Market Values of Thrift Institutions." *Journal of Finance* (December), 37(5):1259–1275.

Davidson, Wallace N. III, P. R. Chandy, and Mike Walker. 1984a. "The Stock Market Effects of Airline Deregulation." *Quarterly Journal of Business and Economics* (Autumn), 23(4):31–44.

—— 1984b. "The Impact of Deregulation on Natural Gas Firms: An Empirical Study." *Journal of Extractive Industries Accounting* (Summer), pp. 83–96.

—— 1984c. "The Stock Market Effects of Trucking Deregulation." Unpublished Manuscript, North Texas State University.

Dunham, Constance. 1983. "Unraveling the Complexity of NOW Account Pricing." *New England Economic Review* (May–June), pp. 30–43. Federal Reserve Bank of Boston.

Eisenbeis, Robert A. 1983. "New Investment Powers for S&Ls: Diversification or Specialization?" *Economic Review* (July), pp. 53–62. Federal Reserve Bank of Atlanta.

Flannery, Mark J. 1983. "Removing Deposit Rate Ceilings: How Will Bank Profits Fare?" *Business Review,* Federal Reserve Bank of Philadelphia (March/April), pp. 13–21.

Gilbert, R. Alton and A. Steven Holland. 1984. "Has the Deregulation of Deposit Interest Rates Raised Mortgage Rates?" *Economic Review* (May), pp. 5–15. Federal Reserve Bank of St. Louis.

Gomez-Ibanez, Jose A., Clinton V. Oster, Jr., and Don H. Pickrell. 1983. "Airline Deregulation: What's Behind the Recent Losses?" *Journal of Policy Analysis and Management,* 3(1):74–89.

Hayssen, Jonathan. 1977. "Competition Among Financial Institutions: A Survey from Maine." *Issues in Bank Regulation* (Summer), pp. 13–20.

Hendershott, Patric H. 1975. *The Impact of the Financial Institutions Act of 1975.* Washington, D.C.: Department of Housing and Urban Development.

Hester, Donald D. 1983. "Deregulation and Locational Rents in Banking." *Journal of Bank Research* (Spring), pp. 96–107.

Jaffee, Dwight M. 1972. "The Extended Lending, Borrowing, and Service Function Proposals of the Hunt Commission Report." *Journal of Money, Credit and Banking* (November), pp. 990–1000.

Jaffee, Dwight and Kenneth T. Rose. 1979. "Mortgage Credit Availability and Residential Construction." *Brookings Papers on Economic Activity,* 2:333–76.

James, Christopher. 1983. "An Analysis of Intraindustry Differences in the Effect of Regulation: The Case of Deposit Rate Ceilings." *Journal of Monetary Economics,* 12(3):417–432.

Kaufman, George G., Larry R. Mote, and Harvey Rosenblum. 1982. "Implications of Deregulation for Product Lines and Geographical Markets of Financial Institutions." Staff Memoranda 82–2 (April). Federal Reserve Bank of Chicago.

—— 1984. "Consequences of Deregulation for Commercial Banking." *Journal of Finance* (July), 39(3):789–803.

Kilcollin, Thomas E. and Gerald A. Hanweck. 1981. *Regulation Q and Commercial Bank Profitability.* Financial Studies Section. Board of Governors of the Federal Reserve System.

Kimball, Ralph C. 1976. "Recent Developments in the NOW Account Experiment in New England." *New England Economic Review* (November–December), pp. 3–19. Federal Reserve Bank of Boston.

Koehn, M. and B. Stangle. 1980. "The Effect of Deposit-Rate Ceilings on Bank Risk: A Comment." *Journal of Banking and Finance,* 4:381–86.

Marcus, Alan J. 1984. "Deregulation and Bank Financial Policy." *Journal of Banking and Finance,* 8:557–65.

Meyer, John R. and William B. Tye. 1985. "The Consequences of Deregulation in the Transportation and Telecommunications Sector." *American Economic Review,* Papers and Proceedings (May), 75(2):46–61.

Metzker, Paul F. 1982. "Future Payments System Technology: Can Small Financial Institutions Compete?" *Economic Review* (November), pp. 58–67. Federal Reserve Bank of Atlanta.

Michel, Allen and Israel Shaked. 1984. "Airline Performance Under Deregulation: The Shareholders' Perspective." *Financial Management* (Summer), pp. 5–14.

Mingo, John. 1978. "The Effect of Deposit-Rate Ceilings on Bank Risk." *Journal of Banking and Finance,* 2:367–78.

Morrison, Steve A. and Clifford Winston. 1984. "The Welfare Effects on Travelers of Airline Deregulation." Working Paper, Northeastern University and the Brookings Institution.

—— 1985. "Intercity Transportation Route Structures Under Deregulation: Some Assessments Motivated by the Airline Experience." *American Economic Review,* Papers and Proceedings (May), 75(2):57–61.

Nelson, Richard W. 1983. "Economies of Scale vs. Regulation as Determinants of U.S. Banking Structure." *Proceedings of a Conference on Bank Structure and Competition.* Federal Reserve Bank of Chicago.

Paulus, John D. 1976. *Effects of NOW Accounts on Costs and Earnings of Commercial Banks in 1974–75.* Staff Study no. 88. Board of Governors of the Federal Reserve System.

Petersen, William M. 1981. *The Effects of Interest Rate Ceilings on the Number of Banking Offices in the United States* (February). Banking Studies Department. Federal Reserve Bank of New York.

Peltzman, Sam. 1976. "Toward a More General Theory of Regulation." *Journal of Law and Economics* (August), pp. 211–40.

Rose, Peter S. 1985. "The Impact of Financial-Services Deregulation: The Hypotheses and the Evidence from Metropolitan Markets" (August). Research Paper. Texas A&M University.

Scott, William L. and Peter S. Rose. 1977. "The Bank Failure Problem Reexamined." *MSU Business Topics* (Winter), pp. 5–10.

Shull, Bernard. 1972. "Multiple-Office Banking and the Structure of Banking Markets: The New York and Virginia Experience." In *Proceedings of a Conference on Bank Structure and Competition,* pp. 30–40. Federal Reserve Bank of Chicago.

Simpson, Thomas D. and Patrick M. Parkinson. 1984. *Some Implications of Financial Innovations in the United States.* Staff Study no. 139 (September). Board of Governors of the Federal Reserve System.

Smirlock, Michael. 1984. "An Analysis of Bank Risk and Deposit-Rate Ceilings." *Journal of Monetary Economics,* 16:195–210.

Spellman, Lewis J. 1980. "Deposit Ceilings and the Efficiency of Financial Intermediation." *Journal of Finance* (March), pp. 129–36.

Stigler, George J. 1981. "The Theory of Economic Regulation." *Bell Journal of Economics* (April), pp. 121–58.

Taggart, Robert A. 1978. "Effects of Deposit-Rate Ceilings: The Evidence from Massachussetts Savings Banks." *Journal of Money, Credit and Banking* (May), pp. 139–57.

Waite, Donald C. III. 1982. "Deregulation and the Banking Industry." *Bankers Magazine* (January–February), pp. 26–35.

Walker, David A. 1982. "Effects of Deregulation on the Savings and Loan Industry." *Financial Review,* pp. 94–110.

Wall, Larry D. and Robert A. Eisenbeis. 1984. "Risk Considerations in Deregulating Bank Activities." *Economic Review* (May), pp. 6–19. Federal Reserve Bank of Atlanta.

Whitehead, David D. 1983. "Interstate Banking: Taking Inventory," *Economic Review* (May), pp. 4–20. Federal Reserve Bank of Atlanta.

Index